To
My dearest
one of God's warriors
in high heels.

May you be blessed in
everything you do.

I love you very much.
H. 16/5/10

WARRIORS IN HIGH HEELS

The Genesis 3:15 Commission of God's Women to Warfare

Zaidie Crowe Carnegie

Copyright © 2007 Zaidie Crowe Carnegie

WARRIORS IN HIGH HEELS
The Genesis 3:15 Commission of God's Women to Warfare
by Zaidie Crowe Carnegie

Printed in the United States of America

ISBN 978-1-60266-368-8

All rights reserved solely by the author. The author guarantees all contents are original and do not infringe upon the legal rights of any other person or work. No part of this book may be reproduced in any form without the permission of the author. The views expressed in this book are not necessarily those of the publisher.

Unless otherwise indicated, Bible quotations are taken from The Amplified Bible Large Print. Copyright © 1987 by the Zondervan Corporation and the Lockman Foundation. Published by Zondervan. Scripture marked KJV are taken from the King James Version of the Bible. Scriptures marked NIV are taken from The Holy Bible New International Version. Copyright © 1973, 1978, 1984, 1988 by International Bible Society.

www.xulonpress.com

TABLE OF CONTENTS

INTRODUCTION ix

1. LET THE BATTLE BEGIN 17
2. THE FIRST COMMISSION OF THE HUMAN FAMILY 45
3. THE IMPERFECT WARRIOR 91
4. THE HOPE OF THE AGES 109
5. BIRTHING THE SEED OF REVOLUTION AND RESTORATION 131
6. ULTIMATE OBSTACLE COURSE 157
7. A MEDUSA HEART 175
8. DYING OF THIRST AT THE WELL 191
9. WATER, DEATH AND LIFE 207

10. THE IMPORTANCE OF EFFECTIVE
    COMMUNICATION 227

11. EMPTY WOMBS AND OPEN ARMS 249

12. FAITH, FOCUS AND VISION 263

13. CALLED TO SERVICE..279

14. SEEKING AFTER WISDOM 295

15. SINGLENESS OF MIND..309

16. ENGAGING THE ENEMY 333

17. WOMEN WHO KNOW ARE THE
    WOMEN WHO BLEED 353

18. GOD GIVEN GIRL POWER 369

19. ON THE WARPATH 385

20. POLITICS, POSITION AND POWER 407

21. DRESS TO IMPRESS 433

DEDICATION

To Mama

This book is dedicated to my mother, Mrs. Merdel Crowe, the first and best warrior of the Most High and of His Kingdom of Love and Righteousness that I have ever known. She taught me love, obedience, commitment and loyalty to God first and then to family, community and country. I have always called her a 'Womanist' for her steadfast belief that in God there is absolute equality. She passionately believed that only in God are we truly completed as women with passion, purpose and destiny according to the Will and favor of the Father. She was very opposed to service to God being determined other than by a calling of God by the Holy Spirit. She was a warrior who fought a good fight, completed her course and is now at rest awaiting the glorious resurrection to be with her Lord forevermore. You are my hero and my role model. I love you Mama. (1934 -1978),

INTRODUCTION

There is a deep need within every person that I know to have a rock solid comprehension in their inner being of exactly who they are and the purpose and destiny that is their portion in life. I have spent many years of my life following my dream, trying to fulfill my ambition but there was always a part of me that would search for an anchor to which I could permanently tie my identity and fulfill my destiny. When I gave my life to the Lord and became an obedient daughter of my heavenly Father, I gained a certain amount of stability from my new identity as a Christian; I committed to worship God first and to seek after righteousness with my whole being.

At the time that I gave my life to God I was a single mother striving to live according to the godly principles that I was being taught. There was an understanding, seldom voiced but firmly believed between myself and other sisters in my position that God would bless us with a husband according to His will in good time. In the meantime we would stay faithful to the Word to seek after righteousness and serve God with all our hearts, strength, mind and soul. But nevertheless, there was perhaps an unspoken feeling that we were in a holding pattern awaiting our blessing of a partner in order to be accepted by the established church cliques as living fully in the will of the Lord.

As it turned out, within two years I met and married my husband, a newly baptized man who expressed a desire to grow in the ways of the Lord. I moved to the United States with the two youngest of my three children to start a new life as a wife and at the same time as an alien, far removed from all my usual comfort zones. Within a short period of time I felt as if I had slipped my moorings and was in danger of getting lost; my mind, my identity, my self worth were being diminished by the challenges of my new status, my usual support network, my loved ones, my culture, my community and my Church which had kept me grounded was literally pulled from under me. The only things that remained the same that I was able to take with me were my relationships with my sons and my God, everything else was new.

    I had somehow imagined that serving God as mother and wife, honoring any calls that the church made on my skills was all that I had to accomplish. In the face of the challenges which presented themselves in my move however I was in desperate need of answers from God about His divine purpose for my life. Operating under the circumstances I now faced could not be it for me! But I had to believe that God had a plan for my life and I knew that even if I had made a mistake either in my marriage or my move, in His mercy He would work everything for good to those who love Him. I had proved Him over and over in the past and I was not about to stop believing in Him now.

    Therefore, in the last two years my experiences have resulted in a very personal search for a closer walk with God and a clearer understanding of His designs for my life. Most especially I needed to understand the role I was made to perform and the destiny my Father had assigned me. I wanted to be sure that I clearly understood my place as a wife, mother and child of God according to the Word, not according to man. I began to search the Scriptures diligently, asking the Holy Spirit to show me myself in the Words, eyes and heart of the Father. What I discovered has been summarized for this book. I did not set out to write a book but the Holy Spirit impressed on me the words in **Habakkuk 2:1-3** to write the vision; the revelation that I was being blessed with and to make it plain because it speaks of the appointed times at the end of days. This was repeated in my spirit so often that I began to transcribe the notes from my Bible study.

A culmination of all the circumstances that have taken place in my life has resulted in the birthing out of this my very first book. I began with a question about the desire of woman for the man as stated in **Genesis 3:16**...paraphrased it says simply that her desire will always be for her husband and he shall rule over her. What did this mean, would I be cursed with all my sisters to hunger after my husband's attention, affection and perhaps even validation and place my God next in line to this "need, craving, desire" imposed by the Divine Himself? Did my gender as female and my position of wife mean that I was limited in certain things and denied others within the body of Christ? How important was the status of wife in a Christian setting? Did this explain why young women even before marriage spent so much time thinking/talking about getting a husband? Was there a biblical explanation of this or merely a cultural, political one?

And if the Lord loves me, and I am sure He does, what were these horrible curses in **Genesis 3:16** all about? I needed to touch the heart of my Father. Of course, because He first loved me and drew me to Himself with His everlasting love, He touched my heart and began to reveal to me the insights that I am sharing with you. Not only did He begin to teach me through His Word and by the Holy Spirit, He began to deal with me at a level of relational intimacy that I had never known before. This search, this study, this journey was strictly between the Lord and I and as it was impressed on me any other of His daughter sharing the same concerns I had.

Ideally, being loved, cherished, honored, respected, treated as Christ treats His bride, the church, to the laying down of His life, is the beauty of a marriage, a true unity. To share such love is to really catch a glimpse of the unconditional love of God and yet for all that we see, understand or comprehend, the sum total is a pale reflection of the smallest portion of the immensity of the Lord's divine love. If real love between a husband and wife can be so satisfying, then is not the love of God to be so much more desired? Love is God and God is Love and love flows inexorably from Him to men and women alike. But most importantly, His love is not dependent on whether our status is that of being married or single, male or female.

Imagine a love that is extended towards one's enemy; one who has done all that they can to reject you, push you away, oppose you and take the lies of your enemy as truth concerning you. Imagine that you have given all things to such a one, including your Kingdom authority over your creation and imagine that all this is handed over to the instigator of rebellion in your Kingdom, how would you feel about such a person? I know that our natural human response would be to destroy such a person if we could; treat them as the enemy because in reality, they are just that and leave them to their own evil ways and the ultimate consequence of their actions. Our Lord was in just such a position with His human children. As the Creator, He could have wiped the slate clean after the fall in Eden and start over again but He did not take that route. Instead He set in motion a plan to redeem and to restore the rebels into a relationship of right standing with Him. **'For while we were yet sinners, He loved us and gave His only begotten Son to die for us, to draw us to Him with His everlasting love'.**

When we recognize and accept that He loved us even when we were unlovable and that He has given everything to make us understand this divine love then how can we refuse so great a love? Loving God with our whole being and surrendering to His mercy and His grace is our only reasonable response. Unity with Him will restore perfect communion and the love within that bond will go from glory to glory as God is magnified. The first male and female were established as a holy union, the perfect example of the working and experience of oneness. So let us use the marriage relationship to understand God's plans for women.

Where there is love in a marriage union, a true union with the Lord as the third cord, every act of love becomes an act of worship: of praise and thanks giving to the Lord Most High. It is He who created your spouse, who designed every characteristic and feature that delights the senses. He is the Originator and Giver of the gift of love which binds. Each moment of pleasure heightens the awareness of God's care, interest and love. Every unfolding of deeper depths of love is a delight that only the Divine could mastermind because He is Love. Every act of the beloved is a tender, profound reminder of the beauty and joy of the love of our Creator and Father.

God's divine plan for man was the only purpose and occupation of Adam and Eve in the pre-rebellion garden paradise. That original plan proclaimed by God has never changed but mankind sinned, alienating the Creator. They lost their God-focus and turned away from life; abundant, God-appointed living. Instead they allowed self-centeredness and idolatry to overtake them and destroy their heritage. Satan, the enemy of everything good and the source of all evil, achieved his mission to disrupt God's Plan and the First Parents' Paradise home.

The perfect union was mangled and mankind became a biological weapon in the devil's arsenal against the righteousness of the Holy One. The devil continues to attack the human family starting in the home with marriages and families in order to create dysfunctional, distortions of a divinely ordained union and in the process he uses counterfeit alternatives to attract humans into opposition to the plan of the Almighty. Every effort is expended to foster an environment of acceptability of alternate lifestyles that excludes, neglects or deny the role of God as essential to a happy, loving and holy partnership.

Unless a man or woman love God they cannot claim to have a true and lasting love that transcends the carnal mind. Adam and Eve, by ordination, first had a loving relationship with God, one on one, before being brought together as husband and wife. They were each equally balanced and secure in their relationship with God and could therefore be equally balanced, loving and complete together. That's right, their individual desire was for God first and then equal delight in sharing each other's love, interests and responsibilities to govern the earth as directed by the Lord and to propagate His love and fulfill His purpose through the birth of children.

It was only after the devastating, diabolical deception of the devil, which violently severed their divine connection that God declared a change in the balance, harmony, and order of the desire that they had for each other. Eve was the first of the pair to lose her God-focus so God decreed that every wife's desire thereafter would be for her husband as long as iniquity and sin prevailed in the lives of His created beings. Briefly then that was the answer to the question of desire. But my search did not end with this revelation. The Holy Spirit took me to God's declaration in **Genesis 3:15** and began to open my spiritual eyes concerning identity, purpose and divine destiny.

The Lord revealed that **Genesis 3:16** is not just an imposition of the consequences of sin; it is a scenario that the heavenly Father turns from its intended evil to work for the good of His children. The conditions attendant to our disobedience has become the training and preparatory tools that will make of womankind warriors of the Most High in the earth realm. Notice that the decree of spiritual warfare was proclaimed before the conditions and consequences of sin were pronounced in **Genesis 3:16.** Therefore sisters, before we start to get into **the how**, we must grasp hold of **the what**! What is our purpose, our calling, our job, our divine commission as decreed. Once we have the answer to these questions then everything that follows will fall into its proper place and its purpose will become clear.

Before the Lord even started to deal with the result of disobedience, He gave the serpent notice that there was to be a continuous state of hostility, hatred, warfare between him and the woman, between her seed and the serpent's. The Lord also declared and decreed that the Seed of the woman would defeat and utterly destroy the serpent and his reign of evil. **Genesis 3:15** then is a declaration of war; war between Satan and the human family through the special role and appointed assignment of the woman. She is the divinely appointed, chief opponent of the devilish warfare set in place by Satan in the Garden of Eden. The earth thereafter is enemy territory and the people of God, operatives, soldiers, servants and warriors against the rule of the dark kingdom and the prince that holds court therein. God's declaration was announced to all of His creation, out loud; not quietly whispered to the woman only. It was spoken by the Eternal One even before He specifically and directly addresses the woman. There is a war in progress.

In addition, God decided that both Adam and Eve needed to be trained, prepared and experienced in identifying the deceitful and disguised assaults of Satan, the consequences of sinful bondage and how to find victory in God. They had lost the first battle but God in love had another plan. The consequences of sin required the establishment of a hierarchy in which the male and female could operate to fulfill the **Genesis 3:15** commission. The new ranking/order required Eve to always desire her husband; that is, to be obedient to the law of God despite her emotions and submit to the rule of the husband in their homes and in the earth realm. It is the promotion of her emotions above the law of God which led to sin, shame and expulsion from the presence of God and the Garden of Eden. Now she must learn to subject those emotions to the sovereign law of the Eternal. The principle of godly submission can only operate where there is agape love; that is, unconditional love, faith and wisdom in the Lord as well as the heart of a servant, of the Christ.

The Lord knew that the discipline, the values, the character development and the testimony that the woman would acquire during her difficulties, challenges and life experiences would equip and empower her to stand in the Lord, take on the enemy and not flinch in the face of his onslaught. She would come to appreciate and emulate the character of God, be a worthy opponent of the adversary, willing to sacrifice and die for her children. The Almighty decreed in the presence of the whole of the cosmos, the seen and unseen, a royal war commission for women, and a special call to serve in the arena of spiritual warfare. That warfare was being waged by the forces of evil against the Kingdom of Righteousness. After "the Fall" it is now the warfare of the human family also.

The **Genesis 3:15 Commission** applies to all women whether we are single or married, young or old; wherever we are, whether we know it or not, we are on the frontline and Satan and sin is our enemy! The serpent knows this and will attack us at every given opportunity. But we must also know that we know that we know exactly who we are in this war against us and against the Lord our God. We must also know our purpose and our destiny in this Great War according to the will of God. Despite our appearances, positions or challenges, we are frontline spiritual warriors. Let us go forth fully armed with the spiritual weapons of our warfare, appropriately dressed with the righteousness of the Christ and standing in His might, His power and His victory.

It is my prayer that the Holy Spirit will work in and through every person who reads this book to hear, answer and sound the Clarion Call to God's women that the time is **now**; behold now is the acceptable day of the Lord! We are wives, mothers, daughters and sisters but we are also God's warriors; we are not merely victims of the devil we are his conquerors through Christ Jesus! There is no time for confusion, delusions, distractions and delays. We must make a stand for the Lord wherever we are because wherever that may be, make no mistake it is a frontline position. Draw a line in the dirt, in the grime, in the sink, in the ink, in the mess or the pristine order and tell the devil, come no further, behind this line is holy ground on which the Lord's anointed stands!

I have always been amazed at the sacrifices that soldiers will make to plant their country's flag on a piece of land, enemy territory, to claim or reclaim it as the territory of their country, state or kingdom. As warriors of the Kingdom of God we too must reclaim territory for our Lord and King and count it all a privilege to live and die for this great cause of the Christ. All this territory for which we fight belongs to Him in the first instance but the enemy has taken occupation. Therefore sisters, arise as God's warriors, warriors on the frontline, rise up in the name of the Lord Jesus and claim victory in and through Him.

> **You did not choose Me, but I have chosen you and appointed you to go and bear - fruit that will last. John 15:16 (NIV)**
>
> **But when He, Who had chosen and set me apart [even] before I was born and had called me by His grace (His undeserved favor and blessing), saw fit and was pleased to reveal (unveil, disclose) His Son within me so that I might proclaim Him. Galatians 1:15-16.**
>
> **And afterward I will pour out My Spirit upon all flesh; and your sons and your daughters shall prophesy ... Even upon the menservants and upon the maidservants will I pour out My Spirit. Joel 2:28-29.**
>
> **The Lord gives the Word [of power]: the women who bear and publish [the news] are a great host. Psalms 68:11**

CHAPTER 1

LET THE BATTLE BEGIN

2. Then the Lord replied: Write down the revelation and make it plain on tablets so that a herald may run with it. 3. For the revelation awaits an appointed time; it speaks of the end and will not prove false. Though it linger, wait for it; it will certainly come and will not delay. Habakkuk 2:1-3

Before The Earth

In the eternities before the beginning, the one and only God, the Omnipotent, Omnipresent Jehovah God, created. He created the heavenly hosts and He created their worlds. His creation worshipped Him in the beauty of holiness and His praise was continually in their mouth. All of His creation was governed by His Law of Love and by the administration of His Righteousness. He made the hosts of the angels and gave them free will so that they were not mere automatons but could freely exercise their ability to reason and reach independent decisions concerning their actions. They worshipped from choice, in love, with perfect joy.

The Law of Love by which God bound Himself as well as the members of His Kingdom could only operate on the premise of self-determination. There was freedom of choice for all His created beings. The imposition of any rules or code of conduct to mandate compliance with divine protocols, kingdom laws or to demand worship of Jehovah God would be in opposition to the operation of the defining, foundational principle of love.

Therefore since God is Love, to force or demand obedience, respect, honor, worship and praise would be inconsistent, contrary to, and in conflict with the very essence of His nature. So the angels and all created beings enjoyed the gift of free will by their Creator; a gift which facilitated freedom of attitudes and actions of love; obedience, worship and exaltation of a holy, righteous and loving God. It was and remains the delight of angels to glorify and adore our God day and night. However, before the beginning of earth time, there was one angel, most beautiful and gifted, entrusted with high office at the Throne of God, but by his conduct he came to demonstrate the full scope of the operation of this principle of free will in the Kingdom of Love.

The Enemy

This angel was incredibly adorned in the most precious jewels imaginable by God, full of wisdom and perfectly gifted to praise and worship the Lord God Most High. But pride entered into the heart of this angel. He envied the praise and worship given to the Most High Creator and the honor and adoration bestowed on the Beloved Son of our God. He desired to receive all the glory to himself.

This angel was called Lucifer; the shining one. **Isaiah 14:12**. His thoughts and attitude finally materialized into open rebellion against his Creator and Lord. One third of the angelic hosts was corrupted by him and gave allegiance to his treacherous cause. Joining together, they waged war against their Creator God and against the remaining faithful, righteous two thirds of the angels that did not succumb to the evil of Lucifer but remained faithful to the Creator God. **Ezekiel 28:13-19.**

So there was war in the Kingdom of Jehovah God. Lucifer, now called Satan, the devil and serpent waged war against our God. But righteousness prevailed. The 'Glorious Two Thirds' were triumphant and Lucifer and the one third of his dark angels were cast out from the Kingdom and from the continual Presence of Jehovah God.

> **7. Then war broke out in heaven; Michael and his angels went forth to battle with the dragon, and the dragon and his angels fought. 8. But they were defeated, and there was no room found for them in heaven any longer. 9. And the huge dragon was cast down and out – that age-old serpent, who is called the Devil and Satan, he who is the seducer(deceiver) of all humanity the world over; he was forced out and down to the earth, and his angels were flung out along with him. Revelation 12:7**

God's Own Image

In His wisdom and because of His great love; a love that moved Him to share Himself, Elohim, the Creator God conceived in His heart to make 'man'. He also purposed in His mind to make man a physical, material being and to provide a physical place for the abode of His new creature; that place was the earth. Mankind would be given dominion and authority to stand as God's Regent over all the earth, and over all the living things that would exist on the earth. The government of the earth would be according to the laws of the Kingdom of Righteousness, its constitution, operation and organization exactly according to the decrees, directives, mandates and rules of God's Sovereign Authority.

So it was that the heavens and the earth were created. They came into existence by the Word of God and the oversight of the Holy Spirit. Then God said

> **Let Us make man in Our own image, and after Our own likeness. And let him have dominion over the earth …. So God made man. …male and female created He them. Genesis 1:26.**

The entity man – male and female - was created with freedom of choice. They were given the ability to reason for themselves and to make whatever choices they wanted. It was the will and the nature of God and His Law of Love that man, like all His other created beings, would not be compelled to obedience or to worship. Their decisions would have to be personal, motivated and activated by, and flow out of their love of, and for their Father the Creator.

Shattered Reflection

The Fallen angels, the ignoble one third, were not pleased with this new development. Their leader, Lucifer, was incensed. He was determined to destroy the Kingdom of God and His Righteousness, by whatever means necessary. He was not prepared to see new beings come into existence, choosing to love God and acting in obedience to His laws. That would make his rebellion a selfish lie and would demonstrate that his behavior was evil self-promotion. The devil devised a plan to turn 'the man' away from obedience, loyalty, patriotism and faithfulness to the Kingdom.

His first words to Eve were phrased to raise doubt concerning God's commands and to undermine belief, confidence, trust and faith in the Almighty. There was an implication that God was not being honest, truthful or fair with Adam and Eve. To impugn the character of the Creator and to undermine, challenge or destroy the foundation of love that exists between Creator and created beings; this exemplifies the very spirit of the anti-Christ even in today's world.

And he [Satan] said to the woman, Can it really be that God has said; you shall not eat from every tree of the garden? Genesis 3:1b

The serpent, Satan, formerly Lucifer, was determined to dispossess man of the position of authority, favor, and love given to him by the Creator; he determined to do all that he could to turn everything good to evil. He determined to establish the rule of his dark and evil kingdom in the hearts of man and in the earth realm given to man;

both conditions diametrically opposed to the will and sovereignty of Jehovah. Satan is in rebellion against the very government of Jehovah God and seeks to replace Him by whatever devious plot and evil plans necessary.

13. And you said in your heart, I will ascend to heaven; I will exalt my throne above the stars of God; I will sit upon the mount of assembly in the uttermost north. 14. I will ascend above the heights of the clouds; I will make myself like the Most High. Isaiah 14:13, 14. (NIV)

It is the inherent nature of Lucifer and his Kingdom of Darkness, to bring about rebellion, treason, pain, suffering and annihilation to every righteous thing that exists. Disharmony, disloyalty and deception are his trademarks. It is his only interest, his ultimate desire **"to steal, to kill and to destroy". John 10:10.** That is the fullest extent and the precise intent of his interactions with the human family.

As long as Satan is able to separate us and keep us separated from the love of God, he is satisfied. He is the enemy of the Lord God and therefore he is the enemy of humanity. The creation of humans is an outflow and an overflow of the love of the Lord; a love which Satan seeks to repudiate. Therefore it is and will always be his work to organize and promote our destruction just so he can dishonor, displace and ultimately replace our Lord.

1. ... Satan, standing at Joshua's right hand to be his adversary and to accuse him. 2. and the Lord said to Satan, the Lord rebuke you, O Satan! Even the Lord ... rebukes you! Zechariah 3:1-2

The Bible catalogues the violent and aggressive tactics and strategies that the devil has used to cause eternal separation between God and mankind. His first apparent success took place with the First Mother and Father of the human family in the Garden of Eden. I say apparent because much to the chagrin of the serpent, that was not the end of the matter.

God is and always will be God. **Exodus 34:6-7** is God's publication of His moral character and this declaration sets the tone for all of His actions, attitudes and approach to mankind. **Exodus 34:6-7**

> **6. And the Lord passed by before him, and proclaimed, The Lord! The Lord! A God merciful and gracious, slow to anger, and abundant in loving-kindness and truth. 7. Keeping mercy and loving-kindness for thousands, forgiving iniquity and transgression and sin, but Who will by no means clear the guilty.**

His ways are past finding out by our limited carnal reasoning, logic, philosophy and sciences. God knows all things because past, present and future are as clear to Him as 'this present moment'. Although He knows our future, it is not pre-destined by Him but rather is determined by our choices and actions. He was not surprised by the events that transpired in Eden; disappointed, hurt, heartbroken even, but not surprised.

Elohim is all powerful and He could have destroyed us for our transgression and proceed to His next creative act. But this would be in opposition to His character. Instead, out of His love, mercy and grace, He implemented another plan, purposed even before the foundation of the earth was laid; a plan to redeem the human family from the death-hold of the serpent and restore Paradise.

The execution of His Plan of Redemption could not be understood, undermined, delayed, disrupted or destroyed by the adversary of God and man. God's plan remained solid, certain and true. However, in His judgment against the devil, He forewarned him of the divine plan to redeem humanity through the offspring of the very woman that had been cruelly deceived by the serpent's seditious lies. A human descendant would be Redeemer of the human family and Destroyer of the devil, his allies and his presumptuous plot to step into God's shoes.

Our God is awesome and His words never lose their efficacy, their power and prophetic fulfillment. Satan was put on notice by God. **Genesis 3:14-5** finds the Lord speaking His first response to the sad situation of disobedience and betrayal by Adam and Eve, directly to the devil who master-minded the deceptive plot that led to rebellion, transgression and destruction in Eden. God's words were words of judgment, prophecy, promise, warfare and destiny.

When I travel back to Eden in my mind, I can see the scene replayed and I weep. But there is hope and there is purpose in the Father's words. The most comforting thing that comes from this tragic scenario for me is the absolute wonder, joy and affirmation of the heart and character of God, whose 'Plan of Redemption' was formulated even before the creation of the earth; the creation of Adam and Eve. The Creator's plan is designed to restore to man the inheritance stolen by the **"Father of Lies"**; lies that we believed and so, doubted and distrusted a loving God and Father.

You are of your father, the devil ... He was a murderer from the beginning and does not stand in the truth, because there is no truth in him. When he speaks a falsehood, he speaks what is natural to him, for he is a liar [himself] and the father of lies and of all that is false. John 8:44

Thank the Lord that because of His character, His attributes, totally because of Who He is and not because of our own personal merits, we have a certain hope that one day the reign of the devil will come to an end. When it does, and it will, we will be free forevermore from the possibility of a repeat or re-run of the wickedness and devastation that invaded and infected this earthly realm. There is no provision for the salvation of the devil and he knows this; a truth that makes him all the more determined to dominate this earthly domain through his dark designs and to ultimately depose and dispossess the Divine Sovereign God of all His authority. A place of final judgment has already been prepared for the devil, the fallen angels who support and carry out his work, as well as that section of the human family that refuses salvation and instead chooses eternal separation from God.

Then He (The Lord) will say to those at His left hand, be gone from Me, you cursed, into the eternal fire prepared for the devil and his angels! Matthew 25:41

We have a choice, we have always had a choice made certain by the grace of God either to join the devil in his revolt and earn a place with him in the final death, or, to make a stand for God and be rewarded with eternal life. The eternal fire is prepared for the devil and his angels, not for mankind but we do have freedom of choice and that includes the consequences of those choices. God the Father implores us to choose life that we and our children might live and reign with Him in the eternities.

15. See, I set before you today life and prosperity, death and destruction. 16. For I command you today to love the Lord your God, to walk in His ways, and to keep His commands, decrees and laws; then you will live and increase, and the Lord your God will bless you in the land you are entering to possess. 17. But if your heart turns away and you are not obedient, and if you are drawn away to bow down to other gods and worship them, 18. I declare to you this day that you will certainly be destroyed. You will not live long in the land you are crossing the Jordan to enter and possess. 19. This day I call heaven and earth as witness against you that I have set before you life and death, blessings and curses. Now choose life, so that you and your children may live 20. And that you may love the Lord your God, listen to His voice, and hold fast to Him. For the Lord is your life... Deuteronomy 30:15-19. (NIV)

Lost Chance and Last Chance

Satan was full of wisdom and knew the exact nature, extent and evil of his actions. He tried to put himself on God's throne, in God's place. **Isaiah 14:12-15.** He had been successful in turning one third of the angels against the Lord in heaven and so he set out to achieve sinful revolt in these new human beings that were the expression of God's love. The devil was determined to demonstrate that God was unjust, unfair and unyielding in His commands, partial in His favors and tyrannical in His love. In spite of being cast out of heaven, he was still in pursuit of his diabolical scheme to dishonor, disrespect and de-throne the Almighty Creator and Lord. Man became his pawn, his ransom, his trophy. **Revelation 12:9-13**

If we foolishly accept the explanations bandied about by so called intellectuals; scientists, teachers, and philosophers that Satan is a figment of fertile imaginations or a symbolic representation of wrong-doing in society, we will be lost forever. He is real and his subversive propaganda to lull sinners into a false sense of safety is a satanic strategy of immense and successful proportions. That serpent seeks only to mislead, misdirect, manipulate and maneuver us to our own destruction. If for one moment we choose to believe that his devilish plot has ever changed since his ejection from heaven or his actions in Eden, or buy into the lies concerning his existence, identity or his character, we will continue to be his victims, his spoils of war.

If we fail to acknowledge the truth of the Scriptures that tells us that he is a real, created being and informs us as to his character, his motives, purpose, plans and his ultimate end, we will find ourselves in continued opposition to the will of our Creator for our lives and our destiny. The evil one is at war with our God and has enjoined the human family through his deception and our disobedience and complicity. When we breach divine law, we are giving our allegiance to the devil and voluntarily take on a mantel of slavery, subjection and subjugation to the originator of evil, the father of lies, the mastermind of our misery and downfall and our alienation from our loving Creator.

A God of the Second Chance

In spite of our enmity with God, He continues to love us and while we were yet sinners in rebellion against Him and His Kingdom authority, He proceeded with His planned second chance for the human family. The chance that God ordained was for the deliverance, salvation, sanctification and restoration of the entire human family through the "Seed of the woman". Jesus is that Seed, the Messiah of lost humanity. He broke the yoke of bondage to Satan by giving His sin-free body to be broken, humiliated and punished for our transgression against the laws of God. His sacrifice encompassed the inevitable consequences of disease, suffering, pain and death that sin brought in its wake.

He was wounded for our transgressions, He was bruised for our guilt and iniquities; the chastisement [needful to obtain] peace and well-being for us was upon Him, and with the stripes [that wounded] Him we are healed and made whole. Isaiah 53:5

Jesus the Christ lived a perfect, pure and sin free life by making God's business and His Law the first priority; the only choice always and regardless of circumstances, conditions or cost. He lived in obedience to His Father and because He **"was without sin', Hebrews 4:15,** He was able to pay the price for our redemption with His blood sacrifice and His righteousness.

After all, the **"wages of sin is death", Romans 6:23,** and divine justice, grounded in divine love demands that the debt be paid if we want to have a second chance of Eden. Sinful man is incapable of paying the price of his own redemption. Yet, it was necessary that a 'son of Man' accept the judgment and pay the debt that would purchase freedom from the curse of sin for humanity. The shedding of blood was mandatory if there was to be remission of sin. But the blood sacrifice of animals was not sufficient and was instituted of God merely to provide a memorial and temporary type of offering that fore-shadowed the ultimate sacrifice that the Messiah would have to make for the propitiation of sin and the work of cleansing that He would accomplish on our behalf in the heavenly sanctuary by His ministry as our High Priest.

That is why God's Plan of Redemption was to be achieved through the Seed of the woman; fully man, innocent, pure and untouched by the stain and stench of sin. Only such a Man could become the acceptable Sacrifice, taking the place of sinners; our place on death row; for **'we all have sinned and come short of the glory of God.' Romans 3:23**.

The Messiah, Jesus our Lord is the spotless and pure Lamb of God and so death had no power to keep Him in the grave. He arose from the grave a Living Conqueror, an All-powerful Redeemer and a Sufficient Savior for all who will accept His act of atonement on our behalf.

20. But the fact is that Christ (the Messiah) has been raised from the dead, and He became the first fruits of those who have fallen asleep [in death]. 21. For since [it was] through a man that death [came into the world, it is] also through a Man that the resurrection of the dead [has come]. 22. For just as [because of their union of nature] in Adam all people die, so also [by virtue of their union of nature] shall all in Christ be made alive. 1 Corinthians 15: 20-22

We are not compelled to accept the liberty that He won for us; God's love prevents compelled compliance even if it is to secure freedom from the slavery of sin and Satan. The Gift of God, salvation through Jesus the Messiah is freely offered to humanity and the choice to accept or refuse is still ours. I love the phrasing of the King James Version of the Scriptures that records John the Baptist's proclamation of joy, awe, entreaty, deliverance and destiny when he declared **"Behold the Lamb of God that takes away the sins of the world"! John 1:29.** Behold is such a powerful word here and invokes the concepts of focus, faith, vision, discernment, direction, love, atonement, sacrifice and salvation. Behold the Promise, the Seed, the Redeemer and the King; Victor over our sworn enemy, Satan!

The most profound realization for me however, and I pray for you also, is that Jesus the Christ did everything that He did because of His complete, unconditional love for God the Father. Obedience, ministry, humility, submission and death were all embraced by the Christ because of the divine, agape love that He shared with the Father;

- ❖ The love of God for the Son.
- ❖ The love of the Son for the Father
- ❖ Their love for the human family
- ❖ Love for all of created life.

Jesus' work of redemption was not perfected because of His religious observance of God's law. Rather, His love of and for God manifested itself in His obedience. The love came first and from that love, obedience naturally followed. There used to be a popular saying years ago that "Love means never having to say you are sorry" and in this case, 'God-love' (agape love) means just that; if one is filled with God-love then one will not break any of God's law or commands, cause Him pain, grief or a broken heart or have to ask for forgiveness. Love is unity not separation, obedience not rebellion, dependence not independence, godliness not idolatry, loyalty not treason.

After the fall in Eden, we were unable to get back to a no-sin situation by ourselves or live in holiness again without God's loving intervention. Enters Jesus the Christ centre stage; a love gift from God, an open Door back to righteousness, communion and paradise! Because of the love-bond between Son and Father, Jesus also shared the depth and breadth of the love that His Father had for us. This bounteous and infinite love took Him to the Cross of Shame to purchase our liberty; it is agape love, God-love that took the Christ all the way to the grave and God-love that raised Him up in triumph on resurrection morning!

Man was created from love, by love and offered salvation through that same love. This is the mystery of love; it is eternal, it can never die, it gives life, it is life, it is God! The miraculous victory of Christ's resurrection was a fruit of divine love. The power and the authority given to Him upon His Ascension by the Father, flows from the same love that Jesus had for the Father and therefore for us; we are **"so loved"** by God that **"He gave His only Begotten Son"** for our restoration to His Presence and to the privileged position within His Kingdom that He appointed and apportioned to us from the genesis of the earth. **John 3:16**

Is it any wonder then, that Jesus prayed that we might all come to know and to share agape love, the God-love that He has with and for the Father and the Holy Spirit; a love that He extends to us also?

20. My prayer is not for them alone. I pray also for those who will believe in me through their message,

21. that all of them may be one, Father, just as you are in Me and I am in You. May they also be in us so that the world may believe that You have sent Me.

22. I have given them the glory that You gave Me, that they may be one as we are One;

23. I in them and You in Me. May they be brought to complete unity to let the world know that you sent me and have loved them even as you have loved Me.

24. Father, I want those you have given Me to be with Me where I am, and to see my glory, the glory you have given me because you have loved me before the creation of the world.

24. Righteous Father, though the world does not know You, I know You, and they know that You have sent Me.

26. I have made You known to them, and I will continue to make You known in order that the love You have for Me may be in them and that I Myself may be in them. John 17; 20-26. NIV

Whoever claims to live in Him must walk as Jesus did. 1 John 2:6. NIV

If we love one another, God lives in us and His love is made complete in us. 13. We know that we live in Him

and He in us, because He has given us of His Spirit. 14. And we have seen and testify that the Father has sent His Son to be the Savior of the world. 15. If anyone acknowledges that Jesus is the Son of God, God lives in him and he in God. 16. And so we know and rely on the love God has for us. God is love. Whoever lives in love lives in God, and God in him. 17. In this way, love is made complete among us so that we will have confidence on the day of judgment, because in this world we are like Him. 1 John 4:12 (NIV)**

If we share agape love then we will be willing, honored and blessed to give up every earthly thing, even to the laying down of our lives for the Lord, for our brethren, for the Kingdom of Love, knowing that love endures; it is eternal and we will be raised up to life everlasting with Christ, even as He promised. And His promises are certain. **Titus 1:2**

Satan's mission to disprove, defeat, and destroy the God-appointed authority, mission, measure and meaning of man's existence, received its final and fatal blow on that resurrection morning, when the Lord came forth from the grave with the keys to death, the grave and hell.

17. ... He laid His hand on me and said, Do not be afraid! I am the First and the Last. 18. And the Ever-living One [I am living in the eternity of the eternities]. I died, but see, I am alive forevermore; and I possess the keys of death and Hades (the realm of the dead). Revelation 1:17-18

Just as sin came into the world through the first man, so also life eternal is regained through one sinless, pure and unblemished human being; that man is Jesus, Beloved Son of God, born into the human family, wrapped not only in the swaddling clothes of the infant in the manger but supernaturally in the divinity of deity. It is the restoration of righteousness, purity, obedience and therefore of love, that is the substance, spirit and sum total of the redeeming work of Christ on behalf of the human family

> **10. In bringing many sons to glory, it was fitting that God, for whom and through whom everything exists, should make the Author of their salvation perfect through suffering.**
>
> **11. Both the One Who makes men holy and those who are made holy are of the same family. So Jesus is not ashamed to call them brothers.**
>
> **13b. And again He says, 'Here am I, and the children God has given Me'.**
>
> **14. Since the children have flesh and blood, He too shared in their humanity so that by His death He might destroy him who holds the power of death**
>
> **15. And free those who all their lives were held in slavery by their fear of death.**
>
> **16. For surely it is not angels he helps, but Abraham's descendants.**
>
> **17. For this reason He had to be made like His brothers in every way, in order that He might make atonement for the sins of the people. Hebrews 2:10, 11, 13b-17 (NIV)**

It is only when we become united in purpose with God, turning away from the things of the flesh, that humanity and divinity can walk in love again, under the New Covenant of the Christ, according to all the original decrees, statutes, ordinances, laws and instructions of the Creator God, established to govern His Kingdom, "**on earth as it is in heaven**". Matthew 6:10.

God's Covenant, His Promise contained in the **Genesis 3:15** decree, to send a Redeemer to crush the serpent's head, finds its fulfillment in the person of Jesus Christ. The true gospel of the Lord Jesus Christ is that He came to earth to:

- ❖ Restore the broken relationship between God and the human family

- ❖ Re-establish the shattered dominion and displaced authority of the Kingdom of God in the earth realm as administered by His appointees; heaven's sovereignty over earth's affairs.

- ❖ Renew the Kingdom of Love in the hearts and minds of the peoples on earth who are all a result of the outpouring of the love of the Father; the Source of all things in all the worlds, seen and unseen by us, and, the foundation of God's reign.

- ❖ Redeem the legacy of Love, Eternal Life and all other privileges bestowed on the citizens of God's Kingdom

- ❖ Re-instate union and open communion between the Creator and the created.

The Lord Jesus achieved His purpose by redeeming us from the bondage of sin and by wresting the keys and the ultimate control of the administration and government of the earth realm from the corrupt, despicable abuse of the Prince of Darkness. The final conclusion of the process of the re-instatement of God's Kingdom authority and reign in this realm is drawing near. The sign of the times and the urgency with which evil is operating in the earth tells us, unequivocally that the rule of sin is in its final stages. The ending of this dispensation is cause for us to look to our salvation and the saving of souls for the Kingdom of God. Our Lord and His government and rule will soon be here!

6. For unto us a child is born and unto us a Son is given and the government shall be on His shoulders. And He shall be called Wonderful Counselor, Mighty God, Everlasting Father, Prince of Peace. 7. Of the increase

of His government and peace there will be no end. He will reign on David's throne and over His Kingdom, establishing and upholding it with justice and righteousness from that time on and forever. The zeal of the Lord Almighty will accomplish this. Isaiah 9:6 (NIV)

There is great urgency in the commission to labor for God's Kingdom and there is no time to be wasted in pointless denominational divisions and theological, doctoral debates while souls are perishing at the hands of the enemy. The War has already been won and the Victor already revealed. But there are still battles to be fought for His Kingdom here on the earth while He makes final preparations in the heavens to return and declare judgment, justice and jubilation for the righteous.

The Church; His Bride and His Body, is vested with the mission of redemption and its accomplishment by the power of the Holy Spirit. The mission and ministry of Jesus is the mantel the Church inherited on His ascension; He and the Church are one in the same way that husband and wife become one flesh. His sacrifice and suffering for the salvation of souls is ours to share when we accept Him as our Lord and become one with Him in the Spirit. It is a relationship of deepest, purest agape love. The Body is inseparable, indivisible, and unidentifiable apart from the Son; the two are one unified whole. **Ephesians 5:23-32**

Life in the Battle Zone

Just in case you are skeptical about the truth of this Scriptural summation of separation, sedition and salvation, too educated to be placated with biblical facts, too enlightened and progressive to be saved by grace, let me hasten to assure you, evidence of the toll taken by this Great War is the very history of the human family. **Revelation 12:7**. The war originated in the heavens when Satan challenged God's authority and sovereignty. When the human family was created, it too came under attack by the adversary of the Lord. Satan was determined to prove that none of God's created beings could live according to His law. Proving this would in turn allow Lucifer to justify his arrogance, pride and hatred of divine rule.

You do not have to take my word for it. Just look around you and see for yourselves all the signs and sins of warfare. They are everywhere and they are distressing, divisive and destructive. Brothers are fighting against brothers, sisters against sisters, parents and children have become sworn enemies; communities, tribes, and nations have turned against each other. All over the world people perish for a lack of knowledge, understanding and wisdom about the true nature of evil and the real identity of the sole enemy that engineered its entrance into our lives.

Satan disrupted our Edenic paradise of love and intimacy with the divine Creator purely to propagate his wickedness and manipulate us into joining his revolt. We need to strip the deception and lies away, open our eyes to see and our ears to hear the truth, and direct our every effort, purpose, mission and ambition towards defeating him, our deadliest enemy. Instead we are misdirected, convinced and convicted by the evil that has infected our hearts and invaded our lives into destroying the very members of the family of man with whom we should stand in unity, harmony and shared purpose against our mutual foe.

The inescapable truth is that the first assault launched by the enemy was planned to wipe out man's allegiance to their Maker; to enslave us to the bondage of sin and death forever thereby making us enemies of the rule of God and His righteous reign. This would in turn lead to the exaltation of the devil instead of the Lord. This was the choice that faced man in the Garden of Eden; the glory of the Father or the promotion of the enemy. Unfortunately, we chose to believe the enemy of God and the enemy of our own happiness, prosperity and liberty; which states of being are blessings that exist only in the Presence of the Most High God and under His rule of Love;

In Thy Presence is fullness of joy; at Thy right hand there are pleasures for evermore. Psalms 16:11. (KJV)

Consequently, man became an active participant in the war that has been raging since the great rebellion in the Kingdom of God and now even more so as it approaches its climatic conclusion. The whole human family has a part to play in this 'War of all wars' and not one of us are exempt, excluded or excused.

Then the dragon was enraged at the woman and went of to make war against the rest of her offspring – those who obey God's commandments and hold to the testimony of Jesus. Revelation 12:17 (NIV)

A Personal Journey Begins

As a servant of God, born into His family through the redeeming love of Jesus Christ, my 'Kinsman Redeemer', it became a matter of life and death for me to understand my role in this war. I wanted to know for myself what God had purposed for me to do and be; not the perceived, pre-conceived or imposed definitions of family, community, culture, history, religion or even my own selfish, egotistical so-called wisdom.

When I began this study, I had only recently gotten married. Within this institution, my faith came under the severest attack I have ever encountered. The very foundation of my identity, self esteem and value as a human being and a child of God was being challenged, tried and tested. I was going through the fiery furnace of purification, walking through the valley of the shadow of death and I needed to find answers, fast. As a result of my vocational training and experience, my personal methodology when I am in search of understanding concerning a subject has always been to start at the beginning of the matter and go on from there.

Believing with my whole being that all human beings are created by God the Father translated into the Bible as my first resource and the First Parents of the human family, Adam and Eve, my point of origin, and my ground zero. I knew there was a purpose for my life, a purpose common to all mankind, and that I was a child of God through Jesus Christ my Lord. But every possible form of spiritual attack was being aimed at me and I needed to study line upon line and precept upon precept to come to a full knowledge of my worth in God's eyes. It seemed to me that these assaults were gender related and endemic to the roles that being female entailed. I was a daughter, a sister, a mother and a wife and it appears that these roles carried with them some pre-determined, pre-set rules and expected behavior that I had not previously considered or perhaps even learnt in some instances. This was especially apparent with the new role of wife that I had acquired!

I began prayerfully and diligently to search the Scriptures beginning with Genesis. I felt a deep and passionate need to pursue this study so that I would be worthy of the call that I felt certain God had placed on my life. I realize now that the desire to seek out and come to a divinely inspired understanding, under the guidance, supervision and teaching of the Holy Spirit was not of my own origin but came from the Lord. I am so grateful to God that He would grant me this honor. I found myself uniquely positioned with the opportunity to immerse myself in the Word and to be more completely at the feet of the Lord. I was a very long way from home, from everyone I hold dear, in a strange and new environment, an alien in a foreign land, unemployed, isolated and alone with my children and my husband. My 'home where the heart is', was many thousands of miles away, across the Atlantic Ocean in the United Kingdom.

My physical, emotional, mental, psychological and spiritual comfort zones had seemingly disappeared in the thousands of miles that separated me from home. The challenges that I faced left me feeling vulnerable, hurt and eventually broken. But glory to God, one day when I felt the broken pieces of my mind, heart and spirit slipping into that dark place of insanity, I experienced a gentle tugging of love that transported me back to another moment, another time and place in which I had rested in the Lord and surrendered my all to Him. My brokenness brought me to a point of release in which I was able to relinquish self and surrender again to God, this place of surrender is my true abode; my home where the heart must be!

Another Place and Time

Only a few months previous, while I was on my honeymoon, I went through a time of unexpected, intense pain, severe suffering and belief that my life had run its course and it was time to leave this mortal body behind. The realization that this was possibly the moment of my death immediately caused me to do a speedy inventory of my life, a brief feeling of fear surfaced but was gone within a split second and just as rapidly replaced by a feeling of great love, safety and peace flooding into my heart and mind; the kind which only the Spirit of God can bring. I recognized His touch and immediately I was comforted, peaceful and joyous in His rest.

As I felt myself drifting off into unconsciousness, I began to worship my God, praising Him, giving thanks for countless blessings and committing my loved ones to His care. Then I heard the Lord and felt the unspeakable peace of His Presence. He spoke to me words of love and assurance and then reminded me, gently, insistently and firmly that **'He had given His angels charge over me to keep me in all my ways and they would bear me up lest I dashed my foot against a stone'. Psalms 91:11, KJV,** paraphrased. I was spiritually reassured and physically restored; my recovery was completed in a very short while thereafter. From that time forward I knew that my life and everything, every aspect of my being and my living was His alone.

It should not have been possible it seems, yet only a few short months later I found myself in the very depths of despair and depression, walking through the valley, a broken thing. But again and again the sweet assurance of His words would resonate through my pain and bring comfort, reassurance and promise. He was my strength, my hope, my love and my life. I was determined to keep faith with Him who is holy, faithful and righteous; whatever problems would beset me and whatever storms would threaten, I would not let go of His promise, a personally whispered promise to me. I stumbled and fell but His Word and His law was a lamp to my feet and I knew that the weapons formed against me would not, could never prosper. In my weakness and my pain, I found His strong arm!

Let the weak say, I am strong [a warrior]! Joel 3:10. (NIV)

9. He said to me, "My grace is sufficient for you, for My power is made perfect in weakness". Therefore I will boast all the more gladly about my weaknesses, so that Christ's power may rest on me. 10. That is why, for Christ's sake, I delight in weaknesses, in insults, in hardships, in persecutions, in difficulties. For when I am weak, then I am strong. 2 Corinthians 12:9-10. (NIV)

We are hedged in (pressed) on every side [troubled and oppressed in every way], but not cramped or crushed; we suffer embarrassments and are perplexed and unable to find a way out, but not driven to despair; 9. We are pursued (persecuted and hard driven), but not deserted [to stand alone]; we are struck down to the ground, but never struck out and destroyed; 10. Always carrying about in the body the liability and exposure to the same putting to death that the Lord Jesus suffered, so that the [resurrection] life of Jesus also may be shown forth by and in our bodies. 2 Corinthians 7: 8-10

I held fast to His promises, praying without ceasing, encouraging myself in the Spirit, seeking the prayer of the saints and turning to the television ministries of His anointed servants for blessed impartations to my spirit. After much study, meditation and prayer, I have been privileged to receive a level of intimacy, communion and fellowship with the Lord by His grace and favor and the office of the Holy Spirit that I had never known before and will never live without again.

The most astounding, ground- breaking, earth-shaking, mind-blowing revelation for me, came in the realization that the women of the Kingdom have been specifically named, commissioned, called up, appointed and anointed by God the Creator to be warriors, front-line activists, and final victors through the Christ, in the War of Righteousness.

I was a "Warrior Princess" and I never knew it; never understood that there is a Spirit of Warfare given to me by the Father that had been suppressed, silenced and subjugated by the strategies of Satan in our societies and social institutions including the Church of Christ! How many daughters of the Lord were similarly in the dark about this; lacking the confidence, conviction, power and passion that knowledge of our divine military commission would supply in grounding our identity, fueling our service to the Lord and empowering the pursuit of our God-given purposes?

Military Call Up

The specific military commission that was assigned to women in the Garden is one that will be in effect until the time when the Seed of the woman, the Messiah, Jesus the Christ returns a second time, to declare final judgment on the serpent and his evil reign and rebellion. I will even venture so far as to declare quite boldly in every place and at every given opportunity that it is because of this divine 'Military Order', that women have been subjected to wholesale opposition, oppression, suppression, accusation, degradation, humiliation, rejection and death throughout all the ages and the history of man on the earth.

In today's world, this opposition to the rightful, equal standing of women in the spiritual realm, commences at conception and carries on throughout our lives. And, regardless of the many guises and forms by which it has been perpetuated, perpetrated and imposed on the females of the human family, every single attack continues to be the implementation of the strategies, tactics, plots and plans of the enemy, Satan himself. **Revelation 12:17.**

Per se, we might identify the source of the opposition and hostilities directed against us as originating in the vessels, medium, circumstances, politics, culture, religion, philosophy, chauvinism and sadism in our various communities. But finding ourselves in a personal relationship with the Savior will open our eyes to the commission and the plan that He established in the very beginning for us. And with the Light of truth we can identify the real enemy that stands behind the attacks directed at women all over the world.

The Body of Christ must strive to achieve maturity in the Lord. This will enable us to look beyond the natural and clearly identify and engage the enemy of our world. There was a time when God would wink at our ignorance and childishness but that time is long gone. In all our obsessions to get material wealth, positions of influence, power, status, societal recognition and standing as proof of our holiness, we have lost sight of the Kingdom and the Kingdom purpose of Christ's ministry and our calling to serve in the battlefields and on the frontlines of the War of Righteousness.

What we need to be passionate, obsessive and persistent about, is godly vision and divine wisdom, the acquisition of a full knowledge and understanding of the Word, and the divine purpose of worship and witness. **In Hosea 4:6, we hear from the Lord, "My people are destroyed for lack of knowledge"**. In a world in which we celebrate and bask in the international super highway of communication with finger-tip access to the world's archives of human knowledge, we have overlooked the corresponding imperative to be equally grounded and excessively equipped with super-natural knowledge of divine teachings, impartations and revelations of the Word of God through the cosmic supernatural medium of the Holy Spirit

> **For the Word that God speaks is alive and full of power [making it active]; it is sharper than any two-edged sword, penetrating to the dividing line of the breath of life (soul) and [the immortal] spirit, and of joints and marrow [of the deepest parts of our nature], exposing and sifting and analyzing and judging the very thoughts and purposes of the heart. Hebrews 4:11**

We are not fighting against flesh and blood, so acquisition of the trinkets and trophies of material and carnal measures of success are useless in this time of warfare. Instead, we must be prepared, practiced, professionally armed to the hilt with the weapons of our warfare, which are spiritual not carnal, as we have been ordered by God.

12. For our struggle is not against flesh and blood, but against the rulers, against the authorities, against the powers of this dark world and against the spiritual forces of evil in the heavenly realms. 13. Therefore put on the full armor of God, so that when the day of evil comes, you may be able to stand. Ephesians 6:12. (NIV)

The aim, objective and effect of our royal assignment from God is to have a clear vision, unwavering acceptance, a state of preparedness and unobstructed, unimpaired focus on the fight and the prize to be won when the war ends. We can achieve these by the Spirit of God through active orchestration, participation, implementation and fulfillment of any and all actions that will curtail, disarm, eliminate and defeat the deceiver and destroyer of the human family. We must put on the full armor of God, be practiced in the use of all weapons of our warfare and be ready to employ them against any individual, demon or dark force, any philosophy, power or principality, any creed, culture or constitution that would seek to defeat us, detach or distract us from the assignment to which God has appointed us

It has been decreed since the Fall of Man, that the usurper of our God-given authority, manipulator of our ordained dominion over the earth-realm, and challenger to the Throne of God and His Kingdom authority is to be the focus of all human efforts. This is the only way we can be compliant with the appointment that our Lord declared in Eden. We were openly attacked and invaded in our own divinely created and specifically ordained territory. We cannot, must not, will not surrender our inheritance and then join with the mastermind of our destruction to further oppose our loving Creator, God the Father!

Our God-given position and place in the Kingdom was undermined by the enemy. But God in His mercy has given us another chance and a warrior heart to heed the call to arms and join in the Battle of all battles. **"The Kingdom of heaven suffers violence and the violent take it by force". Matthew 11:12.** God has gifted us with a warrior spirit that might be eclipsed but not extinguished, denied but not destroyed, curtailed but not culminated by the dirty, low-down, detestable plans of our enemy, the devil. Women, rise up and fight every move, motive and monstrous plot that originates from and is generated by the schemes of our arch enemy, that old serpent, the devil.

We have been commissioned and commanded to engage in hostilities until **'the kingdoms of this world (again) become the Kingdom of our Lord'. Revelation 11:15.** Until the Lord is once more in command of this realm with a redeemed, reconciled human family, and the re-instated reign of His Kingdom of Righteousness, hostilities **will** continue. There can be no compromise; no negotiations, no ceasefires or cessation of hostilities until our God is declared Lord of all, forevermore.

And the seventh angel sounded; and there were great voices in heaven, saying; the kingdoms of this world are become the Kingdom of our Lord, and of His Christ; and He shall reign for ever and ever. Revelation 11:15 (NIV)

And so, because the devil is well aware that women are truly his enemies by divine ordination, he does everything in his power to subvert, undermine, railroad and destroy the purpose of God to unify men and women in a single mission and a common goal. That objective is to utilize our combined forces to fight the fight of faith, truth, love and righteousness. Every child of God living in this realm that is under the burden of darkness and the control of the demonic forces of Satan, have been appointed to warfare.

As we will learn from this study, women have a divinely mandated mantel of spiritual warfare that bequeaths us divine and earthly responsibility, duty, purpose and destiny. These duties are directly dictated in God's Word, the Bible. The enemy has never lost sight of this mandate. Consequently, because of his knowledge and understanding of the far-reaching effect that could result from man's acceptance and activation of the mandate, he has systematically set about aborting, diverting, distorting, denying, dissipating and compromising the ability, capacity, potential power and progress of women in the battle for the souls of our children, our family and our heritage.

But sisters all, let us put the devil on notice; we have a divine commission to spiritual warfare, we have the Word of God, we have the seal of authority of Jesus Christ, we have the power of the Holy Spirit, we have the weapons of our warfare, the will, the way, the passion and the perseverance to comply with the divine ordinance of our Commander-in Chief.

10. That in (at) the name of Jesus every knee should (must) bow, in heaven and on earth and under the earth.

11. And every tongue [frankly and openly] confess, and acknowledge that Jesus Christ is Lord, to the glory of God the Father.

12. Therefore, my dear ones, as you have always obeyed [my suggestions], so now, not only [with the enthusiasm you would show] in my presence but much more because I am absent, work out (cultivate, carry out to the goal, and fully complete) your own salvation with reverence and awe and trembling (self-distrust, with serious caution, tenderness of conscience, watchfulness against temptation, timidly shrinking from whatever might offend God and discredit the name of Christ).

13. [Not in your own strength] for it is God Who is all the while effectually at work in you [energizing and creating in you the power and desire], both to will and to work for His good pleasure and satisfaction and delight.
Philippians 2:10-13.

One thing I do [it is my one aspiration]: forgetting what lies behind and straining forward to what lies ahead.
14. I press on toward the goal to win the [supreme and heavenly] prize to which God in Christ Jesus is calling us upward. Philippians 3:13 and 14

7. However, we possess this precious treasure [the divine Light of the Gospel] in [frail, human] vessels of earth that the grandeur and exceeding greatness of the power may be shown to be from God and not from ourselves. 2 Corinthians 4:7

CHAPTER 2

THE FIRST COMMISSION OF THE HUMAN FAMILY AT WAR

The Role of Women

Throughout all times and in all societies, the role of the female of the family has been dismissed, devalued and distorted during various periods of history. Its significance outside the bearing of children has been almost obliterated by the orchestrations and maneuvers of the enemy, the devil. Historically, women have been relegated to the role of chattel; property to be owned or disposed of by men, whether those men are fathers or husbands.

The current position is generally, very similar in practicality for the majority of girls and women across the globe. The ever-increasing incidence of physical, mental and sexual exploitation and violence towards females has reached alarming figures. This summation applies in all areas whether, natural or spiritual, in all nations whether developed, developing or undeveloped, in all cultures whether traditional or modern and almost all religions.

In many countries and societies therefore, the status and position of women is still overtly or covertly regulated and enforced by law, traditions, culture, economics and religion. In others, such as some modern western countries, contrary to the populist view, there are still a large number of women who are treated within their homes and communities as second-class citizens, disposable people of debatable value.

This is amazing in view of the fact that the majority of women share in, and often shoulders the economic, social and psychological responsibility and spiritual training of children, the future adults and leaders of society. The distorted view expressed or implied in most societies, that women have no valuable contribution to make with respect to the important and weightier matters of the governing of the nations, organizations or institutions at any meaningful level is another flawed and flagrant disregard of the authority, power, vision and wisdom the complete unit, male and female in union with God, was divinely designed to achieve together, as one. **"And the two shall become one." Genesis 2:24**

Sedition and Segregation

I believe that this separation and segregation of the sexes that results in demeaning a woman or dismissing her worth is a seditious strategy of the devil. It is designed to keep men trapped in their own idolatrous, egotistical world and to keep women disgruntled, depressed, distracted, disabled and disenfranchised. In turn, this state of affairs will keep us all disorganized, disunited and distant from the real challenges that life in this fallen earth realm presents.

These endemic and evil divisions that are enforced through various cultural, economic, religious and political imperatives have prevented the human family from pouring all of our combined efforts, energies and corporate power, physically and spiritually into the battle against Satan. Regrettably for us but to the delight of the demonic forces that constantly assails us, the status quo that prevails in the organizations and institutions of the world are to a large extent replicated in the organization, structure and functioning of religious bodies including the Christian churches.

Women are perceived as useful, even necessary as foot soldiers, followers, and congregants. But when the time comes to strategize and implement attacks against the kingdom of darkness, women are most often relegated to the periphery of operations. The position of women as frontline warriors is not realized as their positions are not perceived as important enough to be so designated by church hierarchy. On both counts, women are regarded as secondary supporters to the soul work of our male leaders.

It is time now for men and women to catch the vision of the Lord in Eden after the Fall; a united force of humanity engaged on all fronts. We must come together as one force against the serpent; the sneaky, malicious, evil enemy that stole our paradisiacal joy, peace, holy beauty, perfection and unity with God. He stole the very covering of our bodies rendering us naked, ashamed, guilty, lost and alienated from our loving Creator!

Men and women must clearly recognize their God-appointed positions within the family, society and the nations, and reconcile these with their divine assignments to spiritual warfare and ultimately the victorious destiny that waits in Christ Jesus our Lord. We are all called to serve after the example of our Lord. **"Just as the Son of man did not come to be served, but to serve... ", Matthew 20:28**, in the same manner we are called **"to serve one another in love" Galatians 5:13. (NIV)**

The greatest service that the Christ came to perform is the redemption of the human family and its restoration to the Presence and rule of God. It is to this end that we also serve with Christ Jesus; it is the reason for our calling in Christ, our commission to war and our commitment to obey God in love, sharing His love abroad with our fellow man.

"Just as You sent Me into the world, I also have sent them into the world", said the Lord of His disciples in His prayer in **John 17:18**; a prayer which He concludes with the following summation of purpose in **verse 26:**

> I have made Your Name known to them and revealed Your character and Your very Self, and I will continue to make [You] known, that the love which You have

bestowed upon Me may be in them [felt in their hearts] and that I [Myself] may be in them.

As Christians we are all under the authority of the Lord, members of His Body, His bride the Church. Indeed we must respect and honor the person appointed by the Holy Spirit as a shepherd or steward of His church. But we must also remember that the Bible tells us to submit to one another. That means therefore women to men and men to women, young to old and old to young, one caste or class to another, such as leaders to followers and followers to leaders, employers to workers and workers to employers; this excludes a hierarchical order established to divide, separate and elevate sets of people above each other within the body of Christ. Our submission is grounded in the pure love of the heart that is likewise fully yielded in reverence to Christ our Lord. **Ephesians 5: 21**

The Beginning of Hierarchy

At the commencement of human existence on the earth, the exercise of authority and dominion in the earth was placed equally on the shoulders of both male and female. Our Creator also gave joint responsibility for the proper functioning of the marital relationship to the male and female united in love with Him. They both received the heavenly decree to procreate and people the planet within the operation of that relationship, for the further glory of God and the natural out-flowing of His love and theirs. **Genesis 1:28 tells us -**

God blessed them and said to them, Be fruitful, multiply, and fill the earth, and subdue it [using all its vast resources in the service of God and man]; and have dominion over the fish of the sea, the birds of the air, and over every living creature that moves upon the earth.

After all, love is a creative force whose very nature is to increase, to flow, to share and to grow. For example, that is why we feel so driven, so compelled to share the love of God once we give our lives to Him and His love fills our souls through the Presence of the Holy Spirit. God is the only true source of love and the love that comes into our hearts comes directly from Him; it is the very essence, life-blood and spiritual elixir of a child of God. And it matters not whether we are male or female, once we have been reborn into the perfect image of God, through Jesus Christ; we are imbued with the potential to be just like Him. Love is the perfect image of God and the fullness and reflection of love is more love. That is our destiny, to be the perfect image and likeness of love, of God.

Brethren, do you not share in my amazement that despite all the efforts of Satan to separate men and women spiritually, in Christ there is truly no distinction that is stated in His word? Other religions may practice differences in access to, study and worship of their gods but for the followers of Jehovah God, there is no such separation. There is only one Spirit, one Christ, one crucifixion, one resurrection, one salvation, one baptism and one way that we can become children of God.

There is not a different redemption for women and one for men, there is only one Door through which we all must enter into His Presence. Neither do we have different weapons of our spiritual warfare, different character traits to be perfected, gender appropriate spiritual gifts, feminine and masculine fruits of the Spirit, male and female spiritual realms or two robes of righteousness. There is only one way, one truth, one redemption, one atonement, One Holy Spirit, One Christ, and One God.

Our First State

The particular conditions and circumstances that would attend the attainment of the first directives of government and lifestyle given to men and women in their perfect garden state had to be amended by the Lord after sin. The declaration of hostilities against the enemy proclaimed by the Most High in the Garden of Eden firstly, placed a wedge of division, and a demarcation between the devil and mankind and will remain until **"the tabernacle of God is with men, and He will dwell with them, and they shall be His**

people, and God Himself shall be with them, and be their God". Revelation 21:3.

Secondly, it placed a hierarchical structure between men and women in order to better facilitate the additional roles and responsibilities that were given to them after sin entered the earth realm. However, this change was not designed by the Lord as a means of causing divisions, exploitation and oppression between men and women, neither was it meant to indicate superiority or inferiority due to the different areas of responsibility assigned by the Lord to each.

The revelation that we need to understand is that the time for unity in Christ, under His banner of Love and Righteousness, between all sections of the human family; genders, races, colors or cultures, is **Now**. Now is the day of salvation; now is the acceptable time of our Lord. A house that is divided from within cannot stand. Divisions originate with the devil and his strategy of divisiveness breeds mistrust and hatred. Divisions within the Body of Christ can only delay the work of the Gospel and the return of the Lord.

Without a doubt, we are approaching a time of great trials and testing for the people of God. Spiritual battles are intensifying because Satan knows his time is running out. As stated in the Scriptures**, 'he is going about as a roaring lion seeking to destroy as many as he possibly can'. 1 Peter 5:8.** The whole human family needs to 'wise-up' and true wisdom comes only from worshipping God in Spirit and in Truth.

Women, who comprise the largest portion of this earth's human population, need to take up, and be allowed their rightful, righteous place on the battlefield alongside men with confidence; fully conscious, alert and aware of their roles and responsibilities, perfectly trained, prepared, seasoned and passionate to pursue the enemy in the service of the King of kings and the Lord of lords.

Women were given the promise of redemption in the very same decree and at the very same time as she was offered a chance to become an ally of God's Kingdom. We are assured on the authority of the Holy Spirit that when we become children of God through the Christ, we are all are restored to our inheritance in unity and equality with Jesus the Lord.

Nevertheless [the sentence put upon women of pain in motherhood does not hinder their souls' salvation, and] they will be saved [eternally] if they continue in faith and love and holiness with self control, [saved indeed] through the Childbearing or by the birth of the divine Child. 1 Timothy 2:15

It is only by having faith in the atonement of the divine Offspring, Jesus the Christ, can women, or men, secure salvation from our sinful, fallen state and be born again into the state of perfection that God originally placed us and intended for us to abide. After Paul speaks on the position, posture and propriety of women, he makes it clear that our calling and election is made certain in the Messiah, the Seed of woman; His birth, sacrifice and triumph restores us to our former unity and equality with men and righteousness in Christ Jesus.

Therefore, [there is] now no condemnation (no adjudging guilty or wrong) for those who are in Christ Jesus, who live [and] walk not after the dictates of the flesh, but after the dictates of the Spirit. 2. For the law of the Spirit of life [which is] in Christ Jesus [the law of our new being] has freed me from the law of sin and death. Romans 8:1-2

Men of God need to open their eyes to the handicap caused by the prevailing hypocrisy that allows a demarcation and a distinction between:

a. Who may or may not be called to the battlefield of our Lord
b. Where that battlefield is located
c. Treating one battle location as superior to another
d. Decided according to gender rather than the appointment of the Holy Spirit.

Service to God should never be determined by the preferences and prejudices of God's people. **Galatians 3:28** expands on the equality that lies in the Cross and in Christ the Messiah:

There is [now no distinction] neither Jew nor Greek, there is neither slave nor free, there is not male or female; for you are all one in Christ Jesus.

Women of God have a responsibility to avoid the entrapment of the enemy who will always bombard us with his diabolical diversionary tactics. It is time to put on the character of Christ and the full armor of righteousness and boldly step to our responsibility as God's anointed and His royally appointed warriors. Every woman is destined to experience training and preparation for warfare through the every day conditions and circumstances of her life as female. I refer to these experiences as our 'Spiritual Boot Camp'. God made sure that the circumstances and conditions attendant on our roles as mothers, wives and warriors will equip and empower us to recognize the enemy in all situations and wage spiritual warfare without fear or favor and with intent, purpose, passion and determination.

As God's warriors, our **Genesis 3:15** orders came with the assurance of victory through the divine Offspring, the Messiah. Women of God in ages past, before the actual, physical birth of the Christ, looked forward with the eyes of faith, believing in their deliverance and triumph in the Promised Child. Since the earthly ministry of Jesus, women of today are able to look at His first coming, His Sacrifice for sin, His victory over its consequences of bondage to death, disease, suffering and destruction and with certain knowledge and faith in His word, receive Him as Savior and Lord. We can now look towards His soon return in glory, power, authority and final triumph over our enemy. We have the proof that God's promise, prophecy and providence declared in **Genesis 3:15** are faithful. This should inspire us with even greater faith in the importance and weight to be attached to His commission to warfare that He decreed for womankind at the same time as the Promised Messiah!

It does not matter what positions we hold or how we are regarded by men in our societies, how we are dressed or addressed, whether we are wearing our sexy high heels, our most comfortable floppy sandals, beaded bedroom slippers, boardroom power pumps or running barefooted from the bullwhips of oppression, exploitation, degradation and ignorance. The time to be who we are destined to be in Christ is right now.

Our destiny lies only in the Christ and the way and Cause of the Cross. So who are we women of God? We are God's warriors, the warrior women of the Kingdom of the Most High. As women we have always paid a very high price just because we are born female. And if we must continue to pay with our very lives, even as our Savior, the Son of God, paid with His life, then let it be our portion; we overcome by not being afraid to lay down our very lives for our Lord. So leaving the past and all those things which held us captive, thus preventing our full and satisfying relationship with the Lord, we press on to the higher calling; our reward is with the Lord and our victory is assured in Him.

13. I do not consider, brethren, that I have captured and made it my own [yet];but one thing I do [it is my one aspiration]; forgetting what lies behind and straining forward to what lies ahead, 14. I press on toward the goal to win the [supreme and heavenly] prize to which God in Christ Jesus is calling us upward. 15. So let those [of us] who are spiritually mature and full-grown have this mind and hold these convictions; and if in any you have a different attitude of mind, God will make that clear to you also. 16. Only let us hold true to what we have already attained and walk and order our lives by that. Philippians 3:13-16

Preparation for Battle

In today's world there is no time to play at serving God or to be maneuvered or compromised into ineffectual fighting postures and positions. Women must take up their assigned rank as warriors. This is not a new or fashionable direction or development orchestrated by modern women. Neither is it a call for changes in doctrines, schools of thought, teachings, theologies or the adoption of an attitude or approach to appease modern sensibilities. This is not a promotion to reward feminism, the educational achievements, economic power or political will of women, or a product of the so-called enlightenment of the times in the name of progress or the pressures of political parties and peers.

But, it is a timely intervention of the fruition of the words of prophecy and the revelation of the will of God to this latter day generation, for a sign of the times in which we live. Recognition of the **Genesis 3:15** call to spiritual warfare, to which the Almighty God appointed the females of the human family in the Garden of Eden, is a reality, a responsibility and a necessity that all the peoples of God must embrace in love and obedience; for us to be at enmity with God is death while to be at enmity with the devil is life eternal!
Romans 8:7.

The Lord God directed, declared and decreed the commission of women to warfare in the Garden of Eden to Satan, even before He spoke to the woman and the man. All the hosts of heaven and the un-fallen worlds bore witness to this declaration, even as the Bible records it for our instruction. **Genesis 3:15** reads as follows;

And I will put enmity between thee and the woman, and between thy seed and her "Seed"; it shall bruise your head, and thou shalt bruise His heel. (KJV)

The modern translations of the Bible use the word "Offspring" in place of the word "Seed' but I must confess to having a preference for the word 'Seed' because of all the connotations attached to that word and the images that it conjures in my spirit. God promised that the Seed of the woman would crush, destroy and defeat the serpent while Himself suffering bruises, hurt and pain in the process, but never annihilation. The final victory of the Seed of the woman is the desire and certain hope of the ages; it was so during the times spoken and written of in the Old and the New Testaments, as well as taught, preached and prophesied today and it will remain so for all the tomorrows until the end of this dispensation.

The contents of the **Genesis 3:15** decree necessitates the training, preparation, equipping and empowering of women for warfare. It is also the source of the fear that drives the enemy to commit great atrocities and perpetuate extremely hateful acts against women in the past and as well as today. Even with the birth of the "Offspring", Jesus our Lord, His triumphant ministry on earth, the serpent is still terrified of the unity, agreement and joint assault of the army of man; the righteous, blood-bought, Holy Spirit filled people of God. He still tries to destroy any opportunity for consensus, agreement and obedience to the will and commands of God that will bring the family of man together as one united force against his evil designs and his empire of darkness. But we must unite and fight; our orders have already be issued in the Garden of Eden and re-affirmed by the Messiah.

The Genesis 3:15 Commission

The following is a brief summary of the content and the consequential implementation of the Commission.

1. It declares the commencement of hostilities between the serpent and the human family.

And I will put enmity between you and the woman. Genesis 3:15. (NIV)

And the huge dragon was cast down and out – that age old serpent, who is called the Devil and Satan, he who is the seducer (deceiver) of all humanity the world over; he was forced out and down to the earth, and his angels were flung out along with him. Revelation 12:9. (NIV)

2. Commissions the first spiritual warriors from among the human victims of the enemy.

34. He teaches my hands to war, so that my arms can bend a bow of bronze. 35. You have also given me the shield of your salvation, and Your right hand has held me up; Your gentleness and condescension have made me great. 39. For you have girded me with strength for the battle; You have subdued under me and caused to bow down those who rose up against me. Psalms 18:34 -35 and 39 (NIV)

Blessed be the Lord my Rock and my keen and firm Strength, who teaches my hands to war and my fingers to fight. Psalms 144:1.

3. Indicates the start of a military operation manned by the citizens of the earth.

I have commanded my holy ones; I have summoned my warriors to carry out my wrath – those who rejoice in my triumph. 4. Listen, a noise on the mountains, like that of a great multitude! Listen, an uproar among the Kingdoms, like nations massing together! The Lord Almighty is mustering an army for war. 5. They come from faraway lands, from the ends of the heavens – and the Lord and the weapons of His wrath – to destroy the whole country. Isaiah 13:3 (NIV)

4. Earth and its citizens becomes a battlefield; the kingdom of darkness pitched against the Kingdom of Light.

14. For really they are the spirits of demons that perform signs (wonders, miracles). And they go forth to the rulers and leaders all over the world, to gather them together for war on the great day of God Almighty. 16. And they gathered them together at the place which in Hebrew is called Armageddon. Revelation 16:14, 16

And he (Satan) will go forth to deceive and seduce and lead astray the nations which are in the four corners of the earth – Gog and Magog – to muster them for war; their number is like the sand of the sea. 9. And they swarmed up over the broad plain of the earth and encircled the fortress (camp) of God's people (the saints) and the beloved city. Revelation 20:8, 9

5. Instituted military training for warriors to prepare them for spiritual warfare.

Behold I have refined you but not as silver, I have tried and trained you in the furnace of affliction, and, No weapon that is formed against you shall prosper... Isaiah 48:10, 54:17.

Beloved, do not be amazed and bewildered at the fiery ordeal which is taking place to test your quality, as though something strange (unusual and alien to you and your position) were befalling you. 1 Peter 4:12

6. Established an Armory of spiritual weapons that are the necessary fighting equipment of His warriors.

3. For though we walk (live) in the flesh, we are not carrying on our warfare according to the flesh and using mere human weapons, 4. For the weapons of our warfare are not physical [weapons of flesh and blood], but they are mighty before God for the overthrow and destruction of strongholds. 2 Corinthians 10:3 and 4

7. Decreed the emergence of the final WMD (Weapon of Mass Destruction); the Seed of the Woman, the Messiah.

6. For unto us a Child is born, to us a Son is given; and the government shall be upon His Shoulder, and His name shall be called Wonderful Counselor, Mighty God,

Everlasting Father (of Eternity], Prince of Peace. 7. of the increase of His Government and of peace there shall be no end ...Isaiah 9:6, 7

Jesus approached and, breaking the silence, said to them, All authority (all power of rule) in heaven and on earth has been given to Me. Matthew 28:18

8. Announced the inevitable losses and casualties of the war to be expected and accepted.

9. Then they will hand you over to suffer affliction and tribulation and put you to death and you will be hated by all nations for My name's sake. 10. And then many will begin to distrust and desert [Him Whom they ought to trust and obey] and will stumble and fall away and betray one another with hatred. Matthew 24:9, 10

So then, any of you who does not forsake (renounce, surrender claim to, give up, say good-bye to) all that he has cannot be My disciple", says the Lord. Luke 14:33

And so it is that "By faith Abraham, when he was put to the test ... was ready to sacrifice his only son". Hebrews 11:17.

9. Proclaimed the conclusion and the outcome of hostilities and the War.

They will wage war against the Lamb, and the Lamb will triumph over them; for He is Lord of lords and King of Kings – and those with Him and on His side are chosen and called [elected] and loyal and faithful followers. Revelation 17:14

I have told you these things, so that in Me you may have [perfect] peace and confidence. In the world you have

tribulation and trials and distress and frustration; but be of good cheer [take courage; be confident, certain, undaunted]! For I have overcome the world. [I have deprived it of power to harm you and have conquered it for you]. John 16:33

The Numbers of Divine Love, Purpose and Plan

There is a symbolism that is attached to certain numbers and which, in the example of the numbers 3, 1, and 5, allows us to have a quick insight into the ministry of the Messiah, His message and its meaning for our lives; as this Scripture in Genesis directly relates to the mission of His warriors still on earth and the Plan of Redemption.

- The number 3 represents the Triune Godhead.
- The number 1 is the number that represents unity, and,
- The number 5 represents Grace, the grace of our God.

The Triune God: Everything begins and ends with God, Elohim, the Triune Godhead; The Father, Son and Holy Ghost present together at the creation of the earth and man. Genesis records the beginning of all life forms, fauna and flora as well as the origin of human institutions and social relationships on the earth. All the Persons of the Godhead were present and participative in the creation process. Elohim said **"Let us make man"**. Every member of the Godhead created.

Unity: The expression of divine love is manifested through the foundational principle of unity. The most important revelation that we take for granted is that the three Persons of the Godhead are all together, God. This Tri-partite oneness is represented throughout God's creation so that our one universe is made up of time, space and matter; the sun is composed of light, heat and energy. Another important example is Time, which is divided into past, present and future, a linear measure that enables us to chart our experiences according to the natural order of our universe as instituted by the Creator.

Grace: Without the grace of God we would be forever lost in sin. Grace is His unmerited favor towards us that flows from His love and His mercy. We cannot earn His blessings with our own righteousness, which is just as filthy rags in His sight. **1 Timothy 1:14** points out that the grace of our Lord is exceedingly abundant. It is the grace of God by which He planned for our redemption and restoration. Because of the love that God has for us, He has given us freely of His grace, loving us when we were His enemies, when we sided with the adversary and revolted against His Lordship in our lives.

Humanity: The numbers 1 plus 5 is equal to the number 6 which could be another way of regarding 1 and 5. The number 6 is the number for human weakness, sinful man, who since the disobedience of Eden has come short of perfection. It is no surprise to read that the number of the Beast is the number of a man; 666. I believe that the number 6 is stated three times in order to emphasize the plot of Satan to set up a counterfeit to impersonate the Triune Godhead; three Persons in 'One', as outlined above.

> **This calls for wisdom. If anyone has insight, let him calculate the number of the beast, for it is man's number. His number is 666. Revelation 13:18 (NIV)**

The revelation then concerning the numbers in **Genesis 3:15** may be summarized and expressed in the following statement:

From the very beginning, God the Father, the Son and the Holy Ghost have determined on a divine plan to re-unite and restore the unity that existed between the Creator and His created before the Fall of man in the Garden of Eden. This Plan of Redemption is offered to us, the human family, by the grace of God through Jesus Christ, the Second Person of the Godhead who offers us atonement for our sinful rebellion.

This is the motive, the impetus, the reason, the purpose and determination of God that led to the commission of every woman of God in **Genesis 3:15**; to be engaged in continuous warfare against the devil and to hold fast to the promise that through her Seed, final victory is certain. God's enemy is our enemy; His war is the war of all His children. Satan is as much against God our father as he is against the human family. **Psalms 139:21, 22**

Fruits of the Spirit: This is a postscript to the revelation above concerning the symbolism of the numbers that appear in the biblical text that is the **Genesis 3:15 Commission.** The sum total of the numbers, 3, 1 and 5 is 9. The number 9 has attached to it the fruits of the Spirit. Acceptance of the **Genesis 3:15** 'Call to Service' is first of all, an acceptance that we are sinners in need of a Savior. It is a call to repentance for our sins. Next, it is a call for us to make a complete surrender to the will of God in and for our lives. Then, it requires from us a total regenerative acceptance of Jesus Christ's atonement for our personal salvation and the redemption of the world.

Acceptance of the Lordship of the Christ and God the Father in our lives and our world leads to spiritual rebirth with the consequential endowment, receipt and indwelling of the Holy Spirit. As we are filled with the Holy Spirit, we pursue obedience to the will of God and willingly embrace His purpose for our lives. At the same time, as we live and walk by the Spirit, the fruits of the Spirit will become manifested in us for the glory of our God and a living testimony of His love and His grace. The character of God's warriors is developed to show the character of Jesus the Christ by the working of the Spirit in instructing, teaching, preparing and sanctifying us to effectively war against evil. **Galatians 5:22-25**.

This is the conclusion of the numerical symbolism and importance of the **Genesis 3:15** commission; all things, all our experiences, struggles, pains, travail, trial and testing, work towards a single purpose of preparing and empowering us to be warrior women of the Kingdom of Righteousness during our life-time and to pass on this same call, spiritual culture and commitment to each succeeding generation.

The Fear Factor

Men have generally sought to deny or distort the interpretation, importance and application of the **Genesis 3:15** commission of women and instead have used the events of the Garden as reason and excuse for centuries of misogyny against the females of the human family. The enemy's deception has driven a wedge of division between God and man, and equally deadly between male and female. He even tried to engineer a division between the Father and the Son during the temptation of Christ in the wilderness. Satan has so perfected the art of 'divide and conquer' that the Body of Christ falls prey to the many variations of the same theme. If you don't believe me, count the number of Christian denominations that prevail in our world today.

In this devil-induced division, man has unwittingly sided with the destroyer abusing their roles as the head of families and communities. They have used the events of Eden as an excuse to bolster their belief that the positions of stewards, shepherds, overseers and leaders in the world, extends to the organization of the Church resulting in the loss of the meaningful, dynamic, potential contribution that women bring to the service of the Kingdom.

Women have generally accepted the limitations placed on them by the religious institution called 'the church'. We have either completely agreed with this position and therefore have no concerns or, although we feel that this teaching/doctrine is not divine truth, we feel powerless to affect any change. There are two promises in the Word that women have been able to rely on in the face of opposition. The first is that God is going to have His Way in the end.

> **We are assured and know that [God being a partner in their labor] all things work together and are [fitting into a plan] for good to and for those who love God and are called according to [His] design and purpose. Romans 8:28**

Secondly, the Psalmist goes further, exhorting us to patience, perseverance and trust in the purposes and prophecies of the Lord.

Wait on the Lord and be of good courage and He shall strengthen your heart, wait I say on the Lord. Psalms 27:14. (KJV)

So women have waited, occupying themselves for the Kingdom in the ways accessible to them; they have accepted the mantels of sacrifice and suffering, living holy lives acceptable to the Lord. We have held our ground in such ministries as prayer, hospitality, and praise and worship. Many have suppressed their convictions and their desires to respond affirmatively to the call to leadership and have only given expression to their service to God in ways that does not incite opposition, fear and antagonism from our brothers. But the Lord assures us in His Word to put on the **"full armor of God"** and having done all that we can, **"to stand"** and be witnesses to the move of the Holy Spirit that will tear down barriers and remove stumbling blocks to individual and corporate revelation, regarding the true identity of the Father's daughters as spiritual warriors. **Ephesians 6:12.**

Women have recognized and supported men in the assignment the Lord have given to them. After all, the men of God are assigned to confront and combat opposition in the earth realm from natural and man-made disasters, as well as from those engineered by demonic forces. Rightly, women have accepted and fulfilled our role as helpers to our men. However, the overwhelming evidence everywhere in the Church of Christ supports the fact that men have not accorded equal honor, appreciation, facilitation, or acceptance of the call that God has placed on women.

Generally speaking, the male or male dominated hierarchy of the Church has refused to consider that the traditionally held interpretation of the role of women in the work of the Gospel of Christ may be off the mark. Or else, they have shown only partial or grudging acceptance or acquiescence of women's call to leadership and spiritual warfare, even with the inescapable evidence of fully surrendered lives and the anointing and special gifts of the Holy Spirit.

This opposition however is contrary to the expressed will of God. We all have a duty to share in the mission of Jesus Christ to save lost souls and advance Kingdom authority in the earth. Instead what has actually happened is that men have carried their leadership roles as husbands, administrators, protectors and providers in this natural earth realm over into the spiritual realm. There seems to be a conviction that to admit that God has called us to serve with equal purpose as His warriors in the spiritual realm will diminish men's authority, effectiveness and their superior status within the earth realm. May I suggest that this is pride where there ought to be humility, ignorance where there ought to be godly knowledge and understanding, and arrogance where there ought to be acceptance of divine order in all matters spiritual.

> **Submit to one another out of reverence for Christ. 22. Wives, submit to your husbands as to the Lord. 23. For, the husband is the head of the wife as Christ is the head of the church, his body, of which He is the Savior. 24. Now as the church submits to Christ, so also wives should submit to their husbands in everything. Ephesians 5:21-25. (NIV)**

Men and women are equally commissioned to fight in the spiritual realm as God's warriors against the forces of evil. However, our brothers have used their appointed positions of leadership within the family and in the natural world, as a reason to deny the right of women to stand as equals in the task of organizing and leading the saints in spiritual warfare against our joint enemy. As **"the weaker vessel"**, women are expected to remain in the ranks behind the men while they lead the war against the wiles of the enemy; the same way that they lead and control the organizations of society, generally. But God's ways are different to men and the way of the Spirit is different to the way of the flesh. This is made clear in the bible and finds expression in the God-breathed words of the Apostle Paul in **Romans 8:5-11.**

But the simple fact is that God has chosen the weaker vessel to be a spiritual warrior. I am convinced that one of the reasons is that there will then be no room for mistake in whose Person all the glory, the honor and the praise should be placed. God's strength is demonstrated in the weaker vessel because it is apparent that such victories as can be attained could only be achieved by divine appointment or intervention. If men believe that women cannot be frontline opponents of the devil because we were deceived in Eden, by that same rationale, what should be said of men who were not deceived but deliberately sinned? But the truth is we all sinned and in Christ Jesus we are all equally forgiven and redeemed if we choose Him.

Since God's way is different to the ways of mankind, it comes as no surprise to find that the War of Righteousness is not subject to the same rules or conditions that apply in the wars that erupt between men and nations on this earth. We do not have to go very far in the Scriptures to discover that when the Children of Israel went into battle against their enemies under the direction of Jehovah God, their warfare was not 'natural' or typical according to the military planning of other peoples. Consider for example, Joshua and the battle for Jericho, the heroic exploits of Gideon or even David against Goliath and the Philistines.

It is no surprise therefore, to discover that spiritual warfare is governed by a higher law and by the order of a Supernatural God. And when we become children of God, we become **"partakers of the divine nature"** and subject to His laws, His way. **2 Peter 1:4**. We know that the ways of the Lord are not the ways of man and are beyond the ability of our carnal minds to comprehend.

8. For My thoughts are not your thoughts, neither are your ways My ways, says the Lord. 9. For as the heavens are higher than the earth, so are my ways higher than your ways and my thoughts than your thoughts. Isaiah 55:8, 9 (KJV)

There is organized opposition, resentment and bitterness towards God's women becoming pastors, bishops, apostles, elders, and like officers, within certain sections/denominations in the Body of Christ; despite the absence of any such prohibition detailed in the Scriptures. The qualities required for stewardship positions are gender neutral, requiring only a character that reflects the character of the Christ. The attitude, behavior, language and theology that have been targeted against women in leadership in the church, most often does not reflect the love or the will of God.

> **Let all bitterness and indignation and wrath (passion, rage, bad temper) and resentment (anger, animosity) and quarrelling (brawling, clamor, contention) and slander (evil-speaking, abusive or blasphemous language) be banished from you, with all malice (spite, ill will or baseness of any kind). 32. and become useful and helpful and kind to one another, tenderhearted (compassionate, understanding, loving-hearted). Ephesians 4:31, 32**

Many women that have been reborn into the family of God are denied so-called leadership roles in the Church despite being obviously blessed with the gifts and qualities of those offices by the Holy Spirit. But the Word of God tells us that all the gifts of the Holy Spirit, in whomever they reside, are to be used for the benefit of the Body of Christ and the glory of His name. No one is to be prevented from edifying the Body of believers.

> **11. It was He (Jesus) who gave to some to be apostles, some to be prophets, some to be evangelists, and some to be pastors and teachers 12. To prepare God's people for works of service, so that the body of Christ may be built up. 13. Until we all reach unity in the faith and in the knowledge of the Son of God and become mature, attaining to the whole measure of the fullness of Christ. Ephesians 4:11-13.**

Furthermore, the Scriptures also declares that there will be an equal outpouring and granting of the gifts of the Spirit to God's children, male and female, in these last days and this is a sign on the earth that the glorious "Day of the Lord" referred to in **Isaiah 4:2-6** is certainly at hand.

In **Acts 2:17-18** we find the Apostle Peter on the Day of Pentecost reminding the people that they are witnessing the fulfillment of prophecy:

17. In the last days, God says, I will pour out my Spirit on all people. Your sons and daughters will prophesy, your young men will see visions, your old men will dream dreams. 18. Even on my servants, both men and women, I will pour out my Spirit in those days, and they will prophesy. (NIV)

I want us to note that when Peter spoke these words, he was referring to that specific time, that specific day of Pentecost as the time in which the prophecy was being fulfilled. The Holy Spirit came upon the one hundred and twenty disciples, male and female. **Acts 1:14** records, there were women and men together in the upper chamber; waiting and praying for the Holy Spirit. **Acts 2:1-4** goes on to make it clear that there was no distinction when the Holy Spirit fell on them; they were all filled, indiscriminately, equally. The Holy Spirit was not bestowed for personal aggrandizement but for the work of spreading the Gospel message.

The Apostle Peter felt it necessary to remind the listeners of the prophecy of Joel that men and women would both receive the outpouring of God's Spirit. It can reasonably be inferred that as there were women among the body of believers that day, filled with the Holy Spirit and professing Christ. Women expounding the Word would have raised concerns and perhaps disdain and dismissal of the disciples' message because of the presence of women. No doubt that was the reason Peter felt it necessary to answer objections that might or did arise, given the nature of society and the status of women in those days.

It is also wise that we take note of the fact that it is the absence of division; the disciples in the upper chamber being of one accord that is the pre-requisite for the Lord to pour out His Spirit and His power on His worshippers as a corporate body. Divisions and distinctions between believers that have nothing to do with holiness mean that there cannot be 'one accord'. And it was their unity that created the right spiritual atmosphere for the outpouring of the Spirit on Pentecost and the power that followed, resulting in the salvation of over three thousand souls for the Kingdom that day.

We do not need to fight for the fulfillment of prophecy; that is the Lord's responsibility; it is a battle that belongs to God. In the same way that the Lord spoke through His prophet to re-assure King Jehoshaphat, we too must be encouraged, we **need not be afraid or dismayed ... for the battle is not ours, but God's. 2 Chronicles 20:17.** Heaven and earth will fade away before one single utterance of our God is returned to Him void. He has declared the way things will be in the last days, and so they shall be. The Word of the Lord assures me, assures all women that the fight to banish division within the Body of Christ is already won. For if our God spoke then it is already a done deal.

You shall not need to fight in this battle; take your positions, stand still, and see the deliverance of the Lord [Who is] with you. 2 Chronicles 20:17.

As women, we are not at war against men, institutions, prejudices or politics. Our fight is with evil and with the source of all evil. The devil uses his demonic forces and his human agents in all his assaults, attacks and manipulations within the earthly and heavenly realms. But it is for us, as God's warriors, to discern his cunning and craft through the Word and the Spirit of the Lord. We must study and search out his schemes in the heavenly places and identify, intercept and nullify his plots by employing our training in spiritual warfare and its weapons provided us by our Lord.

The devil is our enemy. Being able to see beyond ourselves and the people who are being used to do the enemy's dirty work is absolutely fundamental and urgent to the Cause of Christ. At any time and in any situation that challenges us, we must be spiritually ready so that our words, attitudes and actions can be Spirit-filtered and focused on the source of the assault not on the manifested symptom or its servant. Jesus rebuked Satan, not Peter, when the disciple seemingly tried to prevent the Lord's final stage of His earthly ministry because He was looking beyond the natural and plainly seeing the subtle, disguised hand of Satan in Peter's outburst. We must maintain our God-vision and direct our hostilities at the true adversary. We are God's warriors and the Lord will go before us.

Psalms 18:29, 34-39 and 46-49.

> 29. For by You I can run through a troop, and by my God I can leap over a wall. 34. He teaches my hands to war, so that my arms can bend a bow.
> 35. You have given me the shield of Your salvation, and Your right hand has held me up; Your gentleness and condescension have made me great.
> 36. You have given plenty of room for my steps under me that my feet would not slip.
> 37. I pursued my enemies and overtook them; neither did I turn again until they were consumed.
> 38. I smote them so that they were not able to rise; they fell wounded under my feet. 39. For You have girded me with strength for the battle; You have subdued under me and caused to bow down those who rose up against me.
> 46. The Lord lives! Blessed be my Rock; and let the God of my salvation be exalted. 47. The God Who avenges me and subdues peoples under me.
> 48. Who delivers me from my enemies; yes, You lift me up above those who rise up against me; You deliver me from the man of violence.
> 49. Therefore will I give thanks and extol You, O Lord, among the nations, and sing praises to Your name.

So as I have previously stated, the revelation that is written herein is not new or modern but it is revolutionary. It is the declared and manifested will of the Lord actuated on the day of Pentecost. It should have taken root in the Church of Christ from its inception then, and come down to us through the ages but it did not. We must be aware of the times in which we live and awake to the battle call of our Lord.

> 11. You know what [a critical] hour this is, how it is high time now for you to wake up out of your sleep (rouse to reality). For salvation (final deliverance) is nearer to us

now than when we first believed (adhered to, trusted in, and relied on Christ the Messiah).

12. The night is far gone and the day is almost here. Let us then drop (fling away) the works and deeds of darkness and put on the [full] armor of light.

13. Let us live and conduct ourselves honorably and becomingly as in the [open light of] day, not in reveling (carousing) and drunkenness, not in immorality and debauchery (sensuality and licentiousness), not in quarrelling and jealousy.

14. But clothe yourself with the Lord Jesus Christ (the Messiah), and make no provision for [indulging] the flesh [put a stop to thinking about the evil cravings of your physical nature] to [gratify its] desires (lusts). Romans 13:11-14

As we face the final challenges of these latter days it is imperative that the revelation of this weakness in the battle plans of God's people be openly and honestly addressed and corrected. There is a need for laborers, for all hands to the plough; the fields are white and the Lord of the Harvest is calling us to hard labor in perilous circumstances. Every child of God is a servant of the Kingdom and the cause of advancing righteousness.

Do you not say, 'four months more and then the harvest'? I tell you, open your eyes and look at the fields! They are ripe for harvest. John 4:35

37. Then He said to His disciples, 'The harvest is plentiful but the workers are few. 38. Ask the Lord of the harvest, therefore, to send out workers into his harvest field. Matthew 9:37, 38.

Roadblocks to Revolution

In fact, where we do have women standing on the authority of the Holy Spirit, shepherding the spiritual soldiers of the Lord's army and waging warfare wherever they may be placed in society, many people do not realize or acknowledge the authority and power of their appointment. Instead the institutional barriers and negative attitude of men can be a hindrance and a stumbling block to the will of God and the ministry of women. Many women are handicapped, manipulated, maligned or cowered into submission by structures of opposition and by attitudes of control and criticism. This is cause for a revelatory pause; a caution to those who are arbiters of opposition to the revealed will of the Lord.

Be careful, however, that the exercise of your freedom does not become a stumbling-block to the weak. 1 Corinthians 8:9. (NIV)

Scriptures that were directed to marriages and the management and organization of the home is taken and applied wholesale to the Church. **Genesis 3:16** says quite clearly that the wife's desire will be for her husband and **"he will rule"** over her. The Scripture does not say that the man will rule over all women but rule over his wife only. Neither is this rule of the man applicable to the order of God in the heavens, in the spiritual realm, where we must all stand against the powers of darkness and evil. So then, the headship of the man over his wife and his home has nothing to do with other women who are not their wives, or with men being the only leaders in the organization of the Church.

The commission of women to warfare is universal and is applicable to married and single alike. But the conditions attached to; child birth, the raising of children, the order or rank between husbands and wife and the ordering of the home, after Eden, applies most specifically to married women and is beneficial for their training and preparation for warfare. There are other issues which are gender specific which affect single women most especially and provides the challenges that will prepare and equip their characters as spiritual warriors also.

The home provides a training ground where preparation for warfare in the Kingdom begins. The following is a list of some of the inherent issues that women must traverse by the Spirit and the grace of the Lord.

- ❖ Marriage
- ❖ Motherhood,
- ❖ Sexuality (including physical and emotional issues)
- ❖ Pornography
- ❖ Promiscuity - Fornication & Adultery
- ❖ Gender discrimination,
- ❖ Exploitation,
- ❖ Violence and abuse,
- ❖ Idolatry

This is just a few of the more obvious areas of special concern, struggle and decision that all women warriors face. There are some which are specific to married women and the remainder relates to all women, regardless of marital status. The specific challenges of womanhood must be confronted and resolved in Christ Jesus, the Author of our faith who began the good work of redemption in us. After all, He is able to finish it by equipping us to recognize what is the good and perfect way, in Him. **Philippians 1:6-11**

The sole or exclusive rule of men does not apply to the Body of Christ either. The Body of Christ is manifested in its physicality in the institutions of worship and spiritual warfare, namely the churches, temples, synagogues and meeting houses of the saints and soldiers of God. Here, women and men are to be ruled over by the Lord and governed by the perfect law of His Kingdom. It is only the Lord's appointments within His Church, His anointing by the Holy Spirit and His call to service that is of any consequence, worth, authority or spiritual recognition.

To interpret the Scriptures in a manner that implies, imports or implements division is a contradiction of the declaration of the Most High. This misinterpretation leads to confusion and oppression and can never be the will or desire of the Lord, for our God is not a God of confusion. I am convinced that the **Genesis 3:15** commission of women was a shock to the devil. It was contrary to his intent of turning man against God and recruiting them to his cause forever. Neither would he have anticipated that the very woman that he was able to charm and lead into temptation would be designated his arch enemy, his nemesis. Despite his deception, the heart, mind and spirit of the woman would always challenge him and battle against his evil influence wherever it reared its ugly, evil presence.

Therefore, when women stand their ground according to the prompting, gifting and selection of the Holy Spirit and take on a leadership role in the Cause of the Cross, they are often treated as though they are enemies of the men and rebellious to the teaching and will of the Lord. Like the accuser of the saints, women are constantly reminded of their past in being originally deceived by Satan in Eden but when we are reminded of our past we need to point to the atonement of the Seed of the woman, an atonement which according to God's time was completed from the foundation of the earth!

But every warrior of the Lord's army, by their very nature, training and calling are and must be leaders in opposition to evil. It does not require positions of leadership, as men decide on leadership, for women to be frontline warriors. In every place, every position that we occupy, we are on the frontline and we are leaders in warfare. That is the effect of being born of the Spirit and honoring our God-given assignment to be at enmity with Satan. Later we will look at examples of women who were channels and vessels of great change, vision, power and leadership for the Lord, the edification of His people and the advancement of His Kingdom. They were not all in recognized positions of leadership according to the world's definition of that position but they were warriors and they were frontline warriors.

Let me say this again, the role of females within their families is divinely determined and the assignment of women as spiritual warriors is equally and even more importantly decreed by Deity. There is no need for conflict or confusion to be illegally imported or drafted into the interpretation and fulfillment of these duties and responsibilities. It was plainly stated in the Garden of Eden and reaffirmed in the ministry and the mission of Jesus, He made no distinction; we are all one in Him and partakers of the one Holy Spirit.

Furthermore, women are equally covered by the blood of the Lamb of God which takes away the sins of the world. Women are equally redeemed, equally called, anointed and commissioned to fight the good fight until the Bridegroom returns in power, glory and majesty to receive His Bride to Himself, so that where He is, we might be also. In all of the Scriptures, there is nothing that says that salvation is different for men than for women. The Bible tells us of only one, non-discriminatory way to be saved. We must all confess our sins, believe in our hearts that Jesus died to cleanse us from all unrighteousness, ask His forgiveness and welcome Him into our lives as Lord and personal Savior. Repentance and conversion are equal opportunity principles. And the call to work for the establishment of the Kingdom of Love is also equally extended and indiscriminately available to all who will come to the Christ for salvation. **Amen.**

Equal from the Beginning

In the beginning, when God had completed His work, males and females in their created perfection were the true reflection and representation of His image and likeness. What God had set out to do, He achieved and so He was very pleased.

And God saw everything that He had made, and behold, it was very good (suitable, pleasant) and He approved it completely. Genesis 1:31.

Adam and Eve were gifted with the resources, qualities, characteristics and knowledge needed to subdue the earth, have dominion and authority over all life-forms as well as to multiply the human family, in order to replenish the earth and conform it to the model of the Garden that God planted east of Eden for their home. **Genesis 1:28-31.**

After sin entered into their lives, both Adam and Eve and their descendants were given a promise of ultimate victory, as well as royal commissions to oppose their enemy, through total submission to the grace and the strength of the Lord. They had already discovered the dire consequences of relying on their own reasoning; the result was a loss of the Presence of the Almighty and severance of the direct communion that they had enjoyed up to that point, with the Lord.

However, God granted them an opportunity to choose to be on His side in the war, or to oppose Him and continue to serve with the rebels against His Kingdom. He also added challenges, conditions and circumstances to their lives that were not previously there, in order to prepare them to meet their enemy fully armed and dangerous. If at anytime in their lives, humans would repent and turn to God and take up arms as soldiers in the army of the Lord, they would find that their life experiences were training opportunities for spiritual empowerment. In other words, the conditions attendant on the lives of women in a post–Eden world are in effect, training exercises designed to develop the expertise necessary to shape, develop and strengthen our character to fulfill our God-ordained assignments in the war against the rule of Satan.

Now the judgment (crisis) of this world is coming on [sentence is now being passed on this world]. Now the ruler (evil genius, prince) of this world shall be cast out (expelled). John 12:31

You might say that the tests and temptations, pain and sufferings that would become an everyday part of the lives of women, was destined to imbue them with the very qualities, skills and expertise planned and purposed in the divinely ordained Training Manifesto of the warriors of God. The experiences that would be gained from the four main conditions added to the roles of married women for example, would develop the character of God in us, teach us the wisdom, foresight, obedience, commitment, dedication, loyalty, surrender, selflessness, righteousness and perfection needed to overcome the devil and his plans of destruction and death, and ultimately bring the fruits of the Spirit to full fruition, manifestation and maturation in our lives. **Genesis 3:16-19**

Therefore, despite any devilish denial, however and by whomever spoken, preached, published or enforced, women, like men of God, must seek to follow their military orders. I must point out however that the devil has in fact exacerbated and used these same conditions to attack women by inspiring men to exploit and abuse the impact, extent and operation of the conditions imposed by God in **Genesis 3:16** as a means of dismissing or diminishing the role of women in the spiritual battlefield for the souls of men.

Divide and Conquer

Distinguishing between the appointment to different ranks in the natural and the physical realms is the sticking point when it comes to carrying out our duties as soldiers in the Lord's army. The right to engage the enemy at all levels of spiritual warfare is not questioned. What is distasteful, controversial and divisive is the issue of the right of women to serve God in all capacities, areas or arenas of spiritual matters, as organized and manifested in the world or in the spiritual realm.

In **Genesis 3:15**, Jehovah God clearly commissioned women to make war with the devil and He promised that she would produce an Offspring, a Redeemer, the Ultimate Solution to bring about the serpent's final destruction and the end of all spiritual battles. This prophecy was of course fulfilled with the coming of Jesus the Christ, the birth and emergence of His Bride and the present continuation of Christ's commission until He returns. The Church of Christ is still at war with the enemy and must battle to bring fallen man back to the full knowledge of their lost heritage and the love and grace of their Redeemer and their God.

In **Genesis 3:17-19,** God gave Adam the responsibility to wrestle against and bring a world and nature (that was now in rebellion) into submission; after Eden the world is plagued with the added interference, destructive influence and attacks of the devil who usurped man's dominion over the earth realm. As He did with the woman, the Lord attached the necessary conditions that would provide the training, skill and experience that would likewise equip man to achieve what God ordained for him as His ambassador and His warrior.

God's appointments to men and women ensured that His fighters were positioned to engage the enemy on all fronts, at all times. God created and appointed natural as well as a spiritual heritage to the human family. The attack of the enemy was aimed at destroying man's inheritance in both domains and therefore hostility exists in both, requiring action; the male in the natural, physical realm and the female in the spiritual. That is also the reason that Jesus' ministry and victory had to be accomplished in both realms, restoring the severance wrought by sin

Although the man and the woman were given equal ranking in the earth under God's perfect administration, now with the entrance of sin into the realm, God established a temporary, revised administrative and military order. The purpose of this was to counteract the divisive tactics of the enemy as well as appropriately prepare and enable men and women who choose to join the Lord, to utilize their skills and resources in such a way that would effectively progress the fight on all fronts against the enemy and frustrate his desire for destruction, chaos and confusion.

The rule of the man over his home, wife and family would imbue in him a sense of responsibility, foresight and wisdom while at the same time provide the woman with the opportunity to understand the importance of submission to the Lord, learn the value of obedience, fully understand the true extent of love, nurture and bring to maturity the gifts of the Spirit and achieve understanding and wisdom in the ways of God. These lessons would in turn properly prepare and empower her for the spiritual warfare that is her direct duty, obligation and destiny, if she would serve the Lord.

It is also important for us to realize that presently, the kingdoms of this world are ruled by the devil and subject to his tyranny. On the other hand, the Kingdom of God operates according to the laws of divine wisdom, righteousness, justice and love and is not to be confused with the **'way that seems right to a man but which leads only to death'. Proverbs 14:12**

All those who are appointed by the Holy Spirit to positions of spiritual stewardship are subject to the Lord. If this is the case and it is, then why is there such consternation if the Holy Spirit works through the male or female who are reborn of the Spirit, as children of God, His heirs and joint heirs with His Beloved Son, Jesus the Christ? Surely the only and most important thing is that no one tries to usurp Christ's position as head of His Church. As I will discuss in greater details later on, the Church came out of the body of Christ and is therefore His own body in the same way that Eve came from Adam's body and the two became one. As the saying goes, 'If you cut one, the other bleeds'!

A. Therefore shall a man leave his father and mother and shall become united and cleave to his wife and they shall become one flesh. Genesis 2: 24

B. For the husband is the head of the wife as Christ is the Head of the Church, Himself the Savior of [His] body. Ephesians 5:23

It is equally important for us to understand that we cannot dictate to the Holy Spirit whom He should call to fulfill the purpose, plan and work of the Lord. **Romans 9:15-18.** Each child of God is of equal importance in their assigned tasks and their assigned position, whether as Usher or Pastor, male or female; it is solely the remit of the Office of the Holy Spirit to determine. Obedience to His call, His law, His decrees, His commission, is the only requirement for membership of the family of God.

The Devil Knows

The devil is in no doubt about the commissions that God gave to His people. He most certainly remembers the words God spoke to him in Eden. And as a result of what God said to him, he has tailored his actions, both overtly and covertly. He knows the character of

Jehovah and He knows that what He decrees cannot be revoked, altered, diminished or changed.

Satan has taken to heart the exact content, intent and remit of God's judgment in **Genesis 3:15**. To counteract the effectiveness of the commission and prophecy concerning the role of the woman in his downfall; he has expended every cunning and plan to keep women incapacitated, ineffectual and intimidated. This way he disables half the army of man that can fight against him. And man has, by and large, accepted his deceitful philosophy.

There is a feeling in some quarters that it is exceptional, unusual, and outstanding, as well as perhaps, a credit to the personal strength and perseverance of the particular woman, who leads out in a mighty way for the Lord. There is even a feeling that the female spiritual warriors that have emerged today and are even now accomplishing a wondrous work in the Body of Christ are merely a product of the post modern society of the western world. But to credit man with this move of God, so that chance and happenstance are regarded as the arbiters of our divine destiny is idolatry! God is being denied the glory.

In truth, there is a time and a season for everything under the sun; a time and a season to be determined by God so that we do not divert praise and glory from Him. We must give full credence to divine prophesy which says that the Spirit of God will be poured out on men and women in the last days. Neither should man's rationalization detract from the fundamental truth of this issue; it is the season for transition and revolution in the Church through the revelation and reintroduction of this timely realization of God's direction for the destiny of His people.

The time to think as children is long gone. As the Church of Christ approaches its maturity; it must put away childish things. **1 Corinthians 13:11.** We must now be partakers of a diet of meat. Facing the hard truths about our immature practices that have hindered rather than advanced Kingdom business to date must be dealt with under the spotlight of the Word and discarded for exactly what they are, devilish obstacles and demonic roadblocks in the war against our God and His Kingdom rule.

Seek the Lord [inquire for Him, inquire of Him, and require Him as the foremost necessity of your life], all you humble of the land who have acted in compliance with His revealed will and have kept His commandments; seek righteousness, seek humility [inquire for them, require them as vital] ...Zephaniah 2:3

What a joy and a relief to know that as the body of believers grows into maturity, we are becoming more receptive to greater enlightenment, illumination and revelation from the Holy Spirit as He continues to teach and convict us of the perfect will of God. God's plans, His law, decrees and designs are not new; they have always been the same. He is constant in His desire and He never changes. It was and is His will that women do not keep their light hidden in their closets but that we are forthright in our stance and our actions against the enemy in whatever way God defines and determines.

Blindsided

If we were operating according to godly principles of love, there would be no reason or room to fight against each other and to use divisive methods and tactics to elevate or maneuver ourselves into positions of so-called leadership, importance and fame. Challenging the understanding and interpretation of the Word of God is an old technique of the serpent. It first comes to light in the paradise home of Adam and Eve and continues throughout the history of the human family. "Did God really say that!?" is the question that is a catch-all for arrogant, self-assertive, wayward, stiff-necked and deluded men and women.

War is not of God neither is division amongst human beings. It therefore follows that all wars and their strategies originated with the first being to engage in a war against the Kingdom of our Lord God, Satan. Surely the very act of division itself, which separates brother from sister and husbands from wives etc, is a devilish strategy that has been employed time and again, effectively.

Every hierarchical society and oppressive regime established by man since the beginning of time, have always known that the way to defeat and control a group of people is to fabricate differences that separates them into opposing, conflicting sides. There is victory in unity and defeat in division. I believe that is why Jesus tells us that by having love for one another, we demonstrate to the world that we are His disciples indeed. **John 13:35.**

Love unites brothers and sisters together in the Body of Christ, so that we will lay down our very lives for each other should the need arise, and it will come during the testing trials that man will face at the end of the ages. One is the number that symbolizes unity and unity is one of the most important principles in the Kingdom of our God. It is the foundation and purpose of every relationship within the Holy Scriptures. A section on the importance of the number one in the matters of the Spirit follows in a later section.

In order therefore, to lessen the effectiveness of those who would align themselves against him, the devil sets out to eliminate, disqualify or handicap them even before they have a chance to be engaged in the battle. Denial of opportunity to an equal voice in the war against the enemy and division along the lines of gender, or any other visible distinction for that matter, is abhorrent to the Spirit of God and merely undervalues and invalidates the service of women while serving the devil's purpose.

The Lord God gave Adam charge of the natural realm. To Adam is due all the respect of the created things of the earth. It is his to order, organize, categorize, develop, maintain, maximize and enhance. This was Adam's job even before Eve was made. When God completed the creation of man, by forming Eve, He gave them both authority and dominion over all His earthly creation. This authority and dominion was appointed to man; both male and female before the Fall and was never changed, rescinded or revoked by the Lord, after the Fall in Eden.

After the Fall however, God declared that man would have to struggle, suffer and fight to subdue and have dominion over the earth realm, which would rebel against us and contain aspects injurious to our well-being and comfort. **Genesis 3:17-19.** In fact, if he was to succeed in his God-appointed commission, to exercise authority over this realm, he must battle the very devil that treacherously gained authority and has become the Prince of this world.

We gave away our birthright to the adversary when we disobeyed God's injunction in the beginning. The story of Jacob and Esau, and the destiny of their descendants clearly show us the natural consequence of dealing lightly with one's birthright within a specific family unit and by analogy, spiritually within the family of God, man's first family. **Genesis 25:31-34.** Mankind's carelessness is still impacting our lives and its ripple effect has encompassed all of creation. The changes that occurred after the great disobedience, in respect of man's original, heavenly commission to man the earth, so to speak, occurred because we allowed the enemy access to and control of our dominion key. God's Word did not become void because man sinned neither did He revoke His proclamation concerning man's authority just because we allowed it to fall under the control of the enemy.

> **God is not a man, that He should tell or act a lie, neither the son of man, that He should feel repentance or compunction [for what He has promised]. Has He said and shall He not do it? Or has He spoken and shall He not make it good. Numbers 23:19**

One of the results of the devil's deception was to get situated, poised and positioned to steal, to destroy and finally to usurp God's rule on earth as delegated to man. Jesus taught us to join with Him in purpose and prayer to restore the stolen authority;

> **Thy Kingdom come, Thy will be done on earth as it is in heaven. Matthew 6:10**

> **The earth is the Lord's and the fullness thereof, the world and they that dwell therein. Psalms 24:1, 2**

The serpent's arrogance, betrayal and conceit is so complete that he even offered the earth as a reward to the Lord Jesus provided the Son would acknowledge the devil's sovereignty over earth and consequently his ability and authority to gift it. In other words, he wanted the Son of God to pay him homage and acknowledge his sovereignty over God's. But God never gave up His title to His creation and the devil does not have legal ownership. The temptations of the Christ provides us with another example of Satan's divide and conquer strategy at work and the perfect way of countering this strategy as demonstrated by the Master. **Luke 4:5-7**

Challenges to Man's Authority

When Adam and Eve sinned they became slaves to the "Master of Sin", captives of death and subject to all the consequences of sin, such as disease, violence, crimes, oppressions and wars. In effect, this translated into the following consequences as far as man's rule and role in the earth.

1. A great effort would be needed to overcome the obstacles that man would face in subduing the natural realm, since nature too was in rebellion to the order, peace and harmony that God had originally created

2. The control and authority that man allowed the devil to seize over the human family itself and therefore over the realms appointed to him, became the prize to be recaptured and restored by the "Seed" of the woman.

3. Man's enslavement to sin and so to "the father of sin", Satan, would engage man's internal and external resources in a constant Freedom Fight with the Prince of Darkness and his kingdom.

4. Since nature itself was now in rebellion against man, he would have to sweat, suffer and bleed to achieve the sustenance that the earth was created to

provide for him and his family before sin entered the world.

5. The energies of the mind, body and spirit of the male would be consumed with the task of survival but yet he would have to fight through consuming occupations to serve a God that truly loves and cares passionately, faithfully and honestly about his well being and his divine appointment to authority in the earth realm.

6. The earth is still the Lord's; He is its Creator and legal title has never been given over by Him to anyone else, not even man. Man was the appointed regent of the Lord in the earth realm not the owner.

7. The enemy's army is illegally occupying the earthly territory of the Kingdom of Righteousness and influencing and controlling this domain's governments.

Sweat and Tears

Despite the objections that might be raised at this, following on from what I have previously stated above, I am led to say, with all conviction that God instituted a division of responsibility and duty within both the earth and the spiritual realm after the Fall. Sin is chaos and confusion and the devil is the author of both. Once sin entered the world, so did the signature of sin. The Fall necessitated the establishment of a base of military opposition in the earth and in order for His people to function in enemy-occupied territory, God put in place a hierarchical structure of divine order that would facilitate and accommodate His Plan of Redemption.

All things on the earth were originally made subject to the authority of man and there was no exertion involved in gathering food, protecting against wild animals, guarding against enemies, anticipating natural, destructive disasters, insuring against tragedies, contemplating death, experiencing sickness, pain or suffering or any other negative or detrimental experience. All of this changed when sin took charge. Inherent in the order to labor for the provision of food, is the responsibility of organizing the institutions necessary to bring the earth under the control and the rule of God through man.

The challenges that the man must face are overwhelming and require all of his brains, brawns and even brute force. Without the help of God, a total dependence on His favor, the guidance of the Holy Spirit, the grace, mercy, and blessings of the Creator, man could not, cannot succeed. The consequences of man's failure to include God in every aspect of his struggle to tame, till and take charge of the earth realm is beset with tragedy, disappointment, disaster and death.

Through the challenges that beset him, he must work out his salvation and his victory in Christ, the Redeemer. So that even the establishment of governments, legal institutions, social organizations and the like must invoke the help, guidance and influence of God's law so that the will of God may be fulfilled in the earth for the benefit and the well being of mankind. The record of the exploits of the various kings of Israel shows us the result of governments that are for or against the Kingdom of Righteousness.

The same spirit of rebellion that man allowed to control his mind and his actions in Eden is the same spirit that now prevails among all the life forms of earth in nature itself. In the face of hostility and rejection, the same as that which man showed to God, great exertion, energy, sacrifice, suffering and sweat are the conditions that sinful man must experience, work through and learn from in order to be equipped for battle against the devil; that seducer who led him into the path of sin against the Lord God. **Genesis 3: 17, 18.**

The decree given to Adam does not rule out the assistance of women in carrying out his responsibility in the earth, after all, the woman is his helper in the true, godly sense of the word. Neither does the woman's commission exclude the participation of the man. What it means however is that the primary arena of operation designated as Adam's and his sons is man's training ground, his boot camp for preparation for spiritual battles and warfare.

The responsibilities allocated to man are specifically suited to aid him in the fulfillment of his roles as husband, father, provider, protector, ruler and warrior of the Kingdom of Righteousness. To be successful, the strength of God, His guidance, counsel, wisdom and pre-eminent place in all of man's undertakings and decisions must be sought constantly and earnestly. He must also make God his focus and the centre of his life, placing obedience to God above all other considerations. His battles within the earth realm will also manifest in spiritual warfare against the devil who will try to thwart man's efforts every way possible. The weapons of spiritual warfare and the purpose of divine training is the same, whether the warriors are male or female but the experiences and conditions of training are different.

Eve's original roles remain unchanged but like Adam, she too faced additional obstacles in order to accomplish the additional task of warfare to which she was appointed. For example, Eve would still bring forth children into the earth but she would only be able to do so through much pain and suffering. **Genesis 3:16**. The heartache of rearing children in a hostile, physical environment with an inherent, inborn tendency to listen to and be influenced or ruled by the devil; a consequence of the sin of our First Parents, is the perfect scenario to learn and exhibit qualities such as patience, forbearance and self-control, all fruits of the Spirit of God.

The new challenges that man would face outside of Eden were declared and decreed by the Creator Himself, not I believe merely to punish as generally thought and preached, but because these are the natural consequences that flow from sin. However, at the same time they are profitable to chastise, discipline and properly prepare us all for combat in the arenas of warfare that the Lord specified and decreed. Man did not have to become entangled in the Great War; but by choosing to listen to and side with Satan; the choice of war was made. I know that many wonder if there is a difference between punishment and chastisement. The revelation I have received is that there is a significant difference, spiritually.

Spare the Rod, Spoil the Child

Punishment is the imposition of sanctions that naturally occurs when there is a breach of a rule or law that has been disclosed or publicized. That is, it is inflicted for the sake of the breach and is not necessarily predicated on whether it leads to changes in one's attitude or other desired outcomes enunciated by the authorities such as rehabilitation or re-education. On the other hand, chastisement is action that is imposed and implemented to impart, teach, change and restore to a right way of thinking, behaving and being, the person in receipt of it. Chastisement results in the acquisition of knowledge, wisdom and understanding. It flows from a heart motivated by love in order to correct, instruct, improve and train a person in the right way to approach, deal with or manage a situation or circumstances, to achieve a positive and beneficial outcome and a just conclusion for all parties involved.

The Bible teaches us that those that our Heavenly Father loves, He chastises and there is no doubt that He love us, His children. **Galatians 3:26 and 27** says in paraphrase that we are all sons of God through faith in Christ Jesus, for all of us who were baptized into Christ have clothed ourselves with His robe of righteousness that admits us into the family of God. In other words who Christ is, we become through faith in Him. And, if we are children then the Father will treat us as His children.

Know then in your heart that as a man disciplines his son, so the Lord your God disciplines you. Deuteronomy 8:5. (NIV)

The Lord's chastisement is aimed at enabling us to grow up in Him, to recognize, understand, appreciate and accept our true identity, position and responsibility in His Kingdom. Since chastisement is motivated by love, its imposition demonstrates the care which the Father has for His own and His steadfast faithfulness in guarding and guiding our footsteps and drawing us back to His loving providence, protection and Presence.

The Lord also desires that we come to know Him; His real identity and complete character. He wants us to really get it; that He created us out of His love and set His commandments in place for our protection, joy and liberty. To really know God is to love, worship and adore Him; submitting ourselves in love to His Will, His Way and His Word!

It is also necessary and important that we develop the wisdom to discern the true identify of the enemy; his influence, his lies, his attacks, his ambushes and guerrilla warfare, his wickedness and his destructive purposes. Finally we must come to the knowledge of the consequences of sin in its utter destructive and vile nature. Satan is not, nor ever will be our friend and he can never be trusted. It is opposed to his nature to speak truthfully. He cheats, violates and destroys everything good.

God's disciplinary decree and declaration ensures a clear experiential understanding of the difference and the effect of good and evil for the male as well as the female.

6. For the Lord corrects and disciplines everyone whom He loves, and He punishes, even scourges, every son whom He accepts and welcomes to His heart and cherishes. 11. For the time being no discipline brings joy, but seems grievous and painful; but afterwards it yields a peaceable fruit of righteousness to those who have been trained by it [a harvest of fruit which consists in righteousness – in conformity to God's will in purpose, thought, and action, resulting in right living and right standing with God]. Hebrews 12:6, 11

As I said before, I have a deep desire and interest in understanding what God has destined for me. I am well aware of the limitations that have been imposed by society, due to my gender, both on my potential and on my ability to participate in the social, political and economic organizations of the society. This is not my concern or the focus of my study of the Word and the will of God, right now. There is a time and place for everything.

My present concerns are for those matters pertaining to the special warrior appointment of women in the Kingdom of God. I do not want to become bogged down or entangled with political posturing or politeness, or with the government of man and the god of this world; rather I want to focus solely on the laws and business of my Heavenly Father. Because the decrees of the Lord are irrefutable and unchangeable, His commission of women as spiritual warriors in Eden has never been revoked or rendered null and void; His word is always productive and creative and always truth. The Bible tells us that **"God's gifts and His call are irrevocable". Romans 11:29.**

Therefore, I am mindful that it is the aim of the devil to obliterate from the minds, hearts and souls of women and men the operation of the **Genesis 3:15** commission of women. He is scared, terrified that if the whole human family fully appreciates the calling of the Almighty on the life of every single person, male and female, his devilish plot to lead the masses astray will result in fewer victims of his schemes. The united forces of man, (male and female), marshaled against the devil, will result in the multiplication of the numbers of those who are saved from his evil designs and are made ready for the coming of the Lord. One person can cause a thousand to flee but two will chase ten thousand, if they are acting in the strength of the Lord. **Deuteronomy 32:30**

In the following chapters I will look at the specific experiences of women in the Scriptures, beginning with a deeper and more detailed look at Eve, to see how they became God-focused or not, took up their war commissions or not, fought against the Kingdom or got victory for the King through faith in the Lord and in His Promise. We will study their walk; their challenges, choices, sacrifices and successes. We will seek to identify the lessons that each circumstance, situation and choice imparts. And we will learn from the Mothers of Faith how to emulate their examples and be God's women warriors.

Solomon wrote that there is nothing new under the sun and so in the conditions, confrontations and compromises that we must face in today's world as the elects of God, we will run into new packaging, new slogans and a new, updated and more effective version of old strategies. But the substance, content and impact of the wares that the devil is peddling is still the same; captivity and death. The enemy is constantly refining, re-designing and re-marketing his products but they are still meant for disaster, destruction and defeat of the Army of the Lord. Glory to our God, every action of the devil can be "flipped" for the favor of the saints, a testimony and sign of the love of the Lord and His miracle working power.

God will use all our personal and corporate experiences whether they are perceived as positive or negative, to sharpen our vision, focus our energies, deepen our passion and hone our spiritual warfare skills for the work of the Kingdom, if we allow Him. We have a choice and we must be careful how we choose because there is a just and equitable recompense that we will obtain at the final judgment of the conquering Lord Jesus, a judgment that will bring the final demise of the evil system of Satan and those who follow and serve him.

Do not allow anyone to deceive you, there will be a Final Judgment Day and it will not be very long now. We will each be called to account for our choices; a kind of military debriefing after the battles are over. I want to report to the Lord with joy and gratitude the words of Paul in **2 Timothy 4:9, 10, "I have fought a good fight, I have finished my course, and I have kept the faith".** I want to know, to share the assurance with my sisters and brothers in Christ that **"Henceforth there is laid up for me a crown of righteousness, which the Lord, the righteous Judge, shall give me at that day: and not to me only, but unto all them also that love His appearing."**

The universal prayer of God's women warriors is reflected in the words of the Psalmist in **Psalms 27**. This psalm is one of the main prayers that many Jewish women pray during childbirth and it applies equally to us in our labor on the spiritual battlefield for our Lord; **"Though war break out against me, in this will I be confident."**

CHAPTER 3

THE IMPERFECT WARRIOR

A Perfect Beginning

> **Now the Lord God said, It is not good (sufficient, satisfactory) that the man should be alone; I will make him a helper meet (suitable, adapted, complementary) for him. 21. And the Lord God caused a deep sleep to fall upon Adam; and while he slept, He took one of his ribs or a part of his side and closed up the [place with] flesh. 22. And the rib or part of his side which the Lord God had taken from the man He built up and made into a woman and He brought her to the man. 23. Then Adam said. This [creature] is now bone of my bones and flesh of my flesh; she shall be called Woman, because she was taken out of man. Genesis 2:18, 21-23**

Adam had a need, the precise nature of which he was unable to define because he was unaware of what was missing. But His loving Creator was and in recognition of that need, gave form to the need by vocalizing that it was not good for the man to be alone. In the whole of the six days of creation, this is the only time that we see the Lord expressing dissatisfaction by saying something was not good; not pleasing to Him. It would seem that His mission to make man in His image and after His likeness was not yet complete.

There was an aspect, a part of Him that was missing from the being, which He had set out to make in His likeness and after His image. God determined that the missing portion had resulted in an imbalance in the man, an incomplete reflection of Himself and so He took the final steps to finish His creation; the conclusion of the creative expression of His character, physically, emotionally and spiritually. In order to complete the task of man's creation, Elohim placed Adam in a deep sleep.

God knew exactly what was needed to reflect the fullness of His Triune Being and He set out to perfect His reflection in His creation. This was the original plan of God, that man would be a perfect reflection of His image and likeness and it continues to be the desire of God the Father for each of His children. This is borne out by the Scripture that tells us that Jesus, in His perfection was the fullness of God the Father, a fullness that God desires us to have also!

> **For in Him the whole fullness of Deity (the Godhead) continues to dwell in bodily form [giving complete expression of the divine nature]. 10. And you are in Him, made full and having come to fullness of life [in Christ you too are filled with the Godhead – Father, Son and Holy Spirit – and reach full spiritual stature]. And He is the Head of all rule and authority [of every angelic principality and power]. Colossians 2:9, 10**

The Word of the Lord promises that God will supply our every need. At the very beginning of earth's history, when the very first human was created, we see demonstrated this simple truth even beyond what we might imagine. Jehovah Jireh supplies; not only those needs of which we are conscious but even the ones of which we are not fully aware. Since He knows our every need, it is He that can truly bring forth the exact blessing that can best and most thoroughly meet that need. **Philippians 4:19.**

As much as Adam's conscious or subconscious mind might have wrestled to conjure up the form and image of a companion, it would be limited to the life-forms with which he was familiar, which he had himself named. That is why I believe the Bible tells us that after Adam had named all the creatures created by the Almighty, there was not a companion found for him amongst them. He was unable to identify and therefore meet his own need. He needed the divine and loving intervention and provision of God the Father.

And Adam gave names to all the livestock and to the birds of the air and to every wild beast of the field; but for Adam there was not found a helper meet (suitable, adapted, complementary) for him. Genesis 2:20

There is a word of knowledge and of caution in this Scripture to all of us; Adam and Eve did not choose each other; they were formed, chosen, matched and joined together by the Lord. And that is why it is so important to get a word from God in the choice of life partners. It is for this same reason that the Word of God tells us that **"what God joins together, man should not put asunder". Matthew 19:6.**

To put asunder a union, a joining of two bodies as one, which is the intended outcome of a marriage covenant is to do violence to that unified body. Is it any wonder that the consequences of divorce are so catastrophic in most cases and adversely affects all those involved including children? However, I will add that the Scriptures also tells us that it is better to enter into the Kingdom lame rather than lose our salvation while remaining whole of body! This is all I will say on this matter; as to whether and how this applies is another revelation and point of study!

When the Lord set about meeting the need of the man, the Scriptures tells us that He placed Adam in a deep sleep. He was about to bring into Adam's world a divine blessing, a fatherly gift, a perfect fulfillment of all that the man could have desired, hoped, dreamed and prayed for. Adam's limited vision or infantile fantasy was not an asset in the process of creating a companion and so it was not allowed to get in the way of what God planned for him. God knew perfectly what was needed to complete and compliment him.

It was God Who made him and knew everything about him. Since Adam was made in His image, He was the best qualified for the role of divine Matchmaker. Therefore, Adam's anesthetization, his deep sleep, the quieting of his mind and body while God fashioned a suitable partner for him, removed man's contribution or obstruction of his own best interests. When we try to usurp God's authority in this or any other aspect of life, we become idolaters. The privilege and honor to create in His own image and likeness belongs only to God and so the choice of the individual that will complete our divine image is God's privilege, providence and pleasure!

Adam's sleep can also be seen as a parallel, a shadow, a type of death; the sleep of death that Jesus the Christ entered in the tomb following His crucifixion - a sleep necessary for the birth, formation and emergence of the Church; the Bride of the Lamb. After all, unless the seed is planted, buried in a dark place, it cannot bring new life. After this manner, Jesus died, was buried, and then was resurrected for the Church to be born. Adam was placed in a deep sleep, like the 'sleep of death', in order to give new life, to allow the Lord to bring Eve into life.

The Season of Overflow

There comes a season in everyone's life when we need to allow the Father to put us into a deep sleep, a place of perfect rest and "unknowingness", so that He can take out of the deepest recesses of our being, our spirit, the form and substance of that which is needed to complete us unto perfection in Him. The Father always knows what is needed because He placed the need in us but He also provides the seed, laid up in us to meet that need in due season. For this reason the Lord of the Harvest is the only One that can bring the seed to life. We may try to counterfeit the process but the end product is not the real thing and will eventually fade and fail to satisfy; it will disappoint and disillusion. That is why having a personal relationship of trust, faith and communion with the Lord is essential to distinguishing between real and fake, flavor or favor, a fantasy, or a divine vision.

It is God's desire to perfect us and sometimes, He has to move us out of the way so that He can do what He needs to do for our completion in Him. Our imagination, dreams, ambitions and activities can get in the way of God's will for our lives. He most certainly knows what we need better than we ourselves, and He wants us to attain to an abundant life through Jesus Christ our Lord. **Matthew 6:8** states that our **'Father knows what we need before we ask Him'**. That is why when Adam was awakened and presented with Eve, he was overjoyed; God had just moved him into his overflow!

The creation of the woman was the final part of God's design of the earth realm. She enjoyed the Presence, love and attention of the Divine, solely and totally. It was her special, favored time with her Father, the Lord God. Her first and foremost relationship was with God. They were alone in perfect communion while the man was still in a deep sleep. Eve was in a place of pure love, perfect communion, peace, harmony and joy. It was only after this personal one on one time with the Father Creator that Eve was ready to be presented to the man, her husband.

It has always been the Father's plan that a girl would grow into womanhood under the guidance and tutelage of her parents and the authority of her father's home; nurtured, shaped, instructed and prepared for her role as a wife and mother. It was intended that she would have a firm foundation and a perfect relationship with, her heavenly Father, devoting to Him a position of first priority in her life always. The Lord's will, His order and His desire for His daughters have never changed.

It is God's perfect plan that at the time of her maturity, a female would be presented to her husband from her fathers' hands and his home; both her earthly and her heavenly fathers. We see a remnant of this practice still remaining in wedding ceremonies where the bride is still traditionally "given away" by her father, or his proxy. After all, the first bride to be given to her husband was Eve and she was given by her Father, the Lord our God, to Adam. This is the ideal model and pattern designed by God the Father for all daughters of Eve. This is the very model that the devil endeavors to distort and bring into disrepute so that women reject the way of the Lord; acting in spiritual immaturity, ignorance, arrogance, devilish delinquency and outright rebellion.

Perfect Beginnings

14. But as for you, continue to hold to things that you have learned and of which you are convinced, knowing from whom you [learned]. 15. And how from your childhood you have had a knowledge of and been acquainted with the sacred Writings, which are able to instruct you and give you the understanding for salvation which comes through faith in Christ Jesus [through the leaning of the entire human personality on God in Christ Jesus in absolute trust and confidence in His power, wisdom, and goodness]. 2 Timothy 3:14, 15 -

Eve's first relationship reminds us through revelation, that many children start life in godly homes with a proper upbringing and guidance founded in the Word of God. They are taught a righteous 'Way' of life but later they fall prey to the wiles and lies of the enemy. The enemy, Satan, focuses especially on the children of the saints of God and despite the foundations of the children's upbringing in a relationship with the Lord, many loose their way to the delight of the destroyer.

I stand as an example of this painful and sad reality. I was brought up in a Christian home with a God-fearing warrior woman for a mother. In my early adult life, I strayed from the path on which my feet had been planted in childhood and wandered through a variety of lost, fallen experiences for many years. But people of God that are parents, let me exhort you to take heart. There is substance, succor and truth in the Word of God that admonishes us to train up a child in the way of the Divine so that the preparation and knowledge that has been poured into them will again bloom and bear fruit in their later life. This is the importance of wise, godly training and that is why it receives so much emphasis from the Lord. The training that a child receives is the foundation of a parent's legacy and the building blocks of a godly character. **Deuteronomy 6:7 and Proverbs 22:6**

There is still another aspect to this revelation. Many of us are redeemed from our sins and find our new beginning in a close and personal relationship with God, yet somewhere along the way, we allow ourselves to be ensnared again by the enemy and backslide. We lose sight of the Lord and of our salvation as we become enamored with the things of the world, again. We fall away and replace our God with the false idols of the world; many times we are still observant of religion and its rituals, seemingly still living as children of the Most High, attending church just as regularly as we ever did.

But in reality, we have become distant; alienated from intimacy with the Lord, having a form of godliness but denying its power to transform and renew, save and satisfy. **2 Timothy 3:5**. We allow the enemy to nullify our actions and turn us into double agents; seemingly serving God or having served Him, lose faith, living ineffective warrior lives, making a lie of the goodness of God and the fulfillment that comes from being in His Kingdom, under His sovereignty. Instead, the devil is given the opportunity to parade us as his prize, a reproach to the love and patience of God, a mockery of His grace and a stumbling block to our brethren in need of salvation.

Cradled in a Dark Place

In our society, scientists are able to claim great breakthroughs in medical research. We are all familiar with such topics as in-vitro fertilization, stem-cell research and even cloning. But as astounding as these breakthroughs claim to be they all start off with living tissue, created by a Supreme God in the first instance. In the same way I understand that when God made Eve, she was made from living matter, harvested from the side of Adam.

Adam already had the spirit of the living God in his being when Eve was made from him. Eve was not created from the dust of the earth in the same direct fashion as man; she was one step on in the process. She was never an inanimate form waiting for life to be breathed into her nostrils in the same way that Adam was but rather she was fashioned from already living tissue. She was created from a part of the completed, living, breathing, fully functioning man. And so she had always been alive physically and spiritually.

From her very beginning the woman was possessed of the life, the spirit that flowed through Adam's body; fully alive, fully aware, and fully worshipping. I am convinced that just as the starting point of the conscious, self-aware life of the male and the female was different; their spiritual legacy from the Father was also different yet compatible and complementary to each other, amounting to the whole package of the character and nature of Elohim.

Like Eve, Adam too had spent the earliest time in his life with God. He was then appointed to familiarize himself with his domain and to begin exercising authority over it by naming the animals and all the created life forms that God had placed on the earth under his office. He was given direct responsibility and primary charge of them all; flora and fauna. On the other hand, Eve was the final life form created by God after Adam had completed his task of naming. God fashioned the form, substance, physical and spiritual endowments of Eve to complete His perfect reflection, a reflection of the Godhead in this physical, material realm. Together with her husband, she was given authority and dominion to fulfill the office of regent, representative and ruler of the earth realm according to the Laws of the Kingdom of the Eternal God.

In addition, the woman was designed, appointed and anointed to carry new life within her that would physically populate the earth and make of it a total paradise after the fashion and design of the Garden, which the Creator planted East of Eden. This was the first family's first residence. The revelation here is that the woman was a physical and a spiritual conduit, a channel through which God deposited and demonstrated the operation of the principle of love; intimacy, companionship, selflessness, fellowship, unity and other relational attributes that were essential to reflecting the totality of His likeness. That is to say, through this spiritual umbilical cord would flow spiritual, emotional, mental sustenance that would continue to enrich, enhance and endow the spirit of man with the nutrients necessary for growth into a mature realization of their divine identity and the fullness of the moral character of God.

Both the woman and the man together would reproduce new life; more humans to increase the human family of God and bring honor and glory to His name. But it was the woman that the Creator fashioned to carry, cover, protect and hide the new life while it grew into its potential to maintain physical viability outside her body. Once the child is born, the primary responsibility for its care is the mother's. She would watch over, nourish, nurture and sustain the child emotionally, spiritually and physically, teaching and training the child in way of the Lord; His love, His law. God's plan was the extension of His earthly domain through the reproduction of more sons and daughters to share His love. The multiplication of that love would be the central theme of instruction, preparation and celebration by the earthly and the heavenly parents.

The heart, mind, body and spirit of the woman were specially designed to carry out this task of pro-creation, perfectly. The revelation here that I need to emphasize is that even the woman's first sense of being in the physical was an experience of being hidden in a dark and secret place, enclosed, protected, nurtured and kept safe until an appointed time. In other words, the female's first experience was of being hidden in **"the Secret Place of the Most High"**, **Psalms 91:1**; the deep and secret place of her male companion.

It is still the foremost emotional need of every human being to seek out and be in a secret place. Born from the wombs of mothers; that safe and secret place devised by the Lord to develop and grow new life, there is an emotional as well as a deep abiding spiritual imperative, to seek out a place of quiet rest, security and refuge. For example, a wife has a need to be in the secret place of her husband's heart, his mind and his love. Conversely, husbands share the same need to find that secret place of rest and repose in their wives. But beyond the emotional need, at the level of spiritual awareness, each individual will experience a longing; we might even call it an ache, for a place in the garden of rest and perfection with God, their first and Supreme Love. Our first home was in the Presence and Abundance of Jehovah and of necessity we must seek after that Eden always, whether we recognize and accept our need and our search as such.

> He that dwells in the secret place of the Most High shall remain stable and fixed under the shadow of the Almighty. [Whose power no foe can withstand]. 2. I will say of the Lord, He is my Refuge and my Fortress, my God; on Him I lean and rely, and in Him I [confidently] trust! 4. [Then He will cover you with His pinions, and under His wings shall you trust and find refuge; His truth and His faithfulness are a shield and a buckler. 8. Only a spectator shall you be [yourself inaccessible in the secret place of the Most High] as you witness the reward of the wicked. Psalms 91:1-2, 4, 8.

Only in His secret place can there be security, satisfaction, joy, belonging, unity, harmony and peace. In Christ is the divinely appointed meeting place of the body, mind and spirit of men and women of God. It is the place of ultimate communion and holy union between 'man' (male and female) and God; a place of abode which is covered by God's protection and maintained by His covenant promises. Unfortunately, so many people do not realize that the place of peace for which they yearn is located in the heart of God. Our creation flowed from His love and He knew us before we were in the wombs of our mother because we were first hidden in Him; a place to which we have a chance to return through Christ the Lord!

> He made darkness His secret hiding place; as His pavilion (His canopy) round about Him was dark waters and thick clouds of sky. Psalms 18:11

> 3. For [as far as this world is concerned] you have died, and your [new, real] life is hidden with Christ in God. 4. When Christ, Who is our life, appears, then you also will appear with Him in [the splendor of His] glory. Colossians 3:3-4

Once a Mother always a Mother

Throughout their lives, mothers continue to operate in counseling, advisory and supportive capacities to their children; even when they become adults and have children of their own. The first mother Eve had been endowed with the gifts of motherhood; physical, emotional and spiritual, by God the Father. He taught her everything that she needed to be a mother, a role He modeled on Himself and which she was designed to reflect when perfection prevailed in Paradise. A mother's love can never be over estimated and her instinct to protect her children is perhaps the best example of her warrior spirit at work; another trait reflective of our God.

Through the character of woman, God manifests His constant, sustaining, uplifting love for mankind in the physical realm as well as in the spiritual. He is always a Father with a father's loving heart. Earthly parents can and often disappoint and fail their children but in His perfection, He is the Parent that never fails. **Isaiah 49:15-16**

The attributes of motherhood is a reflection of the attributes of the character of God. It is not surprising therefore to find that the word which is used by God to define and describe the companion of man, "helper or helpmeet", is the same word in the Hebrew language used many times to describe God and His relationship with man!

The female was formed in the image and likeness of God to bring man into overflow. It is not that Adam was not wonderfully and perfectly made but rather that our God is Abundance. And abundant life is His original plan and gift to man, so that we can be a true and complete reflection of Him. This is the reason that Jesus' mission statement includes the paraphrased clause that **'He came so that we can have life and life more abundantly'**; a state of being originally bequeathed to man by the Father and lived in the perfection of Eden and now once more made attainable by the ministry of the Lord Jesus. **John 10:10.**

The Lord created and destined the human family to have an abundant life in Him. And it is in keeping with our Father's character that He supplies our every need long before we experience lack. After all, God is an All-sufficient God; there is no lack in Him. This is also an aspect of His Person that we were created to reflect despite all the efforts of the enemy to keep us in poverty of spirit, mind and body.

Beloved, I pray that you may prosper in every way and [that your body] may keep well, even as [I know] your soul keeps well and prosper. 3 John 1:2

It therefore follows that Adam was not created with a lack because the element that was needed to bring him into overflow was already deposited inside him at his creation; a part of his essential being, hidden, in the deep, secret places of his spirit, his heart. It merely required the direct surgical expertise of a loving Creator to bring to fruition the seed that was hidden in him, **"bone of his bone and flesh of his flesh; woman!" Genesis 2:23**

We can only ever realize the fullness of God in our person once more, as modeled by the Christ, if we allow our Divine Creator to extract from our deep and secret place, our purpose, our ministry, and our call to the battlefield; our divine destiny. The Lord holds the key to unlock the potential, the power and the resources within us that can meet our needs, whatever they may be, tangible or intangible, bringing us into His overflow.

The word of revelation bears repetition; if we have a need, God has already buried the seed within us that can be quickened by the Holy Spirit to bear fruit, manifesting the fullness, wisdom, power, and the glory of the Creator. Within the Holy Spirit we will never be able to birth the seed that supplies the means or the end to our need. This is also the reason there was a 'Seed' of the woman, hidden within her, that was quickened by the Holy Spirit, manifesting in the physical realm as the very Son of God, the Promised Messiah.

Then the angel said to her, The Holy Sprit will come upon you, and the power of the Most High will overshadow you [like a shining cloud]; and so the holy (pure, sinless) Thing (Offspring) which shall be born of you will be called the Son of God. Luke 1:35

It is important for us to grasp this principle; first God places the seed within us and then, when a need manifests in our lives, the Holy Spirit will quicken it to maturity, and we come into our harvest, our overflow. I will even go so far as to say that the presence of a seed does not necessarily signify the emergence of a need. The seed may be the source of your overflow, your purpose, your calling or ministry and will be brought forth in due season for the work and the glory of the Kingdom and our Lord.

Let me just interject a little note here about God's overflow; the woman that was providentially supplied with enough flour and oil each day to feed herself, her son and the prophet of God was in overflow! In other words the revelation I am trying to impart is that overflow is not about physical excess or numerical abundance but rather about a supernatural meeting of our needs and desires as determined by the Lord, that is, needs and desires that He has placed in our hearts and minds! God is a God of pre-emptive provision and that is why fulfillment can only be attained in Him. This is a revelation of God's wisdom. **See Luke 1:35:**

Breach Birth

The severing of the spiritual as well as physical umbilical cord that connected God and man was a direct result of the violent intervention and interruption of sin and its progenitor and propagator, the devil. The Fall was the physical representation of the rebellion of man both naturally and spiritually. Just as in a breach birth the natural order is turned around and carries with it an attendant risk to the life of both mother and child, so too the assault that resulted in man going against the orders established by the Divine, resulted in severe, costly and painful consequences to mankind.

22. We know that the whole creation [of irrational creatures] has been moaning together in the pains of labor until now. 23. And not only the creation, but we ourselves too, who have waited and enjoy the first fruits of the [Holy} Spirit [a taste of the blissful things to come]

groan inwardly as we wait for the redemption of our bodies [sensuality and the grave, which will reveal] our adoption (our manifestation as God's children. 24 For in [this] hope we are saved ... Romans 8:22-24

The love, harmony, peace and communion that God intended was shattered and the relationship that men and women were created and destined to enjoy and share through and with their children, was attacked and imperiled by sin and Satan. The travail of the earth and all its life-forms began as they all became subjected to the consequences of sin; they were all made subject to man by the Creator God. The ultimate price for sin is death. God warned that in the day that man ate from the forbidden tree, he would most certainly die, **"For the wages of sin is death". Romans 6:23.** Man was taught not only the law of God but the consequences of breach and the sanction that inevitably followed. And so when man chose death in Eden, he also made the same choice for the entire earth realm.

Death and killing became characteristics of the created world because these became the characteristics of sinful man. The nature of sinful man does not exclude **any** sin, regardless of how vicious, heinous, gross, repugnant or disgusting it might be when measured against the moral standards of the Almighty. Sin originated with Satan and is therefore reflective of his character and his kingdom. All evil is the manifestation of the essential nature of Satan and consequently of human beings who succumb to his rule in their lives.

12. Therefore do not let sin reign in your mortal body so that you obey its evil desires. 13. Do not offer the parts of your body to sin, as instruments of wickedness, but rather offer yourselves to God, as those who have been brought from death to life; and offer the parts of your body to Him as instruments of righteousness. 16. Don't you know that when you offer yourselves to someone to obey him as slaves, you are slaves to the one whom you obey – whether you are slaves to sin, which leads to death,

or to obedience which leads to righteousness? Romans 6:12, 13 and 16 (NIV)

God's warriors, fathers and mothers, must engage the enemy to fight for the lives and souls of their children. The devil does not want children to be born into this world who will be trained to oppose him. So he puts the necessary machinery in place that will lead to the deception, demoralization and destruction of women. One example is the institutionalized propagation of the falsehood that has led to millions and millions of abortions.

In addition, Satan has infiltrated and polluted the minds and hearts of the cultures of many nations to legitimize and propagate falsehoods that undervalue the life of female children to the extent that millions are murdered every year. In other instances, pornography, prostitution, sexual exploitation, domestic slavery and abuse has taken the hopes, dreams and future of millions more women the world over. The issue of sexuality which is a natural component of the gift of womanhood and child-birth continues to be a rich avenue for the implementation of the concerted efforts of Satan to destroy his nemesis, woman.

But, we are God's warriors and we must fight back with the spiritual weapons of our warfare. We must learn to recognize our attacker from a distance, anticipate his tactics and be ready offensively and defensively. God would not declare hostilities, call and commission us to do battle, train and prepare us for action, equip us with an armory of spiritual weapons and then expect us to sit back, cower under attack, excuse or exclude ourselves, sulk or sorrow in self-pity and allow the enemy free reign! It does not really matter where we are positioned or stationed; the place in which we stand is a battlefield, the frontline of the war. It is time for us to take the war to the enemy, re-capture territory for the Kingdom and sack the strongholds of Satan.

It is, **"not by might nor by power, but by My Spirit, says the Lord Almighty"**, (Zechariah 4:6) that we are conquerors, even more than conquerors. The final outcome has already been decreed by God; victory will be His and through Him, ours also. Finally, that day will come when our Lord Jesus will return all power in heaven and earth to the Ancient of Days at the conclusion of the War, having secured the Kingdom and its citizens from any further attacks from the enemy. We cannot allow our spirit of warfare, gifted us by the Eternal One to be diverted to the arsenal of the enemy; we cannot be traitors to our God.

We must serve our Lord and answer the Clarion Call of duty and the deep desire of our warrior hearts to destroy the evil that is wrecking the lives of our children, our communities and our countries. We need to face the evils of our societies and accept that the battle is not just a physical one but rather an ongoing warfare in the Spirit realm and its effects are evident everywhere that we look in the physical realm. The devil desires to steal our joy, our salvation, our souls and our future in eternal fellowship with the Lord.

The adversary might propagate the lie that it is all hopeless, that we live in a world that is lost in sin, crime, degradation and death on every side, but we are not involved in a futile effort; God gave us the Seed of Hope for Salvation in the same declaration in which He gave us our papers to report to duty on the frontlines. I am imploring all women warriors to report to the Spirit realm, to stand and be counted as women under divine orders with a commission to engage the enemy under the Banner of Righteousness; delay is death!

> **Arise [from the depression and the prostration in which circumstances have kept you – rise to a new life]! Shine (be radiant with the glory of the Lord), for your light has come, and the glory of the Lord has risen upon you! Isaiah 60:1**

> **9. ... Asking to be filled with the full (deep and clear) knowledge of His will in all spiritual wisdom [in comprehensive insight into the ways and purpose of God] and in understanding and discernment of spiritual things.**

> **10. That you may walk (live and conduct yourselves) in a manner worthy of the Lord, fully pleasing to Him and desiring to please Him in all things, bearing fruit in every**

good work and steadily growing and increasing in and by the knowledge of God [with fuller, deeper and clearer insight, acquaintance and recognition]. Colossians 1:9-10.

CHAPTER 4

THE HOPE OF THE AGES

Warriors of the Lord

We are blessed that God is Who He is; a God of mercy and love, unwilling that even a single human being should suffer eternal death and separation from Him. He places equal value, worth and importance on the individual as He does on the corporate whole.

> **He is long suffering (extraordinarily patient) toward you, not desiring that any should perish, but that all should turn to repentance. 2 Peter 3:9.**

The simple but mind-boggling truth is that men chose to become God's enemy. But while we were yet His enemies, He loved us and made a way of escape for us from our own, self-chosen captivity as slaves to the destroyer of all righteousness.

> **17. Therefore if any person is [in grafted] in Christ (the Messiah) he is a new creation (a new creature altogether); the old [previous moral and spiritual condition] has passed away. Behold the fresh and new has come.**

18. But all things are from God, Who through Jesus Christ reconciled us to Himself [received us into favor, brought us into harmony with Himself] and gave to us the ministry of reconciliation [that by word and deed we might aim to bring others into harmony with Him].

19. It was God [personally present] in Christ, reconciling and restoring the world to favor with himself, not counting up and holding against [men] their trespasses [but canceling them], and committing to us the message of reconciliation (of the restoration to favor). 2 Corinthians 5:17-19

Both men and women have been offered a chance and a choice to fight against the enemy of our salvation or to fight with him against our Lord and His Kingdom of Light, Love and Liberty. Eve was created to represent an aspect of God's character that was full of expressive love, gentleness of spirit, sensitivity to emotional matters, in tune with the higher spiritual realm and all things spiritual. She was the perfect partner for the intimate expression of love, generosity, and relationship; friendship, fellowship and communion. In other words, she enabled the manifestation of the relational aspect of the Triune God and the fellowship so essential to the holistic well being of man.

After the great disobedience of Eden, God out of a heart of love for His daughter commissioned womankind to perform an additional duty. If there had been no sin, then this role would never have come into existence. But now, this divine appointment is one that will remain until the end of time when Christ the Lord shall re-establish the sovereign rule of His Father's Kingdom, on the earth as it is in heaven. He will disband the war units and the warrior princesses can return to the position and status of heirs and rulers of their Father's Kingdom together with the Christ. In that day, there will be no need for us to "study war", anymore. **Micah 4:3.** The Word of the Lord according to the Prophet Isaiah beautifully reflects that state of being to which we look forward in Christ Jesus;

Cry aloud and shout joyfully, you women and inhabitants of Zion, for great in your midst is the Holy One of Israel. Isaiah 12:6.

Every woman of God, that is, all females who are on the Lord's side have one divine, spiritual mission; that is, to engage in spiritual warfare with the devil by any and all means necessary and to do so regardless of what sacrifices might be required to the very laying down of this life. It does not matter in which arena we utilize our abilities and our energies, whether at work or play, we are always on duty for the Kingdom and must remain focused on the job that the Lord has given us to do. Whatever it might look like to the natural eye, every woman of God is a warrior on call, on the frontline of spiritual warfare.

So women of God, whether you are in the board room or at the marketplace, you are God's spiritual warrior, always on duty, always operating under code red. Our enemy never takes a break, he never gets tired and he will never quit. We can be no less vigilant, dedicated and persistent in our pursuits. That is why we must take to heart the Scripture that tells us that we **"must pray without ceasing". 1 Thessalonians 5:17.** Prayer is one of the most powerful weapons in our arsenal and we must be perfectly clad therewith and at peak performance all the time because the enemy can **"come in like a flood", (Isaiah 59:19)**, like a thief in the night, and we must be ready to repel his attacks. Preparation, prayer and Holy Spirit power are our watchwords.

Both the male and the female are God's warriors and must work equally hard and with equal preparation, passion and power in pursuit of their God appointed purposes. Together, operating in unity under one banner of love, the male and female will be able to effectively engage the enemy on all fronts of his destructive advance against the human family and the Kingdom of God. All of our experiences are designed to allow us to come to the full realization that of ourselves we can do nothing **"but with God, all things are possible if we only believe'. Matthew 19:26**

The enemy will try to convince and convict us with his lies and his propaganda. He will even use doctored data and false interpretations of the Word of God against us, challenging the very foundation of our faith, identity and service to the Lord. For example, let us consider what has happened to the definition of the word that God Himself used to describe the female companion of the male, in the beginning.

A Note about being a "Helper"

As I briefly intimated earlier in Chapter 3, to be a "help-meet" or a "helper" to Adam is a blessed, privileged and God-ordained position; it is our nature and design to fulfill the role of "helper or help-meet". God named us helper to the male and so that is who we are; that is who He set out to create and that is who we will continue to be in Christ now and in a restored earth under the Christ. The confusion, division and destruction that the various interpretations of this word have birthed and the connotations attached to it have resulted in confusion, rejection and often, anger against man and God. **Genesis 2:18**

In the restored Kingdom reign of our Lord, all will again be as it was in Eden. As I have stated in this study, the abuse and the misunderstanding between the sexes that has prevailed in all levels of our societies is a manifestation of the war strategies of our adversary. These are the divide and rule tactics intended to de-humanize, devalue, disrespect and dismiss the potential of women in the Cause of the Cross.

Eve's role as "helper" to her husband was always supposed to be one of emotional, mental and spiritual support. **Ecclesiastes 4:9-12.** Eve's primary function when she was created by the Lord was not merely to cater for the physical needs of Adam such as cooking, cleaning, washing and so on. And although to look after the physical needs of one's spouse is a joint privilege and a shared honor, a pleasure that flows from any loving relationship, it was not the only purpose for which God created the woman.

The woman's part in biological reproduction was also a shared privilege and again not the main purpose of her creation. Rather, she was created to bring God's abundance of love, a love to be shared spiritually, emotionally and physically in order to manifest the joy of a relational experience on the earth, in the same way that the Father enjoys the relational experience of love, harmony and agreement with the Son and with the Holy Spirit in heaven.

In **Genesis 1:26** the Lord said, **"Let us make man in our image and our likeness"**, clearly announcing the unity and consensus of the Godhead in the creation project. His Beloved Son also reminds us of this Tri-partite relationship when He often taught His disciples that He and the Father God are One with the Holy Spirit. For example as stated in **John 10:30.** He also desired and prayed for that same unity to co-exist with His disciples; read **John 17:21, 22.**

Eve was called Adam's 'helper or help meet' by the Lord; **Genesis 2:18b.** And contrary to the popular belief that this word by which God defined the female's person, character and being, denoted an inferior or lesser status, a ranking below that of the male, it means something altogether different. This use of the Hebrew word for helper is the very same word that is used in a number of other instances in the Scriptures to refer to the Lord God Almighty and His relationship to us, in many situations and under various circumstances. For example, He is referred to as **'our very present Helper in the time of trouble'. Psalms 46:1.**

God can never be regarded as inferior, subservient, a possession or chattel to be bought or bartered for, property to be dispensed with or disposed of at will or whim. Even His enemies can never put such a spin on this attribute of God's Person merely because the Scriptures tell us that He is "our Helper". **Hebrews 13:6.** Yet, it is the very same word in the original Hebrew language of the Old Testament which is translated as a description of Eve, by God.

There is good reason for the Lord to use this attribute of His divine nature and personal character to describe and define the being that He was making to complete the entity, man. Woman was made to possess and represent those same aspects of God that He displays as our Helper. For this reason alone, if for no other, helper should not be misinterpreted to belittle and belie the worth of women or impugn their equality in status and standing with men. When God named the female, help-meet for the man, He was announcing the stamp of His image and His name on her for all times! It is certainly in keeping with the treachery of Satan that he would inspire disdain, disrespect and disregard for the name of God!

Misinformation, misinterpretation and a misogynistic approach to the designation 'helper' as descriptive and definitive for wives, should not be allowed to justify the adoption of a devilish stratagem or to facilitate the egotistical, spiritual suicide bid of our male counterparts to incapacitate and deplete the army of man in the War of Righteousness. Once we have been born again as spiritual children of God, there is no excuse for continuing to maintain the subservient posture, slave mentality and careless attitude of the degenerate, sinful mind and heart of fallen man. Like Paul and his fellow workers for the Kingdom, we must be aware of Satan's schemes so that he cannot befuddle, baffle and outwit us with his deceitful strategies and dangerous, destructive games of semantics. **2 Corinthians 2:11.**

Once we have come into a personal relationship with the Lord, we are no longer slaves to darkness; we become partakers of the marvelous Light of salvation in Christ Jesus our Lord. We can no longer be counted among the unbelievers who are:

Darkened in their understanding and separated from the life of God because of the ignorance that is in them due to the hardening of their hearts. Ephesians 4:18

In **John 14:7- 11,** Jesus confirms to His disciples that He and His Father are One; whatever is said or done is to be received and honored as coming from the mouth of God the Father. Therefore, if we are uncertain and want to determine God's thoughts, attitude and affection for women, we can examine Jesus' discourse, actions and words during the course of His ministry on the earth two thousand years ago. There are no incidences or evidence of unfairness, inequality, exclusion, dismissal or disdain directed at women anywhere in the Gospels of the New Testament by Jesus.

Instead we see instances in which Jesus seized the opportunity to show-case the faith of women; for example, He applauded the faith of a non- Jewish mother, a woman with a warrior spirit battling for her daughter's well-being, before He granted her request of healing.

This woman, described in **Matthew 15:21- 28** demonstrates that God is indeed no respecter of persons. He is not convinced or coerced into compliance with the prejudices and injustices of man's system. He is only concerned that we should worship Him in spirit and truth so that we may have salvation, renewal, rebirth and restoration to our original relationship with God.

Jesus described another long suffering woman as a **"Daughter of Abraham"** declaring her entitlement to the blessings of God's Covenant with the Patriarch, implying her equal heritage and standing with the men. It is no surprise to find that this met with fierce objection by the men of a society that assigned a menial, de-humanizing, subservient role to women. **Luke 13:10 – 17.** But Jesus' mode of address to the woman was merely a divine ratification of her true identity; everything that the Son said or did was in agreement and unison with the Father. All women who come to the Christ through faith are become God's covenant children, heirs to the blessings of Abraham, a peculiar people and a nation of priests. Please realize that nation does not refer to one ethnic group but rather to a mixed ethnicity; people who share a common heritage, culture and government. So that the people of God are a nation unto the Lord, a nation of priests!

Practical Spirituality

The practical effect or consequence of **Genesis 3:15** is that God assigned the woman the task of battle in the spiritual realm; to be in continuous, confrontational engagements with the serpent, to be at enmity with him, to be a warrior in the spiritual warfare that the human family has enjoined. She has a mandate to defeat, disable and ultimately, de-throne and destroy the enemy once and for all eternity, through the birth, life and death of her Kinsman Redeemer, Jesus the Christ.

After the divine decree, womankind was appointed to a mission of resistance, attrition and hostility against the devil and his endeavors to enslave the human family. This special commission from the Most High did not mean that women were relieved of their other duties, responsibilities and privileges in the earth realm, but this commission must take precedence; it is our overriding purpose and primary spiritual mandate in war time and we are still at war.

- ❖ In order to fulfill her duty to her King all the woman's experiences must train and equip her to be spiritually prepared, armed and on battle alert at all times.

- ❖ She would need to confront and accept her own weaknesses and recognize the need to rely on God's strength, provisions and wisdom.

- ❖ She must come to fully know herself and her true identity in God beyond a shadow of a doubt.

- ❖ She must learn to recognize the enemy and his diabolical designs and disguises in order to successfully engage him.

- ❖ She must be able to multi-task as mother, wife, and woman of God but never lose sight of her primary mission for the King; warfare

- ❖ The woman should be cognizant of the truth that every aspect of her life experiences provide training opportunities to hone the skills needed to effectively engage and defeat the devil and his demons in the world.

- ❖ She must learn total, unquestioning obedience to the commands of God in and through all experiences, circumstances, challenges, privileges and blessings that is the sum total of her life.

- ❖ The spiritual warfare to which she has been appointed takes precedence at all times and must never be compromised, deprioritized, neglected, avoided or repudiated or abandoned even in the face of the fiercest opposition.

❖ Finally, every woman warrior of God must know her true calling, purpose and destiny and stand firm in that knowledge regardless of the status she is assigned by community, culture or custom in her home, society, country or church.

All of these goals or objectives however, can only be accomplished if women first seek God; search for Him, follow in His way, recognize and accept His divine authority, submit to Him completely, honor and obey Him even if it means the loss of everything and everyone dear, or death. It is only imperative that we make the Lord the focus, center, purpose, ambition and all-consuming desire of our hearts, minds and souls.

God's warrior woman must learn to live and die by faith in the Messiah, to exercise self-control over her emotions, bring all her thoughts into subjection to God and be in agreement with the plan and purposes of God in every single aspect of her being. In other words, she must learn to be in submission to God every second of her life, at all levels and in all realms of His Kingdom. She will learn through her training, challenges and experiences as mother, wife and warrior how to make the ultimate sacrifice of love, to share in the fellowship of suffering of our Lord, to discern the spirit of the anti-Christ and to employ the spiritual weapons of warfare that God provides to His followers.

God is consistent and He is just. He tells us, **"There is no other God besides Me, a rigidly and uncompromisingly just and righteous God and Savior. Isaiah 45:21.** Therefore I am certain that Eve's appointment, her commission, her assignment to spiritual warfare was merely a continuation of the relationship she shared with her husband and with her Lord before the Fall. I am persuaded that God would not have assigned her a commission in spiritual warfare unless this was a realm with which she was already familiar or in which He trusted her to succeed. This could also be one of the reasons that she was the primary object of the serpent's attack. Whatever the reasons may be however, God knew that Eve was the 'man' for the job!

The Enemy Preys.

The devil has made it his top priority to undermine and usurp the divinely appointed commission of woman. It is no surprise that womankind was and remains his main target. The woman has always been a prime object in his strategies to defeat the Most High God. In the Garden of Eden, the serpent set out to deceive the woman into disobedience. He reasoned that his success would cause the man to follow her lead and the direct link between God and man would be severed forever. That plan was only partially realized, certainly not in the manner that the devil had planned or anticipated. No-one, not even Satan could fathom or comprehend the mind of God and the extent of His love.

God is a merciful and loving God. He already had a Plan of redemption in place even before the foundation of the world was laid; before the deception and sin in Eden. This plan of Redemption would be activated through "the Seed" of the woman. The weapon used by the devil to bring about man's downfall would also be the means of his destruction and defeat. I always find it so amazing when God uses the very thing that the enemy intended for evil to carry out His good will and His purpose. This is the act of the Omnipotent God that we serve.

But as for you, you thought evil against me; but God meant it for good, to bring to pass, as it is this day, to save much people alive. Genesis 50:20

As the battle lines are being drawn in today's world between the Lord and our arch enemy, the destroyer of souls; the handmaidens of the Lord are being called out to honor their commission and serve wherever they are positioned. We do not have to be in so-called positions of influence and power in the world to be leaders in the work of the Kingdom and the Cause of the Cross. The work of the Kingdom is subject not to the laws of the world but to the Law of God.

Leadership is not to be defined only by the positions of headship that one occupies but rather according to the Word of the Lord Jesus and the reality of the spiritual realm. In every post, position or place that we find ourselves, we are on the frontline as God's warriors. And if we stand up or stand out in the estimation of the devil by interfering, interrupting or inhibiting his evil work to destroy souls, we are leaders in the spiritual realm and will come under attack. This however does not exclude the need for women to be involved at the very heart of spiritual battles being fought by the Church. This latter-day urgency to allow women equal access to stand side by side and serve with the men of God in whatever capacity that she is called and gifted by the Holy Spirit is in agreement with the fulfillment of end time prophesies, such as that stated in **Joel 2:28, 29:**

28. Afterward I will pour out My Spirit upon all flesh; and your sons and your daughters shall prophesy, your old man men shall dream dreams, your young men shall see visions. 29. Even upon the menservants and upon the maidservants in those days, will I pour out My Spirit.

Handicapping God's Army

The misconception, misinformation and misdirection that declares that women may not be leaders in the Kingdom business of our Heavenly Father, has been extensively practiced on a society ruled by the devil. This false teaching has been allowed to infiltrate the arena of the spiritual and gain authority and credence as though it is godly principle. It is not but the strategy has succeeded in incapacitating millions of soldiers in the Army of the Lord of Righteousness. The misunderstanding of the Word, the misconstruction of the role of leadership and the misappropriation of the Leadership of Christ over His Church, is nothing less than the work of the adversary.

The Body Corporate of Christ need to realize that there is no limit as to what the Lord will call any woman, or man for that matter, to do by His Spirit, His grace, His power and His authority. It is the incontrovertible right of the Potter to decide which of the vessels that He has created will undertake what task or be made for what specific purpose. Can the pot say to the Potter why and wherefore? In the Gospel of **John 15:16,** Jesus told His disciples;

You did not choose Me, but I chose you and appointed you to go and bear fruit - fruit that will last. Then the Father will give you whatever you ask in My name.

In **Ephesians 1:13, 14,** we learn that the Holy Spirit is the Seal of Christ.

And you also were included in Christ when you heard the word of truth, the gospel of salvation. Having believed, you were marked in Him with a seal, the promised Holy Spirit, 14. Who is a deposit guaranteeing our inheritance until the redemption of those who are God's possession – to the praise of His glory.

And according to the Apostle Peter, believing, witnessing and quoting the Prophet Joel, the Holy Spirit will be poured out on God's people in the last days; on women and men equally, '**a deposit of our inheritance**' of eternal life and a place in the Kingdom of God. All the children of the King; His princes and princesses, have received the Royal Seal that marks them as holders of Kingdom authority through their heavenly Father.

When we have the Royal Seal, we stand in the power and authority of the King whose Seal we possess. That is why the Pharaoh in appointing Joseph gave him his ring; his seal of authority in the Egyptian Kingdom and when the prodigal son returned, his father gave him his ring, his seal, a mark of the son's return to a position of honor, privilege and authority in his father's house!

All of God's warriors must heed the call to arms and rise up! Women are to engage the devil at all times, strip away every disguise in which he masquerades, at whatever personal cost to our physical bodies. It is factually correct that in respect of numbers and therefore potential effectiveness and striking force, women make up the greatest portion of the human family. There is no time to delay or to waste in selfish pursuit, idle philosophies, vain undertakings and godless living. We must make our calling and election sure. As a matter of fact, we are all on the frontline already; the frontline of the adversary or the frontline of the army of the Most High. We are in one camp or the other. In this war, neutrality is not an option and there is no safe or neutral territory, secure from attacks of the enemy. Every place is a frontline and that is why God's women are positioned even in places that might appear demeaning, detestable and even distasteful. Sisters, turn it around, flip it for favor; recognize the frontline and stand in the Spirit of the Lord for the reinstatement of the sovereign rule of the Lord in our lives and the lives of all members of the human family.

Before we can fully understand and embrace our appointment, we must understand the necessity of overcoming the trials and tests instituted by Jehovah Gibbor to equip, prepare, empower and sustain us to press towards the ultimate goal; the triumph of the will of the Almighty in our battle assignments. We are soldiers and were appointed to do battle whilst we were yet within the loins of Mother Eve. Equally important, women must understand that in addition to the conditions of pain, suffering and submission that God imposed for us to work through and learn from, there are constant challenges and obstacles fashioned by the devil to keep us out of the war zone and out of the war council.

Appointed and Anointed

Each and every woman of God who takes up the mantel of spiritual warrior receives an anointing by God, in the same way that all who are born again, not of the flesh but of the Spirit are given the gift of the Holy Ghost. It is this gift that enables us to overcome the attacks of the enemy and to do **"all things through Christ Jesus"**. Without the Presence and indwelling of the Holy Spirit, we cannot stand against the devil and his forces of evil. **Philippians 4:13**

However, to be anointed is to be filled with an extra portion of the Holy Spirit in order that we can carry out the duties of our divinely appointed posting. The word anointing is usually used in reference to the outpouring of oil. In the same way, the oil is represented by the Holy Spirit and to be anointed is to have **"power after that the Holy Spirit is come upon you"**. **Acts 1:8**. In other words, after the

Holy Spirit is poured out upon us, we will have the anointing, the special power needed to fulfill our spiritual assignment

The revelation here then, is that the person that God appoints, He also anoints. For example, Sarah when she conceived Isaac, the promised heir of Abraham, at the grand age of ninety, received a special anointing of God that enabled her to have the strength needed to bring a child into the world, at her advanced age.

Because of faith also, Sarah herself received physical power to conceive a child, even when she was long past the age for it, because she considered [God] Who had given her the promise to be reliable and trustworthy and true to His word. Hebrews 11:11

It took that extra anointing from God, a supernatural gift of endurance, for a woman of Sarah's age, whose so-called biological clock had stopped ticking many years previous, to have the stamina, health and emotional fortitude to carry her baby to full term, successfully, and make it through the labor and birthing process without a C-section or pain-relieving drugs! Only divine favor could achieve the miracle that was the birth of her son Isaac, the child of promise, of covenant with the Almighty God.

Most of the women we meet in the Scriptures, whose lives fulfilled the will of God, evidenced that special empowerment that only He can give to accomplish that which He has ordained. These women did not please God by their works only but their faith in the Father, led to their obedience to His commands and success in their appointments, fuelled by the power of the Holy Spirit. In the case of Elizabeth, the mother of John the Baptist, she was a woman that had long given up on becoming a mother. Both she and her husband Zachariah were old and she was resigned to being childless. But a special Spirit-anointing from God soon turned things upside down!

The Lord made the impossibility of the natural realm a simple matter through His supernatural intervention. Elizabeth's son was the fore-runner of the Messiah, the greatest prophet that ever lived according to the testimony of the Lord Jesus Christ Himself. **Luke 1:5-60.** It is no coincidence therefore that Elizabeth was reminded in her spirit of other women of God who likewise received a miracle child and so we hear her echoing the substance of the praise-song of Rachel whose womb had been closed by God but was later favored with a child. **Luke 1:25.**

The Lord has done this for me, she said, in these days He has shown His favor and taken away my disgrace among the people.

Remember, Rachel was the much loved wife of Jacob. **Genesis 30:23.** She gave birth to her firstborn Joseph who was also "a forerunner"; he prepared the way for the survival of his extended family in Egypt. The family of his brother Judah was among all the other Children of Jacob (Israel) who benefited from the advance provisions of God expedited through Joseph's sojourn and received protection from the effects of the famine, in Egypt. It is from the lineage of Judah that Jesus is descended. Joseph, this son of Rachel was a type of the prophet John the Baptist; John was also born to be the forerunner of Jesus the Christ, Savior of the world.

76. And you, little one, shall be called a prophet of the Most High; for you shall go on before the face of the Lord to make ready His ways.

77. To bring and give the knowledge of salvation to His people in the forgiveness and remission of their sins.

78. Because of and through the heart of tender mercy and loving-kindness of our God, a Light from on high will dawn upon us and visit [us].

79. To shine and give light to those who sit in darkness and in the shadow of death, to direct and guide our feet in a straight line into the way of peace. Luke 1:76-9

Joseph was a savior in this physical realm of his kinfolks as well as his Egyptian hosts and all other surrounding nations that purchased grain from the pharaoh's store-houses in order to survive the great famine that prevailed. In Joseph were those nations of the earth blessed. In Jesus, all of mankind is offered salvation from sin, redemption from rebellion and restoration to their inheritance bequeathed by God when He created the earth. Unlike the operation of high finance that was involved in purchasing Egyptian grain, all the peoples of the earth may secure salvation **"without money and without price"! Isaiah 55:1.** The inspiring, faith-building story of Joseph may be read in **Genesis Chapters 37-50.**

Our Lord Jehovah always gives His people just what they need to carry out His purposes. Without the anointing of the Holy Spirit we can do nothing of ourselves. However, with God **"all things are possible to them that believe." Mark 9:23.** If you have not received the anointing for a mission you are purposed, then I would suggest that you have not been appointed by the Lord for that mission, yet. The anointing always precedes the appointment.

Seek God and listen to His instructions through the Holy Spirit if you would know His will and your appointed position on the frontline. And it is not that we cannot do work that we are not specifically or specially anointed to do in the Body of Christ, it is that to do it well and under guidance of the Holy Spirit, God must have selected and anointed us for that particular assignment. That is why I say, no anointing, no appointing from God.

When Jesus emerged from the water, the Holy Spirit like a dove descended upon Him and the voice of God declared, **"This is my Beloved Son in whom I am well pleased". Matthew 3:17.** Jesus then went into the desert to prepare for His earthly ministry. What is the revelation from this episode in Jesus life concerning the anointing? Let us get real here, if the Seed, the Anointed One, the Son of God who was without sin, was granted the anointing, an extra portion of the Holy Spirit at the beginning of His ministry, how much more are we not in dire need of the anointing to carry out our commission? **Luke 3:21, 22**

The Father equips and anoints us **'to fight the good fight of faith', 1 Timothy 6:12** and to **'finish the course'** He has put before us. Just be sure that you are on the course laid out by the Lord! **2 Timothy 4:7.** The final outcome of this war is graphically, colorfully and specifically detailed in the Book of Revelation of our Lord Jesus Christ as disclosed to the apostle John. All that remains is for us to decide who will receive our loyalty and support. With Joshua, I invite you to join me in a solemn declaration right now; chose the lord and master of your life, Jehovah God or the prince of darkness but **"as for me and my household, we will serve the Lord"**. **Joshua 24:15.** Who is on the Lord's side cried the psalmist David? Are you my sister, my brother? Are you willing to fight, under orders from the Lord, whatever the cost? Consider the cost of obedience to the Levites; warriors and priests of Jehovah God, and consider the reward of their commitment and dedication to the will of the Lord as stated in **Exodus 32:26:**

25. When Moses saw that the people were unruly and unrestrained (for Aaron had let them get out of control, so that they were a derision and object of shame among their enemies),

26. Then Moses stood in the gate of the camp and said, whoever is on the Lord's side, let him come to me. And all the Levites [the priestly tribe] gathered together to him.

27. And he said to them, Thus says the Lord God of Israel, every man put his sword on his side and go in and out from gate to gate throughout the camp and slay every man his brother, and every man his companion, and every man his neighbor.

28. And the sons of Levi did according to the word of Moses; and there fell of the people that day about 3000 men.

29. And Moses said [to the Levites, By your obedience to God's command] you have consecrated yourselves today [as priests] to the Lord, each man [at the cost of being]

against his own son and his own brother, that the Lord may restore and bestow His blessing upon you this day.

Restoration of Hope

Adam was a type (prefigure) of the One Who was to come [in reverse, the former destructive, the Latter saving]. 15. But God's free gift is not at all to be compared to the trespass [His grace is out of all proportion to the fall of man]. For if many died through one man's Falling away (his lapse, his offense), much more profusely did God's grace and the free gift [that comes] through the undeserved favor of the one Man Jesus Christ abound and overflow to and for [the benefit of] many. Romans 5:14b

Through Adam, death came to all his descendants, after the same manner life eternal is made available to all who will choose Christ Jesus as Savior because this choice means a new birth; a spiritual regeneration of a dead body into the joint heritage of a heavenly birthright, the birthright of the only Begotten Son of the Living God. The final destruction of the devil is guaranteed by the Word of God and the victory of our Christ, for he will be thrown into the lake of fire along with death and hell and all those who follow after him will likewise share his fate. The present system of things will pass away and everything will become new under the Lord Jesus and the Kingdom of God. **Revelation Chapter 21** beautifully describes this new heaven and new earth for the redeemed human family; a return to Eden, Paradise and the sweet Presence of the Lord forevermore!

This new beginning applies to individuals on a very personal level. If anyone:

- Believes in the Lord Jesus Christ as the Son of God and Redeemer of mankind
- Repents of sin and disobedience to the laws of God,

- Is baptized as a testimony to the world and the devil of the change of allegiance to the Lord of Righteousness, then
- Their carnal, sinful nature dies with Christ on Calvary
- He/she is raised with Him into a resurrection of eternal life,
- That shall find its ultimate expression in citizenry of the Kingdom of our Lord; it will be established at the end of this present system of evil.
- A new creature is created in Christ after the pattern and design of God in the beginning; that is, 'after the likeness and in the image' of the Divine Creator.
- Old things are passed away and everything becomes new – a new life begins in the service, love and worship of the Lord Jehovah.

A thorough reading of **Ephesians Chapter 4** and **Colossians Chapter 4** will give full clarification of the wonder and blessing of becoming born-again, brand new creatures and citizens of our Father's Kingdom. The new person now born of the Spirit and of the blood becomes a beneficiary of the New Covenant of God in Christ Jesus. There is no more condemnation for sin because the former lifestyle is transformed and a new child of God emerges, no longer ruled by carnality. **Colossians 3:1-10**. Rather, such an individual has achieved the greatest desire of both body and spirit; that is the desire for God first and always.

Blessed are those who hunger and thirst after righteousness, for they will be filled. Matthew 5:6.

Seek first the Kingdom of God and His righteousness and all things will be added unto you. Matthew 6:33

For men and women, this is the only sure way of overcoming the obstacles that blocks or blurs our God-vision, restoring us to a right relationship with Jehovah. Choosing Christ over carnality re-establishes a deliberate, personal, intimate and fulfilling relational experience with Him that was originally ours in Eden. Jesus is the only

Way, the only Door through which we can gain entrance into true liberty, the liberty of salvation and redemption. **Hebrews 10:12-23**

As the children of God, we can no longer be bound by our desires for the things of this world; things that imparts death not life. For to triumph over death we need the Holder of Key to hell and death to grant us our liberty; **"whom the Son sets free is free indeed". Romans 6:18.** In gaining Christ and His righteousness we have attained the greatest desire of our spirit, mind and soul; a renewed, regenerated personal relationship with God. Our old, sinful nature with its carnal mind-set was in rebellion against God and is incapable of anything else, but our new man is the temple of the Living God; acceptance of the gift of salvation means acceptance of the Lordship of Christ and His Presence with us always by the indwelling of the Holy Spirit.

> **Do you not know that your body is the temple (the very sanctuary) of the Holy Spirit Who lives within you, Whom you have received [as a Gift] from God? You are not your own. 1 Corinthians 6:19**

When we surrender our willful, selfish nature to the Lord Jesus, we are redeemed by His saving grace and righteousness. We are now able to come into agreement with His plans for our lives, fulfill His purposes and take up service in His Mission. Our reborn, Spirit-filled souls are ready to 'kick butt' in the spiritual battles that lay before us. As partakers of the New Covenant, personified in Jesus the Christ, we are God-focused and Holy Spirit empowered to effectively engage and rout the enemy. Every child of God, whether male or female, born of the Spirit, is a warrior armed with weapons of destruction targeting the kingdom of darkness and its evil ruler, Satan. **Ephesians 2:10-22.**

Abiding in Christ Jesus allows us to be solely, firmly focused on God and the things of God. This singleness of vision leads to obedience to the Almighty and His divine commandments. After all, our obedience is an outward manifestation of our God-faith in action. That is why the direct connection between God and man was severed in Eden the moment that Eve's faith in God was replaced by belief in herself. She gave in to the conceit and egotistical self-delusion that she had the ability, the knowledge and the wisdom to decide right and wrong over and above the laws laid down by our Creator.

The devil deceived her into sharing his own idolatry,to stand in the place of God.

And when the woman saw that the tree was good (suitable, pleasant) for food and that it was delightful to look at, and a tree to be desired in order to make one wise; she took of its fruit and ate; and she gave some also to her husband, and he ate. Genesis 3:6

We cannot claim to love God and yet be in breach of His laws, His Word, His Will and His Way. A rejection or loss of God-focus followed by acts of self-will leads only to destruction and death. A pursuit of selfish ends is a repudiation of the Lordship of Christ. This is clearly illustrated by the history of the human race and our relationship with the Creator as chronicled in Bible times and continuing through into our own desperate, sin dominated times.

The Lordship of Christ in our lives allows us to work ceaselessly at defeating the plans of the enemy; plans which are designed to achieve our destruction and the dissolution of God's sovereign rule. Every good soldier learns how to follow orders and we are the same. We are soldiers under orders. It could not have been easy for the Levites to carry out the command of God when they came face to face with a brother or a son, yet they did exactly as they were asked in total submission. This is the way of the warrior; total obedience to the orders of the Commander-In-Chief.

But unlike soldiers in their country's army, we do not have to consider the plausibility of conflicts whether ethically, morally or religious. God is Truth, Righteousness, Justice and Love; there is no measure of failing in Him. We can trust in His Word and obey in love and faith. This is the fortitude, determination and commitment that obedience brings through the anointing power of the Holy Spirit. Don't forget, the Levites were priests and warriors and their act of obedience consecrated them to the Lord. The same applies to us; we are a "royal priesthood" but we are also warriors of the Lord, our portion is in the Lord because He is our legacy. We must consecrate ourselves to the Lord and to Him alone.

CHAPTER 5

BIRTHING THE SEED OF REVOLUTION AND RESTORATION

∽

Battle Training for Warriors

13. "Now therefore, I pray You, if I have found favor in Your sight, show me now Your Way, that I may know You [progressively become more deeply and intimately acquainted with You, perceiving and recognizing and understanding more strongly and clearly] and that I may find favor in Your sight. And [Lord do] consider that this nation is Your people.

14. And Moses said – "For by what shall it be known that I and Your people have found favor in Your sight? Is it not in Your going with us so that we are distinguished, I and Your people, from all other people upon the face of the earth?

15. And the Lord said to Moses, "I will do this thing also that you have asked, for you have found favor, loving-

kindness and mercy in My sight and I know You personally and by name". Exodus 33:13-17

Every warrior of God must know Him, know His Law and His Way and live therein. We are His people, a peculiar nation, consecrated and holy unto the Lord. We must abide in His Will and cease from pursuing after our own designs. Without developing the Character of Christ there will be no conquests over sin and without possessing the weapons of spiritual warfare the fight will be lost; that is, if it even gets started. In **Genesis 3:16**, immediately following their assignment to spiritual warfare, God imposed certain harsh conditions on both the man and the woman designed to provide the discipline, character and expertise that a warrior would need in order to be faithful and effective.

Colossians 3:12-18 expands the effect and impact on our character of learning these lessons which are lessons of spiritual maturity and empowerment, of experience, training, preparedness, as well as expertise in the weapons and ammunition of God's army. We must develop a Christ-like character if we are to be His effective warriors.

12. Clothe yourselves therefore, as God's own chosen ones (His own picked representatives), [who are] purified and holy and well-beloved [by God Himself, by putting on behavior marked by] tenderhearted pity and mercy, kind feeling, a lowly opinion of ourselves, gentle ways, [and] patience [which is tireless and long suffering, and has the power to endure whatever comes, with good temper].

13. Be gentle and forbearing with one another and, if one has a difference (a grievance or complaint) against another, readily pardoning each other; even as the Lord has [freely] forgiven you, so must you also [forgive].

14. And above all these [put on] love and enfold yourselves with the bond of perfect-ness [which binds everything together completely in ideal harmony].

15. And let the peace (soul harmony which comes) from Christ rule (act as umpire continually) in your hearts [deciding and settling with finality all questions that arise in your minds, in that peaceful state] to which as [members of Christ's] one body you were also called [to live]. And be thankful (appreciative), [giving praise to God always].

16. Let the word [spoken by] Christ (the Messiah) have its home [in your hearts and minds] and dwell in you in [all its] richness, as you train one another in all insight and intelligence and wisdom [in spiritual things, and as you sing] psalms and hymns and spiritual songs, making melody to God with [His] grace in your hearts.

17. And whatever you do [no matter what it is] in word or deed, do everything in the name of the Lord Jesus and in [dependence upon] His Person, giving praise to God the Father through Him.

18. Wives, be subject to your husband [subordinate and adapt yourselves to them], as is right and fitting and your proper duty in the Lord.

In essence, the bigger picture is beyond the mere suffering, experiences, conditions, and circumstances that a woman will have as she lives her life as wife, mother and warrior. It is the importance of the experiences in shaping the character of Christ within, purifying unto righteousness and the perfecting of the woman for her destination, the Kingdom of God, that is of primary significance and purpose in the Lord's decree in **Genesis 3:16**. Sin was the catalyst that led to the woman's appointment as warrior, and the consequences of her weakness are the raw materials to be used to deliver training in:

a. The weaponry of spiritual warfare,
b. Development of Christ-like qualities, that is, the gifts and fruit of the Spirit,

c. Bearing testimony of salvation through the Redeemer,
   d. Manifesting the power of the blood of the Lamb to renew and recreate a new creature through the Holy Spirit and,
   e. The manifestation of God's strength through the weakness of women typically, the "weaker vessel' of the human family.

Example: The experience of travail, pain and suffering attendant on child birth and child rearing that was imposed by the Lord, gives all mothers a special, intimate and experiential insight into the pain that we inflict on the Lord by our disobedience. The experience of birthing can provide a bond of love so much deeper and stronger than any other in human to human experience.

It also allows us to appreciate the love of God for us when He gave His Son as a sacrifice, to suffer and die for us; a sacrifice that a mother in particular would prefer to make personally, rather than see her child suffer such pain and humiliation. **John 3:16.** By God's divine example and by the experiences of motherhood and marriage, women learn selflessness and sacrifice even if that leads to the forfeiture of life. Our experiences are designed to teach us total submission in love and reverence to God. He is not asking us to give more than He gave for us. He placed His love for us first, even above the life of His Beloved Son. How can we do less than make our love for Him, the number one priority in our lives!

Spiritual Fruits

   22. But the fruit of the [Holy] Spirit [the work which His presence within accomplishes] is - love, joy (gladness), peace, patience (an even temper, forbearance), kindness, goodness (benevolence), faithfulness, gentleness (meekness, humility), self-control (self-restraint, continence). Galatians 5:22-23

Love is the final but most important of the Spiritual Gifts that Paul lists in **1 Corinthians 12** and it is also the foremost of the nine

Spiritual Fruits listed above. However, it is clear that the eight fruits of the Spirit which are stated after love are really variations in our experiential understanding and manifestation of the nature of love. It the work of the Holy Spirit to conform us to the image, the character and the loving disposition of the Lord Jesus and in so doing we will come to manifests the fruits of the Spirit.

All the conditions and consequences of our experiences should aid in purifying, establishing and refining us, so that we produce without pause or thought, the fruits that proclaim the presence and sanctification of the Holy Spirit within us. As believers, servants and warriors, Jesus the Christ is Savior, Lord and Supreme Commander in whose image we must be made again so that we will be Holy even as He is Holy, Perfect as He is Perfect, heirs and joint heirs to the Kingdom of God, bringing many children to the Father as it pleased Him in love.

The Seed of the Woman

In mankind's bleakest moment, the Creator unveiled His Plan of Redemption. He was not prepared to give up on the human family. His love would not let Him. In His wisdom, God saw fit to use His gift of pro-creation to women combined with His chastisement as the vehicle of His love and His mercy to affect man's redemption. He granted to women the privilege of ushering in the Architect of the re-birth of His Kingdom rule on the earth and the extinction of the reign of the kingdom of the serpent, Satan.

As we know, the female had played a major part in the disobedience in Eden and in God's plan she was given the opportunity again, in fact chosen and trusted again, to be a major player in the Redemption Story. The Savior would be "born of a woman", not of man and woman, but "the Seed of the woman". Eve was already gifted with the ability to birth new life for the increase of the human family. Now this gift with the accompanying pains and peril to life added after sin, would serve the cause of atonement and restoration. Hers and the Lord's would be this redemptive sacrifice.

The sacrifice of the Father in sending His only begotten Son is beyond our comprehension but mothers have the best opportunity to glimpse a measure of His love for His children and the pain of loss or anticipated loss. If a mother looses a beloved child, after the experiences of pregnancy, travail, labor and child birth, comfort can only be found in the Lord and in His love. A bereaved parent would give anything to get their child back. And so it is with our Lord. In order to save us from eternal separation and extinction, He was willing to risk everything; He sacrificed His own beloved and only Begotten Son.

As mentioned previously, the experiences attendant on the life of women have been exacerbated, aggravated and manipulated by the enemy to oppress and oppose the entrance of women onto the battlefield for the Lord. But even the worse abuses can be turned around and serve as tools to teach, enlighten and allow us to appreciate at the human level, the pain that we, as God's creation, inflicts on Him and the sacrifice required to redeem us from our enslavement and service to the devil. **John 8:34.** The truth is, regardless of how much we suffer and hurt in this life, it does not compare to the suffering of the Christ. If in His sinless state, He suffered so much on or behalf, how can we consider it anything less than a privilege and honor to join with Him in the Fellowship of Suffering?

Since Jesus was the **"Lamb slain before the foundation of the world", Revelation 13:8,** the woman's destiny to birth the Redeemer was also pre-ordained, pre-conceived and pre-planned. Out of the pain and pangs of child-birth, the minefield of emotions and the humility that women experience in marriage is birthed the qualities and character of a warrior; Christ-like character and personal qualities that line up with the fruits of the Spirit, taking on the image of the perfect Christ; fitting us for warfare and peace in the Kingdom of the Lord.

A Promise Honored

The promise of redemption by the Most High God has been fulfilled in the birth, life, ministry, death, resurrection and sovereign ruler-ship of Christ Jesus our Lord. He is the Son of Covenant, "the Seed of the woman"; not of the male and female human together but of the woman and Jehovah God; wood overlaid with gold, humanity wrapped in divinity.

17. So it is evident that it was essential that He be made like His brethren in every respect, in order that He might become a merciful (sympathetic) and faithful High Priest in the things related to God, to make atonement and propitiation for the peoples' sins. 18. For because He Himself [in His humanity] has suffered in being tempted (tested and tried), He is able [immediately] to run to the cry of (assist, relieve) those who are being tempted and tested and tried [and who therefore are being exposed to suffering]. Hebrews 2:17, 18.

Women all through the ages have suffered as they have seen and experienced the affliction, destruction, designs and diabolical schemes of the enemy to destroy humankind; to destroy the very lives that they brought into the world. In like manner but multiplied to infinity, God has suffered immensely as the adversary has worked to bring about the eternal destruction of everything that is of God. The earth and every thing that God created therein came from within the very being of God and the devil has systematically set out to destroy it all. Unfortunately, sin makes us Satan's allies in his diabolical campaign.

Man had enslaved himself to sin and death and if we are to gain our liberty from the bondage of sin and our slave master, a blood price had to be paid. Divine law requires a blood sacrifice, (the life is in the blood!) **"For without the shedding of blood there is no remission of sin." Hebrews 9:22**. Man, born to sinful human parents, is born in slavery to death. But God has never known death, He alone is life eternal. Only God could infuse us with life; so it was that the plan for God to be made **'manifest in the flesh' (1 Timothy 3:16)**, as **"The Seed of the woman", (Genesis 3:15)** was formulated by the God-Head, Elohim.

Only the Son alone was worthy; only He could redeem us by His righteousness and His obedience as man. Only He was willing to empty Himself of His greatness and become "the Seed" of the woman born to do battle for the fallen human family; only the Lamb of God was willing and able to take up the assignment as a Living Sacrifice. In fact, according to the Apostle Paul in **Hebrews 4:15, 16**

15. We do not have a High Priest Who is unable to understand and sympathize and have a shared feeling with our weaknesses and infirmities and liability to the assaults of temptation, but One Who has been tempted in every respect as we are, yet without sinning.

16. Let us then fearlessly and confidently and boldly draw near to the throne of grace (the throne of God's unmerited favor to us sinners), that we may receive mercy [for our failures] and find grace to help in good time for every need [appropriate help and well-timed help, coming just when we need it].

This blessed and miraculous event took place some two thousand years ago and now the Seed of the woman is the Messiah, the Commander-in-Chief of God's army, not only in heaven but also on the earth. To Him has been given the authority to judge the earth, as it is His blood that was shed to redeem it from the power and bondage of sin, death and hell and He that is touched by our infirmities, was tempted in like manner as we are and faced death as we must, also.

11. Then I looked, and I heard the voices of many angels on every side of the throne and of the living creatures and the elders [of the heavenly Sanhedrin], and they numbered ten thousand times ten thousand and thousands of thousands.

12. Saying in a loud voice, Deserving is the Lamb, Who was sacrificed, to receive all the power and riches and wisdom and might and honor and majesty (glory, splendor) and blessing!

13. And I heard every created thing in heaven and on earth and under the earth and on the sea and all that is in it, crying out together, To Him Who is seated on the throne and to the Lamb be ascribed the blessing and the honor and the majesty and the power (might and dominion) forever and ever (through the eternities of the eternities)!

14. Then the four living creatures (beings) said, Amen (so be it)! And the elders [of the heavenly Sanhedrin] prostrated themselves and worshipped Him Who lives forever and ever. Revelation 5:11-14.

The Seed Revealed

According to God's law, every single seed holds within it the potential for new life after its own kind. This law of creation applies to every living thing that God caused to be on the earth including the man, Adam. But the seed's potential can only be realized if the seed is planted in the right soil under the right climatic conditions and tended by the nurturing care of the farmer.

The Seed that would produce the Conqueror of the serpent had to be "the Seed of the woman". An angel could not stand in the place of the sinner and neither could any other spirit-being. The seed of the man, though it brings forth life when planted in the nurturing 'soil' of the female womb, sparks a life, which like the grass, withers and dies after a season. Each seed already has the blueprint of its identity embedded in its DNA and can only produce after its own kind. That is why an apple seed will grow into an apple tree and produce apples, not oranges, naturally. Any other order is against God's design.

In the same way, mortal man and woman together gives birth to another mortal offspring; together they produce only fruits of sin and of the flesh that carries within it the infection of death, never the seeds of eternal life.

47. The first man was from out of earth, made of dust (earthly-minded); the second Man [is] the Lord from out of heaven.

48. Now those who are made of the dust are like him who was first made of the dust; and as is [the Man] from heaven, so also [are those] who are of heaven (heavenly-minded).

49. And just as we have borne the image [of the man] of dust, so shall we and so let us also bear the image [of the Man] of heaven;

50. But I tell you this, brethren, flesh and blood cannot [become partakers of eternal salvation and] inherit or share in the Kingdom of God; nor does the perishable (that which is decaying) inherit or share in the imperishable (the immortal). 1 Corinthians 15:47-50:

The Seed of the woman needed to bring forth an Offspring with the DNA of Deity. The Holy Spirit overshadowed Mary in the same way that it hovered over pre-earth at creation. **Genesis 1:2.** The Seed of the woman, when finally placed in the bosom of the earth, needed to have within it the very Spirit of the Ever-Living God, so that it could spring up again; the first-fruit of many brethren, bringing new life and producing a new crop, a new harvest of souls. These souls, born of incorruptible Seed will possess the Spirit of God which gives life eternal.

20. But Christ has indeed been raised from the dead, the first-fruits of those who have fallen asleep. 21 for since

> death came through a man, the resurrection of the dead also comes through a man. 22. for as in Adam all die, so in Christ all will be made alive. 23. But each in his own turn: Christ, the first-fruits; then, when He comes, those who belong to Him. 1 Corinthians 15:20-23. (NIV)

In the same way, the Bible tells us that the only fruits that are pleasing to God are the fruits of the Spirit. The seed, which is the Word of God, when it is planted in receptive, fertile hearts will be quickened by the Holy Spirit and bring forth life.

> **22. But the fruit of the [Holy] Spirit [the work which His Presence within accomplishes] is love, joy (gladness), peace, patience (an even temper, forbearance), kindness, goodness (benevolence), faithfulness,**
>
> **23. Gentleness, (meekness, humility) self-control, (self-restraint, continence).**
>
> **25. If we live by the [Holy] Spirit, let us also walk by the Spirit, [If by the Holy Spirit we have our life in God, let us go forward walking in line, our conduct controlled by the Spirit]. Galatians 5:22-23**

And only a woman, focused on God, fully submitted to His will and committed to His plan, could embrace the honor, the privilege even at the risk of losing earthly prestige, to become the vessel in the natural that would bring forth the ultimate WMD; a destruction that will ultimately be accomplished in the physical as well as in the spiritual realms. Mary from Galilee was such a woman, at the appointed time, in the right place with the right qualifications.

Focused on the Kingdom

Mary the mother of Jesus was fully informed by the arch angel Gabriel of the nature and purpose of her pregnancy and the Child that she would birth. **Luke 1:31-33.** It was made clear to her what His mission would be and she rejoiced in the honor bestowed on her. She was familiar and prepared for the role of warrior in the spirit realm, as well as that of mother, wife, nurturer, nurse and teacher in the natural world. After all, only someone with a clear, uncluttered, unobstructed comprehension of the assignment given to women by God in Eden, could be privy to, and willingly participate in the strategies of spiritual warfare that were required then as now, in the battle for souls.

Mary was no passive soldier following orders without any understanding of her own position in the divine strategy to achieve annihilation of the enemy. She was both able and capable of discerning the movement of God that apprehended her. As a cousin to Elizabeth, born into the family of the priesthood, we can surmise that she had grown up with the teachings of the prophets and the patriarchs so that when the angel appeared to her, she obediently embraced the assignment offered her, in knowledge and obedience. **Luke 1:46-55.**

Mary was God-focused. To be God-focused means giving Him our undivided attention and loyalty. It is an active not a passive posture. It is about yielding our minds; our thoughts, will and our emotions over to sovereignty of the Almighty. It is impossible to be God-focused and still desire the things of the world.

15. Do not love or cherish the world or the things that are in the world. If anyone loves the world, love for the Father is not in him.

16. For all that is in the world – the lust of the flesh [craving for sensual gratification] and the lust of the eyes greedy longings of the mind] and the pride of life [assurance in one's own resources or in the stability of earthly things] – these do not come from the Father but are from the world [itself].

17. And the world passes away and disappears, and with it the forbidden cravings (the passionate desires, the lust) of it; but he who does the will of God and carries out

His purposes in his life abides(remains) forever. 1 John 2:15-17

God-focus is about relegating everything but one's relationship with God to the peripheral boundaries of the mind and heart and the authority of the laws, statutes, regulations and design of the Lord. Focus requires the corporation, participation and performance of the whole self in God's plan for one's life. Focus is total submission so that we come into complete agreement with God in all things. And not just coming into agreement as an intellectual exercise but rather as a mindset, a lifestyle, a philosophy and a reason for being. It is us that must come into agreement with the plan of God and not the other way around!

The mother of Jesus knew who she was in the Lord. Her identity as a daughter of the Promise and as a potential candidate to birth the Messiah, was buried deep within her. **Daniel 11:37**. She understood the place of women in the scheme of spiritual things and what was on the table. She was a God-focused woman ready to fulfill her divine commission for the Kingdom of God and His Christ. Mary made God the true center and focus of her life choices and all her desires were to serve Him. She was a woman of God, available to the Lord and the cause of righteousness, regardless of the cost in this earthly realm.

As a daughter of Abraham, of the nation of Israel, God's covenanted people, taught to watch and pray for the coming of the Messiah; Mary was well aware that only the Messiah could assure us ultimate victory over the adversary. She could have refused the commission offered her by the arch-angel especially if one considers the possible consequences of a pregnancy outside of marriage. See **Deuteronomy 22:20, 21.**

Joseph could reject, expose and disgrace her for being pregnant with the child of an un-revealed man; she could be stoned to death, ostracized, made an outcast and labeled as a woman of ill-repute, according to the laws and customs of the Jewish people at that time. This is still the fate of millions of women the world over in societies where sexual impropriety or immorality is not tolerated.

Or, Mary could have preferred to focus on the love, protection and provision of a home, a name, reputation and economic security and status that her marriage would bring her and refuse the invitation of God to be the mother of Jesus, the Messiah. After all, the position of women in her society was very low and being married was at least a personal promotion to a recognized, respectful status. She could have been skeptical, selfish or sinful, preferring to focus instead on materialism and idolatry, esteeming the things of man more than the things of God.

Instead, her vision remained fixed only on the God of her heart and her heritage. She welcomed the opportunity to serve Him and the human family. I believe that entry into the earth realm by the incarnated Lord only became possible when God found a woman ready to submit self-will and self-determination to the higher purpose of His plan of redemption. The spirit of idolatry overtook Eve and Adam in the Garden of Eden and manifested itself as a rejection of the will and the way of God. Mary took the reverse stance and path.

The mother of the Messiah was totally yielded to God first, discarding her own natural desires, dreams and ambitions that conflicted with her surrendered life; giving precedence to God's will and purpose. It was only by choosing God first, above all else and being available to Him that divine liberty would be possible. Mary had to take her eyes off the institutions of man and the carnal things that distract, distort and deceive us into idolatry. Instead she deposited all her affections and faith in God, demonstrating her willingness to be used as God's woman to bring about the timely realization of His redemptive plan for mankind.

At that time, in the culture and customs of the day, as well as the status of women in that society, Mary's submission to the Almighty would appear to be a great sacrifice when viewed with the natural sight of man. After all, a woman's position as a valuable member of her society was dependent on her marital status. Being a married woman was the ambition of every single woman. But faith is seeing that which is unseen and believing in those things which are not as though they are; believing they already exist because they have already been determined by God. **Hebrews 11**

Mary did not hesitate to accede to the will of God for her life. She did not consider her own needs apart from God's purpose for her womanhood. If it meant that she had to fight for her life and that of the Child then she was willing. Her warrior mentality was at the ready and whatever it took, she would pay the price to be obedient to the will of God.

Then Mary said, Behold, I am the handmaiden of the Lord, let it be done to me according to what you have said. Luke 1:38.

As a result of her selfless surrender to God, Mary was still blessed with the espousal love, support and protection of Joseph until the day he died, as well as with other children. Mary surrendered her all to the purpose of God but regained everything she could have desired; more than she could have imagined with the limited vision of the natural mind. This is the kind of Father that we have in heaven; a Father willing to give us even more than we can ask or even imagine and Who rewards us according to His riches in glory.

The Privilege of Sacrifice

For us to gain the very thing we crave most, we must be willing to offer it up as a living sacrifice to the Lord. This is obedience; His commandments must take precedence, His purpose and plan for us, first priority. But take a moment dear brethren and rejoice that you have something dear and precious to offer on the altar to your Lord. The very thing that we give up in faith is the very thing that the Father multiplies back to us, exceedingly, abundantly. There are a number of Scriptures that remind us of this promise that I have included below for our re-assurance and appreciation of God's provisions.

And everyone who has left houses or brothers or sisters or father or mother or children or fields for my sake will

receive a hundred times as much and will inherit eternal life. **Matthew 19:29**

Whatsoever you do, do it heartily, as to the Lord and you shall receive the reward of the inheritance. Colossians 3:23, 24.

The Lord recompense thy work and a full reward be given thee of the Lord God of Israel. Ruth 2:12

4. There is a reward for the righteous. [That is, those who are in right standing with God doing His will and obeying His commands]. Psalms 58:11

The Principle of Godly Submission

The Principle of Godly Submission is the very foundation on which obedience and faithfulness to the Lord is rooted and grounded. Submission to God means surrender to the way of righteousness, to divine direction, the Lordship of the Christ and the operation of God's Kingdom authority. Unless and until we surrender to God, we cannot claim to love Him and we certainly cannot serve Him. This fundamental principle is the very cornerstone of our divine inheritance and the building block of our faith.

Eve begrudged God's wisdom. She wanted to be as wise as Him. She was not prepared to yield herself to God's agenda, His plan and His timing. Rather, Eve was self-willed, conceited and foolish. She decided that she would acquire some devil-determined, carnal comprehension of wisdom other than through the will and definition of the Almighty. Her decision however made her "a thief and a robber" and a fool; willing to challenge God's commandment, His authority and His right to determine her boundaries. She accepted the lies of the serpent above the truth of God and decided to rely on her own carnal reasoning, judgment and logic in her self-appointed pursuit of a self-defined wisdom, purporting to be the wisdom of the Lord.

In succumbing to the devil's deception, the woman proved the folly of the carnal, rebellious nature. Her ability to abide in godly wisdom was undermined by her susceptibility to vain appeals to human pride. In the same way today, the ambition and drive of some women, to be hailed as achievers and high flyers in society is perhaps reflective of this carnal inclination of pride, and praise. The need for self-elevation, self-glorification and self-aggrandizement still drive many women to compete with each other and with men. Eve, the first woman, sought to elevate herself to the status of godhood by rebelling against the Eternal One's ordinances and embracing the misrepresentation that she could become like her Creator by eating the very fruit that He had forbidden her to eat.

The enemy targeted Eve instead of Adam and the Bible tells us that Eve was deceived but Adam was not. She was caught in a web of deceit that planted a seed of doubt; that she was in a state of mind-poverty engineered and enforced by God's command to stay away from the forbidden fruit. The seed quickly brought forth a harvest of disobedience, rebellion and self-centeredness. In a short time Eve was ready to sacrifice paradise and she did! She was no longer in submission to God; she had just sold herself into slavery to sin's master. It is amazing how quickly a garden of flowers can be taken over by weeds, thistles and thorns. In the same way a seed of doubt is fast-growing, taking root and springing up to quickly choke out the growth of life itself. Satan's deceit multiplied exponentially in Eve's heart and eventually it cut her off from the Source of her life, the Creator.

Emotional and Spiritual Poverty

From Mother Eve in the Garden of Eden to her daughters over the generations, women have continued to believe, invest in and nurture a feeling of lack and deprivation. In the Scriptures, we have the revelation that Delilah was a woman who was desperate to change her status. She was convinced that she just did not have quite what she needed to complete her. She was enticed, beguiled and blinded by a desire for fame, recognition and status in her own community and nation and like many of us it appeared to her that money was the answer to meeting her deep longings. In order to achieve her ambition, Delilah was willing to make whatever sacrifice was required.

Judges 16

To Delilah, betraying her man was an acceptable sacrifice to achieve fame and fortune. She had a choice; her decision would determine the fate of individuals and nations. Delilah was not deceived or tricked into the choice that she made. She knew exactly what she was doing when she agreed and then actually disarmed and delivered Samson over to his keenest enemy, the Philistines. Delilah prostituted her honor and integrity for worldly gain. She could have taken the opposite route to the one that she did in her marriage. But a desire to meet some unspecified, unfulfilled need with the things that the world held out as ends in themselves, messed up her mind and caused her to betray Samson.

Delilah, as the wife of Samson had the fantastic opportunity to observe and learn first hand about the true God of the Children of Israel. She knew that the theocracy of the Israelites was different to that of her own people. She also knew that Samson, the Judge and leader of that nation was a very special man. His feats of valor that resulted in the victory of his people were known throughout their world.

However, instead of seeking to follow after the true and righteous God who demonstrated His love, care and interest in the well being of all the Israelites, individually and as a nation specially chosen by Him, to be His witness, self-interest consumed her. She most certainly would have been prompted by the Holy Spirit to consider the merits of following where Samson led spiritually but carnality won out and she decided that the material values and valuables of this world were more desirable and deserved.

Delilah chose Baal; mammon rather than God. She took a short term view of life. She wanted all that she could possibly acquire in this temporary existence. She rejected the gift of eternal life which is the reward of all who truly, spiritually worship Jehovah God. Delilah's diabolical design was the personal destruction of Samson, her husband, and the defeat of the nation of Israel, offered up on the altar of financial gain, social elevation and supposed personal success. This act of betrayal would enlarge her personal standing as well as the territory, influence and power of the Philistines. In the final analysis, the exaltation of Baal above God was the outcome of this hand-maiden's treachery; at least in the short term.

When we choose the things and values of the world above righteousness we are in fact giving glory, authority and pre-eminence to the devil instead of to Him who is the Creator, Provider and Sustainer of our life and our world. We are agreeing with the devil that God is unable to supply our every need, to satisfy all aspects of our personalities and to pour into our lives in the fullness of time, all the gifts that He has in store for us to make us wholly acceptable and perfect in His sight.

Submission Not Subjugation

In a state of rebelliousness, which is the condition of any life that is contrary to the commandments of God, it is literally a declaration of war to say that the woman must submit to her husband. It is like waving a red flag in front of a bull to most modern women especially those of us who live in western societies. The truth is that once sin entered the equation in the Garden, God decreed that the woman's desire would be for her husband and that he would rule over her. This was one of the consequences of sin.

Why then is the pre-eminence of husbands such a difficult concept for women to come to terms with? Why is there so much opposition? Why are women constantly chafing at the bit, as it were, to break free from this perceived yoke of bondage? Could the reason simply be that this is not how God originally created the female of the "entity' to be, and therefore this state of affairs is unnatural, uncomfortable and very often oppressive and exploitative? Or that the terminology has been misinterpreted, misapplied and abused for the nefarious purposes of the enemy to such an extent that even the mere mention of the headship of the husband is an anathema?

As I have said before, God's decree concerning the marital relationship was in complete contrast to God's original ordering of the earthly realm. Originally, He gave the male and female equality in responsibility, dominion and authority. But after sin entered the marital residence, God intervened in the functioning of the union and family unit. Eve had given free rein to her natural, carnal mind, bloated with self-importance, conceit and idolatry. She lacked discipline. Adam had abdicated his duties and responsibilities as God's appointed authority and ruler in the earth realm and subjected himself to the serpent and sin. God's decree concerning the rank of men and women within marriage operates in relation to saved and unsaved people. Regardless of the attitude and behavior of the world in respect of this command, the people of God must strive to uphold the responsibilities and privileges of a marriage and a home based on the order established by the divine directives of our Lord.

For example, it is a spiritual fruit of a God-focused, God-centered, surrendered life for a woman be submissive to her husband. This kind of submission is not the result of weakness, lack or inferiority on the part of a woman. Instead, it is submission which is self-elected and comes from a position of self-control, strength, wisdom, obedience and love, as well as a determination to be Christ-like in all our ways, just as demonstrated by Jesus.

However, the devil has distorted the principle of godly submission and specifically the concept of a wife's submission to her husband to such an extent that there is generally no distinction made between subjugation and submission. However, subjugation is diametrically opposed to submission. The first is imposed from the outside by force, blackmail, violence, threats, coercion, manipulation and other motivators, while the latter comes from the heart and mind of the person doing the submitting and is offered out of love, respect and obedience to God.

Subjugation is of the deceiver but godly submission is of the Christ. Subjugation inflicts sorrow and is a symptom of a sinful or sin-filled mind and a heart of stone while submission is reflective of love and emanates from a heart that bears the stamp of the Lord. Submission is to be honored while subjugation is to be abhorred! In this text we will focus only on submission. Subjugation has no place in the life of God's people and must be uprooted, rejected and ejected from our lives, loves and relationships.

Distortion of truth and opposition to the order that God declared is nothing new for the humans in a society that is ruled by Satan.

Rejection of the biblical counsel that men are the head of families merely exemplifies continued rejection of the commands and the decrees of divine wisdom. In addition, the interchange of the words submission and subjugation is just one of the devilish methods employed to distort God's statutes.

However, a child of God born of the Spirit and adopted into the family of God should have no difficulty with the issue of submissiveness. I say this because the truth is that submission is the principle that underpins godly conduct and is the foundation of Christ-like character. This was perfectly demonstrated by the life of Jesus while He was physically on the earth. His life was a life lived in total, perfect and beautiful submission to the Father. He even went so far as to demonstrate practically, to His disciples, in the ceremony of the feet-washing, the operation of the principle of submission. To be submissive is a sign of love, humility and a life yielded to God. **John 13:4-17.**

Submission is a requisite characteristic of every one seeking to live according to the Royal Charter of Kingdom Citizenship. The Christ was submissive in all things unto the Father and we too must be equally yielded to the commands of the Lord. If we practice and live in submission to God's laws then there should be no difficulty about being in submission to a husband. The choice finally comes down to agape love which is manifested in obedience. An outflow of obedience is submission to the Almighty, while continued rebellion and self-will in the service of sin and Satan rules out any possibility of submission and instead opens the door to subjugation, confrontation, aggression, abuse, pride, denigration and degradation

Liberty lies in living according to the will and purpose of God for our lives; that is, living a Christ-like life that is yielded to the sovereignty of the Lord our God. Being in accord with the divine principle declared by the Word of God should pose no problems when a woman is married to a husband who loves and serves God. Such a husband will also be living according to the principles laid down by the Scriptures so that there is unity in outlook, attitude and approach to the worship of God and fellowship with each other.

As I have heard repeated often, there is joy in accepting a man as head of the home when he would lay down his life for his wife, in the same way that Jesus gave His life for His bride, the church. **Ephesians 5:25**. However, there is great issue taken by many women when they are expected to be submissive to a man who does not fear God or respect the ordinances of a God-centered marriage. The intervention of the Holy Spirit is the only solution to the various nuances and problems that arise. But one thing will remain constant; a warrior of God will rise up against the presence, influence and work of the enemy wherever he is operating against the human family and the Kingdom of Righteousness. She must oppose Satan in whatever guise he appears to the rebuking of loved ones.

Being in submission to God's law is to die to self, not standing on pride, obstinacy, rebellion or revolt against the decrees of our Father Creator. As women, God has appointed us the opportunity of divine schooling within the institution of marriage. We are not called to serve two masters, only one and that one is the Almighty. In a way, we are given a chance to do Eden all over again. Being submissive to our husband does not require us to make the man our master for no-one can serve two masters.

> **No one can serve two masters; for either he will hate the one and love the other, or he will stand by and be devoted to the one and despise and be against the other. You cannot serve God and mammon (deceitful riches, money, possessions, or whatever is trusted in). Matthew 6:24**

Our repentance and our redemption admit us into the family of God once more. Former things are passed away and all things become new. We die with Christ and are resurrected with Him into a new life. In this new life we have the chance to show our love for the Father who so loved us, and for our Redeemer who gave His life for us. Therefore we have no grounds for complaint if God directs that we submit to godly husbands. He said it and that is all that we need to know.

Jesus is our Servant-Priest and Servant-King; setting the standard for us and banishing all our reasons for refusing to rebuke the spirit of rebellion to which we have become enslaved. He broke the chains of sin and has set the captives free. We are the liberated;

purchased by His obedience and submission to the Redemption Plan. How or why would we want to do any less? The Lord will surely beautify the humble with salvation. **Psalms 149:4.**

The rewards of a submissive life may be briefly summarized in the following manner.

1. **Peace** – Jehovah Shalom reveals Himself to us when we are totally yielded to Him. We find divine peace as a result of our adherence to His Way which means a rejection of the way of sin, death and damnation. This peace that the Lord imparts is unlike any peace that we can achieve in the natural. **John 14:27.**

   For the Lord Himself gives us His peace always. **2 Thessalonians 3:16.** There may be storms that will buffet the ship of our lives but the Lord Jesus is not careless concerning our welfare but abides with us if we abide in Him.

2. **Joy Unspeakable** – There is a joy which comes from being filled with the Holy Spirit which is the very presence of the Lord Himself. It means that whatever is going on in the world, in spite of the clutter, clamor and challenges of everyday life, the joy of the Lord is our strength. **Nehemiah 8:10**

3. **Salvation** – Unless we are willing to surrender our whole being and everything that we possess to God then we cannot be saved. Salvation means surrender and if we are surrendered to God then He is able to give us a new life, a life that will lead to a place in God's eternal Kingdom. **Psalms 149:4.**

4. **Exaltation** – The Scriptures tells us that he that humbles himself will be exalted. In fact when the disciples were discussing among themselves who would be the greatest in the Kingdom of God, Jesus plainly taught that unless we are

willing to humble ourselves to the one considered the least then we cannot be partakers of His glory. **John 13:16.**

In fact He said that the first shall be last and the last shall be first. We must be willing to give up all for Jesus; tangibles and intangibles alike in preference for service and a share in the fellowship of suffering, if we would attain the final goal towards which we press.

The Lord our God equipped us with a warrior spirit and the necessary weaponry to engage the enemy in spiritual warfare. **2 Corinthians 10:4.** God's order reflects the principle of humility and divine order that He is not a God of confusion. Chaos is a characteristic of the adversary's world and His Kingdom and the Kingdom of Light has nothing to do with the Kingdom of Darkness.

In establishing His order, God gives authority to the man in this present system of things. He places the man in charge of earthly institutions and this includes the marital home. Hence the Scriptures state, **'man is the head of the wife even as Christ is the head of the church'. (Ephesians 5:23)** Man, whether male or female, is not the head of the Church of Christ. No-one places another in authority over his own body or his over his bride. In the same way, Christ did not relinquish His place of authority over his Church but remains the head of the body for which He gave His very life.

There are many obstacles that can impede the ability of a woman to see clearly the mission and the purpose that God declared in the Garden of Eden. All of these when properly viewed through a "God-scope" can be seen, not as hindrances or curses, as has often been stated but as opportunities for preparation, training and equipping for success in the spiritual warfare that is our portion since Eden's gates were closed behind us.

Seek the Lord [inquire for Him, inquire of Him, and require Him as the foremost necessity of your life], all you humble of the land who have acted in compliance with His revealed will and have kept His command-

ments; seek righteousness, seek humility [inquire for them, require them as vital]. Zephaniah 2:3.

The Bible has provided us with many examples of some of the women who faced the challenges of being God-focused with the God-faith and vision to overcome the enemy. Their victory provides wise instruction, role-models and warnings for all of us who desire to be restored to a right relationship with the Creator. What might be considered a sacrifice in the eyes of the world is a privilege when offered to the Lord in submission.

I am honored to take this opportunity to share the revelations that the Lord has blessed me with concerning His saints, the Matriarchs of the Scriptures. I do not profess theological training or knowledge as taught in the esteemed seminaries, but I know that the Lord has given me revelation that is applicable at the very personal level of salvation, service and worship. I will make further references to a few of the women who exercised their choice against the Kingdom of God just for illustration of the consequences of wrong decisions. The lessons that I have been taught by the Holy Ghost, is written here with the certain hope that at least one daughter of my Father and yours will be succored and encouraged to be an effectual woman of God, a spiritual warrior, in and for His Kingdom of Righteousness.

The women of the Bible are no different to any of us today. Their experiences; the challenges and obstacles that they faced left them in positions that required them to push against the foe to secure a right relationship with God. There is so much that we can learn from their experiences and in the process, be edified by adopting their models of behavior, attitude and action. It is only by obedient submission to the law, decrees, directives and plan of the Lord that we can inherit the Kingdom through the Redeemer of the human family. The following chapters will consider the challenges, conditions and circumstances that women have faced and how they worked out their salvation by choosing to be a warrior of God or a minion of the devil.

CHAPTER 6

THE ULTIMATE OBSTACLE COURSE

The Practical Test

As we saw earlier, the conditions and consequences that followed the transgression in Eden serve to prepare God's warrior women for battle against the enemy. The way that this works will be explored in greater details in respect of one of those conditions namely that the wife will desire her husband. This imposed a change in the marital relationship that did not originally exist. In imposing on woman the condition that her 'desire' would be for her husband, read **Genesis 3:16,** God was allowing carnality its full remit, demonstrating to womankind the ultimate conclusion to a desire that overruled and undermined obedience to the Father Creator. The woman had based her reasoning and her decision to rebel against God's command, in the realm of the natural; she gave full reign to the sensual or sensuous, rather than the divine.

> **When the woman saw that the fruit of the tree was good for food and pleasing to the eye, and also desirable for gaining wisdom, she took some and ate it. Genesis 3:6**

After the Fall in Eden, God decreed a hierarchical system in the home. In so doing, He was allowing the woman to experience the fullest extent and final maturity of her rejection of His way and His law based on the exercise of her emotions and reasoning. The work, energy, spiritual focus, fight and commitment involved in the experiences of post-Eden life would be invaluable lessons in agape love and wisdom; obedience, submission, humility, faith and righteousness among other qualities and conduct that must shape the character of a follower of the laws of the heavenly Kingdom.

For our instruction I will look in greater detail at the condition which stated that the desire of the woman would be centered on her husband and he will rule over her. First let me say that I believe that a wife's desire for her husband by itself, without being grounded and filtered through a love relationship with God, is a distraction and an obstruction that could lead to idolatry. As the redeemed of the Lamb, we must be in subjection to God in all things and in all areas of our lives, including our love lives. **James 4:7**

And as Paul tells us plainly in **2 Corinthians 10:5,** every thought, emotion, philosophy and imagining of man must be brought into subjection to God and to His laws, statutes and ordinances. God is a jealous God and He commands that we have no other god before Him. In **Ezekiel 11:19-21** we are told definitively that God will give us a new heart with a new spirit so that we may walk according to His statutes because without the new heart from Him, we cannot attain to His righteousness through Jesus the Christ. Our first desire needs to be focused on, and situated in the Lord.

But seek (aim at and strive after) first of all His Kingdom and His righteousness (His way of doing and being right), and then all these things taken together will be given you besides. Matthew 6:33

Without the grace of God, human beings cannot control the tendency to allow emotions to dictate and rule our thought processes and consequently our decisions and actions. It is only with the anointing of the Holy Spirit and the acceptance of the provisions and responsibilities of the New Covenant that the daughters of Eve can truly triumph in the re-institution of their heritage. **Psalms 51** is a prayer that we should come into agreement with!

Was God's decree concerning desire for the husband, a punishment of the woman? Did He take away her equal standing with man by burdening her with an unhealthy, unbalanced, inharmonious characteristic that would be purely punitive? I must admit that when I started this journey, I was almost persuaded that the answers to these questions were all in the affirmative. Like many women, I had grown up hearing that women were cursed. Even our monthly cycle was nicknamed "the curse"!

Through the guidance of the Holy Spirit I have now come to the realization that God was not trying to belittle, subdue, control or diminish the value, worth or self esteem of His daughters. Such intention or act would be incompatible with the character of God. He was in fact determined that we would develop God-faith, vision, wisdom, patience, understanding, emotional maturity, spiritual muscles and above all, obedience to Him in all things, in all circumstances, regardless.

We were commissioned to warfare by the Lord before He imposed the conditions that were consequential to our sins. So I am led to believe that when the Lord was pronouncing the consequences of Eve and Adam's sin, He had in mind the assignment that they would be commissioned to perform in the service of the Almighty. After all, without these aspects of character development and personal strengths that are the inherent benefits of these experiences, we would be doomed to fail under our own steam. And since God never set us up for failure in any divine appointment, He imposed conditions that would serve as methods, means and experiences of training, preparation and success in the spiritual warfare to which we are assigned.

Desire is only a negative emotion when it flows from our carnality, is motivated by selfish gain and controls our decisions and our actions. When we locate our desire in the wrong thing or when desire becomes perverted and manipulated negatively to the purpose of evil, a problem arises that can lead to our eternal damnation. However, there are desires which flows from a heart renewed by the Spirit of God and these are the desires that He places within and promises to grant. Such a renewed heart will not desire things which are inappropriate, immoral, or sinful in any way but rather, will seek the things which are in keeping with the will of the Lord and His holiness.

The emotion, the feeling that is desire can be a good thing or a bad thing depending on the heart from which it flows and its focus. One thing is certain however; the imposition of a desire, a craving, and a consuming need for our husband is a learning experience for women. It allows us to go through the processes that take us from a starting point that could inherently lead to idolatry and conclude with the triumph or submission of our emotions to the law and will of the Almighty, if we allow God to work His salvation in our lives.

In other words, starting with the choice of a partner all the way through to responsibilities of parenthood, we need to humbly, lovingly accept our continuous and total need for divine guidance before we make any life decisions. The marriage covenant was instituted as a tri-partite relationship; Jehovah is the first party and then the spouses, male and female. Generally, our choice of spouses is motivated by our emotions and whether we find a compatible, loving relationship will depend on how submitted to the Lord our hearts and minds are and how dependent we are on Him to guide our choices.

Given the unreliability of pure emotions as a basis for decisions, evidenced by Eve in Eden as well as the state of marriages and relationships in today's world, we need to commit our emotions and their exercise to the authority and sovereignty of the All-Knowing Father. When God guides our choice of a spouse, the desire of a woman for her husband presents a daily opportunity to selflessly share herself with her husband in a way that acknowledges God as Lord of their lives and does not detract from the greatest commandment of Love declared by Jesus in **Matthew 22:36-38 (NIV)**

36. Teacher, which is the greatest commandment in the Law? 37. Jesus replied; Love the Lord your God with all your heart and with all your soul and with all your mind. 38. This is the first and greatest commandment.

Therefore, in order to achieve our Spiritual Home-coming, our hearts, minds and bodies will of necessity be the battleground where we must confront, defeat, and consciously choose to turn aside from the desires of the carnal man. After all, the natural, carnal desires, that originally triumphed in Eden and led us into transgression against God's law, continues to be the inheritance of every person born into this world.

Victory will only be possible when our desires are in alignment with what God desires for us. The prize towards which we must press is the restoration of communion with the Creator God and perfect union and agreement with His will. God loves us so much that instead of turning His back on us, and leaving us in our own folly and sin, He took the marred vessel and decided to make it again; again in His likeness and His image, this time, born of the Holy Spirit.

1. The Word which came to Jeremiah from the Lord: 2. Arise and go down to the potter's house, and there I will cause you to hear My words, 3. Then I went down to the potter's house, and behold, he was working at the wheel. 4. And the vessel that he was making from clay was spoiled in the hand of the potter; so he made it over, reworking it into another vessel as it seemed good to the potter to make it. Jeremiah 18:1-4 (NIV)

So how do we learn the lessons that God desires to teach, to allow us to come to a place of submission, understanding, wisdom and victory? There are many different paths and diverse experiences and situations that we will traverse and experience before we find the Truth. For example, when we focus all our attention and affections on man, we will inevitably come face to face with his limitations; flaws that do not make him any less lovable but which highlight the imperfections that result from sin, pointing us to the perfection and fullness that lays in the Lord our God.

Even the most 'perfect' man will cause disappointment, pain, or heart-break at some time, either intentionally, indirectly or unconsciously. Guaranteed he will exhibit the short-comings and failures inherent in the sinful nature of mankind. After all, as the prophet declares in **Jeremiah 17:9 the "heart is deceitful above all things, who can trust it?"** This deceitful and dishonest heart is the natural outcome of transgression against the laws of God. Without the heart of God, we will continue to be naturally self-centered, self-serving and self-destructive.

Head over Heart

Submissiveness is not consistent with rebellion and as long as we remain in sin we are in rebellion. Submission to God means obedience and so much more. It is joyfully embracing divine plans and destiny. It is welcoming the opportunity, the privilege and the honor to be in the Way, subjecting our will, our thoughts, desires, and actions to the will, direction and authority of the Almighty. Submission is the knowledge that we have a choice and then exercising that choice by putting God and His Kingdom first, last, always, regardless. In other words, Lordship over our lives belongs to God, we are His, totally.

Jesus made that choice, becoming the **"First-fruit of many brethren"**. He has by His lead, His example made it possible for us to be redeemed through Him, through His righteous obedience to God. He experienced the same emotions that we do and in His moments of loneliness, isolation, emotional and spiritual pain, He could have allowed His emotion to dictate His decision in Gethsemane or at any time during His trial, conviction and crucifixion, but He did not.

Even at the last moment when the face of the Father was hidden and Jesus faced the final separation, a condition never previously experienced; He did not allow His emotions to destroy His obedience. His distress is evident in His cry to the Father, **"Why have you forsaken Me?" Matthew 27:46.** Jesus could have called legions of angels to His aid but He did not give in to His emotions. If He had given in, it would be giving up on mankind and His Father's Redemption Plan for us. Unlike Adam and Eve, He proved the devil a liar to the whole of God's Kingdom, everywhere. Now, when that old serpent tries to use mankind's disobedience as proof that God's Laws are unjust, impractical and incapable of compliance, the Conquering Lion is able to show otherwise.

Unless and until we surrender to God and receive salvation through Jesus our Redeemer, sin is the master of our lives. We become servants of that to which we subject ourselves. Paul declares in **Romans 8:16:**

Do you not know that if you continually surrender yourselves to anyone to do his will, you are the slaves of him whom you obey, whether that be to sin, which leads to death, or to obedience which leads to righteousness (right doing and right standing with God)?

The Perfect Man

It is not the fault of any particular man that he disappoints or hurt. That is the nature of men and in fact of women also; since we are all born in sin and shaped in iniquity. Even, a man or woman of God will stumble and cause hurt and disappointment to loved ones.

Yet, the flip side of this reality is that in sharp contrast, there stands a most perfect Man, the Son of Righteousness Himself, Jesus the Christ, our Lord and Redeemer.

If we see Jesus, then we also see the Father. We will see His perfection, His love, His constancy, His faithfulness, His wisdom, His justice, glory and majesty, a perfect image of the divine Creator. Furthermore, if we look at our loved ones with eyes that are like the eyes of the Lord, we will be better able to love unconditionally; faults, warts and all, just as He does. It is to this Son of Man that our greatest desires should be directed and all our love, loyalty and devotion, first and foremost.

However, our sinful hearts cannot submit to God of its own volition. Only divine intervention can bring about heart-change. The process of getting a new heart may be summarized in the words of Scripture to flow in the following manner:

- ❖ The heart is deceitful above all things, and it is exceedingly perverse and corrupt and severely, mortally sick! Who can know it [perceive, understand, be acquainted with his own heart and mind]?   10. I the Lord search the mind, I try the heart ..." Jeremiah 17:9, 10

- ❖ For the Word that God speaks is alive and full of power [making it active, operative, energizing, and effective]; it is sharper than any two-edged sword, penetrating to the dividing line of the breath of life (soul) and [the immortal] spirit, and of joints and marrow [of] the deepest parts of our nature], exposing and sifting and analyzing and judging the very thoughts and purposes of the heart. 13. And not a creature exists that is concealed from His sight, but all things are open and exposed, naked and defenseless to the eyes of Him with Whom we have to do. Hebrews 4:12, 13

- ❖ So this I say and solemnly testify in [the name of] the Lord [as in His Presence], that you must no longer live as the heathen (the Gentiles) do in their perverseness [in the folly, vanity, and emptiness of their souls and the futility] of their minds. 18 Their moral understanding is darkened and their reasoning is beclouded. [They are] alienated (estranged, self-banished) from the life of God [with no share in it; this is] because of the ignorance (the want of knowledge and perception, the willful blindness) that is deep-seated in them, due to their hardness of heart [to the insensitiveness of their moral nature]. Ephesians 4:17, 18

- ❖ Put on the new nature (the regenerate self) created in God's image, [Godlike] in true righteousness and holiness. Ephesians 4:24

- ❖ Because if you acknowledge and confess with your lips that Jesus is Lord and in your heart believe (adhere to, trust in, and rely on the truth) that God raised Him from the dead, you will be saved. 10. For with the heart a person believes (adheres to, trusts in, and relies on Christ) and so is justified (declared righteous, acceptable to God), and with the mouth he confesses (declares openly and speaks out freely his faith) and confirms [his] salvation. Romans 10: 9, 10

- ❖ Blessed (happy, enviably fortunate, and spiritually prosperous – possessing the happiness produced by the experience of God's favor and especially conditioned by the revelation of His grace, regardless of their outward conditions) are the pure in heart, for they shall see God! Matthew 5:8

- ❖ So repent of this depravity and wickedness of yours and pray to the Lord that, if possible, this contriving thought and purpose of your heart may be removed and disregarded and forgiven you. Acts 8:22

- ❖ Create in me a clean heart, O God, and renew a right, persevering, and steadfast spirit within me. Psalms 51:10

- ❖ And I will give them one heart [a new heart] and I will put a new spirit within them; and I will take the stony [unnaturally hardened] heart out of their flesh, and will give them a heart of flesh [sensitive and responsive to the touch of their God]. 20. That they may walk in My statutes and keep My ordinances, and do them. And they shall be My people, and I will be their God. Ezekiel 11:19, 20

God works all things together for good to them that love Him and are called according to His purpose. He can and will change our hearts so that instead of a handicap, or a curse, the emotional impediment rooted in the hearts of women is cause for rejoicing.

When our emotions flow from the new heart which God gives to us, it will fuel a passion so fierce that we have exactly what it takes to be a warrior; the heart of God. Our weakness is made perfect in the strength of Christ Jesus. **2 Corinthians 12: 9 and 10**

So, if as a woman you ever find yourself awake next to a sleeping husband, feeling as if there is no-one in the world to see your need, feel your pain, understand your feelings of lack and incompleteness; if you have just reached the conclusion that your husband is neither a mind reader nor an emotional telepath, and that even if he sensed your unease, he might not understand it; or if you are blessed with a sensitive man tuned into your every mood, yet he can only offer a salve not a solution to your deepest longings, you have reached the place of your breakthrough, the shores of your own Red Sea or your Samaritan well. You are standing on the threshold of wisdom by the grace of God.

You now have a choice. You can choose to remain in the captivity of carnality or you can surrender to God's control, sovereignty and authority in your life. Surrender of your mind, will, emotions; heart, body and spirit to the Almighty is the only way to freedom and complete fulfillment of your deepest desires and longing for love, unity, understanding, communion, peace and joy. God is the only one that can fill the God-space that is an intrinsic part of our inner being designed from the beginning. Jehovah Shalom is the only one that gives peace eternal. His peace surpasses all understanding and only when we turn our desires to Him can we truly know and have abundant life.

Man, whether male or female, in all their glory is a poor imitation of the majesty, grandeur and might of Jehovah God. We must not exert all our energy, effort and endless worry on the fake and finite pleasures of this world fashioned in the likeness of sinful man, when we can have the real deal that lasts for all eternity in Christ Jesus our Lord. Yet this opportunity for us to realize the limitations of the flesh is not the end of the purpose of God in adding extra hurdles to the acquisition of wisdom. Finally, women are brought full circle, back to our beginning.

In the restoration of our affections in the Person of our first love, in the recognition of His perfection and His ability to supply all our needs, quench our desires, as well as His worthiness of all worship, glory, honor and praise, we come to the fruition and maturity of our desire for man. After all, the Lord Jesus, Immanuel, is the one and only perfect Man. He is our true Covenant with the Father Creator, the right/righteous focus and fulfillment of all our desires. In Him is Life for He is the Bread and the Water of life, the propitiation for all our sins, our Righteousness, the way back to the bosom of our God. Jesus is the Messiah; the Promised Seed is the Delight of all woman-kind and the Desire of the nations.

When we give ourselves completely; hearts, minds, bodies, and spirits without any reservations or reserves, to the Christ, fully yielded to His will, dedicated and consecrated to Him, He gives us power to become children of God, living our lives in Him.

1 John 1:12. The Lord will grant us the desires of a surrendered heart, because those desires will be according to the dictates of the Holy Spirit's direction. It is only the work of the Holy Spirit that gifts us with the ability to surrender to the Lord. It is He that **'draws us to Himself with an everlasting love'** and binds us to the throne of grace with cords of love that cannot be broken. **Jeremiah 31:3.** In other words, a desire for His favor, His purpose and the manifestation of His glory in and through our lives; **exceedingly, abundantly above all that we might ask or think, according to His riches in glory. John 10:10.**

First Love

Let me set the record straight right from the start. I am not advocating that women loose, deny or distrust their desire for their husbands. Rather, I believe it is the will of God that we indeed desire our husbands but not that we are so consumed by it that God is replaced as Lord of our hearts, minds and lives. There is nothing that should ever distract, detract, diminish or divide our attention or affections for the Divine to the extent that we lose our relationship with our God and self-destruct. In Eden, Eve allowed her emotions to take precedence over the rule and Lordship of Jehovah.

Such a state of affairs translates into idolatry. In a union that places the Lord at the center of our love, our reason for being; the deep desire one feels for a husband becomes a gift of God, a shadow of the awesome love of and from the Father. Marital love is a gift designed to bring greater unity, bonding, love, pleasure and appreciation of ourselves and most importantly of God's love and favor. It is simple; we have to be able to love a person that we can see to be able to love God who is unseen. **1 Timothy 1:17, 1 John 4:20**

The Lord God loves unity and approves the righteous union of His people. He created man and woman to be one; one flesh, one body; "bone of bones and flesh of flesh". He did not need to impose any conditions of desire or craving upon either the woman or the man in the Garden of Eden. Does the left hand crave the right or the head the feet? The man and woman were as one, they walked as one, in perfect harmony and union with the Lord in the Garden of Eden and so they were able to experience fullness of joy and God-love in their marriage relationship.

Where there is perfect love, then there will be no lack, no need, no unfulfilled desire, no imbalance, therefore no craving, no longing, no fear, no wishful, wistful thinking. There will be only harmony, love and joy in pleasing and caring for one another. There will be pleasure in fellowship, sweet communion and honest communication. There will be equal and joint adoration for the Presence of the Lord within the marital bonds.

16b. God is love, and he who dwells and continues in love dwells and continues in Him. 17. In this [union and communion with Him] love is brought to completion and attains perfection with us, that we may have confidence for the Day of Judgment [with assurance and boldness to face Him], because as He is, so are we in this world. 1 John 4 16b-17

Distrust, jealousy, anxiety, dishonesty, deceit, disrespect and other negative emotions will never enter into a relationship of love. The righteous character of a God-focused, God-ordained and God-inclusive union precludes the negative characteristics that plague a marital relationship in which God is absent from the equation. Consider the story of Leah.

Unrequited Love

Leah was the wife of Jacob, the Patriarch of the children of Israel, a man capable of great love, devotion and commitment. For fourteen years he worked to secure marriage to Rachel. In the process he was tricked into marriage with Leah by her father. She had become a wife by default, deception and most surprisingly, destiny. I heard a sermon that gave me a whole new insight into Leah's experience. The following discourse is inspired by the invitation that the preacher extended that we take a close look at the fate and faith of Leah, a woman who got a new heart from God after the old one failed to bring fulfillment.

In **Genesis 29**, we have our first encounter with Rachel as Jacob is introduced to her as she comes to water her father's flock of sheep; she was a shepherdess. Later after serving her father Laban, who is also Jacob's uncle, for 14 years, Leah and her sister Rachel become the wives of Jacob. From the very start, Rachel had all the love, attention and devotion of Jacob that her heart could possibly desire. His eyes were filled with her and she felt secure in his love. She never experienced dismissal, disdain or distance in their relationship. On the other hand however, her sister-wife yearned for such fulfillment in the marital relationship with Jacob but was always disappointed. She must have tried everything that she could to get his attention.

All Leah's time was spent on figuring out a way to win Jacob's love and so satisfy the longings of her heart, a heart totally fixated on her husband. This desire was duly reflected in the names she gave to her firstborn son and then to the two who followed him. Leah's desperate need remained unmet despite the birth of sons to Jacob which his beloved Rachel was unable to give him for a long time.

Somehow, it must have finally dawned on Leah that she would not find satisfaction and peace in her husband. Her desire for Jacob had so consumed her yet it would never complete her. With this divinely imparted revelation came Leah's freedom from the bondage of her emotions. She turned her focus and her affections to God, trusting in Him for the fulfillment of His divine plan for her life. Her fourth son was a testimony to her transformation by faith in God, before all others.

Judah meaning **"Let God be praised"** was the name that declared the pre-eminence of Jehovah in her life and her living. **Genesis 29:35.** The breakthrough that Leah experienced bears witness to the power of being God-focused. She could now love her husband unconditionally, whether he loved her in the same way or not. She did not have to purchase his attention or his care with the birth of her children. And loving him was not dependent on his emotional response. She had invited the missing third partner of the union she had with Jacob and in Him her joy was complete and her praise endless.

Except the Lord builds the house, they labor in vain who build it. Psalms 127:1

Leah found favor in the sight of God and He gave her a new destiny. Judah, not Joseph the son of Rachel, was the progenitor of the royal lineage of David and of our Lord Jesus the Christ. **1 Chronicles 28:4**. In the lineage of the Christ there are some other women who first had to experience the brokenness and the breakthrough of Leah before they could achieve their divinely ordained destiny and complete their assignment on the battlefield for our God.

Having a Wedding, Living a Marriage

Marriage is an institution ordained by the Creator Himself when He gave Eve to Adam for a companion. It was the properly assigned forum to facilitate the divine command of procreation and demonstrate the joys and the rewards of love, union and communion. The marriage of Adam and Eve was perfect in its formation and implementation. It was perfect because it had all the right components.

A marital union according to the Designer of the institution needs three parties to complete the divine covenant. First, there is the man who must cleave to his wife in love, the wife who must honor and respect her husband and thirdly but most importantly, the

Lord our God, the Provider and Sustainer of pure, unconditional love. The relationship thus established is a covenant relationship between God, the male and the female, that is between God and man. **1 Peter 1:17-25.**

The history of the institution of marriage throughout the world right up to the present time, loudly declares and displays the adverse interference of the enemy; interference that started in the Garden of Eden! That perfect equation instituted by God has been severely undermined, altered, damaged, manipulated, abused, exploited, trivialized and side-lined so that it is now in danger of extinction in many western societies.

All across the world there are unhappy marital relationships in which men and women find no love, joy, pleasure or peace with each other. In particular, many women find themselves in marriages where they struggle to achieve the love and respect of husbands. This is especially obvious in communities that accords them little regard above that of baby making machines, domestic servants or accessories of success and status. Let me say in all confidence that true fulfillment and happiness in marriage can only be achieved when God is the central focus of all one's affections. He alone can turn a marriage into a union, a house into a home, weeping into rejoicing, sorrow into joy, and tears into laughter.

Three strands are able to withstand the tests of time and the temptations of the devil much more successfully than two. **Ecclesiastes 4:12.** Never overlook the importance of the fact that God fellowshipped with the first married couple on a daily basis. It was not just a haphazard visit but a scheduled appointment that took place each afternoon in the cool of the day. The three would walk and commune together. No doubt those were occasions of immense joy, love and reassurance for all parties involved.

I am convicted that the Lord also spent time instructing, educating and counseling the newly-weds. The union of Adam and Eve had a Divine Partner who devoted time, attention and care to the relationship. Marriage as instituted, sanctioned and sanctified by the Creator God is therefore a union of three, reflecting or modeling the design that originated with the Godhead, itself composed of three Persons; the Father, the Son and the Holy Spirit; the Triune God.

We must spend time together with the Lord; the husband, the wife and the Lord alone. This time of fellowship and communion is essential for a refreshing, renewal and rejuvenation of the relationship. It is a time of bonding, learning, prayer, worshipping and grounding in holiness. However, our responsibilities and role of wife should not be allowed to take precedence over our assignment as warriors. The roles are complementary not contradictory, inclusive not exclusive, unifying not divisive.

There are many times when the warrior spirit of the woman of God is necessary to fight for and hold onto a marriage, fight for children, maintain a home and keep a family together. The way that the world is going these days the home has become one of the most hostile frontline positions in spiritual warfare that it has ever been throughout human history. In adverse situations, it is also the warrior spirit that will ensure survival after the break-up of the marital relationship or the death of a spouse and parent.

If love is true and genuine between the man and the woman with the characteristics stated in **1 Corinthians 13**, then its only Source is God. The essence of God is love and anything which does not flow from Him is not agape love; the kind that is pure, lasting, and unconditional, a gift from the Almighty. Do not be deceived into accepting anything less than that described and defined in Corinthians. If we do not have love that flows from the Source then whatever we may be experiencing, it is but a cheap and sometimes even an expensive counterfeit!

In order to live in love we must remain in God. All our emotions, our thoughts and our actions must be God-filtered. Our focus must be steadfast on the Lord who promises to supply our every need. In seeking Him first, He promises to add all things to us and that includes happiness in our marriage as well as peace of mind, patience, understanding, wisdom, contentment and His divine Presence.

One is the only Number

When it comes to intimacy in relationships, the divine formula may be expressed in the following way. The sum of all the parts must always be equal to the number **one**. So, in marriage, all the parties to the marriage covenant become **one**. When one becomes a child of God, the result is oneness with Christ being hid in Him and therefore one with the Father, the Son and the Holy Spirit. It is the continuing prayer and the work of the Savior Jesus, to unite His Bride, the Church with the Father so that they may become **one**; the ultimate union between God and man as originally ordained and continuously desired by Deity!

The importance of one is further exemplified by the reality of the Lord's mission to redeem the **one** sin-sick soul that is lost in the kingdom of darkness. The Shepherd seeks after the **one** lost sheep that has strayed from the fold, the widow searches for the **one** coin that was lost, the father longs and watches for the son that erred, the Messiah takes a detour to reveal Truth to one Samaritan daughter thirsting for love and forgiveness and keeps silent to free another trapped in a life of sexual depravity.

The Lord Jesus died on Calvary's cross to save the **one lost soul; mine and yours.** Sin came into the world by **one** man (Adam plus Eve equals one man), and so redemption was purchased by the **One** who died that His righteousness might be the acceptable cloak that covers our filthy rags and allows us entry to the marriage feast of the Bridegroom. It is His robe which is the required dress-code of the Marriage Feast of the Lamb! The pure, unblemished sacrifice of the Lamb of God replaced the countless animals sacrificed by the Levitical high priests, once and for all. **Hebrews 9:22-28**

There are still many other examples of the significance of one in the plans of the Almighty. It took only **one** woman to aid the Hebrew spies in the city of Jericho, **one young** woman to dare a King's displeasure and risk death to save a nation. It was **one** woman that proclaimed that the Messiah was in town, hanging out at the well of Abraham, **one** woman to accept the call to be the mother of the Messiah, regardless of the consequences and **one** woman to proclaim the resurrection of the Lord and declare His appointment with the apostles. So you see **one** is the most important number in the divine mathematics of the Creator of mankind; ultimately every other number adds up to one, the number that symbolizes unity. There is after all only **one** God, **one** faith, **one** baptism, **one** body,

one Christ, **one** Door, **one** Way, one Truth and **one** divine will that counts for all eternity.

3 –Be eager and strive earnestly to guard and keep the harmony and oneness of [and produced by] the Spirit in the binding power of peace.

4 – [There is] one body and one Spirit-just as there is also one hope [that belongs] to the calling you received-

5 – [There is] one Lord, one faith, one baptism.

6 – One God and Father of [us] all, Who is above all [Sovereign over all], pervading all and [living] in [us] all. Ephesians 4:3-6:

5 – For there [is only] one God, and [only] one Mediator between God and men, the Man Christ Jesus,

6 – Who gave Himself as a ransom for all [people, a fact that was] attested to at the right and proper time. 1 Timothy 2:5-6

CHAPTER 7

A MEDUSA HEART

Stone Cold Love

When I was a teenager, I fell madly in love. I had read all the Mills and Boons novels that circulated among my school friends and was certain that love would follow the same pattern described time and again. Of course it did not! Instead I experienced exploitation, abuse, degradation and rejection. My self-confidence was undermined, my self-esteem leeched, my faith in men and love destroyed. It was then that I made a decision that I thought would keep me safe and strong, as well as safe-guard my heart and protect me from the foolish distraction of falling in love with a man who would undoubtedly seek to control, use, rule and mess up my life. To my young and idealistic mind, it appeared that the price of love was too high a cost in respect of my identity, value and worth as a woman.

Although I decided I would have relationships with the opposite sex, I would remain objective, sensible and in full control of my emotions and my actions. In this way my heart would remain closed to the effects of male exploitation and superiority. Unfortunately my relationship with God likewise became distant, detached and head-based. I acknowledged His existence but there was a gulf that existed between us that seemed unbridgeable. He too was male and so I decided to steer clear of His rules which seemed to cast women in a subservient, second class role according to the teachings of the various religions of the world including Christianity.

It was not until I had just passed forty years of age that I met an old acquaintance from high school who was instrumental in persuading me to take another, closer but more mature and unbiased look at God and His plan and purpose for our lives and my life in particular. My friend told me he was a believer and felt that until I had looked at who God really was, who I was and the way that God meant for me to relate to Him, I would be unable to achieve my full potential as intended by the Lord. Choice, he pointed out was a big thing with God and His dealings with the human race.

This blessed friend would spend hours talking, reasoning and sharing with me the love of God. Along the way, I imagined myself in love with him. He occupied my mind, my heart. As I allowed myself to open up to him, I also realized that I was allowing for the Word of God to sink into my heart and take root there. Eventually I came to a crossroad. I wanted to commit my life to God, get to know Him and be in right standing with Him as the Lord of my life. I also wanted to be in a relationship with my friend but that might spoil a good friendship at best or transgress the laws of God. For a while I was torn.

By the grace of God I chose salvation, not because my will prevailed over the desires of my flesh but because my help and my strength came from the Divine One. I turned the decision over to God and He furnished the power that I needed to make the right choice. It was the prompting of the Holy Spirit that placed in me a stronger desire for God than for the rewards of fleshly pursuits. Inexplicably, at that time, there was almost an immediate cooling in the relationship between my friend and me. It was soon followed by the intense heartache that was the inescapable consequence of the end of a close friendship. I sought comfort in the knowledge that I had the love of the Lord and that He promised to never leave nor forsake His own. I prayed for His strength so that I could have faith in His promises. He heard and He answered my prayers, hallelujah!

One beautiful, supportive sister in Christ gave me an invaluable piece of advice for coping with the loss. "Whenever you feel that you are being overtaken with grief or overwhelmed with sorrow, get down on your knees and ask the Father to take the pain away. If you cannot find the words to pray, cry, He understands tears. Finally, when you are spent but still hurting, ask Jesus to pray for you! If that means you are praying 24/7 then that's as it should be, just keep praying." I took her at her words. Her words were life to me and I have continued to cherish and live by her counsel.

One day, as I lay on my bed wracked with the loss of my relationship and trying to understand why someone who was so happy to talk about God would turn away from me just as soon as I committed my life to the Lord, I received an unmistakable revelation from the Holy Spirit that was truly astounding. He told me that God was only able to gain access to my heart because I had come to trust my friend and open up my heart to love. Previous to this encounter, my heart had grown cold and unyielding, as if turned to stone by the stare of the fabled Medusa. Only when I allowed the Word to find an abode in my heart was the Lord able to draw me to Him with His divine and everlasting love.

I had spent many years with my heart closed to love; sealed so tight against the possibility of any real deep hurt that there was no way even the love of the Lord could penetrate. My walls were much like the walls of Jericho, designed to keep fear in and love out; mammon in and Jehovah out. When I allowed the walls that kept all love out to collapse under the insistent sounds of His holy Words, the pathway was cleared for love to flow both in and out, up and down.

Understanding gripped me in respect of the Scripture that says that unless we can love our fellow humans that we can see in the physical we cannot say that we love God whom we do not see with the natural eyes. Jesus taught that it is not possible to love God, whom we cannot see, if we are unable to love our brothers and sisters, neighbors and friends that we can see. This is a truth that I have proven for myself. In fact, this reality is demonstrated in the declarations that Christ makes at the final judgment in **Matthew 25:35-46**

From that day I was healed from the pain of my broken heart. God gave me a heart of flesh so that I would be able to feel His love and hear from Him. As the Word of the Lord often exhorts us, we need to see and hear clearly what the Lord is saying to us at all times. We can only fulfill His purposes and abide by His commands if we are receptive to Him and so to the Holy Spirit. The Word has taught me that without God there is no life, no love, no joy, no peace and no me. I am, only if I abide in the great I AM. In Him only, we live, move and have our being. "To be or not to be" is indeed the question. For me it is simple; to be is God; not to be is the devil. This is the only answer that can be called wisdom. We are God's emissaries. His love is demonstrated, displayed and made real by our lives. We are a living testimony and many a soul will only come to know Christ through the way that we live and how we relate to others.

Getting a New Heart

Women are emotional beings and although many women might take exception to this statement, for me it is a complement not a handicap. Personally, being emotional means; being open to feel, to experience, to learn. It means being reachable, teachable and re-moldable. It means being fertile soil in which "the Sower" can plant His seed for an abundant harvest. I know that the Father designed women to be emotional because in order to be creative one needs to process emotions effectively.

Our emotions facilitate the bonding between a woman and her husband, her children, grandchildren, community, church and country. In fact it is believed that our physical body releases certain chemicals that fuel the emotional engine. For example, the bond between a mother and her infant is enhanced by the chemicals that are released through breast feeding. If this is true then it would make perfect sense that this trait is an essential part of our make-up and was so designed by God with good reason.

I suppose that some women will not be happy with this view because it would mean that all the negativity attached to a woman's emotionality is biologically grounded and therefore an undeniable truth. However, to concede that women are more emotionally conscious or gifted than their male counterparts is not necessarily borne out by the reality. I would even say that if Adam was not being ruled by his emotions, that is, if he was not emotionally vested in Eve, he would not have eaten the forbidden fruit that she offered him in Eden. Now I know this is a whole different debate and I will go no further with it but it is certainly worth some thought when it is claimed that men are ruled by their heads and women by their hearts! However, as I am focused on women, I will continue to discuss female emotionality.

If we concede that as women, we are more open to experiencing, expressing and employing the whole range of our emotional inventory then I would suggest that we are merely making good use of a fundamental part of our assets. This is in-keeping with the intent and design of the Creator God. His ways are beyond question and everything He created is good. That is not to deny that lack of comprehension and control over our emotions can be as devastating as a denial of their existence.

According to the teachings of the Bible, self-control is one of the fruits of the Holy Spirit. To exercise righteous self-control therefore, we must have the indwelling of the Holy Spirit. The Presence of God will only indwell those who have accepted Christ as Savior. Their acceptance brings about death of their carnal nature and resurrection into a new life in Christ, as children of God. Only with the Presence of the Lord, the Holy Spirit, can we walk in obedience.

Desire comes from our hearts according to **Mark 7:20-23** and desire can lead to sin. **James 1:13-15.** So what is desire? Desire is an emotional response that can be either detrimental or enriching according to the thing which is desired, as well as the means adopted to acquire that for which one is desirous. I might even go so far as to say that it was and is the lack of control over human emotions that is the primary cause of the many and varied ills of our society, our lives in the natural, as well as spiritually.

Satan, that serpent, exploited this particular trait of both Adam and Eve, but in such a way that he deceived the woman first and then planned that the man in turn would be enticed to sin by his attachment to her. Eve allowed her feelings, her desire, to control her actions and in so doing committed an act of treason that sold the human family into slavery. She allowed her emotions to take precedence over the righteous law of God and His Kingdom. We are told that Adam was not deceived by the serpent's enticement or lies, yet he also allowed himself, together with Eve, to eat in disobedience to God's command.

The revelation here is that his decision was based on the state of his emotional and physical attachment to Eve when she offered him the fruit. A situation very similar to that which we read about in **1 Kings 11:3-9**, in which we are told in regards to King Solomon that **"his wives turned away his heart from God"**. So from the very beginning of the human family, emotions have proven to be powerful to the point of being overwhelming. They continue to be destructive or productive, negative or positive. They are the power source, the fuel that drives the choices we make. They manifest in our 'motions' that is to say through our actions or inactions, words, thoughts, attitudes and behavior.

The amazing thing about our God is that as well as giving us this capacity to feel, to empathize, sympathize, fear, love among many others, He also installed the mechanism that can control the expression of our feelings. That mechanism is our minds but only minds renewed and regenerated by the Holy Spirit can subdue emotions to the reign of reason, knowledge, understanding and wisdom.

The popular expression, "don't let your heart rule over your head" is not just an idle phrase but a gem of wisdom. In other words, what is advocated is that wisdom rather than emotion should be the basis of our decisions. What I find most comforting is that the emotions can be made subject to the sovereignty of the Lord our God. So as long as we allow God His rightful place of rule in our hearts, then we do not have to fear our emotions, in particular our negative, excessive, destructive emotions, running away with us.

After all, one of the most potent of all our emotions is love, which is also not only a divine attribute of the Creator but is who He is; God is love! The Scriptures vividly demonstrates that God is Love in the Person of His Beloved Son, Jesus the Christ. It was the reign of negative human emotions that led to the rebellion in the Garden and therefore the Fall of man. And it is a godly emotion, divine love, which motivated obedience in the Messiah in the Garden of Gethsemane and activated the plan of restoration for the human family to their right relationship with the Almighty.

It is therefore no surprise to learn how imperative it is that we seek out a new heart from the Lord. The heart is after all the seat of the emotions and therefore all desire flows from the heart. **Mark 7:20-23 and James 1:13-15**. As such, the heart cannot be made obedient to the will of God unless and until God creates in us a clean heart, supplies us with a heart of flesh and remove the heart of stone. **Ezekiel 11:9.**

The old unrepentant heart is one which is insensitive to God's statutes and deaf to His calling; an idol that replaces God in our lives. Only when we have been born again of the Spirit and been given the heart of God, can we truly walk in obedience to the Most High and experience the operation of positive, godly emotions in our lives. The revelation here is that only with the new heart can God find a tablet suitable for Him to write His commandments. So to get our orders, we must have new hearts from Him.

2. You yourselves are our letter of recommendation (our credentials), written in your hearts, to be known (perceived, recognized) and read by everybody. 3. You show and make obvious that you are a letter from Christ delivered by us, not written with ink but with [the] Spirit of [the] living God, not on tablets of stone but on tablets of human hearts. 2 Corinthians 3:2-3

But this is the covenant which I will make with the house of Israel; After those days, says the Lord, I will put My law within them, and on their hearts will I write it; and I will be their God and they will be My people. Jeremiah 31:33

The Sacrifice of Praise

I feel in my spirit that we need to realize above everything else that we ever come to understand as children of God, that God made us to worship Him, to give Him praise continually. As David states, **"His praise shall continually be in my mouth." Psalms 34:1.** What this means for us in relation to the state of our emotions is that whatever may be going on in our lives we must subject our feelings to our duty to praise God.

Whether we are broken-hearted or happy, whether we are facing hurt, pain and sorrow, or we are in the throes of enjoyment, pleasure and fun-filled times, we must give God praise. I have often heard people say that it is easy to praise God in the good times but difficult in the bad or challenging periods of our lives. I can only speak from my own experiences but I have found that we can be just as careless in praising our Lord when we are happy and things are going great, as we can be self-absorbed and self-pitying when we are faced with pain and suffering.

So what does it mean when we are asked to offer the sacrifice of praise? When I first accepted the sovereignty of the Lord in my life and I heard this quote from the Scriptures, I just assumed it meant that we should praise the Lord whenever we get the chance and at a level that is what it means, but it means so much more besides! When I entered into the sanctuary on the Sabbath to worship, I thought that all the singing, praises, prayers and preaching was our sacrifice of praise to God, the thing that we presented instead of the animal sacrifices given by the Children of Israel in their temple of worship. As I have grown in the grace of God and been faced with the practicality of a daily walk with Him, there came a time of revelation when I realized what this wonderful phrase was meant to fully convey to me and to all His children.

There are so many times when we are distracted by the problems, cares and concerns of life or challenged by pain, hurt, disappointment and tragedies. Sometimes we cannot see the way forward and feel that we cannot make another step, overcome another obstacle or fight another battle. Yes, we are warriors but the battle can be so wearying, and the attacks and assaults of the enemy so constant that it feels like we cannot survive another step. On such occasions the words of the Scriptures invites us to praise the Lord, to give thanks to Him in all things.

One revelation of the sacrifice of praise then is to offer up praise when we have to literally make ourselves open our mouths, engage our hearts, minds and bodies and worship our God. This sacrifice puts aside the physical and emotional sufferings and focus on the Lord's love, mercies, grace, blessings and favors that He has, and continues to extend to us. For example, there are times when I say I don't feel like going to Church or I don't feel like praying but I have learnt that those are the very times when I need to act out of a mindset of faithfulness to God; not from feelings that can be so fluid and easily influenced by people and circumstances.

On the flip side, when we are blessed by God and our hearts are filled with joy in our families, communities, jobs, financial well-being and social standing, we can be so content that we are distracted and take it all for granted; our just desserts. It is then that we often forget to direct our grateful eyes to the Provider and the Sustainer, Jehovah Jireh, our God. Yet, it is most especially at these times that we must remember to give praise and thanks. It is then that we need to take our minds away from what is going on about us, dedicate extra time to slip into our closet in order to praise Him for His blessed provisions, providence and prosperity.

Mother Eve allowed herself to be ruled, controlled and propelled into action by her emotions rather than the law of God. In the New Testament, we are counseled to subject our whole selves to God, whether that is our emotions or our thoughts, our actions or attitudes, our speech or our gestures, we must bring ourselves into submission to Him and subjection to His law. It does not matter what we are feeling or how, God's Word must have precedence and direct our footsteps. We need a heart disposed to submission; not following after our own understanding and our own wayward impulses dictated by the desires of our own negative, destructive, death-dealing emotions. **Mark 7:21** and **Luke 15:19**

The Word of God reveals that just as the glorious Presence of our God resided in the Holy of Holies in the Tabernacle in the wilderness or the Temple of Solomon, the Holy Spirit takes up His abode in our hearts as our bodies become the temple of our Lord.

Further, in the same way that the tablets on which God wrote the Ten Commandments was placed within the Holy of Holies, today under the New Covenant, these same laws of God are written on our hearts. **Galatians 4:6.** Therefore we can see how important it is that we realize that the **"love of God is shed abroad in our hearts." Romans 5:5.**

When I looked in the New Unger's Bible Dictionary (Revised and Updated Edition 1988) for a definition of the word "heart", I found the following information which provides a brief summary of the areas that we just covered within the body of this text. "The heart is the innermost centre of the natural condition of man" and to demonstrate this, the following details were offered.

1. The heart holds all the life-power of the body. **Ps. 40:8, 10, 12.**

2. The heart is the center of the rational, spiritual nature of man, important in the decision to act. **Esther 7:5** and **Romans 6:17** say that obedience and by implication disobedience comes from the heart.

3. The heart is the seat of love and hatred. **First Timothy 1:5** and **Leviticus 19:17.**

4. The heart is the center of thought and conception; the heart knows. **Proverbs 14:10** and the heart understands, as in **Isaiah 44:18.**

5. The heart is the center of feelings, affections, and joy. **Isaiah 65:14**, of pain, **Proverbs 25:20** and of fear, **Jeremiah 5:24**.

6. The heart is the center of moral life, so that all moral conditions flow from the highest which is love of God; **Psalms 73:26**, down to self-deifying pride; **Ezekiel 28:2** and are all concentrated in the heart as the innermost center of humanity.

7. The heart is the place where God writes His natural laws as well as the law of grace. **Isaiah 51:7** and **Jeremiah 31:33.**

8. The heart is the dwelling place of Jesus Christ in us. **Ephesians 3:17.**

9. The heart is the abode of the Holy Spirit. **Second Corinthians 1:22.**

10. The heart is where God's peace abides. **Colossians 3:15.**

11. The heart is the receptacle of God's Love. **Romans 5:5.**

12. The heart is the closet of secret communion with God. **Ephesians 5:19.**

13. The heart is the place in which all that is good and evil in our thoughts, words and deeds is formulated and put into action. **Matthew 12:34** and **Mark 7:21.** Contrast **Jeremiah 17:9.**

14. The heart is also the place in which evil lusts and passions culminate. **Romans 7:24.**

The Lord came to restore us to the perfection of God, to live righteously and in obedience to Divine Law, not following after our own devices but in all things being subject to the will of God. Jesus the Christ practically demonstrated the Way to life; liberty from the captivity of disease, sin and death, in His encounter with a daughter of Abraham at the well in Samaria. The lessons from her experience that is in the succeeding chapter is a triumph of the Love of God over lust, the cravings of carnality and the cycle of emotional depravity that manifests in sin.

Warriors must confront the enemy in the body, mind, heart and spirit; warring against sin as much within as without. A warrior must also have a heart that has been made like the heart of the Lord, a heart that facilitates direct communication with heaven by the Holy Spirit and ensures a clear, open connection that keeps us in touch with our Commander-In-Chief.

Acclaim of the World

Ambition and drive; these words are generally seen as positive words in the world. They describe a quality or character trait of an individual regarded as desirable, preferable and an absolute essential for anyone wanting to achieve success in today's world. In fact, I am about to say something which will meet with a lot of opposition but which I feel must be said.

This is it; ambition and success are words which generally reflect worldly, fleshly, carnal concepts, standards, desires and motivation to fuel the thoughts, attitude, words, behavior, actions and goals of an individual. I am convicted that these words are cloaked with legality, honor and respectability in order to trap individuals into formulating and pursuing selfish, egotistical lives for the glorification of carnality and worldly values. I am not advocating that worldly success is a bad thing but that it cannot be the end of all one's exertions and endeavors or the means to validate one's worth or value. It must be one stop on the route to achieve divine destiny.

In the struggle to be taken seriously and given equal opportunities and standing with men, women have ferociously embraced the desire to achieve prestige, power and positions that declare value, worth and standing in society. Far be it from me to say that striving to be the best that we can be or to be diligent, hard-working, efficient and dependable is a bad thing.

There is a difference between excelling at whatever we are assigned to as opposed to seeking to achieve recognition, applause and fame in our own eyes and the estimation of our fellow man. In other words, if we depend on our achievements or successes, so-called, to impute value, worth and respect then we are in big trouble. The only one that we should desire to find us acceptable is the Divine One.

The point I am trying to make is that when the driving force for our actions and endeavors is the acclaim of man, not God's approval, then we are still in rebellion. **"Seek ye first the Kingdom of God"** is an injunction that must govern our lives at all times. Our ambition and our motivation must be a desire to serve our Lord and His Kingdom. That is why the Scriptures say that we must do all things as unto the Lord our God. Only with this conviction, passion, certainty and aim can we bring glory to our God instead of exalting self and Satan.

The approval of the world is a temporary, fragile, fickle, intangible and perishable commodity. There is an aggressive, determined strategy by the destroyer to distract, deceive and destroy the awareness or knowledge of the truth that women need to have if they are to realize their identity and their true vocation, profession, calling and persuasion in this world.

Satan is the enemy of all of the human family and he is especially hateful and afraid of all women. He will do everything that is conceivable and things that are not, to make it appear otherwise. But every temptation, action, thought or pursuit that entices us to act independently of God's will and facilitate or divert our focus, efforts and endeavors away from God and the things of God, is a tactic of the devil that allows him to effectively carry out his aim; to keep the human family in captivity. Any plot or ploy that causes us as women to overlook, neglect, ignore or disregard our role as spiritual warriors for the Lord serves the diabolical design of the devil, who is our arch enemy.

For example, abuse in all its variants: promiscuity, prostitution, careers, materialism, alternative spiritualism, etc. may all be methods, weapons or strategies that engage the minds and hearts of women to the exclusion of a righteous relationship with the Creator. Furthermore, the order, institutions and principles that operate within societies to keep women subordinated to the cruel prejudices and whims of men is part of the devil's intent.

Everything that conspires to make women feel inferior to men and therefore conclude that they are of lesser value to God, so that we take refuge in becoming competitive, driven or obsessed with the desire to prove ourselves equal, amounts to an effective evil maneuver of the devil that is working well. The devil has met with progress in the home, the workplace, the economic, social, or political arenas, and even in areas of spirituality.

If women become so overly pre-occupied with challenging discrimination on all these fronts then we might just overlook the assignment given to us by the Father in Eden. When we join in the farce to prove our worthiness, equality and value to men we are helping the devil to destroy our divine destiny. We become like Delilah who was more concerned with her personal status and her material standing in her society than with grabbing the opportunity to get to know the only God, Jehovah our Creator.

Like Delilah, we too are trading beauty for ashes. We are exchanging an eternity in the perfect, beautiful and Holy Kingdom of our Sovereign Lord, with streets of pure gold and where sickness, death, and decay may not enter for a reservation in the place prepared for Satan and his angels! In contrast, God' place is a Kingdom where we are ageless and eternal and the perfect love of God is the governing principle.

So it is irrelevant what trick, disguise or deception the devil might employ to turn us away from God's purpose for our lives. We must be able to discern truth, life and eternity. We must be able to withstand the attacks of the enemy and do not fall prey to his devilish schemes. We can only do what God desires of us if we submit ourselves to Him completely and come into agreement with His purpose for our lives. His will must become our will as we come into conformity with the example of our Redeemer and Lord, Jesus the Christ as He made that final surrender in Gethsemane to His crucifixion at Calvary.

Our roles as women cannot be compartmentalized, fragmented and separated into family, community, church, country and spiritual calling. God must be the central connecting Presence that empowers us to take on the serpent in every aspect of life. The devil tries to divide and conquer; he instigates and encourages division between, men and women, between different sectors of society, between communities, nations and between humans and the Creator. He utilizes every imaginable form of differences, diversities and distinctions that can be highlighted, exploited and exploded to ensure that we do not realize his true endeavor, which is the defeat of the Lord of Righteousness and His Kingdom authority in the heavens, the earth and the realm beneath the earth. It is time that we wise up to him, get God-focused, steadfast, watchful, faithful and obedient to the will of the Lord Almighty.

CHAPTER 8

DYING OF THIRST AT THE WELL

The Noon-Time Heat

1. O God, You are my God, earnestly will I seek You; my inner self thirsts for You, my flesh longs and is faint for You, in a dry and weary land where no water is,

2. I have looked upon You in the sanctuary to see Your power and Your glory.

3. Because Your loving-kindness is better than life, my lips shall praise You. 4. So will I bless You while I live; I will lift up my hands in Your name.

5. My whole being shall be satisfied as with marrow and fatness; and my mouth shall praise You with joyful lips.

6. When I remember You upon my bed and meditate on You in the night watches. Psalms 63:1-6

Imagine a hot summer's day; a day so hot that you try your best to stay in the shade at all costs. You sit down to rest as you frantically fan your face; perspiration making your skin sticky to the touch. You think it is a good day but how truly hot at the same time. You contemplate ways of getting cool. You wonder how to accomplish all the chores you need to get out of the way. You start to plot and scheme how to fully abandon yourself to the task of cool comfort and malaise and avoid a guilty conscience. It is just not possible to think straight or smart. It feels as if the heat is dissolving your physical and mental capacity, ability and agility.

At this point I am sure that every one of us will begin to desire a long cold drink! Just the memory of such days makes us feel thirsty. If truth be told, on these hot days there is nothing that satisfies as well as a nice, tall, cold drink of water. Even if for some of us that translates into flavored water, so popular to the modern palate nowadays! If like me, you have personally experienced such a day, it will not be difficult to put yourself in the shoes of the woman of Samaria. She made it into the pages of history by way of the Gospels of the New Testament, when she went to draw water at noontime and met the Source of 'Living Water", the 'Cosmic Quencher'. **John 4: 4-42**

Noon is the hottest time of the day in the Mediterranean. If ever there is a time to avoid going to the well to get water, it is at the noon time. But the truth of human experience is that sometimes the very thing we desire to avoid is the thing that overtakes us. In the life of every person there comes a noon time. Let us consider the life experiences of the majority of women. Most, if not all of us, can recall a time or times when we have experienced the burning heat of our own emotional noon time; a time so desperate, desolate and disturbing that we were driven to search for something to satisfy our need at an inexcusable hour and in the most unlikely places.

Whatever the experience, there was no one to share it with, no one to turn to for comfort, for support, encouragement or love. There, I have said it, the most important thing; love. There are times when a person feels lonely, alone, parched, stranded in an emotional wasteland, a desert; burning with desire for that special person just to say:

"It's ok; everything is going to be alright",

"You are not in this alone; we'll work things out together".

"Don't worry; I'll take care of you!"

Or just simply to be there, to hold you, to reassure you that someone cares and knows what you are experiencing, someone to say "I love you", someone whose very presence will quench your emotional thirst at the noon time. If you have ever experienced the situation I just described, then you can relate to the woman of Samaria. Now back to her, to you, to me, to us! Please understand that after much study and prayer, I am inspired to write about her in a rather personal way, inspired by the Spirit to help us walk in her shoes for a while.

The woman of Samaria was in desperate need to get some water. She had put off going to the well earlier with all the other women of the village. From the limited history we have, we might surmise that she was a woman with a soiled reputation, in a situation that did not openly arouse the corporate sympathy or understanding of her fellow villagers. In fact, her record of failed or controversial relationships resulted in an alienation and isolation that sealed her into a waking nightmare of disapproval, disappointment and disillusion. But she had a need that required her to make the punishing journey to the well.

In my mind, I can feel her brace herself emotionally, slip into survival mode; her heart was set, her mind determined and her body steeled against the burning heat of the sun. She would do what was necessary to satisfy her thirst. On her arduous, unaccompanied journey to the well, she would contemplate and ponder the teachings that she had received in happier, more carefree days; religious teachings about the coming of a Messiah to relieve the hardships of life and restore dignity, harmony, peace and joy. Life it seems had robbed her of these very things.

Her people, the Samaritans, called Abraham their Father and so held to the legacy of the promise, which God made with the Patriarch. Like all of us that have experienced disappointments and grieved for lost dreams, she too might have hoped that things would work out for her one day. She wanted to find happiness with her own true love instead of her present situation; stealing someone else's joy. Like us, she probably had called a friend to come over sometimes, go out for a meal, enjoy some good company, and listen to sweet nothings; be wined, dined and bedded in the hope that the thirst of the spirit would be satisfied, even if only for a little while. But just like the water from Abraham's well must be drunk over and over, so too the emotional relief from the bore-hole of carnality is only a quick and temporary fix.

After all, a well taps into the very belly of the earth to access the water that flows in the cool dark places. This water that people must collect over and over provides only temporary relief. It quenches the thirst, meets the needs of the human body to function in this physical plane but only for a while. This physical watering hole in the depths of the earth is representative of the process by which many of us seek to satiate our deepest search and need for the meaning of our lives. The woman of Samaria lived her life tapping into the belly of the earthly or carnal watering hole of mankind, to find the answers to her thirst; always satisfying the symptoms, not treating the cause of the thirst.

After all, thirst is the physical realization of the body's de-hydration; thirst indicates the presence of a lack, a need that should be addressed.

But, the things of the flesh can never bring lasting satisfaction. The 'arms of flesh', of a lover, an acquaintance, a stranger even, will fail. And this is not just in respect of single women; married sisters are not necessarily exempt from the same kind of need that drives a woman into situations that brings pain and guilt. Remember the woman at the well had been married on five previous occasions. Even a husband can fail to meet the deepest needs of the heart, mind or spirit if God is an absent, inactive or irrelevant third party to the marriage union. The glow of satisfaction experienced in your intimate times, will fade away. Then sooner rather than later, another noontime will come and another journey in search of relief will be inevitable.

A Divine Blind Date

On the particular noon time under reflection, the woman of Samaria was taking another trip to the well. But something was different this fateful day; Jesus the Christ was also there. His appointment had been pre-determined, and He **"needs must pass through Samaria."** She did not know it but she was about to come into her transition zone, her breakthrough. Her Deliverer was waiting in the heat of the day, ready, willing and able to offer her a permanent solution.

Jesus the Christ was not concerned about the heat, the journey or the objection that His association or discourse with a Samaritan woman might cause. For this reason He came into the world; to seek out the lost and weary soul, to return even the one lost sheep to the fold. The Shepherd had lost sheep in Samaria that would be forever lost unless He kept a pre-destined appointment with the woman under discussion in her place and, at her time of desperate need, all might remain in darkness.

27. The sheep that are My own hear and are listening to My voice; and I know them, and they follow Me. 28. And I give them eternal life, and they shall never lose it or perish throughout all the ages. John 10:27, 28

What He offered would not cost her anything. **Isaiah 55:1-5.** And this is a point that I want us to think about for a while. Most women will agree that there is a price for being in dysfunctional, temporary or fleeting encounters with men. The cost is oftentimes but not always measurable in physical terms but it can always be counted by its emotional wounds and scars. These relationships require a personal heart-investment and after a series of monogamous but meaningless encounters, the cost is accumulatively devastating, taking a toll on ones' sense of value, self esteem and faith in life, love and the future.

By her own devices, the woman of Samaria had sought to find her own way by indulging her desires and her perceived needs with carnality. Somehow, she felt that she needed to be validated as a woman by her male associations. In a time where a woman's worth was measured by her marital status and her economic well being depended on the economic support of men, she was unable to look beyond the role of wife and partner and see her full worth in the eyes of her Heavenly Father. Like many women, the Samaritan perceived men as the answer to her greatest need and desire for love, security and fulfillment.

Consequently she had already gone through a number of involvements, none of which were lasting or fulfilling since she kept on searching! Unable to look beyond the physical, she had gone from one insufficient, desperate situation to another, from one mess to the next, never finding what she sought in her noon time. But now, as Jesus waited at the well, her day of salvation had arrived. She had a date with the Author of divine destiny.

The Water of Life

The only Source that can provide 'water' which satisfies our every need and springs up inside us, eternally quenching, refreshing, revitalizing, resurrecting, outpouring and overflowing was waiting for her in her noon time desperation. The water that He offered to her and still offers to all of us who are thirsty, springs up in our spirits eternally.

It is the same water that flows in the river running through the heavenly grounds of the Father's Kingdom on whose banks is the Tree of Life. It occupies the very center of God's heavenly abode. It has life-giving properties for the terminally sin-infected, mortal soul. It quenches, satisfies, heals and restores. Who can resist a drink of this water of life? Jesus welcomes us to drink without worry for we are not required to pay a price; He already paid on our behalf. This is the only water that can fulfill all righteousness when we become totally immersed in and filled up by it. **Revelation 22:1-2 and 22:17**

The woman of Samaria had finally come face to face with the futility of the inadequate substitute plumbed from the depths of carnality. In the Presence of the only true Source, of the Water of

Life, she no longer feared the noon time heat. She had found the Fount of Life and would never thirst again, for **"blessed are they which ... thirst after righteousness: for they shall be filled". Matthew 5:6.** It is good to be thirsty if we find ourselves thirsting after righteousness and quenching our need at the right water fountain. For there are fake fountains; soda fountains, dirty, polluted water fountains, liquor fountains and all different variety of fountains that will attract your thirst only to de-hydrate and destroy your soul. **Jeremiah 2:13** warns us of a twin evil against our Lord Jehovah;

My people have committed two evils: they have forsaken Me, the Fountain of living waters, and they have hewn for themselves cisterns, broken cisterns which cannot hold water. (NIV)

The woman of Samaria experienced a paradigmatic shift in her search for personal satisfaction, fulfillment and happiness. She was restored to her God-given, God-appointed and God-ordained position in the battle for human souls. She resumed her commission as a General in the Army of the Divine. She had undergone such a profound experience that she was unable to keep her deliverance and her joy bottled up inside her. Her personal redemption was two-fold. Even as the greatest commandment given by God is that we love and worship Him with our whole being, the second is like unto the first. It is stated quite clearly by the Christ that we should **'love our neighbors as we love ourselves'. Matthew 22:36-40.**

This woman at the well knew what it was like to be thirsty at the noon time with a burning desire for fulfillment. She knew full well that despite appearances and behavior to the contrary, there were others like her with the same need. She was familiar with the revolving door syndrome of the desperate and the lonely that leads only to destruction, disgrace and finally spiritual death.

She also recognized their true state, often denied or buried by many around her who would rather feel superior and disdainful, denying their own desperate needs; needs that manifest in as many different ways as there are different people. But the underlying lack, need or desire is common to many of us, despite appearances. This

Samaritan had met the Messiah who gave water that satisfied her own thirst permanently and so she hastened to her neighbors with all speed, to spread the good news of the "Water of Life" that was available freely and directly from the "Throne of Grace".

> **Wait and listen, everyone who is thirsty! Come to the water; and he who has no money, come, buy and eat! Yes, come, buy [priceless, spiritual] wine and milk without money and without price [simply for the self-surrender that accepts the blessing]. Isaiah 55:1**

> **And He [further] said to me, It is done! I am the Alpha and the Omega, the beginning and the End. To the thirsty I [Myself] will give water without price from the fountain (springs) of the water of Life. Revelation 21:6**

The water that the Messiah still offers to each of us today quenches every kind of thirst. The most severe noon time heat cannot produce a thirst too great for this Living Water to satisfy. Every emotional Sahara can be turned into an oasis by the Source. Immediately the woman at the well received salvation from the Lord Jesus Christ, it began to fill her heart and to flow out towards the lost and the needy, just as the Savior had declared. The force of life eternal which is gifted us by God cannot be contained or suppressed; it cannot be hidden or hoarded. It is an active, vibrant presence that washes away all sin and makes clean and brand new all who partake of it. After all, love is the fuel that powers the process of salvation and love is a reproductive, creative presence that keeps on giving.

The Water-Bearers

> **Whoever drinks of the water that I shall give him will never thirst. But the water that I shall give him will become in him a fountain of water springing up into everlasting life. John 4:14. (NIV)**

In times past and even today, in many developing nations, the task of gathering water for a family's needs, fall primarily to the women. Just about everyday, on the television, it is possible to see appeals for the drilling of wells in countries to provide clean water to many communities and families, especially in Africa where there are long periods of drought resulting in famine and suffering. If you look closely, you will notice that those in search of water are mostly, if not completely, women and children. It is customary in such societies for the collection of water to be regarded as woman's work.

This has made me wonder how it is that the acquisition of water, so absolutely essential for daily survival is treated as woman's work. The role of the woman in the physical is a manifestation of the spiritual so that the task of bringing, nurturing and nourishing new life is a familiar instinct and responsibility for the spiritual women warriors of our Lord.

For this reason, it is desperately important that women are in right relationship with the Lord. We were designed, created and appointed to be channels of life, to be carriers and protectors of the "Living Water" for our families, communities, our world and the Kingdom of God. The woman at the well in Samaria had lost sight of her purpose and her commission long before that noontime when she came face to face with her past, her present and her future. It was by His grace that the Messiah restored her divine destiny, and ratified the call to warfare that God assigned to the daughters of Eve.

Breaking Waters

Our physical bodies are made of approximately seventy-five percent water. Not surprisingly, so too is the planet earth that God prepared for our abode, our domain. Water is an essential, vital element for our very sustenance, our continued existence. In like manner in the spiritual realm, without the Water of Life, we perish. It flows freely through the heavenly home of our Lord and He represented this when He made four rivers to flow through Eden, the perfect home that He formed for man on the earth. **Genesis 2:10-14.**

Jesus taught that **"Unless a man is born again, of the Spirit, and of the water, he cannot see the Kingdom of heaven". John 3:5**. In other words, when we are first born of the flesh, as mortal beings, we are born into bondage, captives of the adversary of our souls. We are inherently partakers of an evil slave mentality, following after the dictates of our master, the devil. We display a natural tendency to oppose the will of God. We do not seek to obey His commands of our own volition. We are born enemies of the Creator Father. Our vision is blinded by the things of this world and the incapacitating effect of sin. But praise to the Almighty, He comes seeking after us, drawing us to Himself with His love. This is the reason that Jesus taught that we must be born again; the natural man cannot serve God. Only if we are recreated after the Spirit of God can we see spiritual truths and understand the love that God has for us and worship Him **"in Spirit and in Truth". John 4:23, 24.**

To signify our rebirth in Christ and into the Kingdom of Righteousness, we enter into water baptism which symbolizes the death of our carnal nature and resurrection into the righteousness of Christ; a spiritual rebirth. This process is sanctioned and modeled by Jesus, who also underwent baptism in the River Jordan by John the Baptist, demonstrating to us as a type of His death and resurrection to bring redemption to man and an example for us to emulate. The Christ was without sin and needed no re-birth but as our Shepherd, in whose footsteps we follow, He led the Way. His death and resurrection was the physical and spiritual actualization of the baptismal experience.

Shew me thy ways, O Lord; teach me thy paths. 5. Lead me in thy truth, and teach me; for thou art the God of my salvation; on thee do I wait all the day. Psalms 25:4-5 (KJV).

There can only be new life birthed into both the natural and the physical realms if there is water. Women are channels through which new life enters this physical, natural world. That is the order Jehovah God established in His wisdom. Immanuel, the Wonderful Counselor and Savior of mankind came into the world by way of a woman's body. Every woman carrying a baby is also carrying water in her womb with her baby. One of the first signs that the baby is ready to leave the safe and secure abode of the mother's womb is the flow of water that is released.

Once her 'water has broken', the mother is generally filled with excitement, joy, anticipation and awe as she enters the final birthing stage. Some of us might also experience some fear mingled in with all the other emotions I just listed! Fear of the possible outcomes of labor; for example all the things that could possibly go wrong. The baby cannot long remain safely in the womb without the surrounding water that the mother has been carrying during her pregnancy. It is the water that keeps the baby safe in a pure, clean, sterile environment.

The breaking of the waters is a signal of impending change both for the mother and the baby. This is the indicator that the baby must make the transition from the internal, protected territory of the mother's womb into the external, physical environment that will enable it to transition to its next level of growth, development and maturity as a human being. In the same way, baptism is the outward indication of a transition from death to life in Christ; a transition that will impact the world, the environment of the redeemed. Water is life; there is no life, physical or spiritual, without it.

In the beginning, Genesis records that the Holy Spirit hovered above the empty, chaotic, unformed mass covered in darkness, that was the earth. Then the Holy Spirit moved upon the waters as the Father Creator called forth light and then everything else that He created. When we lay hold upon salvation through Jesus the Christ and we enter into relationship with Him, we are born again of the Spirit, the blood and Water; the physical representation of this rebirth is water baptism and the spiritual is crucifixion and death of the 'old man', and resurrection into the marvelous light that is the Christ. **Romans 6:3-11.**

Like a baby in the natural, babes in Christ come out of water baptism, having been totally immersed and renewed by the Holy Spirit. But in the same way that physically, human beings need water to live, we are unable to continue growing and maturing spiritually, without the Holy Spirit in us. That is why Jesus Christ said that the water which He gives springs up inside of us and we never thirst again. **John 4:14.** We must not only be washed, submerged in the Water of life, we must be filled up so that it becomes a well within us that never runs dry but flows out refreshing us individually and communally.

But whoever takes a drink of the water that I will give him shall never, no never, be thirsty any more. But the water that I will give him shall become a spring of water welling up (flowing, bubbling) [continually] within him unto eternal life. John 4:14.

In order to be fully prepared for the purpose of God in our lives we must increase in righteousness; from glory to glory. To employ Old Testament symbolism; we must journey from the Outer Court of the Temple to the Inner Court and ultimately into the Holy of Holies (the Most Holy Place). What this process and progression represents is spiritual maturity and none of this is possible unless we are replenished constantly from the Fountain of Life, which is Jesus. That is one reason it was necessary for the Lord to return to the Father in heaven so that He could send the Holy Spirit that would indwell each and every believer; an act that Jesus in His human form would have been physically unable to achieve.

First Campaign

In the spiritual realm, when the woman of Samaria asked for and received the Living Water from Jesus, she could not stop herself from becoming productive; she became a channel through which the Living Water could flow to her neighbors. She was excited, pregnant with the good news and thereby motivated and activated to publish abroad the Presence of the Messiah and the salvation He offered.

She rejoiced in her breakthrough and embraced her change; the change from poverty to prosperity of spirit, from alienation to fellowship, from isolation to communion and from death to life.

She was reborn when; she found herself in His Presence, realized and repented of her sins, sought His forgiveness and received Him as Lord and personal Savior forever. She received from Him the cleansing, refreshing, redeeming Water of Life and became a brand new creation, a woman of God, re-born into the divine family. Her salvation allowed the Spirit of the Christ to regenerate the seed for divine service that God had already buried in her deep, dark place, to be quickened into a life-giving ministry.

She left behind her water pot, a pot representative both of the old man of sin, her carnal nature and the Old Covenant of the Law which condemned her with its ritualistic, legalistic teachings and practices as well as the confused and perverted teachings that man preach as truth. Instead, she embraced the life that the New Covenant offered through Grace and the liberty from the captivity of sin that came with it. She was no longer like **"a deceitful brook, like waters that fail and are uncertain", Jeremiah 15:18b;** the Lord filled her with the water of life that heals and restores all things to righteousness.

With a joyful heart and praises on her lips, she rushed to share the good news of the New Covenant that was inclusive not exclusive, where grace and mercy much more abounded. As the water of life broke over her soul, this woman who had until that moment been feeling desperate, disenfranchised and disempowered, received a spiritual infilling of the Holy Spirit which caused an outpouring so amazing that it was inevitable that it would impact the lives of those around her.

It is impossible to give birth to a brand new life by and through love or become a totally transformed being by that love then keep your joy and gratitude hidden from those with whom one comes into contact. As a result of her testimony and her declaration concerning the Lord, **John 4:39** tells us that

Numerous Samaritans from that town believed in and trusted in Him because of what the woman said when she declared and testified, 'He told me everything I ever did'. (NIV)

What a result for this Samaritan Evangelist. Her first campaign on the battlefield for the Lord brought lost souls into His Kingdom. The change in her must have been so obvious, so apparent, so contagious that people who previously shunned her now believed in her testimony; her publication of the Presence of the Messiah in their neighborhood and His obvious ability to transform the life of a woman who had made an idol of her emotions up to that revelatory, transforming experience at the well. Now they were witnesses of the change that transformed her into a woman unashamedly offering worship and obedience to the only Source of satisfaction, fulfillment and salvation!

She had gone to the well in her filthy rags of unrighteousness now she returned fully clad in the armor of a righteous warrior of the Almighty. All it takes is a choice to bring about change; a change in perspective, a change of heart, a change of focus, a change of dress and a change of address

A Water Bride

When God set about the creation of a bride for Adam, He placed him in a deep sleep. The first Adam was unconscious of the process of creation that was taking place, unaware that God had opened his side and drawn out from within him that which was to be the substance of his bride, companion and helper. In contrast, Jesus the Christ was fully conscious, completely alert, refusing even the draught of vinegar and wine offered by the soldiers that might dull His senses and impair His free will to birth the Church, His bride into the earth and the spiritual realm. **Matthew 27:48**

What has this to do with water? Significantly, in the Garden of Gethsemane, Jesus suffered the compounded, multiplied spiritual and physical version of the travail of a pregnant woman; pains and birth pangs that parallel and fulfills those imposed on and experienced by a woman who goes into labor to birth the future. The depth of His suffering is evidenced by the blood mingled with His sweat that the Bible records. **Matthew 26:38-42.** Further, in the same way that the breaking of the water precedes the physical birth of a child, at Christ Jesus' crucifixion, the water that flowed from His pierced side preceded the birth of His Church and mankind's redeemed future. **John 19:34, 35.**

Before His sacrifice and His victory, we had no life in us, no future to look forward to, only death; eternal extinction. It was after Jesus' crucifixion that the church was birthed out in order that it too could develop, grow, expand and mature as the 'Bride of the Christ'; a Bride that came from within the Secret Place of the Redeemer, born of the blood and the water which flowed from His side on the Cross of Calvary, pushed forth by the spasms and pangs of His pain and suffering, wrapped in a blanket of divine agape love, straight from the heart of God; the promise of a future, designed by God and purchased by the death of His Son for everyone that accepts the gift of salvation.

The Church is still in the development and maturation stages and will continue until the return of the Groom, the Lord Redeemer. At the Lord's return there will be a celebration of the marriage of the Bridegroom and His Bride and she will rule with Him forever. That is the divine destiny of the people of God. **Revelation 19:9.** In the meantime, the Bride remains in the earth realm, with a mandate to carry on the mission of her Lord; just like each and every woman of God must carry out their mandate to fight the devil and his diabolical plans of death to the human family. The Church, the Bride is the Proto-Type of God's warrior woman at enmity with the serpent!

CHAPTER 9

WATER, DEATH AND LIFE

Water Pots and the Key to Survival

In societies where women collect and carry water from wells or other natural sources such as springs, brooks and rivers, a water pot, a container used for collecting and carrying the water is a very special, prized and necessary possession. Traditionally water pots were jars of earthenware in which water was collected, carried and stored. Its possession determined whether there is water for drinking, and washing as well for the performance of myriad household chores in which water is indispensable. Sometimes even the planting and maintenance of a small vegetable and herb garden around the home has to be manually watered with collected water.

The physical survival of a woman and her family depended on her ability to find, collect and carry clean water home. In fact in **Joshua 15:16-19** we read of a daughter's exercise of wisdom in providing for the future needs of her family and a father's love in granting her requests and recognizing the character and awareness of his child. Achsah was the daughter of Caleb who was given in marriage as recognition and reward for the loyalty and bravery of her husband Othniel in battle. However, the land that was her new home was the dry Negeb area and so she sought permission of her husband to return to visit her father and ask a blessing, a gift from him.

When Achsah reached her father she no doubt thanked him for her husband and a homestead but she drew his attention to the thing that she still lacked; a source of water. If her new family, her home was going to prosper then she needed a dependable water source and her father could supply that need. The Bible tells us that her father granted her wish. I believe that this is recorded for our instruction not only concerning applying wisdom and foresight to our natural situations but even more to our spiritual lives.

How many of us, in all our getting, forget the necessity of a dependable source of refreshing water? It is an essential for our survival and renewal in all circumstances. Without a source that renews itself, how can we have security in the future? How can we stand if we lack the Water of Life? We need to take a leaf from young Achsah's book and go to our Heavenly Father. He already has all that we could desire or need to live a prosperous life. We must go on our donkeys, that is in humility and ask Him to give us the Living Water that springs up in our lives; our hearts, spirit, minds and homes forever.

The issue of a clean, accessible source of water is still very much an issue in the developing nations and women are still the water-bearers. In recent years, earthenware vessels have been replaced with metal containers (metal comes out of the earth anyway, so it's the same thing, just packaged differently!) but the need and the responsibility to collect water remains located with the females of the family, most often accompanied by the children of the household. It makes me think of mothers going to the house of the Lord, bringing their children with them to the Water Source!

Like those water pots, so essential to survival, we too are vessels made from the earth and we collect, carry and store within our natural bodies all the experiences and emotional baggage that comprises the very essence of our being. We receive into ourselves all kinds of philosophies, beliefs, practices, superstitions and teachings concerning the meaning of life, our part in the dance and how to achieve a satisfying journey. We entertain a vast range of mental and emotional exploits and we reason and arrive at a set of values, principles, and ethics by which we live, measure our experiences and validate our morals, attitudes, behavior and actions.

We each pursue a variety of different activities all expected to lead to enhanced lifestyles. By this, some of us mean a successful life according to the standards of our family, community, culture, creed and country. Often the majority of us find that we are unable to achieve satisfaction through our own endeavors and many more never have the opportunity to acquire the dreams and ambitions that they aspire to, due to institutional structures and organizations that hinder, prevent or circumvent reasonable access

As a consequence, there are millions of people the world over who persevere with dissatisfied, unfulfilled, mediocre and meaningless lives, in desperate need of the true meaning and purpose that justifies being here. Many have been misled, misdirected, misinformed and their desires misappropriated to serve the very enemy of their souls. There is but one Way, one Truth, one Savior in whom every answer, every longing, every purpose and the destiny of every single person lies; and that is in the Creator of all life. He wrote the manual that details the very essence of our nature and His plan and purpose for our existence. He is the Source of our life, the One Who Sustains and in Whom we can find renewal, rejuvenation, redemption and restoration to perfection, prosperity and paradisiacal eternity in His Presence.

But until and unless we access water from the Source of Living Water that can restore us to the original state that was determined by God, we will always be in lack; lost, and longing for something to quench our thirst, allowing us to reach toward a better life than that offered by carnality, materialism and idolatry. Man was made to be an eternal being in perfect union, communion and harmony with Jehovah God. Our rebellion alienated us from His love and from everlasting life in Him. We have desired and endeavored by our own folly, to recapture that state of being, the resonance of which vibrates at the very core of our spirit. That is the reason that we continuously search for strange ways to alleviate, eliminate and satiate the deepest longings and desires of our hearts and minds, and, the reason that so often we end up in situations and places that leads to dissatisfaction, despondency and death. **Isaiah 53:6**

Our sinful bodies, made from the dust of the earth and assigned to return thereto forever by God if we continue in sin, can only be quickened and brought to true Life by the Holy Spirit. And the Holy Spirit can only have His way in transforming and sanctifying us if we accept that Jesus is the Son of God, the Seed promised to defeat the enemy, the Savior of the world and the Sovereign Lord of our lives.

It is no coincidence that when Jesus performed His first miracle at the wedding at Cana in Galilee, water pots were center stage at this demonstration of God's love and His promises to the human family. This marriage was Jesus' first miracle. Just as God began earth's administration by setting in place a covenant relationship between man, woman and God as the foundational institution of earth's government, the marriage in Cana signified the renewed covenant between God and man; that is, between a wife, a husband and the Lord, the human and the heavenly family. **John 2:6-11**.

The pot represents the human body, a vessel of clay, the same vessel that was marred in the Potter's hand; that through water and the blood, (the wine representing the blood of Christ) we would be made anew by the Spirit of God; a rebirth into the family of the Divine, Triune God, into His Presence, Peace, Joy and Everlasting Kingdom

For as many as receive Him, (Jesus) He gives power to become the sons of God, even those who believe on His name. John 1:12

Wells That Run Dry

Wells in Palestine are traditionally excavated from the limestone rock which pervades that territory. **Genesis 24:16**. They are absolutely essential to any settlement or community as they are the only source of water supply. Without water there is no life for humans, livestock and plants. Not surprisingly, we find in the Bible that the well was often a source of contention. The final separation of Abraham and Lot resulted from disagreements over water supply and an incident at the beginning of Moses' exile from Egypt is another prime example of the problems that access to a well causes.

One of the main reasons that disputes frequently transpired is that the digging of a well took effort, time, resources, skill and experience to detect easily accessible locations with a ready supply of clean water. There were individuals who did not want to invest in the effort and costs required to sink a well but nevertheless wanted to enjoy the benefits. Things are no different spiritually. There are so many routes that people have invented to make their way into the Kingdom of God but there is only one Way and that is the Way provided by the Father Himself in Christ Jesus.

In fact, in ancient times, the people of Israel faced many confrontations and hostilities over water supply. In the same way, spiritually, as God's covenanted people, they were also subjected to a constant barrage of hatred and attack from the usurper through the auspices, actions and antagonism of the neighboring nations that served idols and false gods, namely Satan in disguise. But then as now, as long as God's people remain connected to the Source, the gates of hell cannot prevail and that is why the devil works so hard to cause problems at the very point of access to Living Water, the well.

But although historically and spiritually the well can be a place of contention it can also be a place of transition or conversion. A well is also a figurative representation of our Father God. He is the Source and the Sustainer of Life, physical and spiritual. Jesus Christ is the Rock of our salvation and in Him we should seek to plumb the depths of God's grace and His mercies, even as wells are sunk in the limestone rocks in the region of Palestine to secure a good water supply. That is the reason that Satan employs every device, every scheme, every cunning that he can muster to mess up the minds of men.

If there is sufficient interference, deterrence or confusion concerning the nature, character, identity and disposition of God and divisions and disagreements concerning the path to redemption that He has provided, then human beings can be kept away from true worship and relationship with our only true God and Lord. You don't have to give great thought to this proposition, just do a brief survey of the many paths that humans have invented and follow to supposedly reach God. There are more religions, doctrines, teachings, and philosophies in the world than there are days in a year!

But there is only one Source, One Creator, One Jehovah God, One Son, and One Savior of mankind, One Narrow Way, One Truth, One Life and One Holy Spirit. And therefore, it matters not where you may be located, you have access to the one true Well that is the Lord, the only Source of Living Water. It is to Him only that we must turn for an infusion of new life and its continuous, sustaining overflow. **John 4:10** tells us how Jesus presented 'Life' to the woman at the well of Samaria; **Jesus answered her, If you had only known and recognized God's gift and Who this is that is saying to you, Give Me a drink, you would have asked Him [instead] and He would have given you living water.**

3. Therefore, with joy, will you draw water from the wells of salvation. 4. And in that day you will say, Give thanks to the Lord, call upon His name and by means of His name [in solemn entreaty]; declare and make known His deeds among the peoples of the earth, proclaim that His name is exalted! Cry aloud and shout joyfully, you women and inhabitants of Zion, for great in your midst is the Holy One of Israel. Isaiah 12:3-4, and 6

There are many who will not make the time or expend the necessary effort and energy to tap into the Source of Life for themselves. They are too lazy, too complacent, too smart or more precisely, too foolish to seek for the Way, the Truth and the Life. As a result they are willing to accept the re-cycled versions of truth from false prophets and those possessed with the spirit of anti-Christ, who peddle and preach false doctrines, teach the philosophies of men as wisdom and answer questions on the purpose of human life with the foolishness of man's imagination. This is an affront to our God and a rejection of His blessed provisions to the saving of our souls. He calls on the heavens to be appalled, shocked and horrified at the behavior of the people. See **Jeremiah 2:12**. However, **Jeremiah 2:13** goes on to explain the cause of this outrage:

For My people have committed two evils: they have forsaken Me, the Fountain of living waters, and they

have hewn for themselves cisterns (that is, wells), broken cisterns which cannot hold water.

If like Satan, to whom God bestowed great beauty, glory and wisdom, **(Ezekiel 28:12:17)** we reject the perfection of God's bounty, the newness of eternal life that He offers to us in Christ Jesus and instead, follow after our own devices and imaginations, we are deserving of the consequence of the final death.

No Water Bill

If like the woman of Samaria, we seek the Lord and experience a personal encounter with His saving grace, His mercy, His love and His healing power, we can truly find the eternal solution to our noon day thirst and an end to those repeat trips, that cycle of behavior which draws us into carnality and sin, over and over again. Accepting the gift of salvation, being reborn of the Holy Spirit and being filled therewith, so that we are transformed into new creatures in Christ means also that these earthen vessels, our bodies, become the Temple of the Lord, a place where His Spirit dwells, a holy abode of our God. The Holy Spirit has the power to cleanse, purify and sanctify us for the acceptable service and worship of our Lord. **1 Corinthians 6:19**

And where the Spirit of the Lord is, there is liberty. There is freedom from that burning thirst, that desire to wander out at noontime; there is liberty from the temporary, corruptible things of this world and from the bondage of sin and death. **2 Corinthians 3:17.** In Christ there is freedom to worship in Spirit and in truth, to call on the name of the Lord who is able to supply all our needs according to His riches in glory, there is freedom to focus on God and the things of God and, there is faith that God will provide everything that will fulfill all the desires of our heart and soul.

There is no more waste of energy, time and emotions in search of answers to the demands of lack that walking after the ways of the world inevitably exemplifies. Like the widow whose hospitality to Elijah resulted in a blessing that prevented the oil in her jar from running out, during the time of famine, the Water of Life that is the gift of God will never dissipate, run out, never cease to satisfy, replenish, refresh and renew. It imparts life everlasting to all those who drink.

But whoever takes a drink of the water that I will give him shall never, no never, be thirsty any more. But the water that I will give him shall become a spring of water welling up (flowing, bubbling) [continually] within him unto (into, for) eternal life. John 4:13-14

The woman of Samaria lifted her eyes out of the earth realm, that watering hole dug into the ground and looked to the heavens, the spiritual realm where the One who is the Source of all our needs beckons us to choose life. She refocused, fixed her gave on the Messiah and in so doing restored her link with the Lord and her connection to life eternal. Leaving her water pot behind, that jar of earthenware, that symbol of her unfulfilled passions, carnal desires and legacy of death, physical and spiritual, she rushes to invite and lead others to the Lord. **John 4:28.**

It is an awesome vision to see a woman who is passionately purposed about the work of the Lord; focused on a mission, fulfilling her God-ordained calling. The woman of Samaria had no need and no thought of returning to her previous state. She knew well the sorry state that she was in for that period of her life and she knew well that it held no attraction only dissatisfaction. She had no further use for a water pot that carried the very substance which kept her tied in sin and bondage to the desires of the flesh. She had drunk from the Fount of Living Water; she would never again be satisfied with less, when freely, she can have more, more abundantly! Having once experienced satisfaction, contentment and the peace of God, she could not return to her old condition.

Her unfulfilled desires, that feeling of something missing, that timeless, pervading sense of emptiness that had driven her into so many fruitless, futile experiences, was finally gone. Life had been poured into her spirit and she would never be the same thereafter. Her mind, body and heart were apprehended by the Lord forever.

There was no further reason to cling to the water pots, keeping them around for old time sake; the former things were gone and now she was pressing forward to the things which were ahead; the Will of God for her life and her destiny. **Philippians 3:12-17**

The water that Christ offered to the Samaritan woman still flows freely and is available to all who thirst; and everyone gets thirsty sometime! Jesus is still our Source today as He was back then for the Samaritan woman and He needs must pass our way. He makes Himself available to us all the time, anytime, morning, noon or night.

37. Jesus stood and said in a loud voice, If anyone is thirsty, let him come to me and drink. 38. Whoever believes in me, as the Scripture has said, streams of living water will flow from within him. 39. By this He meant the Spirit, whom those who believed in Him were later to receive. John 7:37-39 (NIV)

Behold, I stand at the door and knock; if anyone hears and listens to and heed My voice and opens the door, I will come in to him and will eat with him, and he [will eat] with Me. Revelation 3:20

This Samaritan woman was not the first woman in the Bible in dire straits, to meet the Lord of our salvation at a well. Let us consider Hagar, the mother of Ishmael, son of the Patriarch Abraham. In her time of great need when she faced death, the Lord provided a well for Hagar, a well that confirmed His earlier covenant with her and her offspring, her son Ishmael.

Hagar's Well of Covenant

The well was the means that the Lord provided to restore life to Hagar and her son physically. **Genesis 16:6-15.** But it was also the place that God manifested His faithfulness in respect of the covenant He made with Hagar in a previous encounter, at a time when she was caught up in her own agenda and arrogant in her self-centered disobedience.

> **For she called the name of the Lord Who spoke to her, You are a God of seeing, for she said, Have I [not] even here [in the wilderness] looked upon Him Who sees me [and lived]? Or have I here also seen [the future purposes or designs of] Him Who sees me? 14. Therefore the well was called Beer-lahai-roi [A well to the Living One Who sees me]. Genesis 16:13-14.**

The Lord brought Hagar to her senses; He questioned her actions, reminded her of her obligation and duty and commanded her return to her appointed station in the household of Abraham with a new attitude, a responsible commitment and a revitalized sense of loyalty. She had experienced her fist personal encounter with Jehovah God, not Abraham's or Sarai's testimony but she came into direct relationship and covenant for herself. The Lord revealed Himself to her and she was the beneficiary of His promise to her and her posterity; a promise honored by the Lord later at the well of Beer-lahai-roi.

Many years later we meet the Samaritans, who were confused about the worship that they offered Jehovah and the operation of the covenant under which they kept faith with Him. **John 4:19-26.** But God is not a God of confusion and that is why it was necessary, according to God's plan, for Jesus to journey by way of Samaria. He brought clarification, illumination and revelation concerning truth and redemption in the Messiah; and He did so in a personal encounter that could not be ignored or confused by second hand reporting.

In the same way that the Lord revealed Himself to Hagar and met her needs at the well called Beer-lahai- roi, He also met the woman of Samaria in her time of lack and freed her from her personal, communal and religious captivity. Hagar is used as a metaphor by the Apostle Paul to represent the bondage of the law under the old covenant in **Galatians 4:24.** And certainly like Hagar, the Samaritans were released from the bondage of traditions, rituals and misunderstandings that held them in sin and error.

Both Hagar and the woman at the well of Samaria were women in bondage to their own needs; the Lord asked the questions that brought revelation and conviction to them both concerning their personal condition. They were both empowered by the Word to bring about change in their lives and their perspectives and in so doing embraced their divine purposes. The Lord also wanted to bring truth concerning personal worship and to clear up the confusion of second hand accounts and experiences that clouds one's knowledge and causes faith to falter in the Person, purpose and proper way of worshipping Jehovah.

Like Hagar, the Samaritan woman's personal encounter established her in a New Covenant relationship with the Christ; truth about her identity and her destiny in the Lord was all that she needed to turn her life around. And this truth is all any of us ever need to reposition ourselves for power to conquer the enemy as Christ also conquered. The personal revelatory experience of the woman at the well echoed Hagar's words when she said of the Lord Jesus, **"Come see a man that told me everything I ever did! John 4:29.** In other words, she too had come face to face with the same Lord as revealed Himself to Hagar, the Living One, the Living Water, who sees everything, knows all things! He came to give all of mankind, all nations, Jews and Gentiles alike the opportunity to be reconciled to God their Creator.

There are a number of similarities between the two women and between the two covenants into which they entered with the Lord. The covenant with Hagar was a personal covenant and extended to her son Ishmael and all his descendants. The invitation to covenant with the Lord was given to one woman and through her extended to all the people of Samaria and beyond who listened and believe in the Messiah; the Lord said the Water which He would give would spring up and flow out, by implication, to others. It does not matter if one comes to Him through hearing her testimony or through a personal encounter, He is the Man that sees and knows everything about us and still bids us come and drink from the Source that never runs dry. Blessed are those who believe the reports of the saints and the testimony of the redeemed and become covenant keepers through personal ratification!

Presence of Water, Absence of Death!

I would also like to pause at this point, to consider the episode in the Prophet Elijah's life that was directly impacted by Jezebel, wife to Ahab, king of Israel. She had given herself over to the false idols and gods of her people, and although she came into marriage with the king of Israel and knew of the God of the people she ruled, she turned her back on Him. Her service to evil found its expression in:

A. The persecution and killing of the prophets of Jehovah God, the God of the Children of Israel, and,

B. The elevation of the false gods that she worshipped. **1 Kings 18:13.**

C. The education and preparation of the next generation of idol worshippers and servants of the kingdom of darkness.

Jezebel used her position of power to convert the people to her evil ways and kill the prophets of Jehovah God. She rejected the opportunity to serve the God of Israel and chose to exalt Baal instead. The man of God, Elijah, was sent to declare a judgment for the murderous idolatry that had gripped the nation of Israel. God's judgment was evidenced by severe drought; a lack of rainfall and the drying up of all the water in the land, thereby inflicting a time of testing and hardship on the people; an extended season of drought. **1 Kings 17:1.**

For three and a half years there was no rain. Spiritually, this also signified the withdrawal of the Spirit of the Lord in the kingdom ruled by Ahab and Jezebel. The anointing of the Lord was neither on the leaders of the nation nor on the people. There was no renewal of life; no new crops and a depleting livestock. There was only death in the land.

The woman Jezebel, in all her vain rebellion, focused only on the carnal pleasures and the fleshly satisfaction that her worship of idols brought. She became a channel of death, physically and spiritually to the Children of Israel. She was not prepared to yield herself to the Lord and embrace the life that He alone offers. Idolatry is the ultimate elevation of self and a declaration of independence from obedience and obeisance to the Creator, God; an overt act of rebellion and covert capitulation to the rule of the evil one. Jezebel was a worshipper of the devil and a human agent that promoted, popularized and proselytized the cause of Satan.

But God in His mercy was not about to allow His covenant people to follow after Jezebel without a wake up call. Whom He loves He chastens and He loves His people with an everlasting love. In the same way that having no water to quench our thirst and meet all the other needs that we have, leads to our physical demise, the withdrawal of God's Spirit from our lives is spiritual death. Wherever there is a drought, in the natural or in the Spirit realm there can be only decay and death. Water indicates life in both realms and its absence signifies death in both realms also.

The drought that the Lord ordered Elijah to declare on the nation of Israel was their rude awakening to the backslidden state of their lives, an opportunity for them to study their evil ways and return to the God who alone has the power to give eternal life to those who are dead in their sins. Jesus is the Water of Life and only His Spirit can cause a regeneration of dry bones.

Jesus, the Living Water sojourned in the Kingdom of Israel, among men, for a period of three and a half years, refreshing, healing, teaching, and renewing God's covenant with His chosen people. He brought life everlasting; abundance not drought, prosperity not starvation, a divine destiny not destruction.

Anyone or anything that replaces God at center stage in our hearts, our lives and our minds, is an idol. It might be physical, material, emotional or spiritual, seen or unseen. Whatever or whoever is the focus of our mind, strength and heart has replaced the only God that is worthy of that place of honor. Idolatry is a clear breach of the Commandments of the Lord Jehovah.

1. Then God spoke all these words: 2. I am the Lord your God, who has brought you out of the land of Egypt, out

of the house of bondage, 3. You shall have no other gods before or beside Me. 4. You shall not make yourself any graven image [to worship it] or any likeness of anything that is in the heavens above, or that is in the earth beneath, or that is in the water under the earth. 5. You shall not bow down yourself to them or serve them; for I the Lord your God am a jealous God ... Exodus 20:1-5.

A Season of Drought

The season of drought was a warning to the people of Israel, designed to turn their hearts back to their true God, the Source of life. We too will experience periods of drought in our lives;

- ❖ **Emotional:** We experience an absence of joy, love, contentment, fellowship,

- ❖ **Physical:** There is a lack of basic needs such as food, clothing, shelter, money to pay the bills and meet our financial obligations

- ❖ **Spiritual:** We are not bearing fruit for the Kingdom of God, not praying, not studying the Word of God, not witnessing, sharing our testimony, not fighting the fight of faith and not living an obedient, abundant, joyous life in the Lord.

At such times we must recognize that the dry season is serving the same purpose in our spiritual walk with God as it was intended to do for the nation of Israel. It alerts us to the absence of the Holy Spirit and our descent into the wide open mouth of hell. In times of drought there is only one remedy; run to the Source of the Living Water. The rains fall from the heavens to refresh and invigorate the earth that it might bring forth its harvest for the physical nourishment of the human body. The water that the Lord Jesus offers springs up eternally.

In **Ezekiel 37:1-14,** we read of the experience of the Prophet in the valley of dry bones. Those bones came alive when they heard the Word of the Lord; they stood up on their feet; a vast army! The Lord taught Ezekiel that the bones are like His people who feel they have no hope. But the Lord declared, **"I will put my Spirit in you and you will live"**. Water is used to symbolize His Spirit and the Spirit of the Lord is His Seal, the sign of His indwelling.

All who keep His commandments [who obey His orders and follow His plan, live and continue to live, to stay and] abide in Him, and He in them. [They let Christ be a home to them and they are the home of Christ.] And by this we know and understand and have the proof that He [really] lives and makes His home in us; by the [Holy] Spirit Whom He has given us. 1 John 3:24

We too must look to the Divine for an outpouring of the Holy Spirit so that we can manifest the principles of fruitfulness and multiplication in winning souls for the Kingdom of our God. Without Christ in us, we can of ourselves, do nothing. We cannot change a single person, not even our self. But we are called to sow the Word of God into peoples' lives; to operate as His agents in enemy territory and by our example, our testimony point souls to Christ and the Cross. The Lord is the Source of life and apart from Him there is only death. The Holy Spirit can bring about conviction, change, renewal and re-birth into the family of God.

A "Gushing" Well is a Testimony!

Sharing the good news of Jesus Christ with our fellow man is the immediate compulsion experienced by all who have come to the Fountain of Living Water. See the experience and example of the woman at the well and all other followers of God from the beginning of the Bible to the very end. The desire to share our testimony with others and bear witness to the redeeming work of the Holy Spirit is an inevitable by-product of our conversion, a manifestation of our restored love for God and one of the mightiest weapons of our warfare. In fact the revelation is that without a testimony we cannot overcome, we cannot win the battle against the devil. Our testimony bears witness to all the universes, the whole of creation about our salvation, our faith, the love of God, His mercies, grace and favor, as well, it testifies of our triumphs and victories through the blood of the Lamb.

Our life and our word is a living testimony and is in fact one of the most powerful weapons in the arsenal of the warriors of God that helps us to overcome the serpent in the heavenly places according to **Revelation 12:10, 11.** It is the weapon to be employed victoriously to culminate the barrage of accusations and charges that the devil brings against us day and night. He is the accuser of the brethren and we shall overcome and cast him out from before our God by our testimony.

The other weapon that is proclaimed and applauded by the heavenly hosts in conjunction with the testimony of the saints is the blood of the Lamb, that all sufficient, one time sacrifice on behalf of the sinful human family for all times. **Hebrews 10:14.** Like the symbolic Paschal lamb, His blood will ensure that Satan and death has no hold on us; the Lamb of God takes away the sins of the world and His blood saves, protects and justifies. **Exodus 12:13.** It stands to reason that the blood is the most powerful weapon on earth as in the heavens. It prevailed in Egypt and it will prevail more perfectly for all times; it is the beginning and the end of our redemption.

The devil is the enemy of our souls' salvation and we must bear arms against him at all costs. The ultimate price was paid by the Christ and now we too must take up our responsibility and follow in His footsteps. If we love Him then we will keep His commandment that we love one another as we love ourselves; thereby sharing in His desire that not one single soul be lost to the devil. **Matthew 22:37-40.** It is this very love which underpins the mandate to engage hostile actions against the devil in the battle for Lordship over the human family. It was the mission of our Lord when He came to earth as the Christ and it remains His purpose; and it is the Great Commission that He has entrusted to us as His Bride, the Church.

Then Jesus came to them and said, "All authority in heaven and on earth has been given to me. 19. Therefore go and make disciples of all nations, baptizing them in the name of the Father and of the Son and of the Holy Spirit, 20. And teaching them to obey everything I have commanded you. And surely I am with you always, to the very end of the age." Matthew 28: 18-20.

Exchanging a Pot for a Box

I am aware that men often joke about the talkative nature of women. They often label women as gossips. But I am convinced that this is merely another plot of the enemy to gag women's natural communicative abilities, and render them ineffective when it comes to passing on the 'good news' of the Christ and the coming of the Kingdom of our God. Enjoying, exploring and employing positive, uplifting communication with others concerning the good things of our King is not idle chatter or mindless gossip.

In fact, it is worth noting that whenever we encounter a woman in the Scriptures and even in our times, who have received the blood-bought salvation of the Christ, she runs to tell these glad tidings to all who will listen. Her natural gifts of caring and communication become an asset in spreading the good news of the Kingdom.

Let her be labeled a 'chatterbox' for the glory of God! As long as she is busy sharing her testimony, giving glory and bringing honor to the Father, then her gift is a blessing not a curse to the human family. The devil would rejoice if he can succeed in 'muzzling' a woman. Her reach tends to be wide and he knows that even if she confined her evangelism to her family, friends and community, she can achieve great strides for the Kingdom of our Lord. And as the saying goes, "the hand that rocks the cradle, rules the world". That is why the enemy will bring warfare into our very homes and we have to recognize it as such and having put on the full armor of righteousness, **stand** on our frontline in the strength of our Lord

Above all else, Satan has reasons to fear a woman of God because she generally has the most influence in bringing up the next generation of spiritual men and women. She can also influence her husband by her example and stance for God, and if Satan can manage to turn all these positives into negatives and so render them null and void, he is delighted.

The devil will do everything he can to prevent us from exchanging our water pots for a box, the 'chatter box' that will keep on proclaiming the mercy, the favor and the love of our Redeemer and Christ. However, we must be aware that even our communicative abilities can be used to achieve the devil's desires if we are not in submission to the will of God. In a later chapter we will see one woman that Satan was able to use to destroy her own family as well as wreak havoc with a kingdom.

Love's Reward

The role of water bearers and water carriers primarily assigned to women in the natural world is also the same in the Spiritual. This is an important role that can only be fully realized if we yield ourselves to the Lord in submission and love, remembering that we do all things as unto the Lord. It is the honor of God's children, a responsibility and a reward of the great love He extends to us that we carry word of His saving grace abroad, challenging every obstacle that seek to prevent us fulfilling His mission.

The well can be a place of transition and transformation. It is a place of new beginnings; where matriarchs such as Rebecca, Rachel, Zipporah and the woman of Samaria met the men who held the keys to their divine destiny. The women are still the ones who must frequent the Well and they number a great host; a great host to publish the word of the Kingdom of God and the Messiah, Jesus the Christ.

So if you find yourself with your water pot, returning over and over to a well that offers only temporary relief or a brief respite from your thirst and the need to search for satiation and sustenance, it is time to find another Source. Look to the Lord and seek His grace which guarantees sufficiency; His Spirit, the Living Water, which is life. You will find salvation and satisfaction, peace that is like a river, joy unspeakable and a compulsion, a passion to publish abroad the good news of the Water that is not from the wells of ancestors but from the Creator Father.

The good news is that the Source of the Water of Life is even now waiting to grant us a refreshing and to fill us with water that is not from the well dug into the depths of the earth by the hands of man. Rather, He is the Water, the Source and Supplier; that completely satisfies for all eternity. In Him, it is unnecessary to resort to our own devices and engineering to build wells that are broken, wells that are temporary resources. There is no need to be filthy or dirty again, to suffer famine, drought, poverty, or lack ever again. False doctrines and traditional practices that allow our allegiance to be diverted to our enemy is represented by the broken cisterns of the Scriptures, wells that we plumb out of the depths of our carnal natures. Carnality can only produce death, but through spiritual rebirth in Christ Jesus we can have life everlasting. In the Source is Life, most abundant and eternal.

And He Who is seated on the throne said ... 6. It is done! I am the Alpha and the Omega, the Beginning and the End. To the thirsty I [Myself] will give water without price from the fountain (springs) of the Water of Life. Revelation 21:6

In the Lord there is an abundance of living water; an overflow that keeps on overflowing! The supply is more than enough for all who come to drink, to wash, to be cleansed, and to water the seeds that are planted; in the same way that Apollos watered after Paul had planted. The water of life is regenerative and reproductive; as it restores and renews, it refills and replaces itself so that the recipient never runs out, suffers no shortage of supply and never experiences a dry season of the soul again.

It is the inherent nature of this overflow in the lives of the saints of God, to share the abundance with others; to see the needs of one's neighbors and to demonstrate our love and the of the Lord for them by telling them about the life we have found in Christ Jesus. The Water that the Lord gives is for the healing of the nations. **Ezekiel**

47:1-12. We have a duty to publish the gospel to the entire world, to win souls to the Kingdom of our Lord so that we hear the blessed words of approval from our Redeemer when He returns;

> **Then the King will say to those at His right hand, Come, you blessed of My Father [you favored of God and appointed to eternal salvation], inherit (receive as your own) the kingdom prepared for you from the foundation of the world. 35. For I was hungry and you gave Me food, I was thirsty and you gave Me something to drink. Matthew 25:34, 35**

CHAPTER 10

THE IMPORTANCE OF EFFECTIVE COMMUNICATION

❦

The Lord gives the word [of power]; the women who bear and publish [the news] are a great host. Psalms 68:11

How beautiful upon the mountains are the feet of him who brings good tidings, who publishes peace, who brings good tidings of good, who publishes salvation, who says to Zion, Your God reigns! Isaiah 52:7

Born to Talk

At this point I would like to pause for a while and share further insights on the ability of women to communicate effectively, an ability that can and is given by the Giver of every good gift, to be used for the glory of God through and by the direction of the Holy Ghost. Let us remember that the Word of God is the spiritual foundry that forges all our weaponry of spiritual warfare. We must place faith in the Word and therein locate the Source of our weapons and the manual for their effective employ in battle.

All women should remember that it was the Creator Himself who gifted us with the ability to communicate with Him first, and then with others. It is not something to make us ashamed, guilty or apologetic when used for the glory of God. It is a gift that is needed by women to fulfill the **Genesis 3:15** Commission. Please recall with me that the Scripture teaches us that at strategic points in His ministry, Jesus commissioned women to publish His words, His instructions and His ministry abroad. The case just considered, namely the woman at the well in Samaria, exemplifies this truth. This woman was an excellent communicator; a witness, a teacher and an evangelist, and because of her testimony and her witness, many souls were led to the Lord. **John 4:39-42**

"I am Woman"

In Genesis we read that the Lord was well pleased with all that He had set out to accomplish in the six days of creation. **See Genesis 1, 2.** His concluding act of creating on earth was to insert the final part of His master piece. The Almighty's final, creative act, on the last day of creation was Adam's helper, the woman Eve. At the conclusion of each stage of His creative process Elohim declared, "It is good" and the angels broke out in songs of praise and worship, exalting His glory and sharing His delight. **Job 38:7.** When God made the male, He said, **"It is not good for him to be alone".**

Then God fashioned a female form and poured of Himself into her mental, emotional, psychological and spiritual nature. She too was in His image and after His likeness, possessing attributes, traits and characteristics of the Lord. He presented her to Adam. She was truly what Adam declared her to be, "Woman". Adam chose these words to name her because he understood that she was **'flesh of his flesh, bone of his bones'**, as much him as any being could possibly be; taken and shaped from his very self, physical and spiritual. She completed "man" and Adam declared, **'she shall be called woman'**. **Genesis 2:23.**

It was to Adam that God had given authority to name all the life-forms with which He had populated the earth. So it was in-keeping with this order, that Adam named the last of God's created beings on the earth. And let us remember that Adam at this time did only those things which were in agreement with his Creator and Lord. She was "woman" to Adam and to God. Later, however, we see that after the Fall of man, and God's declaration of the new role of woman as mother to the Redeemer and warrior in the battle against the serpent, Adam declared that his wife shall be called "Eve", her name reflected her role as mother of all human beings, repository of the promised Seed of redemption; the Messiah that would restore eternal life to the human family.

Although in some countries today, we no longer attach meanings to the names given to children, there are many cultures and family traditions across the world that adhere to the custom of calling a person by a name that declares their parents' hopes and aspirations for their purpose, prospects and heritage. In the Hebrew language the name 'Eve' means "life-giver" and is truly reflective of the hope and the destiny that was hidden within the spirit of the woman. **Genesis 3:20.**

When she was created, Eve was indeed woman, not just the female of the species but "woman", more than a wife and more than a mother. Wife and mother were her roles. I am led by the Holy Spirit to the revelation that when God completed His creative work, male and female were perfect in all respects. As a perfect female, Eve was 'woman' possessing the fullness of God's attributes as helper, and the traits, assets and aspects of a mother, a wife and a divinely appointed and anointed ruler of this realm with her husband.

Therefore, we are only, truly women when we are restored to that former state of being; reborn of the Spirit through Jesus Christ, as women of God, into that perfect state that we first received from God; when we lived and moved and had our being in Him. **Acts 17:28-31.** Once we are redeemed and restored by the blood of the Savior, living a Christ-like life again, being 'perfect even as He is perfect', we are again women, as originally named and comprehensively defined.

You, therefore, must be perfect [growing into complete maturity of godliness in mind and character, having reached the proper height of virtue and integrity], as your heavenly Father is perfect. Matthew 5:48

In other words, when we have a right relationship with God; when He has perfected us again in Christ Jesus, when we are in submission to His will and compliant with His purpose for our lives, in continuous communication and agreement with Him, holy even as He is holy, as originally ordained, we are women indeed, women of God! **1 Peter 1:13-25.** Outside of the atonement of the Christ, we are merely females, our true identities lost, our vision impaired and our purpose buried under our desires for the carnal, for man and things man-made; subject to the rule of carnality, darkness, sin and Satan.

"In my being and in my becoming, I have always been female but I have not always been a woman, that is to say, I have not always been a woman of God."

These words came into my mind and heart as I prayed and waited for an impartation from the Holy Spirit concerning the fullness of my identity in Christ. It was from this starting point; that further revelation concerning the true character and qualities of "woman" was revealed in my spirit. The word woman is commonly used by us all every day, to denote the female adult of the human family. But I believe that we have come to use this word conveniently, flippantly and perhaps even without godly wisdom and discernment.

To truly live up to the meaning and standing of woman is to be in the likeness and image of Eve when she was first created by God and presented to Adam. Or, since our eviction from Eden, to lay hold of faith and through Jesus Christ, the Promised One once again put on His cloak of righteousness and become the children of God. In other words, the word 'woman' denotes all of the following and much more besides:

- ❖ To be a woman of God
- ❖ To have total, all-round maturity physically and spiritually
- ❖ To be possessed of a Christ-like attitude and character

- ❖ To embrace and display a consciousness of our roles as physical and spiritual mothers and wives, princesses, warriors and heirs of God
- ❖ To reflect the character of God as a Helper
- ❖ To be effective, functioning partners in the Kingdom authority bestowed on man by the Creator,
- ❖ To be loving, obedient children of the royal family of God, our Father in heaven.
- ❖ To complete the entity man and together with the male, perfectly reflect and represent the image and likeness of the Triune God in the earth realm

In truth, if we are living in rebellion against God and the laws of His Kingdom of Righteousness, then we have chosen to be less than He created us to be; less than 'woman' as received, welcomed, appreciated and honored by Adam. Outside the will of God, we have lost our true identity, our vision and our place in the Kingdom of God. It is of the utmost importance that every person knows their own, true, individual identity, purpose and destiny as intended by the Creator. But I believe that the first and most important step is to know who we are; not an acceptance of other peoples' description or an acquiescence with external titles, roles, definitions and designations as the final word of authority.

For example, a part of knowing who we are at a biological level is to be acquainted with the true identity of our biological parents, whose genes, DNA and physical characteristics determine our propensities and susceptibilities to diseases and our physicality such as color of hair, eyes, skin and so on. Knowing our personal history which includes the history of our family is a part of understanding ourselves. That is one reason so much emphasis is placed on genealogy in the Bible so that the people of God can identify their lineage among God's covenanted people. However, knowing our biological background is only a part of the equation. Our character, personality and individual dispositions, temperament and quirks as well as our beliefs, attitudes and aptitude are all a part of the mix.

For many people that is as far as it goes. But despite the practice and approach of the world, there are other components and considerations that go to determine one's complete identity. In truth, the personal history of each person begins when the history of the human family began; with the first parents, the progenitors of all the nations on the earth, and the God who created us all. In order to have this complete picture, we must go to the Source, our Alpha, and learn from Him, as a child learns from its parents and elders; all of these together completes the picture and tells us who we are in the Lord. The Word of God, the Son and the Holy Spirit provide the means of our education directly or by inspiration. Knowledge, understanding and wisdom is gifted directly from the Father, and the Holy Spirit indwelling us teaches and reveals divine truth; sanctifying us for the Kingdom.

> **Study and be eager and do your utmost to present yourself to God approved (tested by trial), a workman who has no cause to be ashamed, correctly analyzing and accurately dividing [rightly handling and skillfully teaching] the Word of Truth. 2 Timothy 2:15**

Choose Your Words Carefully

The issue of identity was at the core of Satan's conversation with Eve. He challenged her identity and undermined her confidence and her knowledge in who she was and therefore in her character, her purpose and her destiny. The serpent implied that that she was not created in the image of God but if she ate the fruit she would become like Him.

> **"Now the serpent was more crafty than any of the wild animals the Lord God had made. He said to the woman, "Did God really say, 'You must not eat from any tree in the garden?'**
>
> **2. The woman said to the serpent, "We may eat fruit from the trees in the garden.**

3. But God did say, 'you must not eat fruit from the tree that is in the middle of the garden, and you must not touch it, or you will die'.

4. "You will not surely die", the serpent said to the woman.

5. "For God knows that when you eat of it, your eyes will be opened, and you will be like God, knowing good and evil".

6. When the woman saw that the fruit of the tree was good for food and pleasing to the eye, and desirable for gaining wisdom, she took some and ate it. She also gave some to her husband, who was with her and he ate it.

7. Then the eyes of both of them were opened, and they realized they were naked; so they sewed fig leaves together and made coverings for themselves. Genesis 3:1-7. (NIV)

This discourse was designed to raise doubt and plant a desire for the forbidden fruit in her heart and mind; a desire that would manifest itself in disobedience. It was also a device to turn away her heart, trust, belief, dependence and loyalty from God. Eve believed Satan's lies for a number of reasons, some of which I have previously mentioned but it is evident that the lie that unraveled Eve was the lie that caused her to forget her true identity, an identity which was encoded in her very name, woman.

Today, there are many instances when the devil will try to undermine the children of God by questioning our identity or reminding us of our history and projecting our past onto future actions. In other words, he will bombard us with negative reminders of past failings, present inabilities and future impossibility to abide by God's laws. In turn these failures are highlighted to show our unworthiness for the Kingdom of God, His mercy and His love. These negative inputs and the gravity of our wrong-doing can cause us to lose our identities, our names and our birthright. Eve failed to spot the evil trick and began to doubt her completeness. As a result of her debate with Satan and the guile of his arguments, she lost sight of God's version of who she was and His vision for her; she forgot the Perfect Pattern of her design; **'after the likeness and in the image of God, created He them, both male and female'. Genesis 1:26.**

Likewise, Jesus Christ faced the very same opponent, the same obstacle when He was also tempted along the same lines as Eve. Jesus did not fall for this devilish deceit. Instead the Christ relied on and declared His Father's Words only. He did not hesitate or try to come up with an explanation of His own; neither did He lose sight of His identity, His heritage or His destiny. He discerned the true aim of the adversary and He overcame the temptations by sticking to the Word of God; not adding or subtracting one jot, not debating or discussing its veracity!

That is what we must do when we, like every single human being must, face the deceit, fraud and wickedness of the enemy. We must stand on the Word of God and on His promises. Whatever God declares is truth because of Who He is. His Word is the Sword of the Spirit, a most valuable, successful offensive and defensive weapon of our warfare. We must be ready with our answer whenever we are tempted, questioned, challenged, mocked, denigrated or despised; the answers that we need are written in the Scriptures. For this reason the Scriptures were given to us; it possesses all knowledge, all answers to every question that our hearts and minds can frame. The bible also has the answer to all the questions, arguments or theories that Satan proposes, propagates or publishes in this world.

Another point I would like to make while we are on the topic of similarities and repetition in the devil's deadly repertoire of assaults and attacks against the human family. Satan appealed to Eve's ego by way of her natural, physical, mental/psychological and emotional appetites. He suggested that the forbidden fruit was good to eat with the double whammy benefit of giving her God-like wisdom. So let us consider briefly the power of this enticement to the natural appetite and the pleasure of tasting delicious food as well as the appeal to the intellect; food for the mind.

"A Little of what you Fancy!"

You can talk yourself in or out of sin by selecting your arguments carefully. For example, when Eve was weighing up her arguments, her reasons, considering the pros and cons for eating the forbidden fruit; the appeal of the fruit to the appetites of her body rated high on her list of self-deluded reasons to break God's law. And food is still a big issue with a lot of women even today; just take a look at all the advertisement centered on food and then take a look at the effects of excessive indulgence. It is an interest, a necessity, a tool or an obsession that occupies a great deal of our time, efforts and thoughts. For me, it certainly is the 'cure-all' in the emotional department; an issue that has always been a big personal challenge.

However, together with many other women, we need to be careful that we do not fall into idolatry in respect of food. Problems such as anorexia, bulimia, yo-yo dieting and weight controlling drug use in modern societies, are indications that we are living in an era packed with women who are out of balance not just physically and emotionally but also spiritually. The Apostle Paul states quite clearly that we are slaves to that which controls us. **Romans 6:16**.

Many women, me included, are victims to our 'need' for food. I am an emotional eater, whatever emotion I am feeling, I eat! Seriously, I do use food to comfort me, to keep me company, to reward me, to occupy me among a myriad of other reasons. What this translates to is that food has an unnaturally prominent role in my life and not necessarily healthy food. Thank God, this project has allowed me to recognize that I have food issues that require more than diets but rather a lifestyle change altogether. It is not true that a little of what you fancy will not harm you, kill you!

Jesus, just like Adam and Eve, was likewise tempted with food by Satan when He was physically and emotionally weakened after a forty day fast in the desert. When Adam and Eve took the fruit they were not hungry or lacking in satisfaction from the food that God had provided; so greed and gluttony is part of the list of sins that they committed that fateful day. But Jesus who was most certainly hungry found strength to resist the devil in the Word of God as follows; **"Man shall not live by bread alone but by every word that proceeds out of the mouth of God". Luke 4:4.**

This truth is a solid foundation on which I now strive to stand daily and I would encourage all my sisters and brothers to do the same if they would have victory in the Lord with food or other addictions. The Word of the Lord is powerful, sharper than any two-edged sword and it can certainly cut through the shackles of slavery; namely our addictions, familial dispositions, habits, practices, generational customs and curses, so-called natural propensities, as well as the arguments, accusations and enticements of Satan that leads us to sin.

Jesus went on to re-affirm that our life or death is dependent on our obedience to the will of God expressed through His Word. Like Job, we must reach a spiritual maturity that will have us saying along with him, **'Even if He slays me, I will still trust in God'. Job 13:15.** Again, Jesus has set us the pattern to follow so that in Him we can enjoy the fruits of our liberation from the control of Satan, sin and carnal satisfaction. **Colossians 3:1.**

Abba, Father!

When I was a little girl I remember hearing the adults and elders of my community say that the first word that a child learns to say was always 'Dada"; a short and simple first pronunciation of a term of endearment for "Father". I would not be surprised to learn that there is truth to this belief!

I say this because I feel convicted that the very first words that our first human parents uttered would have been a variation of 'Dada', 'Abba', a word that our Lord Jesus used to call out to His Father and ours. When Adam was created he opened his eyes to behold the face of our God who breathed life into his still, cold, clay form. Eve likewise saw the glorious face of the Lord God when her eyes opened for the first time. The loving, shining face of the Divine Creator must have been an awesome first sight! To think, Eve also spoke her first words to God; "Abba, Father".

It was He who instructed her, prepared her, and taught her the nature of woman and the ways of 'the feminine' before delivering her to her husband. It was the Father who gave her the blueprint to be a wife and a mother for the human family and He modeled godly leadership, authority and dominion to her. He made her perfect in every way. Eve enjoyed a unique relationship with the Divine and through her so did all women, for we were yet in her loins, a truth that gives me joy.

And this is the reason that when we are adopted as children of God through Jesus our Lord and we receive His Spirit in our hearts, it calls out **"Abba! Father! Galatians 4:6.** That is the way that it should be today and the absence of this divine intimacy undoubtedly accounts for the deep longing, loneliness, depression and emotional deficiency that women experience when they are walking outside the circle of divine relationship.

We should speak always with our Lord and allow all the words that come out of our hearts and mouths to be reflective of His communication with us. Our words are very powerful and can speak life or death for ourselves and our loved ones. **Proverbs 18:21.** God's Words are life and if we abide in Him, our words will also communicate life. I submit the caveat that women will speak life, only if we speak the Words of the Lord. As much as I appreciate that generally, women are very good at communicating, whether they are explaining their feelings, giving a testimony or witnessing for the Lord, there are times when we can go off the 'deep end' and stray outside the will of God in our speech! But Paul exhorts us;

16. Avoid all empty (vain, useless, idle) talk, for it will lead people into more and more ungodliness.

23. But refuse (shut your mind against, have nothing to do with) trifling (ill-informed, unedifying, stupid) controversies over ignorant questionings, for you know that they foster strife and breed quarrels.

24. And the servant of the Lord must not be quarrelsome (fighting and contending). Instead, he must be kindly

to everyone and mild-tempered [preserving the bond of peace]; he must be a good teacher, patient and forbearing and willing to suffer wrong.

25. He must correct his opponent with courtesy and gentleness, in the hope that God may grant that they will repent and come to know the Truth [that they will perceive and recognize and become accurately acquainted with and acknowledge it].

26 And that they may come to their senses [and] escape out of the snare of the devil, having been held captive by him [henceforth] to do His [God's] will. 2 Timothy 2:16, 23-26

We must subject our words, our speech, and all our communication to the will of God at all times, a responsibility that can be difficult without the grace of the Lord. In this I am referring not only to what we speak but also to the words we read, hear and write. Furthermore, our minds must be filled with the Word of God so that we will be ready to give an explanation of our faith if we are questioned. **1 Peter 3:15.** If we speak wisely, not foolishly in pride and conceit, then we glorify the Father. In James we are told that if we lack wisdom, we need only ask.

If any of you is deficient in wisdom, let him ask of the giving God [Who gives] to everyone liberally and ungrudgingly, without reproaching or faultfinding, and it will be given him. 6 Only it must be in faith that he asks with no wavering (no hesitating, no doubting). For the one who wavers (hesitates, doubts) is like the billowing surge out at sea that is blown hither and thither and tossed by the wind. James 1:5, 6.

Learning to talk like Jesus

Thousands of years after the incident in Eden, when Satan tempted Jesus, using the identical technique he had used in the Garden, Jesus was not enticed, beguiled, deceived or manipulated into sin. He did not enter into discussion with the enemy at the devil's leading or on the devil's terms. Instead when He spoke, He declared only the Word of God; words that were imprinted in His heart and mind through His constant, focused communication with the Father in submission, prayer and study of the Scriptures

16. Every Scripture is God-breathed (given by His inspiration) and profitable for instruction, for reproof and conviction of sin, for correction of error and discipline in obedience, [and] for training in righteousness (in holy living, in conformity to God's will in thought, purpose, and action), 17. So that the man of God may be complete and proficient, well fitted and thoroughly equipped for every good work. . 2 Timothy 3:16, 17

By His response Jesus has supplied us with our template for the effective use of our "gift of the gab". As women we must learn from the mistake and failure of Mother Eve, and steadfastly follow, precisely, in the footsteps of Christ our Redeemer, who overcame with the right words, that is, with the righteous Word contained in the Scriptures. He was unassailable because He stood on the authority of the Scripture.

Jesus did not depend on His own intelligence, His own logic or His own opinions about any subject. He did not resort to pride, conceit or ego. Rather, with His Sword drawn He perfectly executed the movement, parry, thrust and technique of spiritual warfare which I quite simply call, **"It Is Written Technique"**. **Luke 4:3-12** details its perfect execution.

This technique enables us to resist temptation, overcome demonic opposition and put the devil to flight. The Sword of the Spirit which is the Word of God is a key weapon in our arsenal. The technique so deftly demonstrated by the Lord is essential to the warrior's skills base. Jesus is the Master Swordsman in the Kingdom and His Holy Spirit can train and equip us to accomplish even greater things than He did while on the earth in person. The point of introduction to this technique and its continuing development is the Word of God. The technique cannot be used in warfare unless the Word that is written is first learnt! **2 Timothy 2:14-15**

Unlike the First Mother, we cannot depend on our own understanding or take false pride in our own abilities, our intellect, our extensive vocabulary, logic and reasoning to battle with the enemy. **"Lean not to your own understanding..."** should be our guiding principle. **Proverbs 3:5**. We must depend only on that understanding which is **'past finding out'**, that is, God's divine directions, guidance, instructions and wisdom as declared in His Holy Scriptures and by the Holy Spirit.

God reveals true wisdom to those that diligently seek. Your past, your position, your parents, your patronage and your philosophy are all irrelevant to your call in Christ. Only the word of the Lord is wisdom.

19. For it is written, I will baffle and render useless and destroy the learning of the learned and the philosophy of the philosophers and the cleverness of the clever and the discernment of the discerning; I will frustrate and nullify [them and bring them] to nothing.

20. Where is the wise man (the philosopher)? Where is the scribe (the scholar)? Where is the investigator (the logician, the debater) of this present time and age? Has not God shown up the nonsense and the folly of this world's wisdom?

21. For when the world with all its earthly wisdom failed to perceive and recognize and know God by means of its own philosophy, God in His wisdom was pleased through the foolishness of preaching [salvation, procured by Christ and to be had through Him], to save those who believed (who clung to and trusted in and relied on Him).

22. For while Jews [demandingly] ask for signs and miracles and Greeks pursue philosophy and wisdom, 23. We preach Christ (the Messiah) crucified, [preaching which] to the Jews is a scandal and an offensive stumbling block [that springs a snare or trap], and to the Gentiles it is absurd and utterly un-philosophical nonsense.

24. But to those who are called, whether Jew or Greek (Gentile), Christ [is] the Power of God and the Wisdom of God.

25 This is because the foolish thing [that has its source in] God is wiser than men, and the weak thing [that springs] from God is stronger than men.

26. For [simply] consider your own call, brethren; not many [of you were considered to be] wise according to human estimates and standards, not many influential and powerful, not many of high and noble birth.

27. [No] for God selected (deliberately chose) what in the world is foolish to put the wise to shame, and what the world calls weak to put the strong to shame.

28. And God also selected (deliberately chose) what in the world is lowborn and insignificant and branded and treated with contempt, even the things that are nothing, that He might depose and bring to nothing the things that are,

29. So that no mortal man should [have pretense for glorying and] boast in the presence of God.

30. But it is from Him that you have your life in Christ Jesus, whom God made our Wisdom from God, revealed to us a knowledge of the divine plan of salvation previously hidden, manifesting itself as] our Righteousness

[thus making us upright and putting us in right standing with God], and our Consecration [making us pure and holy], and our Redemption [providing our ransom from eternal penalty for sin].

31. So then, as it is written, Let him who boasts and proudly rejoices and glories, boast and proudly rejoice and glory in the Lord. 1 Corinthians 1:19 – 31

A Father's Heart

Before we were born to our parents, God the Father already conceived us in every possible detail and had a plan for our lives. He decided our DNA, our genealogy, our generation and our special and natural gifts. For example, He even decided the number of hair on our heads and their color, our height and the timbre of our voice as well as our place of birth and the years of our lives. He stands by with love and joy when we are born into this world and gladly declares our potential destiny in His Kingdom. He remains, always, our Father, Abba.

That is the way it has always been and ever shall be. He is available from day one to shape and mold, to instruct and guide, to prepare and assign us to the purpose for which He determined our design. It is with Him that we have our first relationship; before we were in our mother's womb, He knew us! Revel in the joy that these Words written in **Psalms 139:1-18**, evoke in your spirit. Please read with me and be amazed, awed and awakened to your true identity in the Lord!

> O Lord, You have searched me and You know me.
> You know when I sit and when I rise; You perceive my thoughts from afar.
> You discern my going out and my lying down; You are familiar with all my ways.
> Before a word is on my tongue, you know it completely, O Lord.

You hem me in – behind and before; You have laid Your hand upon me.

Such knowledge is too wonderful for me, too lofty for me to attain.

Where can I go from Your Spirit? Where can I flee from Your Presence?

If I go up to the heavens You are there; if I make my bed in the depths, You are there.

If I rise on the wings of the dawn, if I settle on the far side of the sea,

Even there Your hand will guide me; Your right hand will hold me fast.

If I say "Surely the darkness will hide me and the light become night around me,"

Even the darkness will not be dark to You; the night will shine like the day, for darkness is as light to You.

For You created my inmost being; You knit me together in my mother's womb.

I praise you for I am fearfully and wonderfully made; Your works are wonderful, I know that full well.

My frame was not hidden from You when I was made in the secret place, when I was woven together in the depths of the earth,

Your eyes saw my unformed body. All the days ordained for me were written in Your book before one of them came to be.

How precious to me are Your thoughts O God! How vast is the sum of them!

Were I to count them, they would outnumber the grains of sand. When I awake, I am still with you".

This Psalm is such a revelation and a blessing. If ever I need reassurance this is the Scripture that reminds me most beautifully of my origin, my Source, my identity, my standing, worth and completeness in the Lord. My relationship with Him is an intimacy so perfect that it is unlike any other that I will ever be able to achieve in this life time! This is the birthright of every human being if we accept it in Christ Jesus. An intimate, unified relationship with our Father in heaven is always accessible; it is there just for the asking and most assuredly to all the daughters of Mother Eve. And all women, wherever in this world we might be located geographically, economically, socially, culturally or politically, are all daughters of Eve. **Acts 17:26** tells us

> **He (God) made from one [common origin, one source, one blood] all nations of men to settle on the face of the earth, having definitely determined [their] allotted periods of time and the fixed boundaries of their habitation (their settlements, lands and abodes).**

We can turn away from carnality, from our obsession with romantic love, the desires, needs and lusts of the flesh, self-centeredness and egotistical ambitions, from the worship of flawed gods and idols, from the institutionalized oppression of cultures, religion and politics, from rejection, rebellion and insubordination to the Orders of Jehovah God. **Romans 8:5-13**. Instead we can return to our beginning, to the way it was for Eve before the serpent and sin; to a right relationship with our Creator Father who has only plans of prosperity, purpose and perfection for all areas of our lives.

> **16. If we continually surrender ourselves to man and the desire for man, which desire is for carnality, then we become slaves to carnality and the things of the earthly realm, which leads only to death. 13. We must not offer either our physical body parts or our faculties to sin ... Romans 6:16, 13 (NIV)**

It would also be highly instructive for us to pause and carefully study what is written in **Ezekiel 23:1-49** and meditate on how it might be applied to our individual lives as women as well as to the nations on the earth! When we are concerned and consumed by the things that are valued and applauded by our communities, societies and the rulers of this world, all our attention, our interest, our thoughts, our energy, our conversations, actions and focus will be on things of a carnal, temporary, decaying nature that will eventually fade away. There will have been no purpose to our lives because we invested in dust and to dust it will all return.

19. Do not gather and heap up and store for yourselves treasures on earth, where moth and rust and worm consume and destroy, and where thieves break through and steal, 20. But gather and heap up and store for yourselves treasures in heaven, where neither moth nor rust nor worm consume and destroy, and where thieves do not break through and steal; 21. For where your treasure is, there will your heart be also. Matthew 6:19-21 (NIV)

Salvation lies in a paradigmatic shift in focus and a re-configuration of faith in the Father.

We can succeed in re-connecting to the Almighty through believing in the Christ and being saved, and we fulfill His purposes for our lives by accepting His commission to fight for the cause of a righteous Kingdom and a just and loving God.

17. For God did not send His Son into the world to condemn the world but to save the world through Him. 18. Whoever believes in Him is not condemned, but whoever does not believe stands condemned already because he has not believed in the name of God's only Begotten Son. John 3:17-19. (NIV)

There is therefore now no condemnation to them who are in Christ Jesus, who live and walk not after the dictates of the flesh but after the dictates of the Spirit. Romans 8:1. (NIV)

The woman at the well of Samaria abandoned the well that could only provide temporary distraction and limited, fleeting satisfaction. She re-established her God-focus through the Messiah, resumed her original, God-appointed position in the ranks of God's army and proceeded to fulfill her divine commission as a warrior. The obstacles that had been erected to derail her purpose and nullify her status in spiritual warfare were washed away in the Fountain-Head of the Living Water. It is only in the Lord that we can find our true purpose as determined by our Heavenly Father at our divine conception, before the beginning of time.

The woman at the well of Samaria was no longer on the "AWOL List"; she had oriented herself and found her true identity and a new vision; the vision that God had of her all along. She got her purpose lined up with her commission and committed herself to take up arms for the Lord in Operation Love, the spiritual battle for the salvation of fallen mankind. Redemption through Christ Jesus frees us from the bondage of sin, transforming us into **"servants of righteousness (of conformity to the divine will in thought, purpose and action)"**. **Romans 6:18**. The Scriptures continues in **Romans 8: 22-23,**

> **But now since you have been set free from sin and have become slaves of God, you have your present reward in holiness and its end is eternal life. For, the wages which sin pays, is death, but the [bountiful] free gift of God is eternal life through (in union with) Jesus Christ our Lord.**

We are not so different to the woman that Jesus met at the well in Samaria that fateful day. Just like her, we are faced with many distractions that can distort our true image of ourselves. When we look in the mirror of our souls we see only a reflection of what our circumstances, society and religion tell us that we are, rather than the potential warriors of a Divine Deity. But God who knows all things determined that we would be effective opponents against the enemy; that old deceptive, evil serpent that invaded our homes, hearts and minds to the detriment of our standing in God's Kingdom.

Carnality is a weapon of destruction that is aimed at our physical and spiritual well being; our hearts, minds, body and spirit. Consecrating our lives, every single aspect of it to Christ is the only way to be cleansed from the stain of sin, freed from the evil vice of Satan. Under the authority of the Christ, Commander-In-Chief of God's Army, we must bring warfare to the devil; challenging, opposing and destroying his diabolical subversion and treason against the Kingdom of God.

CHAPTER 11

EMPTY WOMBS AND OPEN ARMS.

A Life without Purpose

Hannah was a woman very much loved by her husband Elkanah. In fact, the love he had for her was a source of jealousy to his second wife, Peninnah. He showed his love in every possible way and with every opportunity. He was a priest and whenever he went up to make the offerings, he gave Hannah a double portion of the best meats. This point is worth mentioning in view of the fact that Peninnah had children but Hannah did not. One might assume that given the societal values of the day, the favor would have flowed in reverse order. **1 Samuel 1:4, 5.**

Despite the obvious short-coming of apparent barrenness, negatively regarded in many communities even today, Hannah received the best of everything including an abundance of love and attention from her husband. Quite simply he was devoted to her. For many women, having a doting, devoted husband might have been enough, but not for Hannah. Her womb had never been filled with a promise, a dream, and a destiny either physically or spiritually. Her arms were wide open to hold and cradle love's reward but she remained barren according to God's design.

Hannah's husband was much puzzled that she could not get pass her one source of discontent, children. He made it plain to her and to everyone else that despite her inability to bear him offspring; she was still a much desired and specially loved woman. Let us not forget that in such societies the value of a woman was primarily her child bearing, child rearing potential, ability and skills. Usually it was this accomplishment that would ensure the husband's honor; children were a symbol of his favor, blessings and prosperity. Hannah undoubtedly knew how much she was loved and fortunate not to be despised or discarded by her spouse.

In fact, the Scriptures tell us that Elkanah asked her, no doubt rather frustratingly or plaintively, **"Am I not more to you than ten sons?' 1 Samuel 1:8.** He must have been peeved, a little disappointed that she was not completed by his love for her. It is not hard to imagine that his re-assurances to Hannah went along the following lines:

"I don't mind that we have no children. I love you for you. It might even be a blessing in disguise. Since we have no children, we will just devout all our attention to each other!"

As Hannah listened to his words, she still could not deny the ache that continued to plague her heart. Her inner being would cry out in anguish, strain against the confines of a love that did not fulfill her deepest longings. Hannah spent years crying, praying to the Lord to remedy her problem. She reasoned that if she had a child then her feeling of emptiness would vanish. The taunts of her sister-wife only served to enhance her sorrow, her desire and her desperation. Peninnah's jealousy never abated and she used every chance she got to heap derision and insults on Hannah. But this persecution by Peninnah was the very fuel that drove Hannah to her place of brokenness and into the Presence and ultimately the will of God. Hannah's experience perfectly illustrates the teaching contained **in James 1:2-4**

2. Consider it wholly joyful, my brethren, whenever you are enveloped in or encounter trials of any sort or fall into various temptations. 3. Be assured and understand that

the trial and proving of your faith bring out endurance and steadfastness and patience. 4. But let endurance and steadfastness and patience have full play and do a thorough work, so that you may be [people] perfectly and fully developed [with no defects], lacking in nothing.

Peninnah validated her own worth and showed her insecurity by degrading, belittling, hurtful taunts, comments and spiteful treatment towards Hannah. Peninnah exulted in the inability of Hannah to bear children, to the max! Her words were the darts and arrows of the enemy seeking to undermine Hannah's faith and pervert the course of destiny that was determined by the Lord for her life.

But God the Father had a plan for Hannah. It was He that shut up her womb. His handmaiden was destined to be the mother of a great Prophet who would usher in a new era in the affairs of His people, the Children of Israel. This task required godly fortitude and spiritual muscle power that could only be achieved through the trial and testing, suffering and disdain, the patience and perseverance, the faith and focus that would be the fruits of Hannah's testing, painful experience.

For Hannah to be able to serve the Lord in the way that was necessary to her appointment, her God-vision needed to be clarified, sharpened and focused. A desire for her husband, community applauds and worldly recognition or even a 'slap in the mouth' for Peninnah the jealous persecutor was not the right reason for Hannah to pray for a child. Rather, she needed to be yielded to the purpose of God for her life. Her ego must be subjected to His plan and total trust and faith in His love must be fully embraced. Unless Hannah was able to fight her way through her pain, shame and distractions, she would never fulfill her divinely ordained destiny.

Hannah was a God-fearing, prayer and fasting kind of woman. She had spent year after year in supplication for a child. Undoubtedly, it was the Lord God who had given her the desire for a child even though He closed her womb to allow the process and the pressure to create in her a steadfast commitment to submit to His designs. Finally her yearning led to her yielding. **Philippians 4:6.** I can see

Hannah constantly and persistently praying and petitioning the Lord with words that initially went along the following lines;

"Please Heavenly Father, give me a child so that my arms can be filed with joy and my husband can be proud of me".

"Make me a mother so that everyone can see I am a real woman'.

"Lord, hear my prayer so that I can shut Peninnah up!

I am certain that she often felt discouraged but she never gave up. She kept on talking to the Lord and expecting a breakthrough. She must have exhausted herself many times over; reasoning with God, making promises, reminding Him of His faithfulness to Sarah in her old age, to Rachel, and now here she was asking Him for personal and public deliverance. But the desire that Hannah had for a child was the vehicle of her soul's salvation. She could not shake it, postpone it, deny it or ignore it. She kept on pressing toward the mark, pushing against the brick wall of self promotion, self interest and pride. Finally, something changed inside her as the Spirit of the Lord worked to perfect her for her purpose. The selfish desire of her earlier prayer life became solely a desire to please God.

It is the will of the Father to train us, correct and discipline us, molding our characters so that we are able to fulfill the purpose He has ordained for us. He does this by allowing us to go through challenging experiences and to face difficult obstacles that we can overcome only by reliance on Him and His mercies. **Hebrews 12:5-7, 10.** But He only allows these experiences to enable us to share in His holiness and more than that, He never allows us to face challenges and temptations above our ability to bear except He first prepares a way of escape for us.

Finally, Hannah's persecution birthed a prayer life that positioned her for personal transformation and spiritual transition. The time she had spent in tears, in prayer and supplication to God had allowed the Spirit of God to work a change that took away her pride and conceit, gifted her a new heart and a right spirit. The need for personal vindication, societal status and standing to determine or proclaim her worth and her identity that had consumed Hannah for so long, faded away. Unknown to Hannah, there was a higher power at work in her spirit. During the years of her suffering and her longing for the Lord's intervention in her affairs, she had attained a higher level of revelation in the Spirit realm than she ever had imagined. The tears and the heartache sown in the natural had been translated to the Father by the Holy Spirit and grown a harvest of godly humility and submission in the spiritual.

Spiritual Alignment with God's Plan

Hannah cried out to God, fully surrendering all that she was or ever would be to Him. Her whole attitude, her approach and her vision changed and were now conformed to the will of God. Her prayer now was to fulfill His purpose in her life and as the Holy Spirit gave her the right words to pray, she surrendered to God the very thing she had labored for in the physical and in the spiritual plane, the thing that she prized and sought most, she now surrendered to Him. **Job 5:6-27.**

God's agenda became Hannah's agenda, His will became her joy. She was finally in 'sync' with the Divine. The walls of her Jericho went tumbling down. Hannah had the answer to her husband's question as to his sufficiency and the sufficiency of his favors and material provisions. She finally felt completed when she stepped into a relationship with God that took precedence over the desires of self and made His service the top priority in her life.

Hannah had made the breakthrough from one level to another in the spiritual realm. She tuned into the Holy Spirit frequency and was finally able to receive her assignment, her commission, her divine appointment. I believe that Hannah reached a place in God of total submission and could therefore accept whatever He decreed for her destiny. If she was blessed with a child so be it, if not God would still be her God and she would live in the certain knowledge and joy that He was the true Source of all her desires and the Supplier of all her needs.

As I said earlier, God never gives us an appointment without His anointing. The High Priest Eli, unaware of God's plan for him that day, was nevertheless at hand to witness Hannah's graduation from a self-obsessed, self-seeking, needing-a-child-to-shut-up-Peninnah, kind of woman, to a God-focused, broken, submitted, purpose oriented daughter of the Divine. Eli did not know how long she had been in the race and how her weakness was even then being made her strength in the Lord. But all things work together for good to those that are called according to God's purpose. **Romans 8:28**

Hannah had just received her 'higher calling' from the Creator God. The High Priest, Eli, was there to bestow the Lord's blessing; the extra portion of the anointing of the Holy Spirit that Hannah needed to carry out her assignment. **"The blessings of the Lord maketh rich" Proverbs 10:22 (KJV).** Eli's blessing on Hannah was spoken after the manner of the blessing that Melchisedek pronounced upon Abram. (See **Genesis 14**) Hannah's sacrifice of tears and submission by faith to the will of God was witnessed by the High Priest; her covenant with the Father was duly executed.

My heart just swells up with joy and my spirit magnifies the Lord when I consider this; Hannah immediately knew that her breakthrough had taken place. She had tarried and the Lord now blessed His handmaiden with that 'extra something' needed for the fulfillment of His plan. His blessing was the anointing, the anointing was her empowerment for her assignment; the enablement and ability to bring forth and dedicate to God the last ruling prophet of the Children of Israel. Hannah went on her way, no longer distraught but full of the glow of the Lord's glorious Shekinah, rejoicing all the way home, by faith having already secured her answer. Her desire was fully aligned with the will of God and now her destiny waited.

The darkness, depression and desperation that for so long exemplified her demeanor, was gone. Her tears had all been wiped away; her night was turned into day, her ashes to beauty, and her misery to laughter. She had received her miracle; true intimacy and union and shared purpose with the Father. The pregnancy that came later was merely the physical realization of the move of God that had exploded in her spirit at the temple. **1 Samuel 1:18**

When we line ourselves up with God's plan, there is no need for us to worry. It is only a matter of time in the physical realm. The thing that God has destined for us is already accomplished in the spiritual. Our faith makes the unseen not a future state of being but our present reality. And it is this same faith that is counted to us for righteousness. Read **Hebrews 11.** Hannah's restored communion with God was evidenced by the birth of her son Samuel whose name means "heard of God". He was a living testimony and a witness to all the people of the mercy, the grace, the faithfulness and the glory of the Lord Jehovah to his faithful servants.

A Prophet Consecrated in God's Season

The mother of Samuel kept faith with God. She took Samuel to Eli the High Priest as an offering of first fruit to Jehovah Jireh; promised, dedicated and consecrated to the Lord Most Gracious. **1 Samuel 2:1-10,** records the worship which followed Hannah's honoring of her covenant with the Lord. She re-iterates and acknowledges the rightful place, position and standing of God in her relationship and rejoices in His favor. Notice how **verse 10** is mirrored in the exaltation of Mary, the mother of the Christ. Hannah had finally got it right with God. Her obedience was not predicated on future rewards or spousal satisfaction but only on the Lordship of God in her life.

Hannah's son Samuel was the last great Prophet and Judge in Israel prior to their rejection of theocracy in preference to monarchical rule. The biblical books of First and Second Samuel tells us all we need to know of how mightily Samuel was used of the Lord. He was dedicated before his conception by a mother who had succeeded in getting her priorities right with God by His grace only. The Scriptures also tells us that Hannah's marriage was blessed with five more children and we may infer that her relationship with her husband no longer suffered lack because God had been restored to His perfect, proper place within their union.

Fertile and Fit for the Purpose

The empty womb of a woman whether in the physical or the spiritual, is a potentially fertile space waiting for the seeds of a godly harvest to be planted despite appearances in the physical world. Such a harvest will bring glory and honor to the Lord of the

Harvest. God's ways are mysterious but if we surrender to Him, He will cause a harvest beyond our wildest imaginings so that we do not have enough room to receive it. **Malachi 3:10**

The Father waits with open arms to welcome us into His divine Presence where we can receive fulfillment, completion and total satisfaction through unadulterated, unconditional love and intimacy in reverential worship, obedience and submission to His purpose, plans and port folio for our lives. We were all created to serve the Lord in love and to manifest the glory of His image and the likeness of His character by emulation of His Beloved, Begotten Firstborn, and our older brother.

Sometimes we might be unable to bear children in the natural but that has no relation to our ability to be mothers, especially in the spiritual realm. We can birth spiritual offspring by faith and obedience. Is your heart and mind a fertile and fit environment for a spiritual impregnation? We have established the way to a new heart from God that is truly the heart of God! But, what about the state of man's mind, that is his thoughts, his will and divine duty? An un-regenerated mind must be conformed to God if we would serve the Kingdom. The following Scriptures are the Lord's directions on renewing a right mind within.

> **Do not be conformed to this world (this age), [fashioned after and adapted to its external, superficial customs], but be transformed (changed) by the [entire] renewal of your mind [by its new ideals and its new attitude], so that you may prove [for yourselves] what is the good and acceptable and perfect will of God, even the thing which is good and acceptable and perfect [in His sight for you]. Romans 12:2**

> **But we have the mind of Christ (the Messiah) and do hold the thoughts (feelings and purpose) of His heart. 1 Corinthians 2:16**

> **For the rest, brethren, whatever is true, whatever is worthy of reverence and is honorable and seemly, what-**

ever is just, whatever is pure, whatever is lovely and lovable, whatever is kind and winsome and gracious, if there is any virtue and excellence, if there is anything worthy of praise, think on and weigh and take account of these things [fix your minds on them]. Philippians 4:8

Blessed (happy, fortunate, prosperous, and enviable) is the man who walks and lives not in the counsel of the ungodly [following their advice, their plans and purposes]. Nor stands [submissive and inactive] in the path where sinners walk, or sits down [to relax and rest] where the scornful (and the mockers) gather. 2. But his delight is in the law of the Lord, and on His law (the precepts, the instructions, the teachings of God) he habitually meditates (ponders and studies) by day and by night. Psalms 1:1, 2

For the weapons of our warfare are not physical [weapons of flesh and blood] but they are mighty before God for the overthrow of strongholds. 5. Inasmuch as we] refute arguments and theories and reasoning and every proud and lofty thing that sets itself up against the [true] knowledge of God; and we lead every thought and purpose away captive into the disobedience of Christ (the Messiah, the anointed One). 11 Corinthians 10:4, 5.

Hannah's life story exemplified the 'wonder working power' of God's calling and His anointing in the life of those that hear His voice, focus on Him exclusively and rest their destinies in His hands. She began to petition God with her own agenda and ended up glorifying Him when she brought her desires, her thoughts and her purpose into subjection to His plan for her life. At that point, when His will became hers, she experienced the fullness of a life that belongs to the Lord's anointed. Hannah's patient perseverance in seeking the Lord was rewarded by a loving Father, who always attends to the cries of His children that seek Him with all their hearts. **Jeremiah 29:11.**

It is stated in the Scriptures by the Lord, that He will never turn away any of us that seek Him with our whole heart, mind, body and strength but instead He will bless us abundantly.

If My people who are called by my name will humble themselves and pray and seek my face and turn from their wicked ways, then will I hear from heaven and will forgive their sin and will heal their land. 2 Chronicles 7:14.

Hannah's Prayer Life

The following notes are a summary of Hannah' prayer life that holds very important lessons from which we can all benefit –

1. Hannah went to the Temple in order to find a consecrated, quiet place in the Presence of God. Remember, Eli the High priest saw her by herself. She had separated herself from everyone around her; the family, her husband and other worshippers so that she could be alone with her Lord.

   This kind of isolation allowed her to fully focus on the Lord and to give herself over to her communion with God. Hannah needed to **'dwell, abide, be fully present in the secret place of the Most High"** so that her thoughts, her heart, her fullest concentration would be on/with the Father. **Psalms 91:1**. In this act of separation to God and from the world, Hannah demonstrated her complete surrender.

2. Hannah expressed her adoration and praise to God; **"Hallowed be thy name"** ... **Matthew 6:9, "for there is none like You"** ...Who sees and knows all and is alone worthy of all our praise. **Psalms 95:1-7.**

3. Hannah made her confession to God. In so doing, we acknowledge our sinful natures and agree with God as to the

effect of sin in our lives. As a result of this act of confession and contrition our Lord is able to forgive us, remake us in His image spiritually and bestow His blessings upon our lives. This forgiveness that the Lord gives is our 'Freedom Pass' from the bondage of sin and its consequences.

4. It is the delight and the will of God and the duty of grateful hearts that we give thanks in all things to our Heavenly Father. **1 Thessalonians 5:16-18.** Hannah recognized this truth and so despite her sadness and her pain she nevertheless offered the sacrifice of praise which the Lord is happy to receive from His people. **Hebrews 13:15 and Psalms 51.**

5. It is the will of God that we should seek His purposes and desires for our lives with all our hearts, minds and bodies. This is how we make our supplications known to the Lord. **Philippians 4:6.** If we diligently search for Him then we shall find Him. To find Him is to embrace Him and thereby His plan for our lives.

6. Our heavenly Father implores us to make our requests and petitions known to Him. And by His grace He grants us the desires of submitted hearts. Therefore our prayers should be specific, Spirit directed, intentional and in-keeping with the will of God for our lives. **Romans 8:26**

7. Vague petitions will not bring the desired results. We must state clearly what it is that we are asking of the Lord just as Hannah did in her prayers. We must also refer to the promises and the Scriptures upon which we ground our prayers and our hope. In this way we can be sure that the Lord will hear us and give us what we have asked of Him. **1 John 5:14-15.** God will never fail to keep His word. **Numbers 23:19.** Heaven and earth will pass away before our God dishonors His promises or His covenant with His people.

8. We must rest upon the promises of God. **Matthew 20:32**. Jesus always gave people the chance to tell Him what they wanted from Him. He did not assume what their greatest need or desire might be. Hannah was very precise as to what she wanted the Lord to do for her. As a child of God we have a legally, divinely ordained right to petition the Almighty in the name of our Lord Jesus and to know that the Father will hear us by reason of the name of the Savior.

9. There is no point praying if we do not have a belief in His will to answer our prayers. The Scriptures tells us that whatever we ask in prayer, we will receive it. **Mark 11:24**. If then we truly believe that He will give us what we pray for then we must persevere in prayer until we get our answer. **Daniel 10:10-14**. Hannah did not give up after the first year of prayer but she continued to ask God to grant her the desire of her heart. Perseverance in prayer prepares us for the pursuit of purpose in Christ Jesus.

10. After presenting our requests to the Lord we should remember to give thanks for His response whatever that may be. If we truly believe that He stands by His Word we do not need to wait to give Him thanks but in all things and at all times express our gratitude and our praise.

11. Take action based on the anticipated answer to your prayer. In other words, step out in faith, make room for your answer and expect God's blessing to flow into your life. **Ephesians 3:20** tells us that not only does He give us what we have asked for but even more than we could possibly imagine.

Hannah went away after her prayer with a spirit of happiness and rejoicing, fully confident that her prayer was answered. Indeed it was. **Matthew 9:29**. Not only did she give birth to a son, Samuel, she was blessed with five other children besides him. Truly, her cup ran over and she found herself living in the overflow of God's mercies and His love.

Hannah's life is a perfect illustration of the positive difference that the desires of a heart submitted to God can achieve for His Kingdom. Hannah was a warrior whose life was primarily afflicted and persecuted through the medium of Peninnah. She also had to confront her own pride, fear, selfishness and ego. It is necessary that we first crucify self before we can be wholly God's and available for His service.

The character of a warrior is developed through such things as prayer, perseverance, faith, endurance, and a covenant commitment to the Lord. As women of God we are called into a covenant relationship that requires the qualities and strength of a seasoned worshipper to fit us for the purpose of spiritual warfare. We cannot be His warriors without being His true worshippers. There are rewards from God both in this life and the life to come when we consecrate ourselves to His service, in Christ Jesus.

CHAPTER 12

FAITH, FOCUS AND VISION

Twenty-Twenty Vision

To focus refers to issues of vision. It refers to what one sees in the physical and also what one sees spiritually. In other words, it is that thing, person, object or subject matter upon which one fixes or centers one's attention; devoting one's time, energies and efforts. Being focused is to be single-minded, a state which is preferable and profitable to the believer and to the Lord. **James 1:6-8**

God-focus is to catch God's vision and to persevere against all odds to fulfill it; to be patient, to endure, to hold fast regardless of what may be done or said by others. God-focus is to set one's affections upon God and the worship of God alone. To run with patience and not be weary, to fight but not faint, that is God-focus. To pray without ceasing; to run the race with patience; to endure is God-focus.

God-focus is to be still and know that God is God and there is none like Him. **Isaiah 6:10.** God-focus is walking **"through the valley of the shadow of death"** without fear. **Psalms 23**. To spend the night in the lion's den, knowing joy comes in the morning. God-focus is going into the fiery furnace and still come out smelling like roses, purified and liberated, spiritually and physically unbound!

God-focus is being prepared and determined to fulfill God's plan with fore-knowledge and faith, saying **"if I die, I die"**. God-focus is having your lamp trimmed and filled with oil but still making sure that you are carrying extra in case the Bridegroom is delayed. God-focus is living in agreement with Him on all issues determined by Him. It is living in the overflow of His abundance; abundant mercy, abundant grace, abundant love, abundant provisions, abundant anointing and an abundance of His blessings all round.

Without God-focus, you cannot exercise faith and **"without faith it is impossible to please God". Hebrews 11:6**. Without God-focus there is no God-love, for to love God is to give the fullest attention to everything that touches or relates to the Person and Kingdom of God. Loving God works obedience in the spirit, body and soul; hearing and doing the will of the Lord regardless of the storms of life that rages about us, despite the temptations of the devil to distract, in spite of the pull of the temporary treasures and pleasures of carnality and regardless of the risk to limb and life. God-focus is to remain fixed on the infinite, unconditional love and favor of God Most High. God-faith is God-focus in action. God-love is God-focus in production.

A God-Focused Life

In the Bible, we read that Mary Magdalene would sit at the feet of Jesus all day long. Even when it was that time of day when the women of the house generally got busy cleaning, cooking and undertaking household tasks that satisfy the needs of the flesh, Mary would still be sitting at the feet of the Teacher; Rabboni. She was hungry and thirsty for the things of the Spirit far more than she was concerned with the physical needs of the body.

The Magdalene was God-focused and so her thoughts, emotions, will and actions were secondary to her worship and held in subjection to the Word and will of God. There are important matters of everyday life that demands our efforts and attention but the needs of the flesh must be made subject to the necessity of spending time in the Presence of the Lord and the direction determined by His Holy

Spirit. Again Jesus the Christ is our example and His words and actions were only those that His Father instructed.

> **So Jesus answered them by saying, I assure you, most solemnly I tell you, the Son is able to do nothing of Himself (of His own accord); but He is able to do only what He sees the Father doing, for whatever the Father does is what the Son does in the same way [in His turn]. 20. The Father dearly loves the Son and discloses to (shows) Him everything that He Himself does. And He will disclose to Him (let Him see) greater things yet than these, so that you may marvel and be full of wonder and astonishment. John 5:19, 20; 8:28, 29**

> **So Jesus added, When you have lifted up the Son of Man [on the cross], you will realize (know, understand) that I am He [for Whom you look] and that I do nothing of Myself (of My own accord or on My own authority), but I say [exactly] what My Father has taught Me. 29. And He Who sent Me is ever with Me; My Father has not left Me alone, for I always do what pleases Him. John 8:28-29**

Mary had a God-focus which translated into a '**hunger and a thirst after His righteousness**'. **Matthew 5:6.** Likewise, when we get God-focused, everything and everyone in our hearts and minds, falls into alignment with His will. Idolatry is having tangibles or intangibles occupy, absorb and swallow up that space, that first place in one's life that belongs only to God. The Prophet Ezekiel warns us against **"the idols of the heart" Ezekiel 14:3** and Jehovah commands us **"Thou shall have no other God before me". Exodus 20:3-6**

I often find that our home-making duties, job or career, socializing and or fellowshipping, volunteering and all such activities that fill our minds and our time can actually serve to diminish or deplete the time given to God. For the child of God, the activities that consume our energies may actually be church related and neighborly motivated, yet they leave little if any time for us to focus and devout time to the Word and the will of God. We are so busy trying to prove ourselves worthy of the title "Christian" that we do not hear the Lord telling us that our worth is demonstrated by His sacrifice and all our self-directed actions cannot gain us a place in His Kingdom. **Titus 3:4-7**

We must take time out of our day to just sit at the feet of the Lord, be in His Presence, to be instructed, to listen and learn of, and from Him and spend time in reverential worship, communion, listening and waiting; praise, thanks-giving, prayer, intercession, study of the Word and so on, all according to the prompting, direction and guidance of the Holy Spirit. It is in these periods that we are able to learn from the Lord exactly what His plan is for our daily lives so that we may grow in godly knowledge and spiritual maturity in the Lord.

Whoever speaks, [let him do it as one who utters] oracles of God; whoever renders service, [let him do it] as with the strength which God furnishes abundantly, so that in all things God may be glorified through Jesus Christ (The Messiah). 1 Peter 4:11

Mary had a different perspective on things than her sister. Martha was steamed at Mary because she did not share the same priorities. Martha's choice was her own to make and she did. Yet she felt that Mary should have been similarly occupied as she was, placing the same emphasis as she did on the requirements of the physical body. Martha operated according to what was expected of her by her society, family, friends and even herself. Sometimes our expectations and demands on our self is the heaviest burden that we bear.

Don't get me wrong, the jobs or chores that Martha was occupied with were important.

And so are many of the things that take up a lot of our attention. But, none of these things should ever take precedence over our worship, over the pre-eminence and the prominence of seeking divine direction in our daily living. We might even find that our brethren in Christ have their own ideas of how we should serve the Lord and will frown on any variation in the traditional, customary or accepted ways of service. But their views, opinions or decisions should not be the sole determinant of our service although we must be careful not to cause unnecessary hurt or offense, speaking always in the love of Christ. After all, when the Savior promised to send the Holy Spirit, He declared that the Holy Spirit would guide us into all truth.

Ask your spiritual leaders to pray with you about your divinely inspired assignment, and be especially careful to be submissive to the revealed will of God in your life; it is His will first and foremost that matters. We are all uniquely created, individually gifted and personally called to serve as members of the Body of Christ. Paul implores us to pray without ceasing and we are admonished to do all things as unto the Lord. So even in the midst of all our living activities God must be the focus, motivation, reason, result and delight of our engagements and activities at all times; each breath that we breathe, every thought, word, or deed must be one of worship, obedience and purpose in Christ. **Ecclesiastes 12:13, 14**

Setting your Priorities

Martha was serving the Lord. She was occupied in preparing for the physical needs of the Lord and His disciples who were guests in her home. She must have been extremely busy and would have no doubt benefited from some extra help from her sister. Was this her only reason for complaining to the Lord about her sister's behavior? **Luke 10:40**

The fact that she expressed herself in a seemingly churlish, petulant and finger-pointing manner would seem to indicate the presence of a negative attitude or emotion. Did Martha find joy in her duties? Was she not worshipping the Lord through the joy she had in carrying out her hospitality? Perhaps her complaint therefore manifested an absence of joy in her tasks and revealed an attitude to service that could deny her the blessings that were hers. For was she aware that in all things that we do, we are serving the Lord?

Mary had chosen to set different priorities to her sister while Jesus was around. Her vision was fixed on the things of God, on the things of the spiritual realm that leads to everlasting life. Her eyes, that is, her mind and heart were so filled with the desire to learn from the Lord that she could not be concerned or distracted by the hustle, bustle and demands on the household that the presence of guests required. **Luke 10:41, 42**

Mary was not selfish or thoughtless as it appeared to her sister but she had taken to heart the words of the Redeemer **"Seek ye first the Kingdom of God and His righteousness and all things shall be added unto you". Matthew 6:33.** She was not unmindful of physical needs and the necessity of hospitality but she recognized a unique opportunity to learn at the Master's feet and grabbed her chance. The Lord was not always with them! So she seized upon the thing that was the desire of her heart and in so doing put God first.

We all need to have some Mary discernment and attitude in us even if we also have some Martha conviction and mentality of service provided we take delight in that calling. The purpose of our life and all its pursuits must be worship and we do this by coming into personal relationship with the Lord. Even if we are busy serving in the Body of Christ, our service must not be the end but only the means by which we show and share our love of the Eternal One.

It is no surprise to find Mary with the Christ all during His ministry. **Luke 8:2.** She was there at His trial, His crucifixion and His death. **Matthew 27:55, 56.** I will look at these events in more detail later. But the point I want to emphasize here is that we see the outcome and the full maturity of the time that Mary invested in seeking and listening to the Lord, graphically demonstrated on Resurrection Morning. The seed that was sown in her heart grew into a passionate pursuit, promotion and publication of the revealed will and plan of the Lord Jesus.

The disciples and all the other followers of our Lord Jesus were distraught, uncomprehending, deflated and in despair. The Lord had been put to death by the authorities. Their hopes of messianic rule had died with Him on Calvary's Mount. They were confused, unsure of what came next, like sheep without a shepherd. Mary too was a devoted follower of the Christ. She had spent most of her time listening, learning and pondering the Words of the Lord in her heart.

Mary was uncertain as to the manner in which her Lord would manifest His triumph but she knew that He would, despite the way that things appeared to the natural eye. She had witnessed the many miracles that He had performed. Her own brother had been called from the grave after being dead for four days. As difficult as it was to see the Christ hung so disgracefully on the despised Roman cross, she had a hope in her heart that this business of Jesus as the Messiah was not yet over. She had stored up His teachings in her heart and He had said He was **"The Resurrection and the Life"**, a truth which He not only taught but showed in her Brother Lazarus' case. **John 11:25**

There were many things that were unclear to Mary but there was one thing of which she was absolutely certain; she needed to be near to the Lord, to abide in His Presence, regardless. She knew that if there was a place to be in troubled times, it was next to Jesus. She had proven Him to be a Refuge and a Fortress, a Shield and a Strong Tower. His words spoke life to her soul and despite the look of things in the natural; Mary discerned in her spirit that things were not what they seemed. She knew that Jesus, the Christ was about far more than physical appearance.

The seeds planted in her spirit by the Master were growing. It is impossible to have the Word in your spirit and it fails to bear fruit and increase your faith crop unless the enemy is allowed to come in and spoil the crop with His evil tricks of contamination, pollution and suffocation of the faith-seed. Faith comes by hearing the Word of God and faith as small as a mustard seed can move mountains including mountains of obstacles, doubt, problems and pain. The Word is life and the 'seed- word' has within it an indestructible, regenerative essence; the Word of God is productive and when planted in fertile soil and kept well-watered, will produce a bumper crop for personal salvation.

I am led to believe that there was a 'quickening' in Mary Magdalene that held the promise of a new beginning, a change that was about to overtake the world and the way it related to Jehovah God. If I might be so bold as to declare Mary Magdalene was experiencing that 'certain feeling' that many women often have; a sixth sense if you like, an instinct that tells us there is more to a matter than meets the eye; whether in the physical or in the spiritual. Often times I express it as the, "I can't quite put my finger on it, but, feeling". But what it really amounts to is a prompting of the Spirit of God.

Mary would not, could not make herself stay away from the tomb of Jesus. Even when she discovered it was empty, she could not walk away or give up on that feeling inside that said something was happening with her Lord and she just had to get closer to Him, wherever they might have laid His body. There had been many occasions when she had gone to Jesus with her questing, searching heart and He had always filled her with truth. Now, even when faced with an empty tomb, Mary tarried in communion with the Lord. Her faith was like that of God's women who when they come up against the physical reality of barrenness, continue to believe God for a birthing celebration

I believe that as Mary wept and waited, she prayed ceaselessly; her pain the very thing that would birth her purpose. Jesus had taught His disciples to pray; after all, He is the foremost practitioner of prayer. She had been storing up His teachings in her heart and this was a most opportune time to put them into practice; this was the first major test of her faith in the power of prayer. So I am led to believe that Mary prayed as she tarried outside the tomb of the Lord

Seed-time and Harvest

Mary is an excellent example to us all. We must learn from her behavior and the attitude she displayed in the deperarately difficult and sad circumstances that she was experiencing. When we come face to face with an empty tomb, a barren womb, a lonely bed, a dead end, a place of distress, dejection or defeat, we need to pray, weep and wait on the Lord. When we find ourselves at a graveside facing a dead situation, we don't have to wonder what is next.

We have Mary's persistence to guide us and Jesus' miracle to reassure us. He too wept at the tomb of Lazarus just before performing one of the greatest miracles that has been manifested in the earth realm. We need to realize that it is time to get ready; prepare ourselves for a revelation and a resurrection. This is the moment in time when we need to turn our total focus on God the Father. Such a situation is the perfect and proper season for prayer and fasting; for waiting, being still, and standing securely on the promises of God and then, having done all, to "just stand".

Putting all our trust and faith in the ability of the Lord to bring about His divine purpose is the cornerstone of a Christ-centered relationship. Look closely at the women in the Scriptures such as Sarah, Leah, Hannah, Ruth or Elizabeth; then look around at the women of God about you such as the sister that always finds something to praise the Lord about. We must take the experience and the lessons of travail and labor in the natural realm and apply them equally to our labors and battles in the Spirit realm.

29. He (God) gives power to the faint and weary, and to him who has might He increases strength [causing it to multiply and making it abound].

30. Even youths shall faint and be weary, and [selected] young men shall feebly stumble and fall exhausted;

31. But those who wait for the Lord [who expect, look for and hope in Him] shall change and renew their strength and power; they shall lift their wings and mount up [close to God] as eagles [mount up to the sun]; they shall run and not be weary, they shall walk and not faint or become tired. Isaiah 40:29 -

Now back to Mary. She had a God focused, Christ-centered relationship with her Savior and she was not prepared to let a little thing like a tomb, even an empty one impede her vision and destroy her faith in the Messiah, the Savior of mankind.

"Let me know where you have placed Him", she implored. What she was really saying is;

"I need to be near Him, to be in His Presence wherever that might be".

We can only imagine how Mary's heart must have soared when the voice of the Christ finally registered through her pain and her prayer-filled mind and she heard Him gently and lovingly say, **"Mary"**! Mark 16:9. I wonder how many times the Risen Lord said her name before she heard Him? Sometimes, when we are distressed and distraught we do not hear the Lord as He gently calls our name. Sometimes we forget that He knows our name and so we are not expecting, not listening and we do not hear. But God is patient and He will persist until He gets our attention.

My sheep hear my voice, and I know them, and they follow Me: And I give unto them eternal life; and they shall never perish, neither shall any man pluck them out of My hand. My Father which gave them to Me is greater than all; and no man is able to pluck them out of My Father's hand. I and My Father are one. John 10:27-30

Consider how the seeds, the Words of Jesus sown into Mary's heart had so taken root that they transformed her approach, her perspective and her focus so totally that even with the absence of a living Christ in the flesh, she did not loose her faith in God. The effect of knowing and believing in the power of the Word prompted her spirit and propelled her into action. As soon as the Sabbath was over, she hurried to the place where last she saw her Lord. She hastened to be near Him. Not even the sight of His bruised, battered and lifeless body was enough to discourage, dissuade or deter her. He was her Lord and she was not defeated by what her physical eyes could see. Rather, I believe that Mary was motivated, activated, and spurred on by what she saw through the eyes of faith, fuelled by the Words of life spoken by Jesus. She also had personal experience of His miracles in healing, restoring life and renewing hearts and minds for Kingdom citizenry.

It was Mary's gift to be the first of the Lord's followers to see Him after His resurrection. She had refused to be distracted by the pain and the loss that resulted from Jesus' crucifixion, to be ambushed by the despondency or disappointment of the disciples at the death of their dream of Messianic rule; a vision limited to triumph in the natural world, ruling an earthly kingdom of Israel with Jesus. Even the sight of an empty tomb did not deter her search for His Presence. She tearfully inquired for His whereabouts so that wherever they had taken Him she could make her way there also! Her perseverance was justly rewarded. **John 20:11-17**

Her great desire had not diminished even in the face of seemingly insurmountable odds. Sometimes, like Mary, we have to stand vigil outside the empty tomb and wait for our change, our deliverance, our breakthrough to manifest. Sometimes the very place where all our hopes and dreams lie buried, dead to all intents and purposes, sometimes that is the very place that resurrection is going to take place, the very location that our phoenix is going to rise from the ashes of despair and declare the might and glory of our God. That tomb is the very place that will give birth to a new beginning, a new life, and a new direction. Often times, it is from a painful, desperate experience that our ministry and our divine purpose are birthed.

Jesus declared **"I am the resurrection and the life"**. **John 11:25.** There is no dead situation, circumstance, undertaking, or challenge that He is unable to renew. There is no heart that He cannot revitalize, refresh, and recharge. There is no sin-sick soul that He cannot make brand new in the Spirit. He is the Restorer of all things dead because He is the Source of all life. **"In Him is life and His life is the light of men"**. **John 1:4, 5.** In Him only can we find our brand new beginning; resurrection into newness of life and revelation of God's purpose for our lives.

Mary Magdalene was in the practice, of necessity, of seeking after the Lord daily, diligently, dutifully with passion, perseverance and purpose. This remained despite physical evidence that militated against the plausibility and possibility of satisfying her desire. She was the first of Jesus' followers to receive an assignment, a commission from Him, after His resurrection. His other disciples, distressed, deflated and dismayed needed to hear a Word. For just such a time, Mary Magdalene was positioned in the right place at the right time and given the right word by the risen Savior. As I have pointed out above, this was not by chance or coincidence. She had consistently and consciously put the Lord first in her affections, affliction and affirmations. He was her greatest desire; a desire that grew out of the words of the Lord that had so often been poured into her.

Happy Feet

Like all seasoned and skilled warriors, Mary was in a state of preparedness. She had been released from the influence and control of seven demons by the Lord and only vigilance in the spirit kept them out. Is it any wonder that she seized on every opportunity to fill her heart and mind with the Teacher's words? She had removed all the obstacles, cleared out all the junk, buried the busy-ness of daily living, sought after the righteousness of the Lord and developed a personal relationship that made Him and the things of His Kingdom her top priority. Mary was ready, willing and waiting for a revelation of the divine plan and purpose of the Lord for her future and the future of His followers.

Of all the people that might have been expected to be the first to whom the risen Lord would make His appearance, I wondered how many expected it to be Mary Magdalene? Surely, one might, if pressed, speculate that it would be to one of the eleven that He would first appear. But it was the honor and the privilege of womankind, the woman Mary Magdalene, to be the first to see Him, to bear direct, personal testimony of His resurrection, to learn of the next stage of His ministry and work, to minister to, direct and declare His message to the disciples.

Eve, the first woman of God was the first warrior commissioned to warfare in the great War of Love, and for love's sake, she, in the person of her daughter Mary Magdalene was the first to witness the actual resurrected Messiah, a state which was the physical manifestation of His victory over the Serpent! His first word to her was simply her name but it spoke volumes to her heart.

Is there any single message, any gospel more glorious to be conveyed, to be proclaimed throughout all of time and all creation than the resurrection of the Messiah? Jesus the Christ is alive! **"Oh death where is thy sting, oh grave where is thy victory?" 1 Corinthians 15:55.** Mary was euphoric, her weeping, her wanting and her waiting vigil was over. That undefined feeling she had inside, that seed imparted directly to her soul by the Lord now manifested as joy unspeakable. Jesus, the Messiah, the Redeemer of mankind, the conquering Lion of Judah was alive! But still, this was not all there was to the communion that took place between Mary and the Lord.

By His declaration at the tomb, He made it clear that He would not be remaining on the earth, in person for long; the next part of His ministry was in heaven. **John 20:17, 18.** Far from being the end of His assignment, His resurrection heralded the beginning of another phase, another level in the Plan of Redemption. In His words to Mary concerning His next step after His resurrection was the revelation that He must go to His Father in heaven. She must not try holding onto Him in the physical.

The next level of His work for the Salvation of mankind was elsewhere; at the throne of His Father and in the heavenly Tabernacle which had provided the model for that built on earth by the Israelites. He was required to administer the offices of High Priest, Advocate, Mediator and Sovereign Lord at the right hand of the Father in heaven. A thorough reading of **Hebrews 8, 9 and 10** will further explain, expand, inform and instruct us concerning the fullness of Jesus' ministry in heaven on our behalf.

The Magdalene was then given the essential information that needed to be communicated to the disciples; Jesus the Savior is alive! Not only was He alive but He had to report to His Father and ours, His God and ours before appearing to them. There was an important order and protocol that was being reinforced in His communiqué to the disciples. The Commander-in-Chief of an army takes special care in choosing the emissary that will be entrusted to get His orders through to his commanders, generals and soldiers. Jesus acted similarly. Mary was His emissary, His mouth-piece, trusted to deliver His instructions to His soldiers, His warriors. That was her assignment and the gift of communication given by God to womankind kicked in for a divine mission!

Mary must have ran all the way; rejoicing, shouting hallelujahs as she went, declaring to everyone, whether they were listening or not the news that the Christ was risen from His grave. To the casual observer, she must have appeared as a mad, crazy woman. She must have been laughing, crying, rejoicing all at the same time. The song by the gospel singers "Mary, Mary" with the words, "Take the shackles off my feet so I can dance" would be a most apt description, I believe. Mary Magdalene must have felt that the shackles of grief, loss and pain had fallen from her heart and her feet. I imagine she would pause momentarily to do a jig, then catching herself and the import of her assignment, start running again.

I am certain of one thing, though; Mary Magdalene was not quiet, not circumspect, composed and conservative. She must have been crying and shouting over and over: **"He is alive; Jesus my Lord, our Messiah is alive"!** Have you ever noticed that when a person is under the anointing, on a mission for the Lord, they often appear to be mad, crazy or intoxicated? That is why I believe that Mary Magdalene must have appeared to casual observers, who did not recognize the glory of God that illuminated her features, as completely insane or totally drunk!

However, the Scriptures tell us that some of the disciples, specifically some of the brothers, did not believe Mary Magdalene. How wrong they were for not accepting her testimony and her news. They failed to hear the first Message of the Messiah because they did not believe the Messenger! Whatever the reasons, prejudices or pre-conceived notions that closed their minds and caused their dismissal of her mission is not revealed in the Scriptures. However, it is enough of a warning that the Lord God caused this piece of information to be recorded in the Bible for future generations of believers; including us, the present generation.

There are many people who should beware this level of mistake; that is failure to hear the Word of the Lord because they disapprove of His messenger. We must search our hearts and make sure that we possess the word-seed; the Word of God that will shout 'yes' and leap for joy in the Spirit, when God's servants in dresses or trousers, male or female, yellow or red declares His truth. **John 3:3- 4** The Truth is not tailored to fit types and satisfy delicate sensibilities. If we belong to the Lord, we will always be able to hear His voice regardless of the garb, generation or gender of the speaker as the

Holy Spirit gives utterance of and bear witness to the Truth. Jesus the Christ declared to Pontius Pilate:

This is why I was born, and for this reason I have come into the world, to bear witness to the Truth. Everyone who is of the Truth, [who is a friend of the Truth, who belongs to the Truth] hears and listens to My voice. John 18:37b

The questions we need to answer for ourselves are simple. Are we ready and available to God? Do we continue in His Presence until we get a revelation from Him? Are we prepared and waiting for His assignment to us? Is the fulfillment of His plan and purpose in our lives the number one priority in our hearts and minds?

If we are to follow the example of Mary Magdalene then we must make the Lord our God the greatest desire of our being. We must listen, learn and rely on the Word of God; stand firmly on His promises and hold on to the vision of victory revealed through the eyes of faith. Nothing less than total commitment, total dedication and total surrender to God will be sufficient to attain the higher calling of spiritual warrior on duty for the Lord of Hosts.

Every warrior must understand that tarrying and travailing in the Spirit is an essential element of birthing a mission or a ministry, fulfilling an assignment or a plan, deliverance from diseases or demonic influences, teaching or preaching the Word, living the Way of the Cross or dying the death of the redeemed. The battle that we fight takes place on all fronts and we all have our positions somewhere on the frontline; in the direct line of fire. The weapons of the enemy are trained on our positions and he plans to take us. We will suffer casualties but soon the war will be over and the warriors of the King will reign in a Kingdom at peace forevermore.

CHAPTER 13

CALLED TO SERVICE

It Is Never Too Late

The Bible tells us that both Elizabeth and her husband Zechariah were **"upright in the sight of God, observing all the Lord's commandments and regulations blamelessly. But they had no children, because Elizabeth was barren; and both were far advanced in years"**. Luke 1:6, 7. (NIV)

It is quite clear from the Gospel of Luke, that Elizabeth was a God-fearing, God-focused woman. Like her husband, she had come from a family of priests. Her upbringing was among the people appointed by God to serve in His temple. No doubt, Elizabeth must have been heartbroken at her barrenness. She would never have the opportunity to produce a son that would continue in her husband's footsteps and serve the Lord God of their fathers Abraham, Isaac and Israel. But Elizabeth had not turned away from God in despair. She found purpose in faithfulness, serving God despite her disappointment. God was first in her heart and mind and adversity did not detract from her love, worship and adoration of Him.

The Scripture quoted above tells us that she continued to live according to the will of God, observing His laws and His statutes. I believe that although Elizabeth had grown accustomed to her state of childlessness, she had not completely given up hope of being a mother. I believe that there are many women, who, like Elizabeth, never truly give up hope of a miracle, when faced with the same or similar challenge.

To a woman whose hope is built on Jesus, nothing is impossible with God. If He wills it, it will come to pass, in His season! Such women **"walk by faith and not by sight"** (**2 Corinthians 5:7**) and so Elizabeth found favor in the sight of God; He took away her disgrace among the people. **Luke 1:25**. There had always been only thanksgiving and praise on Elizabeth's lips, gentleness in her hands towards others and love in her heart. She was not closed to the possibilities that service to God might present as evidenced by her testimony and praise. She was available and alert to the call of the Lord on her life..

Although in the physical, it seemed her biological clock had stopped ticking, in the spiritual realm she was ready for an impartation, an impregnation from God. She had been trained and fully equipped to fall in line with His plan, His assignment for her, in the battle that was appointed to her. The Lord can only bless us, fill us up with His anointing and loose us to carry out His plan to the extent that our hearts, our minds and bodies are and remain yielded to His will.

Spiritually, Elizabeth was prepared; her womb was already pregnant with the potential to bring forth a mighty warrior for the Kingdom of God. She was ordained, appointed and anointed to be the mother of the Fore-runner of the Messiah, to give birth to the **"greatest prophet that ever lived"**, according to the words of Jesus in **Matthew 11:11**. Her son, John the Baptist, was filled with the Holy Spirit even before his birth! It was his assignment, his calling to declare the Day of the Lord Immanuel and to prepare the hearts of men for the coming of the Lord, the Messiah. **Luke 1:17**

It is so very reassuring to know that with God there is no 'sell-by date'. He is the designer, installer, and maintainer of the biological clock! If we yield ourselves to Him then the only time that need concern us is God's time and the only date, that which appears on His calendar. God-faith knows that the most important thing is not what we see in the natural realm but rather, that which is a 'done deal' in the spiritual realm.

This faithful, obedient, surrendered, God-focused daughter of the Divine Father was the very first person to whom Mary, the mother of the Lord Jesus rushed when she received news, not only of her own blessing but also that of Elizabeth. And Elizabeth was the first to rejoice with Mary in the knowledge that the Presence of God was with mankind in the physical form of her baby, His Beloved Son. Imagine touching a pregnant belly and feeling the heartbeat of the Lord! Well, it is not an experience totally unique to Mary and those so permitted by her. When we have received a new heart from the Lord, the only act required to feel His heart beat is to touch our own hearts!

Elizabeth and Mary fellowshipped together, shared their testimony of the faithfulness of our God, broke out in praise and thanksgiving to the God of their fathers, shared their faith in God's Promise to Mother Eve and also rejoiced in seeing the fulfillment of God's promises. The first promise was His declaration to the serpent that the woman would bring forth a Seed to destroy him. And the second was to the children of man that God would send the Messiah to redeem and restore us to our original state and the third, that the Anointed One would be birthed through the line of David to **"set His people free"** from the bondage of their enemies, once and for all times. **Isaiah 11:1-5.**

Once again the Lord had shown that the season is never too late, the vessel too old, beat up or weak, neither can it be too used, abused or broken that He is unable to remake and renew it for service in His kingdom. There are many of us, who reach a place in our lives, whether in our walk with the Lord or outside of His fold, who feel that it is too late in the day for us to be of service to God. Wrong; even if we are the weak, the discarded, the outcast, the disposed, despised and disenfranchised of this world, God's strength is made perfect in and through us if we turn our lives over to Him, completely.

Let me assure you right now, if you take time out to search the Bible as well as do a little investigating among the people around you, you will discover there are countless numbers who will testify to the fact that the hour is never too late to labor in God's Kingdom.

Neither is it ever too late for the fulfillment of His purpose and plan for each of His children; the redemption of the human family and the restoration of paradise is the plan of the Divine Father and our Lord Jesus.

Sarah was an old lady, getting ready to die, when the Lord Almighty used her to demonstrate the infallibility of His Word. She was strengthened, through faith in God, to bear the child and heir promised to the faithful patriarch, Abraham. Elizabeth too was advanced in years and it took God's gift of strength for her to carry her son to full term. She was a faithful servant of God in spite of early personal disappointments and although her community no longer expected her to bear a child, God still had a miraculous, divine purpose for her in the motherhood department. She must have had the very credentials that God required for the mother of the Baptist! Each of us can be qualified by the Lord for His service and His Kingdom.

It is of no account that we think that we have either;

- ❖ Done our part already
- ❖ Are not worthy of God's calling to any new appointments
- ❖ Have lived too long in sin to go running to God now that the best days of our lives have passed,
- ❖ Or, that we are just too messed up for God to use.

It is never too late to be of service to God and never too late to turn our lives over to His direction and determination; living and laboring for Him, spreading and sharing His love, sowing, watering or reaping souls for the Kingdom. The devil would like us to think that for one reason after another, there is no hope or use for us in the Kingdom of God. But he is a liar and the father of all liars. God's love does not discriminate or distinguish between those who are called by His name. It is not because of our age, gender, race, social status, education, skills or moral standing that He wants us to come into relationship with Him.

Rather, it is in our acceptance of the atonement of Christ the Lord for our sinful rebellion, a chance to be reborn in the image of the

Divine, coming into a love partnership with the Lord, being covered by the righteousness of Jesus the Christ so that one may approach the throne of grace and offer worship and praise to the Most High. In other words, since the most important thing that God desires is that we come into personal and right standing through an enriching, intimate relationship with Him; it becomes quite irrelevant what we feel that we can contribute by way of service.

I believe that worshipping God, honoring Him with our whole life that is with each and every aspect of self, doing only those things that bring glory to His name is the first and best service we can offer. If we have breath, then we can praise and therefore serve our Lord. As to the rest, our submission to the way of God will allow Him to use even our weakness to magnify His name, power and might.

We had better rethink our opinion and our position on participation in the Kingdom's business. In the Kingdom of God, there is always "room at the Inn". It does not matter what our personal situation may be, in the eyes of God we are all of the greatest importance to Him. **"He is not willing that any should perish"** and He invites all to His banqueting table. **2 Peter 3:9.** The pay is the same for all the laborers in His vineyard, whether you have been working all day long or only in the last half hour of the work day.

With the Eternal One there is neither late nor early, He holds time itself in His hand. It is always "Now" with the Lord. **"Behold now is the day of salvation"** through Christ Jesus our Lord. **2 Corinthians 6:2.** It is never too late to follow Jesus and following Him means loving Him and loving our fellow man as He loves us. Jesus was our role-model while on earth and He still sets the standard for our lives. He serves as Mediator, Advocate, Intercessor, High Priest, Sacrificial Lamb, Lord and King of heaven, earth and the realm beneath the earth. All that He does is done out of a heart of pure, divine love. If any of us would sit with Him in glory we must make His mission of love our own; share in the fellowship of his suffering and war with the originator of rebellion and sin.

A Living Sacrifice

1. I appeal to you therefore, brethren, and beg of you in view of [all] the mercies of God, to make a decisive dedication of your bodies [presenting all your members and faculties] as a living sacrifice, holy (devoted, consecrated) and well pleasing to God, which is your reasonable (rational, intelligent) service and spiritual worship.

2. Do not be conformed to this world (this age), [fashioned after and adapted to its external, superficial customs], but be transformed (changed) by the [entire] renewal of your mind [by its new ideals and its new attitude], so that you may prove [for yourselves] what is the good and acceptable and perfect will of God, even the thing which is good and acceptable and perfect [in His sight for you].
Romans 12:1, 2

As we study the Word of God, it is apparent that the women of substance and spirituality in the bible chose God as the ultimate authority in their lives. This contrasts to practicing a self-centered attitude and approach. Their emotions were brought into subjection to the will of the Lord by a heart transplant operation at the spiritual level, at the hands of the Great Physician; a heart of flesh to replace a heart of stone. Further, their arms are physically and spiritually wide open, raised towards the heavens in acknowledgement of the Lordship of His rule, signifying their willingness to receive His orders, declaring their availability to God and a worshipful, reverential submission to orders, commands and purpose from His Courts.

Extending wide open arms to the Lord signifies our acceptance of the manifestation of God's purpose in our lives in whatever shape, form or framework that it materializes. To be open to the working of God in our life means that we yield total control; spiritual and physical direction to our Lord. Unless we make space in our being, both at the physical and spiritual level, God is unable to find room to impart His instructions, deliver His assignment and bestow His blessings on us. Furthermore, once we have accepted the atonement of Jesus, He becomes Lord of our lives because we are bought with the sacrifice of Calvary. We no longer belong to ourselves and therefore He is the Architect and the Director of our destiny. **Revelation 5:9**

A partial yielding to God that allows Him a little room in our lives because we are otherwise occupied in egotistical self-pursuits is not and can never be enough. But if we surrender to God serving Him with all that we are, all of our time and energy, our love and devotion, our thoughts and our talents, our hopes and our dreams, our resources and our potentials, then He is able to use us for the glory of His name and the advancement of His Kingdom. Furthermore this is our reasonable service. **Romans 12:1**

In today's world there are so many distractions that so occupy and weary us, physically and emotionally, that it takes the Spirit of God to implant in us a desire to look beyond the natural and seek out that which has been ordained as our true, eternal heritage. None of us naturally seek after and desire the things of God unless He first imparts that desire to our spirit, to follow in the footsteps of the Savior.

The Anointing

There can only be a mighty move of God if there is an outpouring, an anointing of the Holy Spirit on those who heed the Clarion Call of services to the Kingdom. Women who are called into battle for the Lord need that special anointing in order to be divinely equipped to carry out their God-given assignment. The anointing is the power to successfully fulfill divine directives. It enables and empowers us to carry through the plan of God for our lives. The parable of the ten virgins is a perfect illustration of this pre-requisite. **Matthew 25:1-13**

The ten virgins who set out to meet the Bridegroom and attend His marriage feast carried oil in their lamps to light their path. David tells us in **Psalms 119:105, "Your word is a lamp to my feet and a light to my path." Ephesians 6:17** tells us that **"the Sword that the Spirit wields is the Word of God"**. Only the indwelling of the

Holy Spirit, with faith in the Word can empower us to stand up for the Lord at all times; to do that which He has assigned to us despite difficulties and challenges. The outpouring of the Holy Spirit is always followed by power. The Lord Jesus assures His disciples,

> **But you shall receive power (ability, efficiency, and might) when the Holy Spirit is come upon you, and you shall be My witnesses in Jerusalem and all Judea and Samaria and to the ends (the very bounds) of the earth. Acts 1:8**

Notice that all the virgins of the parable had oil in their lamps, but there was a lack, a shortfall, a miscalculation of what was needed to complete the final leg of the journey by some sisters. Only the five virgins who had extra oil with them were able to complete the journey and so be with the Bridegroom. They had a supply in there lamp that was seemingly sufficient to their needs but they were also in overflow and so they carried extra with them; making sure that they could complete their journey and achieve their goal of rendezvous with the Groom. Having Christ as our Lord and His Holy Spirit as an internal life-source guarantees enough power to complete the journey that is laid before us and endure with longevity in the fight that is our fate until the final destruction of evil is accomplished in the Lord.

A thief and a destroyer will try to enter into the Fold or the Feast by whatever means possible. When we receive Christ Jesus as Savior and Lord of our life, we receive the Holy Spirit but when we are ordained or called for a special assignment we are given an extra portion; the appropriate gifts of the Spirit to fit us for the task we are given. It is the same if we are going to war. A soldier, fighter, warrior must always be equipped with the necessary weapons that will allow them to be effective in their commission. Even in the wars of men, lack of proper equipment and clothing is a detriment to soldiers.

Only the five wise virgins were in the overflow of the Lord's abundance. The adjective **wise** is our first and best clue to their attitude and behavior in preparing to welcome the Bridegroom on His arrival. Wisdom is the true worship of God. The virgins were worshippers dedicated to the will of God and prepared to endure until His coming, however and whatever it required to do so. The assignment is to reach the final destination, His Presence, at the appointed time. God is Abundance and He is able to give us an overflow of His anointing so that we have oil in our lamps and a surplus if the need arises and it usually does!

As it is with the visible, natural realm so it is with the Kingdom of God. The soldiers of the Lord do not go to the wars without:

- Appropriate training and relevant preparation
- The right hardware, equipment, uniform and arms
- A specific rank, identity tag and rank or position in the army with its attendant responsibilities
- An officially, authorized, assignment or order from the Commander-in-Chief of the King's Army
- And, the authority of His Kingdom and the power to act on His behalf; a spiritual anointing and empowerment for victory in His name.
- The banner and the seal of the country to which one has pledged allegiance.

It is not possible for us to stand against the wiles of the enemy without God's anointing. Our Righteous Example, the Sovereign Lord Jesus received that extra special anointing, visibly. Firstly, at the beginning of His ministry when the Holy Spirit came and sat on Him in the form of a dove, and again as He prepared to face His trial; demonstrated by the woman who anointed Him with oil from her alabaster box.

These visible reminders and representations of the special empowerment that is bestowed through the anointing were designed by a loving Father for our instruction. **John 1:32-34.** Jesus was able to stand against the devil even during the testing and suffering that was His portion. Likewise, in order to run the course that is laid before us, succeed in our divine calling and overcome the enemy of our God and our brethren, we must seek the special anointing of the Holy Spirit. This has always been and still is God's method of endorsement of our assignment. **Those whom He appoints, He anoints.**

Our Father never gives us a task without endowing us with the ability, gifts, talents and resources to accomplish more than we are able to bear, never sends us into the battlefield unprepared, never allows us to be tempted beyond what we are able to endure except He makes a way out for us to overcome; God never sends us out to lose a battle. There are strongholds that we must assault but we can only be triumphant if we stand in the overflow of the anointing through prayer, fasting and abiding under the Shadow of the Almighty.

Sometimes it might appear to the natural mind that we are losers that the devil got the best of a particular situation but sometimes, losing is winning. Sometimes, apparent defeat is victory in Christ Jesus; ask all the martyred saints when they stand before the Throne of our God dressed in robes of purest white, with the imputed righteousness of the Lamb of God! **Revelation 7:14, 15.**

At times when it appears that we are outnumbered or outmaneuvered by the enemy, it is only an appearance of defeat. In Christ Jesus we are always more than conquerors. So even if we die fulfilling our purpose we have the victory. After all, as the Apostle Paul declares, to die in Christ is gain. **Philippians 1:21.** Our Lord holds the key to death and through Him we triumph over the enemy of our eternal inheritance. The most important thing is that we accept our assignment and honor our commission, our Commander-In-Chief, our Creator God and His commandments.

Never too Young to Yield

Mary the mother of Jesus the Christ was a humbly, submitted young woman. She was open to the possibility of a movement of God in her life. It was not a specifically defined movement of God that she was anticipating but she was in an expectant frame of mind, ready and willing to welcome the announcement and the proclamation of the arch angel Gabriel. Mary was taught and knew that the Messiah was the only hope for the Jews living in hardship and subjection to their Roman rulers.

The promise of the ultimate deliverance of the Children of Israel was predicated on the appearance of the long-promised Messiah, who would shoulder the government and rule the Children of Israel; leading them to freedom and victory over all their enemies, once and for all times. It is my strong conviction that every God-fearing woman since Eve, among the covenanted people, must have entertained the dream of giving birth to the Messiah, Savior of their nation and Destroyer of the enemy of mankind, Satan.

Mary, I believe, would have been no different, having been reared in the knowledge of God and having been yielded to His way. Her devotion, her submission, her humility and her willingness to serve God with her whole being, physical and natural made her the perfect vessel for Jehovah God to bring forth the Messiah, the Christ into this condemned world.

We have the authority of the Scriptures and the experiences of the people of God, to declare with confidence that only those individuals who are ready for a miracle, for a move of God, for an impartation from the Divine can and will receive one. I am referring to a Spirit of Expectancy; expectancy of a revelation or a call to ministry, of a much desired gift of the Spirit, the manifestation of a miracle, a mission field to evangelize, a deliverance from a dilemma, the resources to champion so-called lost causes, to move into a position of power, to shake hierarchies, experience economic and spiritual breakthroughs, spiritual transition into higher dimensions of relationship, service and worship.

We know very little of the details and experiences of the life of Mary before the arch angel Gabriel appeared to her. However we do know that she must have been God-focused and overflowing with a God-faith that filled her with the confidence that her destiny was in the hands of the Father; so that she was able to say without hesitation, **'according to His will, let it be with His hand-maiden'. Luke 1:38**

Mary was a woman fully surrendered, totally prepared to let the Lord have His way in her life. She positioned, aligned with the will of God, so that when the appointed time of the Messiah's advent arrived, she was able to yield to the Holy Spirit. Mary had her eyes on the higher calling. She kept herself pure, spiritually and physically because she walked in the Way of the Almighty. Her devotion and her worship were God focused. She was a daughter of the Way! Prepared, expectant, willing, ready and able to roll with the cosmic move of Jehovah!

Mary had cherished a hope, entertained a vision and was properly committed, submitted and prepared for the possibility of service to the Lord. When the manifestation of God's promise in the natural took place, she welcomed the privilege, the honor and the joy of being chosen. How do we know that Mary was God-focused? Well, the Scripture records her response to the proclamation of Gabriel and it spoke volumes about her mind set and her mentality.

Generally, a self-centered young woman, engaged to be married would immediately start thinking of the consequences of a pregnancy that had nothing to do with the results of her wedding night. How crazy would her explanation sound to her relatives and her groom and the disbelief with which it would be received. If Mary was operating purely in the natural it would have only taken a few seconds for her to repudiate arch angel Gabriel's announcement. If she was a modern day bride she might have been made to believe that she might even be experiencing some kind of hallucination brought about from the stress and anxiety of preparing for her wedding!

The penalty for a pregnancy in such circumstances as Mary's, being yet unmarried was possibly death by stoning. Her claim to be pregnant by the power of the Holy Spirit would have met with derision, claims of deception, wickedness and possibly, insanity. She could end up being abandoned to fend for herself, disgraced by her fiancé Joseph, ostracized by her community, an outcast shunned by family and friends alike. After all, there was no precedent in the Scriptures of such an occurrence in all the history of the Children of Israel and neither was the Messiah expected to come into the world by such an unnatural or rather, supernatural method.

Yet, Mary did not protest any of these points or question God's messenger as to her personal well-being and the future of herself and her child. Instead, it is recorded that she rejoiced in God's plan for her life; her faith in God was perfect and not subject to discussion, debate or doubt. She saw only the positive in the situation, namely the will of God to bring forth the Messiah through her. In the midst of an uncertain future and the possibility of rejection and condemnation, Mary humbly submitted and began to exalt the Lord, an exaltation which found its vocal expression in song when she met with her cousin Elizabeth.

That is what being God-focus can do in our lives; it will allow us to know beyond a shadow of doubt that God will make a way for us; any battle that we face in our Christ-walk is not ours, it belongs to the Lord. He promises His people that we 'shall not want' for anything; in the desert or the wilderness, in the valley of the shadow of death or in the land of strangers.

He is the Provider and the Sustainer, Jehovah Jireh. The Red Sea is merely a parting of the waves for the God of our salvation, not a stumbling block to freedom. A read through Mary's exaltation tells us a great deal about her knowledge of God's promise to His people, the honor which she embraced as her own and her awesome love for and commitment to the divine plan that the Lord was unfolding through her, His warrior daughter. Being the natural mother of the Messiah was fraught with danger but Mary never once baulked at her choice to be God's woman on the frontline. **Luke 1:38, 46-55.**

A Living Sacrifice

When God is the center of our affections and the greatest desire of our hearts and minds, we should always expect and welcome the chance to bring glory and honor to His name. The concerns of the natural man; of the opinions of family, friends and community must be abandoned. Obedience to God is the outward expression of our inner submission to Him and, our living testimony that we serve the only God, the Creator Divine.

If we keep the Lord at the center of our vision, He activates within us the courage, the strength and the faith that we need to stand firm and run the race He has laid before us. Once we give ourselves up to the indwelling of His Holy Spirit, He will fill us with desire, drive, passion and determination to serve, to acknowledge the Lord in all our ways, to lovingly, happily obey His commands and adhere to His plan and purpose for our lives.

For women, it is not the fact of a seed planted in our physical wombs that confirms our completeness as women, despite the beliefs to the contrary. Eve was a woman even before she gave birth in the physical because she was already ordained a mother in the spiritual. It is our ability to receive a seed of promise from God and to bring it to maturation so that there is a harvest for the Kingdom that confirms our status as women, women of God.

Barrenness of the spirit only occurs if we are not open to receiving God's gifts, plans, inspiration, direction, guidance or will, in our spiritual walk. In Christ, there is no barrenness. He is the Source of all life, He is the Resurrection and He is life itself. He renews and revitalizes dead things and He is eternal. If there is unproductivity, infertility or barrenness, then we need to do an inventory of ourselves and the things upon which we are fixed in our affections.

Unless we overcome our natural man and empty ourselves of our carnal inclinations and desires, we cannot hold out open arms and fertile, empty wombs to receive divine instructions and to welcome the implantations of the Holy Spirit. We must present our bodies as living sacrifices to the Father, so that His work can be done on this earth for the honor and the glory of His Kingdom. We must make Mary's affirmation our own; **"Let it be to thy servant according to the divine will". Luke 1:38** (paraphrased)

The sentiments of the mother of the Christ would later be repeated by her Son in the Garden of Gethsemane, as He faced the reality of being the Passover Sacrifice for mankind. The promise of **Isaiah 54** applies not only to the physical but also to the spiritual. In both alike, we are ordained of the Creator to bring forth life; to produce fruit from the seed implanted by the Holy Spirit.

We must declare the acceptable day of the Lord. The fields are white and the laborers are few. We are commissioned to be productive, to be the warriors of victorious battles in the might and power of Christ Jesus our Lord. There are ministries waiting to be birthed through us. Our spiritual wombs must be places of fertile production. The Word of God is seed, water and light, assuring us of spiritual productivity according to God's harvest.

Mary the mother of Jesus was already pregnant in the Spiritual realm when the angel of God appeared to her. She was pregnant with the possibility of being favored by God to birth the Savior of the human family. It was therefore not a big deal for her to transition to the next level; to the materialization on the physical plane. Her words of acceptance to the arch angel merely gave voice to her submission in the domain of the Spirit. A spiritual impregnation will always precede the natural manifestation of a move of the Divine Creator.

Another Mary, Mary Magdalene likewise gave birth to a new chapter in the delivery of God's message of redemption to the nations of the earth. Her role after the resurrection of the Christ was to proclaim the beginning of a new level of ministry. She was the first to witness the physical re-appearance and manifestation of Jesus Christ on this natural plane which declared His victory in the Spiritual realm. (See previous chapter)

This miracle, more than any other, confirmed that He was indeed the Son of God, the Redeemer who had won the victory over death and the grave; **"the First-fruit of many brethren"** who had retaken the authority originally given to man by God in the Garden of Eden. Jesus Christ is the Victor over the enemy of man's immortality. And Mary Magdalene was the first to bear direct witness of His resurrection and of His publication of the natural and spiritual result of His victory in the Plan of Salvation as well.

God designed us for a divine destiny and prepares us for our purpose in Him. We can only realize this if we yield ourselves to Him. God the Father takes great delight in opening His hands and pouring out the blessings that are the rewards of a heart that enthrones the Spirit of the Lord.

16. You open Your hand and satisfy every living thing with favor.

17. The Lord is [rigidly] righteous in all His ways and gracious and merciful in all His works.

18. The Lord is near to all who call upon Him, to all who call upon Him sincerely and in truth.

19. He will fulfill the desires of those who reverently and worshipfully fear Him; He also will hear their cry and will save them.

20. The Lord preserves all those who love Him, but all the wicked will He destroy.

21. My mouth shall speak the praise of the Lord; and let all flesh bless (affectionately and gratefully praise) His holy name. Psalms145:16-21

CHAPTER 14

SEEKING AFTER WISDOM

The Foolishness of Children

All of us have been children and we have all been subject to the rules of our parents and caregivers. I would imagine that very few, if any child has grown up without being subject to standards of behavior and expectations of conduct in their homes and in the hallowed halls of the institutions of society. There are some rules that allow us to exercise a certain amount of freedom in comparison to others which are non-negotiable and demand total, unerring compliance. However, they all have a common purpose and that is to prepare us to be adults. As we grow we are expected to achieve maturity, equipped to be productive, participative members of society with morals, ethics, behavior and beliefs that will allow us to be an effectively functioning part of the whole.

As future adults, it will become our obligation to pass on correct moral standards, a sense of responsibility and a desire to be positive contributors to the community of man, to the children that we too will parent, train, guide and, or mentor for the continuation of our posterity. Having stated the ideal let us step back for a moment and consider this question. Is there an individual living today that can truthfully say that they have never questioned the authority, knowledge, attitude, actions or wisdom of a parent or caregiver?

I for one, remember many occasions when I wondered about the way that those who were in charge of me, reasoned. Don't get me wrong, I knew better than to give voice to my objections. Even if I would have liked to I was not prepared to suffer the consequences. 'Suffer' being the operative word! Nevertheless, in the privacy of my mind I would 'kick' against the standards and the boundaries that were set for me, my siblings and my friends.

I am now a parent and have experienced both express and implied disagreement from my children with many of my rules; come to think of it, too many. For example, when I decide that a particular television program is unsuitable for my son and he feels that I am being unreasonable because his friends are allowed to watch it, there may be implied or spoken objection and even disobedience if I am not around. What my son is doing in actuality is questioning my authority and the wisdom of my rule or the standard of behavior that I expect from him. He wants to be the decision maker, for example, the one who says what programs he should watch, in other words, he wants to be me, the parent.

The purpose of this aside into the minor details(a little pun) concerning my son's views of some of my rules demonstrates that we have all been critical of and even disobedient to the rules that our elders set in place for our own good. In fact, we consider many of them unnecessary and silly, thereby implying that they do not know what is good for us all the time or even want us to have good things or good fun sometimes.

In the Garden of Eden, Eve was not very different to my son. Her rebellion marked a desire to be in the shoes of her Father, her Creator, and God. Eve wanted to be the decision maker, to decide if she should eat the fruit of the Tree of the Knowledge of Good and Evil, or not, to be independent of His laws and set her own standards of conduct. She wanted to be God and to exercise His authority. She listened to stuff that she had no business listening to and as a result received the demonic seeds of destruction sown into her heart and mind by the devil. Exposed to the father of lies, his word-seeds quickly matured into a fatal harvest for Eve, Adam and all their offspring to this very day.

Eve succumbed to the lie that she would become like God possessing all His wisdom. This appealed to her rebellious heart and the sin was committed. But rebellion against the authority and wisdom of God is transgression punishable with death. This was a truth that the first pair knew; God did not fashion them with learning difficulties or as fools. They were adults, fully cognizant of their disobedience to God's law and the consequences.

Unlike parents and caregivers in the natural, God's holiness prevents Him from accepting or condoning our sins but God is big on forgiveness and He provided for this through His Beloved Son. However, like natural elders, but even more perfectly and with more certainty, once we seek His forgiveness, He never says no to us. He sacrificed His only Begotten Son for His prodigal sons and daughters, so that we can **again** have the chance and the choice to be His children.

For as many as receive Him (Jesus), to them gave He power to become the sons of God, even to them that believe on His name. John 1:12

Satan goes after our minds and our hearts. If he can control these then he can control our thoughts, actions and our emotions. This explains the basis of the Scripture that entreats us to love the Lord with all our hearts, minds, and bodies and with all our strength. Love of God will manifest obedience to His commands, and His way. If we continue to live after our own way, the natural man, then we will continue in opposition to the Father but when the second Adam came, He made it possible for us to have His Spirit living in us so that we have no problems being in submission to the will of the Father. **2 Corinthians 10:5.**

Self-Serving Motives

The "fruit was desirable for gaining wisdom" was the conclusion arrived at by Eve's limited reasoning capacity; limited because she was relying on her own abilities and not on the Wisdom of God in His provisions, order and law for her life and her future. The false teaching of the serpent was really a manifestation of the spirit of anti-Christ and it found acceptance in Eve's heart. She craved parity with God; coveted His wisdom and His sovereign authority. According to the Bible, she gave the fruit to her husband, who was with her and he shared in her decision to disobey God. Let me just say, women will automatically share whatever they are experiencing and that is why it is so important that we live and move and have our being firmly grounded in and controlled by the Word of God. Adam stood by as she partook of the fruit and when she shared with him, he ate and sinned by so doing.

Let us look closely at what the Lord would have us understand through the Scriptures in regards to the issue of wisdom. We will first look at what is stated in the Book of **Job 28:20-28** for a discourse on wisdom and its acquisition by mankind. We should carefully and prayerfully commit to study the Book of Proverbs and the wisdom of King Solomon contained therein as well as other Scriptures that speak to us of godly wisdom. What we will encounter is a demonstration of how easy it is to acquire wisdom from the Lord our God if we trust Him.

Job 28:20-28

20. From where then does Wisdom come? And where is the place of understanding.

21. It is hidden from the eyes of all living, and knowledge of it is withheld from the birds of the heavens.

22. Abaddon (the place of destruction) and Death say, we have [only] heard the report of it with our ears.

23. God understands the way [to Wisdom] and He knows the place of it [Wisdom is with God alone].

24. For He looks to the ends of the earth and sees everything under the heavens.

25. When He gave to the wind weight or pressure and allotted the waters by measure,

26. When He made a decree for the rain and a way for the lightening of the thunder,

27. Then He saw [Wisdom] and declared it; He established it, yes, and searched it out [for His own use, and He alone possesses it].

28. But to man He said, Behold, the reverential and worshipful fear of the Lord – that is Wisdom; and to depart from evil is understanding.

In the **Epistle of James 1:5**, the Lord makes it plain to us,

If any of you lacks Wisdom, let him ask of God, that giveth to all men liberally, and upbraideth not; and it shall be given to him. (KJV)

The dictionary tells us that -

Wisdom is an attribute of God and is bound up with divine knowledge manifesting itself in the selection of proper ends with proper means for their accomplishment. In men Wisdom is not only the practical understanding of matters relating to life but in the highest sense it is the theoretical and practical acceptance of divine revelation. In the highest sense it is a divine gift. (The New Unger's Bible Dictionary).

The wisest human being that ever lived, and one that was the most honored with the gift of wisdom by the Lord, characterizes wisdom as an evangelizing woman who preaches to everyone and most especially to men. A thorough reading of Proverbs will teach us about the nature and value of godly wisdom. This woman named 'wisdom' calls out to **"Men and the sons of men" "to receive her**

instruction in preference to striving for silver and to receive knowledge rather than choice gold "for all the things that may be desired are not to be compared" with "skillful and godly wisdom". Excerpts from Proverbs 8 and 9

Proverbs 28:28 says that Wisdom is the reverential and worshipful fear of the Lord! Therefore what is foolishness by comparison? It is rebellion against God and dishonor, disrespect and disobedience to Him and to His laws, as well as a failure to revere and worship the Father Creator. The absence of wisdom in this world is evident in the exposition and proliferation of doctrines, philosophies and vain imaginings that we purport to be scientific, undisputable, logical representations of the origin and purpose of man on the earth and the origin of the universes. This is the foolishness practiced by man that is revered and highly regarded in our most esteemed halls of learning, as wisdom. In fact, we were created to worship God and the Bible says that this is the whole duty of man. In other words we were created wise, and to remain wise, in Christ!

Worship was the lifestyle of our First Parents in the Garden of Eden. Everything about their lives was in harmony with God and with bringing glory to His name. The serpent did not approve of this; it highlighted his error, pride and wickedness; it detracted from the validity and substance of his accusations against God and His administration. Eve fell for the lie that her lifestyle of worship was a life of lack, deprivation and subservience. But wisdom, God's wisdom was the birthright of man and was already an attribute that they reflected and demonstrated by their life choices of obedience and worship and by the mere fact that they were formed in the image and after the character of God.

In **Genesis 3:6** we are told that when Eve saw that it was a **"tree to be desired in order to make one wise, she took of its fruit and ate"**. Not only was Eve being disobedient, she was a thief and a liar because by her actions, she implied that God had not been truthful, honest and caring towards her and Adam. She did not have the right to 'take' the fruit but she did and she joined in with the treachery of the Accuser of our God and her own Destroyer.

Adam, like Eve had also replaced the true God with a false idol. He was selfish, self-centered, self-focused and self-willed. He had sinned in his heart even before he ate of the fruit. He had listened and succumbed to rebellion. Taking the fruit from his wife was merely the outward manifestation of the sin that had already been committed in his heart. She had replaced God in his affections, his loyalty, and his trust and this in turn naturally impacted his ability and reasoning in respect of God's truth.

Adam was not deceived by the serpent but by his own carnal desires for the woman. He chose to listen to her words, her views, her reasoning, in order to be with her, rather than observe the divine commandments. God had given Adam all authority over every created thing on the earth and yet, he like Eve, allowed himself to stand by and tolerate the lies being leveled against Jehovah God, keeping quiet while the devil impugned the character of the Lord. Eventually he joined Eve in the final act of treason against the Kingdom of Light. **1 Timothy 2:14**

The Ripe Time, the Right Time

Adam and Eve challenged the authority of the Divine Maker to declare His season, His agenda, and His order in their lives. The time for man to gain greater godly wisdom, enlightenment and understanding of the knowledge of good and evil was for God to determine. God's time is always the best time. Yet **"all we like sheep have gone astray"**, each going our own way and following after our own devices. **Isaiah 53:6**

The Divine began the creation of the earth and mankind with a plan of Love. First He sought to establish obedience, trust, love, fellowship and communion with the first pair. He was in the process of training and preparation of all His creation, including the male and the female. It was important that man abide in His Law by choice. God is not a God of disorder, disarray or confusion. Instead, He is precise and perfect in all His ways. There is a God-appointed season for everything under the sun. Eve's haste, presumption, pride, idolatry and rebellion propelled her act of treason, pre-empting the timetable of God's revelations. **"There is a time to sow and a time**

to reap" declares the wisdom of the Father. Seed, time and harvest are within His control. **Ecclesiastes 3:1-8**

The "Edenic" pair harvested and ate out of season. It was not yet God's time for them to have access to the fruit of the Tree of the Knowledge of Good and Evil. God would inform them in due season; at the right time. However, by declaring independence and following the dictates of their own heart and mind they acted prematurely and so fell into sin.

Eating unripe fruit causes the belly to sour and the children to sicken. Eve and her husband brought sickness and death to the human family by their act of rebellion. God had already decreed a "ripe time' but Adam and Eve stepped out of the Way and acted as thieves of their Maker's authority, His sovereignty and His glory. As my mother often pointed out to us in childhood, a ripe fruit does not have to be picked from the tree. It does not require any violence, aggression or force in its harvesting. For if it is ripe and ready for consumption, it falls, easily, one might even say willingly, into the hand of the one who reaps. It is deliciously satisfying to the mind, body and spirit when consumed at the appropriate time. This is the natural order of things as set in place by our Creator.

So it is that in His season, the Almighty grants us the privilege, honor and blessing to enjoy the fruits of our labor in His vineyard. Mark well the rewards reserved for the redeemed of the Lamb of God. For example, the Scripture tells us that we shall eat from the Tree of Life again, withdrawn from mankind's sinful grasp and gluttony. The same Tree of Life that God protected from fallen man in the Garden of Eden shall be available to the saints of God again. The Tree of Life was kept from man after the Fall lest we magnified and immortalized sinful flesh and be outside God's redemptive plan, formulated before the great disobedience of man.

Our Father never denies his children any good thing but like a good and wise parent neither does He spoil us and allow us to come into ownership of gifts, responsibilities and positions for which we have not yet been prepared, trained and made competent. It is the duty of man to wait upon the Lord and His appointed seasons for our portions, anointing, blessings and inheritance.

The record of Jehovah's relationship with man holds examples of what happens when man acts according to their own agenda instead of waiting on the Lord. The pre-mature action of Moses, that great prophet and leader of the Children of Israel, when he slew the Egyptian soldier out of God's plan and His time is a fine example.

Clearly then, there is a time for the sowing of seeds, a time to water, fertilize, prune, nurture and wait for the growth, development and fruiting of the tree. And then there is a time for reaping! Adam and Eve were like seeds themselves, planted in the eastern end of the Garden of Eden. They were being tended by the Master Gardener Himself who would, in the fullness of time, in the "ripe season" bestow upon them all the praise, privileges, honor and the blessings that He had reserved for them.

All creation is ordered by the Lord. The seasons are His to command and He wills everything according to His wisdom and His love. To act outside of God's will is to deny His sovereign authority as Source, Creator, the Alpha and the Omega. To sin is to put our faith in self or in another, including the devil thereby committing high treason against our King and His Righteous Kingdom.

The Mother and Father of the human family were ruled by their feelings at the point of Satan's temptation. They succumbed to sin because they allowed their emotions to dictate their decisions and ultimately their actions. They rejected the truth in favor of self-will. This is still the challenge that faces us, their children even today. We are our parents' children. We still have a natural tendency to accord greater credence to how we feel at any given moment rather than subjection of our feelings to God and a walk of obedience.

This is so despite the perfect example of the Lord Jesus Christ who suffered a cruel death on Calvary, rather than give in or give up at the point of His Gethsemane desire that the "cup pass" from Him. We continue to elevate our human emotions above our submission to the will of God, yet we repeat the Lord's Prayer, **"Thy Kingdom come, Thy will be done on earth as it is in heaven"**. **Matthew 6:10.** The adversary continues to work on our emotions in order to use them as weapons against us. But if we are to overcome him through Christ Jesus, we must subject our feelings to the Truth, the Righteousness and the Sovereignty of God and His laws in our lives.

Our emotions emanate from our hearts and as I have pointed out in this book, a change of heart is fundamental to change the prominence and operation of our emotions in our choices and our decisions.

The Price of Wisdom

In **1 Kings 10:1-13** we read of another woman whose life's pursuit was the search for wisdom. The Queen of Sheba heard of the wisdom of King Solomon, sovereign ruler of the Children of Israel. So impressed was she with all the stories that had been told her of this gifted ruler that she gathered up vast and impressive amounts of the most highly sought after spices and laden down with still more gifts amounting to a great wealth by any standard, she took a long, arduous and dangerous journey to test Solomon with hard questions in order to:

A. Prove his famed wisdom to herself
B. To discern his relationship with the God of his people
C. And the relationship between these two facts
D. The effect of the above on the prosperity of the Israelite Kingdom

I believe that the Queen of Sheba really wanted to come to an understanding and knowledge of the link between King Solomon's wisdom and his personal, intimate connection with his God. This lady was not a worshipper of the God of the Nation of Israel but it was spread far and wide that King Solomon was wise above all men and was so gifted by his God. **1 Kings 10:24 and 1 Kings 3:12.**

I believe that the Queen had a thirst after wisdom, a thirst which drove her to search near and far, regardless of the difficulty that might be involved. She purposed to reach the king whose judgments were regarded as 'most wise of the ages'. She was a woman of great wealth, power, learning, knowledge, status and command in her own Kingdom. Yet she recognized that she had not attained true wisdom. In keeping with royal protocol and despite the rumored wealth of Solomon's treasury, her retinue of gifts was over and beyond the norm. It was probably a reflection of the depth of the need that she had for wisdom, perhaps an unformed desire to purchase his wisdom or access to his Source.

This approach is still a popular one in our societies where many foster the erroneous belief that we can secure divine favor by or acts, actions or money. The deep need which this lady exhibited is still at the heart of every man's search for meaning and purpose today, a need which only the love of God can place there through the office of the Holy Spirit. Lest any person should boast, a passionate, deep desire, craving and longing for anything godly can only originate with God Himself. It is His love for us which fills us with the disposition to desire good gifts and it also motivates every gift that He gives to us. This is the manifestation of His love for us even when we are in rebellion.

The Queen of Sheba was a well informed lady who questioned King Solomon about the burning issues that occupied her mind and for which she was unable to get a satisfactory answer in her own kingdom. He in return freely shared with her all the knowledge and wisdom that the Almighty had placed in him. He did not hold anything back but shared with her his God-given wisdom. **1 Kings 10:6-10.** The point that we must learn here is that we are blessed to be a blessing, favored to show favor and gifted by the Lord to share the fruits of our salvation with our fellow man, making sure that God gets the glory, not man; that praise be properly located in the right direction and the right location.

In conclusion, the Queen of Sheba acknowledged the extensive blessings of Solomon and his people and then she praised His God in the following words:

Praise be to the Lord your God who has delighted in you (Solomon) and placed you on the throne of Israel! Because of the Lord's eternal love for Israel, he has made you king, to maintain justice and righteousness. 1 Kings 10:9. (NIV)

She came in search of wisdom and arrived at a place where she could be introduced to and come into personal contact with the Source of Wisdom, Jehovah God. He alone was able to supply her need through the agency of His servant Solomon, leader of His covenanted people. King Solomon gave to the Queen of Sheba, everything that she sought spiritually, which no doubt includes the teachings on wisdom contained in the Book of Proverbs and of which we are partakers by the grace and the provision of the Lord! In addition, Solomon also gave gifts to the Queen of Sheba, personally, from his royal bounty. **1 Kings 10:13**.

The Queen of Sheba went in search of the wisdom of God's man, Solomon, and the link that his great gift had to the God of Israel. She was not prepared to sit and listen to second-hand accounts, to wait for what her heart and spirit desired to come to her. She was a seeker after wisdom, truth and understanding at a deep personal level. And because of this need that God had given to her, He provided the resource that would introduce her to His Word, His truth, His wisdom; King Solomon was that resource. God's promises to those who seek are echoed throughout the Scriptures. The wisdom of God that was taught by Solomon to the Queen of Sheba was then reflected in the fact that she and later her nation came to worship the true, Living God. Her legacy remains today in the lives of the Ethiopian Jews; a repository of some of the oldest traditions, practices and sacred copies of Holy Writ.

As a consequence of the Queen's diligence, persistence and readiness to take whatever measures were necessary to satisfy her hunger for wisdom, she received acknowledgement and commendation from the Lord Jesus during His earthly ministries.

> **The Queen of the South will stand up at the judgment with this generation and condemn it; for she came from the ends of the earth to listen to the Wisdom of Solomon and behold, someone more and greater than Solomon is here ... Matthew 12:42**

> **Get skillful and godly Wisdom, get understanding (discernment, comprehension, and interpretation); do not forget and do not turn from the words of my mouth. Forsake not [Wisdom], and she will keep, defend and protect you: love**

her, and she will guard you. The beginning of Wisdom is: get Wisdom (skillful and godly Wisdom)! [For skillful and godly Wisdom is the principal thing.] And with all you have gotten, get understanding (discernment, comprehension and interpretation). Proverbs 4: 5-9

The experience of Adam and Eve clearly demonstrates the folly of relying on the so-called wisdom of man in his base and unredeemed state. Today, we consider ourselves so learned, so wise, so scientific in our acquisition of knowledge that we arrogantly and mistakenly believe that we are a wise people. But the same truth applies today as it did in the days of Solomon; we are wise in our own folly. Unless and until we get the wisdom of God, we are fools playing a fools game with our lives and our destinies.

If any of you is deficient in wisdom, let him ask of the giving God [Who gives] to everyone liberally and ungrudgingly, without reproaching or fault-finding, and it will be given him. James 1:5.

The example of the Queen of Sheba serves to instruct us that even if we have all the wealth of the world we could possibly desire, and if we have achieved the greatest accolades that the world can award us, and even if we have great learning, status, power, influence and esteem in the world, without godly wisdom, it all amounts **to 'vanity and vexation of spirit'**. Every warrior needs to be a wise fighter, filled with the wisdom of God and operating under the direction of Him Who is Wisdom personified. When we seek after and pray to receive the Holy Spirit we potentially receive all the gifts of the Holy Spirit also. Among the nine gifts of the Holy Spirit is the gift of wisdom. Every warrior must pray for this gift if we are to be wise in the ways of the devil, and we must be wise to his deceit at all times! **1 Corinthians 12:7-11**

CHAPTER 15

SINGLENESS OF MIND AND PURPOSE

A Single Mind

The Bible teaches us that the Lord Jesus Christ, the Word made flesh, translated the Father's thoughts into the physical reality that is the earth and all its inhabitants. He was the Person of the Godhead that formed the first man and woman and breathed life into them. Therefore on the birth day of the first woman, the first Person to fill her vision was the Creator Himself.

The first touch that Eve felt, the first words that she heard, the first smile she saw and the first love that she felt flowed from the Lord. All of these firsts took place while the man was in a deep sleep, oblivious of God's work designed to complete and complement him. God made Eve. She was formed, shaped and wired to provide relational experiences of love, care, succor, understanding and companionship to Adam. But that was not all.

God prepared her, nurtured and instructed her so that she would minister to, enhance and elevate man's soul to a greater level of intimacy, worship, adoration and reverence with God in all aspects of their communion, whether physical, emotional or spiritual.

The Lord our God was woman's first love. He was her beginning, the source of her whole being, of all that she was and was designed to become. He knew her completely because He had made her. She basked in His Presence, drank her full of His love, His light, His joy.

The Lord was the woman's first delight, her first joy, her first pleasure and her first truth. She heard words of love, wisdom, knowledge, understanding, encouragement, praise, respect, support and concern from Him before she was ever introduced to man. In Him, Eve was alive; in Him she was all that she could be. The Lord prepared her for her wedding, created her perfect match and blessed her marriage union. She was equipped to fulfill her God-ordained destiny and honor the role assigned to her in the order of His creation.

There is no doubt that this should be the starting point of all women. I can only begin to imagine the confidence and certainty in which Eve walked; no hang-ups, no issues as to her identity in God, no questions as to the completeness of love that was her heritage. We need to have a solid, foundational relationship with the Father; be whole individuals secure with our selves, our value and our purpose before we bring another person in to develop and establish the three-fold relationship which is the marriage union, according to divine design. Seeking the Kingdom of God first and His righteousness allow everything and everyone else in our lives to fit together perfectly. The time as well as the gift of the single status can be the most rewarding, preparatory or productive time of a woman's life.

I refer to the period of singleness and the gift of being single as two different states of being. In the first, all girls and young women will be single before they are blessed with a life partner, a husband. This is a time of development, learning, preparation, maturation and even anticipation of the roles of a wife and a mother. Marriage is a great assignment in and of itself and one which the Lord ordained for women; there was never a time that the woman was alone. She was always hidden in God, in her husband, with the Father and then with the man as his wife; women are relational beings and have been so created from the beginning. And, despite many men's professed views on the issue of marriage, even if it is often in jest, it is a state that is ordained by God for men, also. It's not good to leave men to their own devices after all, there's no telling what they will get up to! The Creator Father declares it!

As noted previously, Eve was prepared for her role as wife and mother by the Divine and He should continue to be an integral part of the preparation of all young women. Center stage of a young woman's life should be occupied with learning and practicing obedience to all His teachings and His directives. A life of study, prayer and service to God whilst all the while facilitating the spiritual maturity and character of a woman of God should be the primary concern and occupation of a single woman. The practical and emotional aspects of motherhood and espousal responsibilities should also form a part of a young woman's education while she is single.

Three of the single women in the Scriptures that come to mind immediately are Rebecca, Rachel and Ruth, the three R's! These women, while they were in their single states, focused on building godly characters and dispositions. So that when God's time arrived for their husbands to come into their lives, they were ready and worthy. We encounter the women busying themselves with work and family responsibilities; they exhibited character traits that were an expression of the fruits of the Spirit. They displayed qualities that indicated their moral fiber and are the essential building blocks for developing into a fully fledged **Proverbs 31** woman of God.

A natural progression from this period of singleness for young women is the state of marriage and motherhood. However, for some of us, there might come a time when we realize that marriage is not our path and we embrace the gift of singleness. The realization that marriage is not a state for which every woman is ultimately destined is a reality and should not be seen as a deficiency, a lack of divine blessing or other negative connotations that society or the church community may attach. This state of singleness might be revealed at a very early age or sometime later with the passage of time.

The Apostle Paul considered it a great blessing to be single. However, married or single, our central focus and concern should always be the Way and the Will of the Lord. If a woman has remained in the single state and has not become a mother, she will not be subject to the challenges and the issues directly related to the following conditions enunciated in **Genesis 3:16**

    a. The pain, suffering and travail of child-bearing/child-rearing

    b. The desire for the husband and concerns of pleasing him

    c. The rule/headship of the husband over the wife

However, in the reality of today's society, singleness of any kind is an equally challenging status requiring a woman of God to strive to be firmly fixed on complete surrender and a relationship of intimate communion with God in order that she may succeed in maintaining her godly integrity. The devil in his diabolical deception to destroy the people of God will heap huge temptations of sexual sin in particular and unbelievable pressures on single women. These challenges will be more commonplace among women who live in communities that allow a high degree of personal freedom from parental, societal, moral and cultural accountability and control. The tests and temptations will come from all different directions and they will all be designed to distract, disrupt and destroy the single woman's relationship with God in order to pollute, dishonor and defile the gift of singleness.

So that just by virtue of being a woman, sexuality, sensuality, promiscuity, pornography, exploitation, oppression, degradation, poverty and their consequences will inherently challenge the female gender and single women more specifically. These must be recognized and dealt with according to the Word of God and by the power of His Holy Spirit. We must be able to expertly utilize our weapons of warfare, constantly and consistently, if we are to be over-comers in the face of these attacks by the enemy.

As humans who often fall short of God's standard, single women often find themselves acting outside of God's will. This can happen with those of us who were brought up by godly parents, are or were in the body of Christ but fall away from His grace or, were brought up outside of the knowledge of God and His commands concerning sexual sins. We may come from many different starting points but one thing is sure, we must get to a place of surrender to God and allow Him to give us the strength and the fortitude to fight the battle on this particular frontline. One status that proliferates in many communities in developed countries these days is the state of single parenthood; my personal status until quite recently. The challenges that this status brings can best be faced when we turn away from our sin, seek the forgiveness of God and make Him the Lord of our lives.

The devil has been so successful in undermining and polluting the 'Way of Righteousness', that even within the body of Christ; single people can be and often are subjected to all kinds of pressure directly related to their singleness. There is an attitude of censure and disapproval, superiority and exclusivity which prevail within the church and can negatively impact the confidence of a woman who achieves a certain age without having acquired a marriage partner. Being a single mother in Christ attracts additional attention and opposition. There is a separation, isolation and exclusion that single women in particular experience in the church that can distract and divert their focus to 'husband-hunting" rather than service, dedication and devotion to their work in the advancement of the Kingdom of God.

Being single enables a single minded pursuit of intimacy, worship, service and surrender to the Almighty. It allows us singleness of mind, affections, and actions in the service of the Lord. The desires of the heart should be directed towards the Creator and the work of His Kingdom. Passion in pursuit of our purpose, as determined, directed and destined by the Lord are the things that should rightly occupy the mind of a single person dedicated and committed to God.

Serving God as a single woman with or without children does not excuse us from the **Genesis 3:15 Commission.** When we belong to the Lord, we fall under His command and therefore are subject to His purpose and His plan. Where there is a former life of sin it is forgiven and forgotten by the Lord and we come into newness of life, a life that begins the day we are reborn as the spiritual daughters of the King. A God-focus that never falters and a God-faith that remains fixed on the Eternal One, will ensure that women remain faithful to the single state and to the call of the Lord on their lives.

But that does not mean that one escapes the attention of the devil. After all one is still a woman and therefore subject to the divine order to engage in hostilities against the enemy. He will still try to undermine and destroy the standing of women as warriors of the Kingdom by every and any means possible. It is likely that you will continue to be faced with ferocious attacks by the enemy given the potential of women warriors. In the natural realm, soldiers and operatives who are single and without children are preferred for deployment to the most dangerous assignments in warfare due to the focus, commitment and dedication that they can bring to their assignments.

This might very well be the same with single people who are not subject to the challenges that being married with a spouse and children presents. This is not to say that there is not equal commitment and faithfulness of all God's children. But the conditions and challenges of each state must be brought into subjection of the will of God.

The devil will use every means possible to draw your attention away from God, derail you with every conceivable subtlety and ultimately destroy your relationship with the Father. That was his greatest achievement in the Garden of Eden when by his deception, he was able to sever the personal, intimate and direct communion that Adam and Eve enjoyed with the Creator God. Paul is an exponent on the responsibilities, benefits and impact on one's relationship and service to the Lord as it pertains to being married or single. **1 Corinthians 7:32-34.**

A Single Purpose and a Single Mind

Every single woman should seek the Lord, abide in His presence; in that special place that Eve occupied when she first opened her eyes and beheld the face of a loving Creator and Father. Imagine the unsurpassable joy of sharing all your intimate thoughts and feelings with a perfect, all-knowing, all-caring, ever-loving God, and no-one else. He never disappoints, never insults or hurts your feelings, is never careless of speech, unforgiving, unfaithful, untruthful, forgetful of your needs or unmindful of your desires. He will never leave nor forsake you and He is always present with you in the good times and the challenging ones also. Being single is a great opportunity to be wholly available and submitted to the purpose and will of the Divine.

Having been single for the greater part of my life and recently having experienced marriage, I now more thoroughly appreciate that singleness is indeed a gift. It presents its own challenges but it is nevertheless a gift from the Lord to be equally valued, understood and appreciated as is the gift of marriage. The pressure that is exerted on single women to be married devalues and under-estimates the God-given state of being single. Singleness as a divine gift can be devalued by the enemy and used as a weapon to attack the worth, self esteem and recognition given to women who are single in the Lord. Such attack can only weaken the body of Christ, not strengthen it. Satan will always try to pollute, corrupt and counterfeit a good thing and turn it around for his evil purposes.

Being single is not a sin, being a single mother is not a sin but a sad, public manifestation of a private sexual sin. That sin can be repented of and will be pardoned like every other sin that we lay at the foot of the Cross, by the One who gave His life to atone for all sins including sexual sin. The contrition of a single woman who has fallen prey to sexual sin is usually reflected in the totality of her submission to the Lord. After all a life outside the marital union that partakes of its ordinances is the manifestation of a spirit of rebellion and so a new life in Christ is equally a reversal of a wayward heart and a humble acceptance of the Lordship of our God.

It is time that we recognize that the ultimate achievement of each state or status of a woman is to make God the greatest desire of her life, the first love and the complete purpose of her existence. All roads must lead to the Divine or else we will all perish; and God is not willing that any of us should perish. He sends us His Spirit to bring us to recognition of the obstacles that impede or prevent us from placing all our affections on Him; stumbling stones that can cause us to lose our focus, our faith and our final inheritance in His Kingdom.

What it comes down to, is that whether single, or married, we must strive to have a singleness of mind, of purpose and of determination to be spiritual warriors of the Lord; always prepared, on duty or on call, ready at a moment's notice to face the adversary. There are many single women in the Bible, apart from those previously referred to, who demonstrate the different challenges and blessings inherent in the single state. It is not one's marital status that will decide whether one is a warrior of the Lord's army or not. It is one's preparedness to choose life or death, liberty or bondage, the Kingdom of God and His righteousness or the courts of the prince of darkness and his rebellious dominion.

When God declared the **Genesis 3:15 Commission**, it was to all women, both married and single. The training schedule may be different but the weapons of our warfare are the same. The Way to eternal life, to choose to be on God's side is by accepting the atonement of Jesus the Christ, Son of the Living God. He came into this world so that we might have life and live it in His abundance. It does not matter whether we are single-unmarried, single-widowed, single-parent or married women, we must serve the Lord as dedicated, focused and single-minded warriors of the Cause of the Cross of Calvary.

The challenges that we each face are designed to train us to carry out our assignments and even when the devil sets traps to ensnare, derail or destroy us, the Lord will turn it around for our benefit so that the seemingly bad experience will provide valuable lessons for our warfare against Satan. **James 1:6-8** teaches us that a double-minded person cannot be an effective warrior of the Lord because of instability, unreliability and uncertainty about everything. It is not our marital status that makes us His warriors; it is our acceptance of His call to service in love, humility and obedience.

Are you an "Orpah" or a "Ruth"?

It is purely by inspiration of the Holy Spirit that my writing is personalized and poetic license exercised in a manner that imputes additional personal details to the characters studied and written about in this book. The details however have been inferred from the information contained in Holy Writ as well as from my personal experience as a woman walking through the same or similar challenges and circumstances. This approach is one that I did not embark on lightly or set out on by my own design but the time spent in study and prayer brought me understanding and empathy with the women from the Holy Spirit in this intimate way. I pray that this method of writing will not cause offense but will help other women to place themselves in the shoes of our mothers of faith and gain a personally applicable understanding of the issues that most of us face today.

Naomi had journeyed to Moab with her husband and two sons to escape a period of drought and famine in her home town of Bethlehem. During the period of her sojourn in Moab, first her husband and then both her sons died. She was bereaved and bereft of hope. Although I am able to empathize with her, it is hard to imagine the loss that she felt. Her husband and both her sons were gone.

Added to this personal loss of family, Naomi faced destitution and poverty. This was not an uncommon situation for widows in those days, a situation made even more acute in the Jewish culture in the absence of a kinsman of her husband to marry her and take the responsibility of her support. Naomi was in Moab, separated from any family members and therefore any chance of salvation by such a kinsman, even if one existed. She had lost everything; her family, status and security. It is no surprise that her mind turned to thoughts of home; to a place where she belonged, to her people, her culture and her inheritance as a covenant woman.

And so a strong desire grew in Naomi's heart until she was propelled into action; to journey back to Bethlehem, to her home, her place of belonging. The famine which had caused her departure to Moab no longer existed. Her desire was further fuelled by the news that **"The Lord had come to the aid of His people by providing food for them"**. Despite the loss of faith in the provisions of the Almighty that drove her family to Moab, to abandon their home and their appointed place, God had kept faith with His covenant people in Bethlehem. Naomi and her family had lost faith in the God of their fathers, Abraham, Isaac and Jacob. God's promises to Israel was lost sight of and , turning their backs on God and His promises they went into Moab, an idolatrous nation. They did not remember that they who seek the Lord shall not want for anything. **Psalms 34:90**. The Word of God admonishes us to wait on the Lord, to stand on His promises even in the face of adverse conditions, God will always come through.

But those who wait for the Lord [who expect, look for, and hope in Him] shall change and renew their strength and power; they shall lift their wings and mount up [close to God] as eagles [mount up to the sun]; they shall run and not be weary, they shall walk and not faint or become tired. Isaiah 40:31.

There had been a change for the better back at home; there was an abundance of blessing in her homeland and perhaps, Naomi reasoned there might be a slim chance that she could find a way to access a more prosperous future and a brighter outlook for herself among her own kinfolks. Her widowed daughters-in-law, Orpah and Ruth, were become to her like her own children. It was expected that once they were married they would remain duty-bound to honor the parents of their husbands.

Naomi, convinced that the future was very uncertain, tried to dissuade the young women from accompanying her. She was ready to release them from their obligations to her. She argued that they would be better off returning to their own families, remaining in their own countries where the customs and worship of their people was familiar and where, their prospects of a new start was much more likely. In Bethlehem they would be foreigners and it was not usual in Bethlehem for the Children of Israel to marry outside of their own people. This was in adherence to the Laws of Jehovah God.

Orpah heeded Naomi's words and as her affections were still in Moab, she gladly returned to her family. She was undoubtedly hopeful of making a new match with another husband and enjoying the security of being provided for and having a family; raising children of her own. These were not unreasonable expectations for a young woman and neither could she be reproached for wanting these things for her self and her future.

Orpah was a forward looking young woman who seized the opportunity to plan her future according to her own decisions and desires. After all, as Naomi had rightly pointed out, she had no material benefits to offer. She was just an old, homesick lady, returning to her homeland because she had heard that God's hand was turned towards His people and she could again live under the Shadow of the God of Israel. The revelation here is that we all have a home to which we must return. Our home is in that state of perfection in the Lord, living in His Presence, His abundance from which states we departed in Eden, the memory of which is buried in our spirits even today.

Ruth however, had a different focus to her sister-in-law and so she refused to leave Naomi. She too would have the same prospects as Orpah of securing a new husband, and the protection and financial well being that went along with that status. But Ruth recognized the real choice that was put before her. The choice that Ruth faced was; the material and espousal security of her old idolatrous life with her kinsfolk and country men or, the uncertain worldly position of her mother-in-law and the chance to serve the God of Abraham, Isaac, Israel and Naomi. She had been learning of the Lord from her mother-in-law and everything in her hungered to know Him even more. **Luke 10:25-27.**

Let us pause for a while and try to put ourselves in Ruth's position. She could choose to stay in her comfort zone. She would be among her own people; practice the customs and rituals she was familiar with since she was a girl. She could stay close to her relatives and not face the possibility of being isolated, ostracized or alienated in a foreign land where she would face cultural, linguistic and religious barriers. Remaining in Moab seemed to be the obvious, smart and easy option. But whether it was easy to choose to stay or not depended solely on what was the deepest desire of Ruth's heart.

Hard, Harsh Facts; Easy Choice

What were the issues that she must deal with if she stayed with Naomi? Well, she would be a foreigner, without the provision and protection of a husband. As things could be reasoned at the time of her decision and the facts that she had available to her; she would certainly encounter prejudice, suffer poverty, have sole responsibility of caring for an aging mother-in-law, be single for the rest of her life, be childless and die without anyone to care for her in her old age. Her chances of having a happy, prosperous life in Bethlehem amount to almost none; zero in fact when viewed with the natural eyes. In Moab she had every opportunity of a fresh start with as much prospects as ever she did before her first marriage. Was there really a choice to be made here? As I said earlier, it all depended on what she desired to achieve for her life. What would your choice be if faced with such a decision?

Seemingly against all logic and good sense, Ruth chose to remain loyal to Naomi but she had not done so without thought. She determined and purposed in her mind and her heart that there was no going back for her. She had received a revelation from the Lord. Her destiny was with Naomi in Bethlehem! She did not know what future she would have there except that of hardship and duty. But the Lord had bestowed on her the spiritual gift of a deep abiding love for her mother-in-law and for everything to do with her; namely her home, her people and her God.

Ruth shifted her attention and her perspective away from self, from personal gains, from the worship of idols of any kind. She had caught a glimpse of the truth and the Life that might be obtained in the Lord Jehovah and she was not willing to give it up, whatever the cost. The God of Love had touched her heart by His Spirit, acting on a seed of love that was already placed there by Him; love for another person, whatever its consequences and costs to self and now that seed began to grow in the Shadow and oversight of the Spirit of God, it began to produce good fruits; the fruits of the Spirit.

Ruth did not make consideration of self her first priority. She was not concerned with her own well being. She had received a divine deposit of the love of God in her heart for her mother-in-law. Motivated by her love for Naomi, she submitted herself completely to the working of that love and so to the will of the Eternal One. God had appointed and assigned her the task of accompanying her mother-in-law back to Bethlehem and she did not shrink from that duty, not because of obligation but out of a deep agape love. Ruth began her walk of faith when she made the choice to accompany Naomi to Bethlehem and leave her Moab behind!

Her declarations of Love for her mother-in-law and her submission to God's will are tendered in words that cannot be surpassed for their eloquent expression of love and devotion. Since I was a very young woman I have loved the King James Version of this passage of Scripture. However, for greater clarity, the NIV version is quoted here for our consideration and our lesson.

But Ruth replied, "Don't urge me to leave you or to turn back from you. Where you go I will go, and where you stay I will stay. Your people will be my people and your God my God. Where you die I will die, and there will I be buried. May the Lord deal with me, be it ever so severely, if anything but death separates you and me. Ruth 1:16 and 17

Ruth was focused on her God-ordained assignment. She had learnt sufficient to know that the Lord was her best choice. She turned away from earthly riches, from the carnal wisdom of self and from the promises of this world that lasts only for this lifetime. Instead she fixed her gaze on the God of all creation, the Provider and Sustainer of life and the one true desire of a heart seeking after the righteousness of God. It is only the way, the truth and the wisdom of the Most High that is worth all sacrifice.

In our lives, we often come to a place of choice and decision that will bring us either life or death. We can choose to follow the way of the world and the wisdom of self. We can choose to be seduced by the promises of worldly riches, status, reputation and a self-determined future. Alternatively, we can choose to die with Christ so that we can also be resurrected in Him to the certain promise of eternal life in His Kingdom. **Luke 14:16**. The choice is simple. The former is a choice for death and Baal, the latter, eternal life and Jehovah God. As Joshua declared to the Children of Israel,

And if it seems evil to you to serve the Lord, choose for yourselves this day whom you will serve, whether the gods

which your fathers served on the other side of the River, or the gods of the Amorites, in whose land you dwell; but as for me and my house, we will serve the Lord. **Joshua 24:15**

The questions we need to answer are simple. Are we ready to leave our comfort zone and commit our lives to God, even unto death? **John 12:25**. Are we pressing towards the mark of the higher calling despite our points of origin? Are you ready to give up your former dreams, desires, ambitions and pursuits in order to take up the purpose and divinely ordained assignment of the Lord for your life; even if that requires you to journey to a foreign land, where the language, the culture and the people are alien to you?

How about if you have to give up your status, standing and lifestyle? Are you a Ruth or are you an Orpah? Is God the Arbiter of your destiny or are you determined to declare your independence from God as you take charge of your own destiny? Have you changed gears, shifted your focus, developed a God-vision or stepped into God-faith in your life? Is your love and esteem of self greater than your love for the lost, weak or imprisoned members of the human family, for our Lord, His mission and His Kingdom? Today, the choice is before you and the decision is yours. I pray that you choose life!

Is your Destination Bethlehem or Moab?

There is still much to instruct us in a continued study of the experiences of the young woman Ruth and the consequences of her choice as discussed above. On different occasions, I have considered the end of a relationship; either my own or that of friends or relatives. Why did things work out the way that they did? For example, for myself I would think, I was faithful, loving and supportive. For some women, they kept a nice home, worked hard and yet still find themselves alone, abandoned, divorced or widowed.

The effect is almost always the same. Our self-confidence has taken a battering; self esteem is a distant memory and faith in finding a partner in the future, too fantastic to contemplate. We feel certain that we are failures or at the very least that everyone else sees us that way. Even when a spouse leaves by death, the deceased partner seems to have cheated and left the survivor behind, unfairly. But what if this is a God-given opportunity to exercise some God-faith? What if this is just your place, your time to make a fresh start, make a decision, a choice, to stay in Moab or take the journey to Bethlehem? Again, the question is; are you a Ruth or are you an Orpah? What is your chosen destination?

In today's world a widowed woman can be any age. This is especially true with the proliferation of disasters, diabolical devastations, diseases and diverse death-dealing situations and occurrences abounding in every place imaginable. Losing a partner and being left to fend for oneself and one's children is an experience that more and more women have to cope with. In truth, it is a devastating time for families left broken-hearted, numb, angry, and sad or, devoid of hope for a happy and secure future.

Within the conundrum of human emotions, as unreasonable as it might appear to be, the death of a loved one can often translate into feelings of abandonment. For example, a husband promises to love and protect, be a companion and friend for life. Now through death, oftentimes sudden, unexpected and unprepared for, he has broken his promise. Reasonableness or commonsense becomes totally irrelevant to the heart and mind of the surviving partner who had placed all their hope and happiness in the person and presence of that individual.

In the final analysis, the feelings and experience of the bereaved person is not very dissimilar to that of a divorced spouse. It may be difficult to grasp while one is dealing with the practical, emotional and psychological fall-out from such traumas, but these valley experiences are God-given opportunities to gain a new perspective on life, pursue a different goal or revisit and revive delayed, discarded or denied dreams or plans.

It is not my intention to make light of the enormity of the hurt or of the task of moving forward with one's life minus a partner but the unit was three strands and two still remain, namely the surviving partner and the Lord! Let me encourage everyone in these situations to view these 'weigh-stations' in life as the perfect time to seek after the eternal; to search for God with all our hearts and get ever more intimate with Him; to get a heavenly outlook and switch to a God-focused life instead of a man-focused one. Every painful experience is a pregnant possibility that can birth life or death to our souls. Seize the opportunity to spend even more time with the Lord; talk with Him more, yield your life to Him, birth a new present and a divinely directed, purpose-filled future.

Naomi Needed No New Name

Naomi had lost not only her husband but her two sons as well. She had two daughter-in-laws left her but no grand-children. The future was looking bleak. Sadness, bitterness, disappointment, frustration and defeat overwhelmed her, making her feel older than her years. Naomi did not like herself or her life in Moab anymore. She even told her friends to call her, 'Mara', a name meaning bitterness. She felt loss and abandoned. When she left Bethlehem with her family to escape the famine, she felt positive about their prospects.

It is amazing how we can make a move to a seemingly better environment, better chances of a full and prosperous life; a better job, a better neighborhood, a better country, only to discover that in the process of advancement or supposed progress one has left behind one's true treasure, the Presence and protection of the Almighty. Is it any surprise then to find that one has exchanged joy for sadness, delight for bitterness, and the Tree of Life for the thistles of torment?

Ruth's mother-in-law felt that she had not and could not live up to the name, 'Naomi', which meant joy. Life and its trials had robbed her of her joy. The pain that she felt was understandably great. Her memories would probably be all that was left to her now, the best years of her life was behind her. Yet, somehow, she had a desire to return to Bethlehem. Perhaps she must have reasoned, it was just wishful thinking on her part that things might be different there, or just a longing for home or yet, just a wish to die and be buried among her own people.

Naomi was not sure why the longing for Bethlehem had come upon her so strongly but it was compelling enough to propel her into action. I will suggest that the desire came from the Lord and it was placed in her heart and mind for the glory of His name. Like all of mankind, she was made to bring Him honor and she was being given the opportunity to be an instrument of His will and a witness of His love and His mercies; not just in her life-time but ours also.

Bethlehem means 'House of bread'. It is also the place of Jesus' birth into the earth realm. And, we learn from the Scriptures that the Lord Jesus is the "Bread of Life". Therefore it is appropriate that when we have wandered and lived out of the will of the Lord; alienated ourselves in our Moab in search of materialism and carnality, an ever-loving Father would place a desire for home, for Bethlehem, for the House of Bread, for the Bread of life within our hearts! We too should be longing for Bethlehem, hurrying to Bethlehem, to the Lord, for the Bread of life; the Bread which gives life eternal and is ours when we receive Jesus as our Redeemer and the Lord of our life. He is the true manna from on high. **John 6:32-33**

Naomi had considered her course after the death of her husband and sons. She was unable to see any joy up ahead of her because she was still in the old habit of depending on self, on human foresight and planning. I am sure however that her heart turned to God in desperate prayer. It is what we do when we have lost everything that we valued most. We cry out, question, harass and harangue the Lord.

Finally, through the grace of our loving Father, if we surrender ourselves to Him, we 'come to our senses' and only then can He energize the seed of our destiny that He placed in us. Naomi came to herself and a desire for the familiarity of her homeland moved her to action. It is irrelevant how convinced and convicted we may be about an idea, a vocation or calling on our lives; if we do not act on it we cannot realize the blessings that it brings. Every seed must first be sown before it can be grown.

So also faith, if it does not have works (deeds and actions of obedience to back it up), by itself is destitute of power (inoperative, dead). James 2:17

Bethlehem was prospering under the renewed favor of the Almighty. Like the prodigal, Naomi arose, determined to travel back to Bethlehem and perhaps find a renewing in the Lord's favor. She felt her need of God's hand in her life, she longed to share in the abundance that He was bestowing on her people and her home, so she packed her bags and started on her way back; back to His presence, His pre-eminence and His plan for her life. As always, when God plants His purpose in our minds, He makes a way for that purpose to be realized; when He imparts a vision and gives us a mission we must get up and get going. He will take care of all the needs that must be met to bring the vision to maturity and fulfillment; He is the Source of all the necessary resources required to achieve His purpose. Naomi got going and so did her daughter-in-law, Ruth.

A Resource for Divine Destiny

Ruth listened, observed and determined not to return to the same lifestyle in which she was brought up; it involved belief in and dependence on idols. It was the custom of her people, the practice of her parents and of the generations before them. She had been taught observance of all the rituals. Yet she came to a realization that the God of the Israelites, with whom she had become acquainted through her marriage, touched a place in her heart and mind that had always been dissatisfied. This was God's love, reaching out, drawing her to Him.

Up to this time, Ruth may have been passive in her belief and acquiescent in her mother-in-law's worship of Jehovah. Now Naomi presented her with the choice that all humans must face. In response, Ruth made a radical decision and put the God of her husband and her mother-in-law in control of her life. Ruth confronted her reality, met her fears head on and turned her back on Baal. She would do whatever the Lord led her to and in this instance it was to stay with, care for and accompany Naomi to Bethlehem.

Ruth was exercising a radical faith, a God-faith and in so doing she was breaking the traditions and devil worship of generations of her ancestors. The journey ahead might prove difficult and the prospects appeared daunting, a little depressing even but she had placed all her hopes; her faith and her future in the God of the Children of Israel. By this, she crucified the flesh and prepared to take it step by step, day by day; motivated and encouraged by her love for Naomi and the power of the Lord Most High working His will through her and for her and Naomi.

And Ruth said ... Thy people shall be my people and thy God my God. Ruth   1:16 (KJV).

Lessons from Ruth

Ruth's experience may be summarized as follows.

1. Ruth came to a place of self-awareness, knowledge of the Most High and personal recognition of her own status and standing as a sinner in need of His love.

2. With her confrontation of herself, Ruth made a decision to turn away from her sinful nature and this included leaving mother, father, relatives, friends, community and country, to follow after God's plans.

3. The rejection of her former, carnal life, culture and religion indicated her acceptance of the Lordship of Jehovah as the ruler of her life. Ruth gave herself to God; a living sacrifice. **Romans 12:1.**

4. Ruth's conviction, action and desire to serve the Lord was a step of faith; she was walking now by faith not by sight when she submitted to the prompting of the Holy Spirit to accompany her mother- in-law, despite the negative prospects that might act upon a carnally minded person.

5. When Ruth heeded the bidding of the Lord and went to Bethlehem, she transitioned to another level in the Spirit.

When she was seemingly destitute and homeless, she actually increased her territory by stepping into her divinely ordained destiny. Unless and until we act on the directions and leading of the Lord we cannot activate God's plan for our lives.

6. Ruth's obedience to God's purpose gave her a new life in Bethlehem. She was blessed by the Elders of Israel with the blessing of Leah and Rachel, the mothers of the twelve tribes of the nation of Israel. And she brought further blessings upon her husband Boaz, even as the word of God promises. **Proverbs 31:10-31.**

I dare to believe that the Lord in His wisdom and in the plans He had for Ruth's life, gave her the deep, strong love that she had for her mother-in-law. I believe also that as iron sharpens iron, Ruth caught the fire of Naomi's desire to go to Bethlehem. Ruth's love caused her to have a strong desire to be a companion to Naomi on her long and arduous journey, as well as a support to her mother-in-law to the best of her ability. These desires grounded in love, led her to her divine destiny. Submission such as she modeled can only originate in the heart of the Lord.

Staying in your Moab has its merits and certainly can offer worldly compensations that are much sought after and highly regarded by the carnal mind. Yet, as our Savior and Redeemer questioned, **"What shall it profit a man or woman, if we shall gain the whole world but lose our souls"? Mark 8:36.** I implore you in the paraphrased words of the Psalmist David to lift up your heads, catch the vision, fill your heart and mind with our God and the King of Glory shall come in and make His abode with you. He comes with a deliverance package; severance of the ties with Moab and the keys to your 'Kingdom Blessings' in Bethlehem, the house of Bread.

Why do you spend your money for that which is not bread, and your earnings for what does not satisfy? Hearken diligently to Me, and eat what is good, and let your soul

delight itself in fatness [the profuseness of spiritual joy]. **Isaiah 55:2**

One final point to note about Ruth before moving on; out of her love and devotion, Ruth was prepared, ready and willing to give up everything that she knew with certainty, for a future that was unknown, unseen and in the hands of the God of the Children of Israel. The life of Ruth exemplifies God-faith in action. She continued to follow the advice and directions of her mother-in-law and to come into agreement with God's plan for her. It was her special favor and divinely apportioned destiny to be married to one of the godliest men and one of the wealthiest in Bethlehem. She was further blessed with children and brought joy and honor to her mother-in-law, to her husband and to her God.

Naomi also came to a place of joy, purpose and fulfillment by returning to the Lord, her home and her first name. In **Ruth 4:14** we read;

And the women said to Naomi, Blessed be the Lord, Who has not left you this day without a close kinsman, and may his name be famous in Israel.

15. And may he be to you a restorer of life and a nourisher and a supporter in your old age, for your daughter-in-law who loves you, who is better to you than seven sons, has borne him.

16. Then Naomi took the child and laid him in her bosom and became his nurse.

17. And her neighbor women gave him a name, saying, A son is born to Naomi. They named him Obed. He was the father of Jesse, the father of David. (KJV)

It is Ruth's great privilege to be mentioned in **Matthew 1:5**, as the great-grand-mother of King David, son of Jesse and therefore an ancestor of our Lord and Savior, Jesus the Christ.

And there shall come forth a rod out of the stem of Jesse, and a Branch shall grow out of his roots: 2. And the Spirit of the Lord shall rest upon Him, the spirit of wisdom and understanding, the spirit of counsel and might, the spirit of knowledge and of the fear of the Lord; 3. And shall make Him of quick understanding in the fear of the Lord: and He shall not judge after the sight of His eyes, neither reprove after the hearing of His ears; 4. But with righteousness shall He judge the poor, and reprove with equity for the meek of the earth: and He shall smite the earth with the rod of His mouth, and with the breath of His lips shall He slay the wicked. 5. And righteousness shall be the girdle of His loins, and faithfulness the girdle of His reins. Isaiah 11:1-5 (KJV)

We never know exactly what the Lord has in store for us but we can be assured that He knows how to give good gifts to His children and that it is His great delight and His plan to prosper us. **Matthew 7:7-11**. We need to listen to the Word of the Lord and turn our backs on our lives of idolatry;

- following after strange gods
- obsession with self
- absorption with materialism
- personal elevation and promotion

Behold, all you [enemies of your own selves] who attempt to kindle your own fires [and work out your own plans of salvation], who surround and gird yourselves with momentary sparks, darts, and firebrands that you set aflame! – walk by the light of your self-made fire and of the sparks that you have kindled [for yourself, if you will]! But this shall you have from My hand: you shall lie down in grief and torment. Isaiah 50:11

Instead we must look towards our Bethlehem, to the One Who is able to save us from our sins and supply our every need. We will earn a new name in heaven, one that will be revealed in the eternities that is our inheritance, because it is the Almighty that offers and sustains life; He is the Bread of Life. Then and only then will we find a new purpose that is aligned with God's plan for our lives and be able to walk in the fullness of life with our Lord.

> **For I know the plans I have for you, declares the Lord, Plans to prosper you and not to harm you, plans to give you hope and a future. 12 Then you will call upon Me and come and pray to me, and I will listen to you. 13. You will seek me and find me when you seek me with all your heart. 14. I will be found by you, declares the Lord, and will bring you back ... to the place from which I carried you into exile. Jeremiah 29:11-14. (NIV)**

CHAPTER 16

ENGAGING THE ENEMY

Boot Camp

The war that is raging originated with Lucifer's rebellion against God and over the last few thousand years has directly invoked and employed the service of man since the 'Great Fall from Grace' of the human family in the Garden east of Eden. All of creation has likewise been affected since and the battles that proliferate take place both in the natural and the spiritual realms.

We battle daily **"against the devil's schemes. For our struggle is not against flesh and blood, but against the ruler, against the authorities, against the powers of this dark world and against the spiritual forces of evil in the heavenly realms"**. Ephesians 6:12.

Man was given authority over the earth by the Creator but due to our disobedient, adulterous hearts, we allowed the devil, that diabolical schemer, to usurp our God-ordained authority. The first parents' downfall had come at the behest of a creature created by God to be in subjection to man. The woman rejected the responsibility of her position as ordered by God and listened and acted on the beguiling words of the serpent. This creature was being used by the devil to undermine God's authority and challenge His commands. The woman failed to exercise her God-given earth realm authority to rebuke the serpent, who was subject to her and instead became prey and prize in Satan's mutiny against heaven. **Genesis 1:28**

However, having been bested by the subtle deception of the devil that resulted in sin, womankind was thereafter possessed of a peculiar experience and a God-given spirit of warfare that would be of great value to the human family in the battles between the righteous sovereignty of our God and the anarchy of sin and Satan. Experience is a great teacher and its lessons are not to be taken lightly, underestimated or under-valued by the warriors of God. Knowing the enemy (and all about the enemy) is the first duty of a good general. The defeat suffered in Eden exposes the determination of our enemy to destroy, at any cost, the Kingdom of our Lord. All his tactics and his strategies involve the deployment of weapons that attacks the, emotional, mental, psychological and spiritual wholeness of man with the consequential manifestation in the physical.

The flesh, the natural, physical man is likewise never spared any and all plots, plans and ploys that will lead to destruction and death. Eve was ambushed and dispossessed by spiritual guerilla warfare; defeated but not destroyed forever, as was the intent, desire and purpose of the devil. What was meant for evil, our God turned around for good. The adversary had succeeded in beguiling the woman. She had fallen prey to his tactics but the Lord was not about to give up on us. **1 Corinthians 13:4-8**

It is the nature of true love not to succumb easily to defeat. Love perseveres even in the face of opposition and rejection. **1 Corinthians 13:7.** Instead of being left to the wiles of the wicked serpent, God decreed that the woman would become his arch enemy. She would have unction to be at enmity with him; oppose him on all fronts, fight against his schemes, evil plans, influences and designs. The aim of Satan is to win supremacy and his plan is to use us, the human family as his pawn and like a chess player he just as easily sacrifices us to defeat the Kingdom. We are called of God to return to Him and to war against our joint enemy with body, mind and spirit and, join the Lord on the frontline in His army of righteousness.

In the greater scheme of our Lord, a woman's experiences may be utilized as teaching aids and tools to recognize and counteract the wiles of the enemy and challenge him at the spiritual level through the power of the Lord. Womankind, once she is freed from the bondage of sin and the shackles of death would be astute, alert, keenly conscious of the ease with which her emotions, appetites, senses and interest can be engaged and used as a weapon against her, and more, as a weapon against the rule of Jehovah.

God in His wisdom and love decreed spiritual warfare to the woman and purposed that the conditions, challenges and consequences of disobedience would make of her life a training ground, a boot camp environment, preparing and equipping her to operate in a hostile territory and to fight the fight of faith against the devil. So it was that in addition to being the vessel chosen to be a partner with God in His plan for man's salvation, God Himself also appointed Eve and all the daughters of Eve to be His spiritual warriors, partners with Him in the fight for the soul of man; warriors with a royal mandate to be on the frontline of the spiritual offensive against the serpent and his fallen angels.

Our assignment was declared by the Lord at the same hour of man's darkest, despairing moment of alienation from the Father and condemnation to mortality. God is not forcing us to fight against the enemy; He has declared a state of hostility but it does not compel or force us to accept the commission. However, if we choose to seek the Lord and be citizens of His Kingdom again; the Lord has made a way for us to stand against Satan, to oppose the oppressor. If we choose to accept it, we will begin a journey back to ourselves, to who we really are, back to being 'women'; God's women. The words that decree our divine duty and destiny are declared with clarity of purpose and an imperative that cannot be denied. The devil is our enemy and our final victory lies in the Seed, Jesus the Christ.

I will put enmity between thee and the woman, and between thy seed and her Seed, He shall bruise thy head and thou shall bruise His heel. Gen. 3:15 (KJV)

The devil's tactics against Eve in the Garden employed intrinsic as well as extrinsic factors to appeal to her ego. He came against her emotionally, mentally and physically. If we are to prevail against him then we must bring all of these areas of our being into subjection to the Lord and to His will and His righteousness. We dare not imagine or attempt to stand in our own strength; the devil proved unequivocally that when we do then are we weak and easy prey to his deceit and temptation. We can only prevail if we stand in Christ, hidden in His righteousness and armed with His strength, His righteousness and the weapons of spiritual war that comes from being on His side. Against all these Satan is unable to triumph! For example, we need to put on the breastplate of righteousness, the righteousness of the Lamb, so that God's love which is in our hearts will be protected from the lies, the darts of doubt, disbelief and hatred directed at us daily by the devil and his demons. The breastplate of righteousness is our shield in spiritual warfare. It cannot be penetrated by the attacks of the enemy; his arrows are evil and his weapons sourced in darkness therefore they cannot penetrate the light of righteousness.

> **And the Light shines on in the darkness, for the darkness has never overpowered it [put it out or absorbed it or appropriated it, and is unreceptive to it]. John 1:5**

The Weapons of Spiritual Warfare

> **14. Stand therefore [hold your ground], having tightened the belt of truth around your loins and having put on the breastplate of integrity and of moral rectitude and right standing with God,**
>
> **15. And having shod your feet in preparation [to face the enemy with the firm-footed stability, the promptness, and the readiness produced by the good news] of the Gospel of peace.**
>
> **16. Lift up over all the [covering] shield of saving faith, upon which you can quench all flaming missiles of the wicked [one].**

17. And take the helmet of salvation and the sword that the Spirit wields, which is the Word of God.

18. Pray at all times (on every occasion, in every season) in the Spirit, with all [manner of] prayer and entreaty. To that end keep alert and watch with strong purpose and perseverance, interceding in behalf of all the saints (God's consecrated people). Ephesians 6:14-17

This Scripture details the armor of the warriors of God; male and female, married and single, big and small without exception. Our training grounds/camps may be located in different experiences but the outcome must be the expert acquisition of the same measure of skill, experience, power, confidence, boldness, character and Christ-like qualities if we are to fight a good fight and win the battles that we face. The following is an inventory, a checklist of the weapons of our warfare which are not carnal but spiritual

1. **The Belt/Girdle of Truth**
2. **Breastplate of Righteousness**
3. **Footwear – Gospel of Preparation & Peace**
4. **Shield of Faith**
5. **Helmet of Salvation**
6. **Sword of the Spirit - Word of God**
7. **Prayers**

1. **Belt or Girdle of Truth**: Jesus declares in the Scriptures that He is the Truth and if we receive Him as Lord, we receive His Spirit and come into all truth. One of the defining characteristic of Satan is lying. The devil seduces and tempts into sin by lies, deceit, and dishonesty in all his communication. As a consequence he can never be trusted. Counterfeit is the manifestation of a sophisticated lie, and compromise is a subtle lie.

If we are in Christ then we can have no part of lies and that is why girding our loins, keeping our garments of righteousness held fast by the belt of truth will stop us from succumbing to lies, deceit, trickery and moral compromises. Truth is every word of God. We must be honest, open, transparent and trustworthy in all our communications with God and everyone with whom we deal or come into contact.

Let your Yes be simply Yes, and your No be simply No; anything more than that comes from the evil one. Matthew 5:37

2. **The Breastplate of Righteousness:** Being reborn into the Kingdom of God through Jesus our Lord requires that we become new creatures, leaving our old carnal natures in the past. For us to be conformed to the image and the character of Christ, we need a new heart of flesh which only the Father can give us. And He will give us a new heart if we ask in Christ Jesus. Once He has given us our new hearts we must protect it from satanic attacks; for example, from appeals to our emotions by the enemy.

He deceived Eve by first undermining her faith and then by appealing to her emotions. This in turn unduly influenced her mind and her decision to sin. Our heart is the seat of our beliefs, for example it is our heart that believes that Jesus is Lord. **Romans 10:10.** The heart is also the ark of flesh that houses the commandments of the Lord. **Hebrews 10:16.** We have looked at the importance of our new heart earlier and the breastplate is not just for keeping Christ in but for keeping the lies of the evil one from penetrating, infecting and corrupting us unto death.

3. **The Shoes of Preparation and Peace:** The five wise virgins were well-prepared to face any problem or eventuality that would delay their journey by making sure that they had extra oil in their lamps. A warrior must always be alert, ready

to move at a moments notice to help, encourage, support; teach, preach, or testify of the gospel of peace that comes from being in covenant with the Lord.

There should never be a time that we are caught off guard or panicked by a storm. It was said in times past that a man who slept with his boots on was always ready, always prepared. We too must be warriors who sleep with our shoes on! Through the authority of the Christ we can command the storms of life to be still and whatever we bind on earth is bound in heaven and whatever we loose on earth is loosed in heaven. **Matthew 18:18-20**

4. **The Shield of Faith:** Without faith it is impossible to please God and with faith even the size of a mustard seed, one can move mountains, says the Word of the Lord. A shield is a protective weapon that literally does what its name suggests; it shields one from attacks of the enemy. The shield operates in situations to repel the 'arrows that fly by day'; the result is that 'a thousand shall fall at your side and ten thousand at your right hand' but they shall not come near you. The Lord is our Shield and Buckler; His truth and His faithfulness. **Psalms 91:4-7**

5. **The Helmet of Salvation:** The helmet which covers the head represents covering and protection for the mind and the will. There is a war that rages within the mind of man between the carnal and spiritual nature for control of our thoughts and our will. The whispering attacks of the enemy can be insistent, confusing, demanding, condemnatory and evil. He wants to gain control so that we will join his rebellion.

The mind is the place in which sin and insanity originates if we fail to bring every thought under subjection to the Lord. The mind will repeat, replay and relive our experiences; the words we hear or have heard, the things we have done, seen, or think; our thoughts, feelings or hurts will be rehashed in such a way that we are held in captivity to our past, to sin and desolation. It is important for us to have the commandments of God, His words fill up our minds: His words are life and the certain knowledge of His salvation will ensure our liberty.

> **Let this same attitude and purpose and [humble] mind be in you which was in Christ Jesus; [Let Him be your example in humility]. Philippians 2:5**

6. **The Sword of the Spirit:** This Sword is the Word of God and the Word is sharper than any two-edged sword; it is a weapon of attack and defense when it is Spirit-wielded and directed. We should store up the Word of God in our hearts, studying them so that we may be found worthy of the privilege of serving the Lord. Jesus the Christ is the Master Swordsman whose expertise and example we must model. Do not forget that the devil also knows the Word of God and can manipulate it to suit every twist and turn in the arguments that he presents for our entrapment, condemnation and defeat.

Since the Sword is the Sword of the Spirit, the Words will not be effective without the co-operation and conviction of the Holy Spirit. In the final analysis, the Word became flesh and lived among us, the world was made by Him and nothing exists without the Word. **John 1-2.** The Word of God creates and it can annihilate, its effect is unlimited and the power of the Word of God is limitless and timeless. It will always accomplish that to which it is directed.

7. **Prayers:** Throughout this study we have learnt that communication, an essential element of union, communion, fellowship and relationship is very important. But the most important communication in which we can participate is the communication that takes place between heaven and earth, man and God, the King and His subjects, the Kingdom and its citizen, the Lord and His Church, the Redeemer and the

Redeemed; in other words all kinds of communication that is prayer.

Prayer allows us to speak with God individually and corporately and to hear Him as He speaks to us. There are different types of prayer (**1Timothy 2:1**) and they are all equally important in the warfare for souls. Prayer is the mechanism that releases heaven's power, personnel, providence and provision to come to our aid on. Jesus' name is the key that opens the doors of heaven and activates divine responses to our petitions and prayers. The Word of the Lord teaches that whatever we ask of the Father in the name of Jesus Christ, believing, we shall receive. **John 16:23 - 26**

Overcoming affliction

In **Mark 5:25-34** and **Luke 8:43-48**, we learn of the woman with the issue of blood. Her condition was so disabling that she was unable to function normally. This disease made her vulnerable; an easy prey of the devil who, like every predator in nature will lay in wait to attack the weak, lonely, isolated, discontent, confused and wayward soul. So it was that the disease of this lady made her self-centered, using up all of her resources; her time, her thoughts, her money and her energy in finding a cure for what ailed her. The illness that afflicted her body had her blind-sided, leaving no space for her to see further than the problem that confronted her. She was as much cut off by her own pride and ego, as by the laws of Moses which made her unclean in her community.

I know it might seem unlikely that pride played a role in her condition but it always does. She was no doubt ashamed of her illness, determined to solve the problem herself. From our reading of the Scriptures, we see that she relied on her own resources, placing her faith in the power of her money to find a physician with the ability heal her condition. I am convicted that she was so busy and so absorbed with running from one doctor to another, trying one remedy after another that there was no time to make God a part of the equation of healing. The Scriptures tell us that sickness in our bodies is due to: physical, mental or spiritual causes. When we place our confidence in the dictates and determinations of our own minds and our faith in man, we are operating out of false, arrogant self-pride, believing ourselves to be in possession of power and wisdom to heal ourselves and put right what sin has wrecked.

I am sure that she isolated herself to avoid the scorn of people and likewise she hid and separated herself from God. Perhaps, she was convinced that this problem was justly deserved for some sin or disobedience; she felt naked, exposed and ashamed. This attitude to affliction was a taught doctrine of the Jewish Rabbis. Therefore it is not surprising that this woman would be focused on herself and setting things right by her own efforts and expense. She would have felt herself beyond the reach or the worth of the mercies and the will of the Living God. She was physically and spiritually impoverished. She must have felt abandoned and under retributive punishment by God, in the same way that she felt alienated and treated as an outcast by her community.

Her heart and mind was fertile ground for the wiles of the devil to wreak havoc. The devil is delighted, exultant and satisfied when we alienate ourselves from the Eternal God. The interposition of self, ego, and pride at the center of our lives excludes the reign and love of Jehovah. By relying on self and the ability of men, we are repudiating God's love for us, declaring our independence from His divine provisions; declining His direction and disdaining His intervention.

Further, our rebellion makes us of no effect in the ranks of the Lord's army. In fact, it marks us as enemies of the Holy One. Only when we can come to ourselves, like the prodigal son, are we able to recognize the full measure of divine love; that even while we were His enemies, God was reconciling us to Himself through the Son of Righteousness. Before the foundations of the world were laid, the Son had already purchased our redemption and restoration to fellowship with our Heavenly Father.

This is the mystery of our salvation. For the Eternal One, time holds no barrier. Yesterday, today and tomorrow are "now". He stands outside of time and so with Him it is always now. **"Behold**

today is the day of salvation", and **now** is the acceptable time of our Lord. **2 Corinthians 6:2.** If we would turn to the Lord, there is not a problem that He cannot solve or an issue too complicated, too shameful, too disgusting, debilitating or destructive that He cannot fix. We cannot fix ourselves; we cannot make ourselves right by our own endeavors in the sight of the Lord. Like the woman with the issue of blood, all our good works and good intentions will still leave us naked, filthy and unholy before the judgment seat of the Jehovah.

Finding God in the Dark and Dirty Places

The woman with the issue of blood was in hiding from the world, from herself and from God. Feeling herself too sinful, unclean and unworthy to be in the Presence of God or to be a recipient of His love. But God is privy to all our hiding places. There is no place so dark, so dirty, and so desperate that His light and love cannot illuminate and fill. **Psalms 139:7-12.** Just as Adam and Eve heard His voice in their hiding place in the Garden of Eden, this suffering woman finally heard God in the depths of her defeat; in her hiding place of shame and despair.

She listened to every word that she heard concerning the Man, Jesus and all that He was doing to the glory of Jehovah God. The stories of His teaching, favor and miraculous healing extended even to the outcasts of the Jewish society and told a story of unusual love; a love that drew the suffering, diseased and discarded of society to Him. She turned her eyes from self and from seeking relief in the performance of men and their science, which pursuit had used up all her resources, financial and emotional, physical and spiritual. Now she fixed her eyes on the Son of God, Who came with healing in His wings. She felt hope rising in her heart and faith in His power to heal and make her whole. **Malachi 4:2**

The moment she decided to heed the prompting of the Holy Spirit which called her to God, and to His Christ, the Lord Jesus, things changed. She re-directed her faith from man to God; came into agreement with what the Lord had already purposed for her and stepped into the possibility of wholeness and victory, a total-person healing in the Spirit realm. It is God's will that we be whole, prosperous in soul, mind and body. **3 John 1:2.** The miracles that were manifested physically by the Lord had already been determined and therefore completed in the invisible realm of the Spirit. He merely clothed with physicality that which God had decreed in the spiritual realm. It was the work of the Lord at the creation and it continues to be His work; to make manifest the Word of Elohim.

Big Faith, Small Act

This woman was so certain that her miracle awaited her that she merely desired to touch the hem of Jesus' garment for her deliverance. In her spirit, she had already accepted her victory in Christ Jesus. She had made up her mind that she would trust God with all her mind and all her strength. Once she had come to see the folly of her ways and her misplaced devotion, she turned to God with faith and determination. She exchanged her fear for faith and when there was a shift in her spirit, a change that aligned with the will of God for her life, her miracle was complete.

It would be difficult for her to get to Jesus physically. After all, she was unclean and therefore unacceptable in polite society. Her physical condition was also very limiting; she would weary easily, become worn out, bloody and repulsive on the journey to the Lord but she would be satisfied just to touch His garment. By this surreptitious act of faith she hoped to get her healing privately.

The Light of God had illuminated the walls of her prison and she was ready to break out. The Christ offered her liberty and there was no obstacle that she was not willing to traverse to receive healing and redemption. Yet, she decided to go unobtrusively. She knew that He healed by His words as well as by His touch. She did not want any public recognition or announcement of her cure. She had received enough adverse public attention over the last twelve years.

This act of healing she hoped would be just between her and her Lord. A touch of His garment would be all that was needed. This she could achieve anonymously in a crowd. As the woman reached out in faith and took hold of her healing with one touch, the Lord, the Author and Finisher of our faith, publicly recognized the restoration of her birthright and the degree of faith that was exercised by this warrior. **Matthew 9:22**

When the Lord performs His work of healing and restoration in our lives, it is always a reason for honoring and glorying in His name. It also stands as a testimony and a witness of His love and His mercy to the human family. It was the purpose of God to provide personal healing for this woman but also to give her confidence, boldness and empowerment in the favor of the Divine. She too was entitled to come for healing and restoration. There was no greater deserving person than her and her faith was as big and as significant as was the smallness of her act of touching the hem of His garment. Yet this one touch resulted in a divine healing, blessing and testimony for the glory of the Lord.

Testimony of Favor

This testimony of faith and favor offers hope to the desolate, oppressed, and down-trodden of this world. This story declares the mighty works that our Redeemer is able to bring to pass for all who exercise faith in Him. He sets captives free from the limitations that they have set on themselves, or that circumstances, sickness or society have imposed; limitations that denies the right to an abundant Spirit-filled, Holy Ghost empowered attitude, approach and appreciation of a God-focused life.

There is so much we can learn from the deliverance of this woman with the issue of blood.

1. There comes a time when we need to break out of our self imposed exile that separates us from the Lord our God and press through the crowds; family, friends, community, society, class, organizations, religions, customs, practices, rituals and routines.

2. There comes a time when we must take our eyes off the problem and look to the Source for the solution, for deliverance, for restoration.

3. There comes a time when we must recognize that without the Lord at the helm of our lives, we are dreadfully lost and we cannot find our own way back to a right relationship with our heavenly Father.

4. It requires a paradigmatic shift in perspective; a change in the way we perceive of ourselves and the role that the Lord desires to play in our lives, for us to acknowledge that we cannot achieve deliverance, healing, or salvation without the grace of God and the Way of the Cross.

We need the Good Shepherd to come find us and return us to the fold. He is always calling us by our names, and if we listen, truly listen, we will hear His voice. And if we hear His voice we must not allow the crowd to prevent us from following Him. So what if the church is a long way away, and what does it matter if your family have always worshipped under some other belief system, and who cares if your friends, family or colleagues think you have gone crazy, reach through the issues that crowd your life and go pass the people whose opinions oppress you and touch the hem of the Savior's garment. You will find peace for your soul and salvation for all eternity. It is the blood of the Lamb of God and our testimonies that will help us to overcome the adversary and stand as the redeemed for the Kingdom of God.

Jesus said, **"I am the Way, the Truth and the Life, no man comes to the Father but by Me." John 14:6. "The wages of sin is death but the gift of God is eternal life'. Romans 6:23.** Jesus our Lord is Life, so make Him your choice every day and for always. Press though whatever hinders you and reach out to Him, in faith. Be prepared to go outside established patterns, practices, rituals, cultures, customs and traditions to achieve your heart's desire to be one with the Savior.

Once this beleaguered woman who **had** an issue of blood for twelve years focused her passionate desire for the gift of God's healing power, she was able to reach out and touch the hem of His garment. Our Heavenly Father gave her the faith, the passion and the perseverance to pursue her personal healing. There is supernatural profit in perseverance in prayer, in supplication and in determination to be in the presence of the Holy One. There is no place for pride when one needs to press through the crowd and make personal contact with the righteousness of the Lord.

Once the woman under discussion decided to brave the emotional, spiritual, social and physical challenges that obstructed her deliverance from her disease, the loving God watched over her every step, ordering her journey. It is our Lord's delight to welcome and to offer us of the bounty of His love to the saving of our souls unto the eternities.

O Lord [pleads Jeremiah in the name of the people], I know that [determination of] the way of man is not in himself; it is not in man [even in a strong man or a man at his best] to direct his [own] steps. Jeremiah 12:23

The steps of a [good] man are directed and established by the Lord when He delights in His way [and He busies himself with his every step]. 24. Though he falls, he shall not be utterly cast down, for the Lord grasps his hand in support and upholds him. Psalms 37:23-24

When He was touched, Jesus knew immediately that 'virtue' had gone out of Him. A lost soul had drawn from the Fount of Life the living water that made whole the body as well as the spirit. Another warrior had just reported for duty, ready to serve. From the Scriptures, we know that healing by the touching of His garment was not a new experience for our Lord. However, it was one that He did not wish to go unmarked, unrecorded or unacknowledged. There was purpose, as always in everything that the Lord does.

All the miracles of the Lord are for the glory of the Most High God and for a blessing to His people. We know from the bible that it was not just the fact that His healing power had restored the woman's physical health that caused our Lord to remark on the miracle that had taken place. Rather, He wanted to acknowledge and congratulate her on the restoration of her faith in God and the "beginning of wisdom" in her thinking, her choices and her actions.

I believe that He really wanted to reach out to the multiplied millions of us today who feel that we are not deserving of His favor, His attention, His love or His redemption and His restoration. He wanted those of us who are made to feel this way to know that just 'one touch' in faith is sufficient to transform and transport us into right standing in the Kingdom of God as daughters, princesses and warriors.

Jesus did not ask for her name; her privacy was maintained and she has come down to us only as "the woman with the issue of blood". It was her challenges and her faith that the Lord wants us to recognize and learn from. She had made a complete turn-about and oriented her thoughts and then her actions onto the truest, greatest and best desire a woman could ever be apprehended by. She was now a woman that **"reverently and worshipfully fears the Lord!" Proverbs 31:30b.**

A Brief Note on Touching

In a woman's life there can be a lot of intimate, passionate, loving, personal contact but there can also be so much unwanted, undesired, unloving, repulsive and abusive touching. But the response that comes when we reach out and touch the Lord is refreshing, renewing and revitalizing; full of love, understanding, acceptance, peace and unspeakable joy because it is the 'virtue' of the Lord that we embrace when we reach out and touch Him with all of our longing, our craving, our strength and our desires.

Virtue is defined as one of the following: a commendable, moral quality of excellence that is highly desirable, chastity and purity in a woman and a power that is both active and beneficial to those that are impacted by it. The Bible account of the woman with the issue of blood tells us that the reason that Jesus was able to distinguish between the different ways of touching of His person in a jostling crowd of people that placed Him at the centre of their attention is that "virtue had gone out of Him" immediately following.

The revelation here is that the Lord was referring to an impartation of healing power that had the effect of refreshing, renewing and purifying the heart, mind and body of the beneficiary. Not only had virtue gone from the Lord it was received, seized even, by the woman with the issue of blood who according to the laws of Moses was impure, unclean and to be separated from other people who were considered clean. **Leviticus 15:19-30.** Her touch was deliberate, determined and fuelled by her faith that Jesus possessed the power to make her whole and clean. We read in the Word in respect of Jesus Christ that He gives power to become children of God to all those who believe on His name and place all their faith and hopes in Him as the Messiah, the Son of God. **John 1:12**

This woman's faith was noteworthy and remarked by our Lord and so she was able to receive virtue, power that is active in transforming death to life; restoring unclean to purity. This was indeed the kind of faith that can move mountains. When we are able to look beyond all the things that distract our attention and instead fill our vision with the glory of God, we are able to receive the virtue that comes in the healing touch of our Blessed Redeemer and Lord. Touching is a natural way of communication for women and it is a very necessary element to our feeling of well-being. Touching the Christ so that we also receive virtue from Him is essential to our walk of faith. The Lord promises this to all who are born of the Spirit.

But you shall receive power (ability, efficiency, and might0 when the Holy Spirit has come upon you, and you shall be My witnesses in Jerusalem and all Judea and Samaria and to the ends (the very bounds) of the earth. Acts 1:8

We communicate so many emotions with our touch. But there are different kinds of touch as demonstrated by the Lord in His response when He was so pressed by the crowds on all sides yet discerned the difference in that touch of the woman with the issue of blood. There is touching and there is touching! It is important that we are able to discern between the touch of the devil and the touch of the Lord. The touch of the Lord is healing, it makes whole, it restores, and it bestows love and peace. Any touch that invokes the opposite is not of God, there is no virtue but vice that is intended by the enemy of our salvation.

The Blessings of Boot Camp

If putting soldiers through their training at 'Boot Camp' is punishment then yes, the emotional, mental, physical and spiritual training grounds ordained by the Supreme One is punishment. But if we approach this with the right attitude and understanding of the divine plan of the Father, then we will appreciate and welcome Boot Camp not as punishment but as an opportunity to learn and practice discipline.

Boot Camp is appointment, preparation, training, equipping, strengthening and confidence building for those who are soldiers in the army of the Lord. Life experiences are the Boot Camp for God's warriors. Trained servants of the Lord must remain focused on God even if the enemy destroys everything and everyone near and dear to us, when we choose God, we choose obedience and we choose Life, this time round.

We will not be deceived as in the beginning. We are fully armored, rooted and grounded in the Lord and we will strategically inflict major damage to Satan's cause of destruction and death. We are redeemed and restored to our first love through much suffering and sacrifice by the Holy Lamb of God. Now, neither principalities, nor powers, nor life nor death will separate us again from the Love of our Lord, our God and Creator. We will be fully armored with our battle gear and weapons and take up our assignment in the heavens, in the underworld, in the terrestrial, sub terrestrial and celestial domains for our Lord, in compliance with His appointment. We do this not by our own might or power but by the Spirit of the Lord our God. For our weapons are not carnal but spiritual.

Not by might, nor by power, but by My Spirit [of Whom the oil is a symbol], says the Lord of hosts. Zechariah 4:6b.

I cannot say this enough; being trapped in sin, in self-centeredness, in worldly pursuits reduces, nullifies and renders of no effect the responsibility of the spiritual warrior of God. The woman who had the issue of blood spent twelve years in the camp of the enemy. She finally claimed her freedom, her liberty and her heritage when she recognized that the Great Physician extends His healing and His call to everyone; He is impartial, no respecter of persons and a lover of the downtrodden and outcasts of this world. In her healing she gained a revelation, a testimony and a restoration to life and service in Christ. **Malachi 4:2**

The Blood of the Lamb

Just like the woman who had the issue of blood, every single person can gain their freedom from the bondage of sin. There is salvation in the blood, the blood of the Christ shed on Calvary's cross once and for all. His blood sacrifice paid the price of our sins and His bleeding stripes is the cure to every sickness, every disease whether of the body or the mind that afflicts humans. But through Him we can regain a right standing with the Father as the righteousness of the Christ becomes our covering in the eyes of Jehovah.

Even as sin came into the world by the first Adam, so the price of sin and redemption was paid by the second Adam, Jesus the Christ. His act of atonement was to achieve restoration of the order, authority, sovereignty and dominion of God through man, the relationship between God and man and, between the domain of man, that is, the earth and the Kingdom of Heaven. Victory, restoration, redemption, harmony, justice and peace can only be achieved through Christ Jesus, our Lord who took the form of man so that He could purchase our freedom from sin, death, hell and the grave by the shedding of His blood and standing in our condemned shoes.

22. And almost all things are by the law purged with blood; and without shedding of blood is no remission.

23. It was therefore necessary that the patterns of things in the heavens should be purified with these; but the heavenly things themselves with better sacrifices than these.

24. For, Christ is not entered into the holy places made with hands, which are the figures of the true; but into heaven itself, now to appear in the presence of God for us:

25. Nor yet that He should offer Himself often, as the high priest entereth into the holy place every year with blood of others;

26. For then must He often have suffered since the foundation of the world: but now once in the end of the world hath He appeared to put away sin by the sacrifice of Himself. Hebrews 9:22-26 (KJV)

We were created to live continually in the Presence of the Lord's abundance. That, after all, is the meaning of the word, "Eden". It is the will of God to restore us to our birthright and to the possessions and positions given to us in the beginning. He came to rescue and cleanse us from our state of sin so that our dominion and authority on earth can prevail and His Sovereignty and His Kingdom can be re-established in peace, harmony, unity and glory forever.

Old things will pass away and all things will become brand new when Jesus returns at the end of days. However, newness of life starts for us the moment we accept Christ Jesus as Lord and Savior and yield ourselves to Him with a repentant heart and a contrite spirit. His gift of a new heart and a renewed spirit is the foundation of our new lives in Him. With the mind and heart of the Lord we will be able to be in obedience to His commandments and His commission.

CHAPTER 17

WOMEN WHO KNOW ARE THE WOMEN WHO BLEED

A Secret Identity

My sheep hear My voice and they know Me and they follow Me. John 10:27

Mary, the mother of Jesus the Christ knew His divine identity from the day He was conceived, the day the arch-angel Gabriel spoke to her. **Luke 1:32-33** It was her spoken acceptance, already manifested in her obedient heart that was yielded to the will of the Almighty and worked together to bring about the physical appearance of the Messiah in the earth as the Son of Man. As I suggested earlier, I believe that Mary was one of many hopeful daughters of Abraham who had dreamt of being the mother of the Promised Messiah. Yet there was a difference; her dream was more than a fanciful dream. Her heart was prepared, her spirit ready to be just such a one. She had committed herself and had lived a holy life that made her a willing vessel; a prepared and ready servant of the Lord our God.

It is impossible for us to truly understand the pain Mary must have gone through when she saw Jesus scourged and finally, dishonorably crucified. First as mother, the agony and suffering of her son would pierce her to the very core of her soul in an almost unbearable manner. In addition, she knew that He was the Son of God, the long awaited Messiah sent to save her people. She witnessed His rejection by the Jewish rulers and the common man in the courtyard of the Roman ruler, Pilate, and heard the judgment pronounced by those who rejected Him.

Mary knew that "The Hope of the Jewish nation" was at that very moment being murdered. How her heart must have bled within her; the anguish that she suffered gripped her tighter than any vice of steel possibly could. I am convicted in the spirit that the women who stood with the Savior's mother at the foot of the cross also knew His true identity. I believe that all godly women of the nation of Israel paid particular attention to the promise made by the Eternal One to Eve. A promise re-affirmed so many times to the prophets and patriarchs of the nation throughout their history; a promise that the Messiah would be born into the nation and would bring their salvation and re-institution as equal partners and joint heirs to the inheritance of the Heavenly Father.

Mary, mother of the Christ was accompanied by a number of women, including Mary Magdalene, who spent much time with Jesus; listening, learning, communing with Him in earnest. The other women at the gathering at Calvary were witnesses to His many miracles and would very likely have heard testimony from Mary of the conception and birth of the Lord Jesus. **Luke 8:1-3**

These women stood together with the knowledge that Israel's only hope lay in the Messiah. Yet that hope seemed to be slipping away even as the life-blood and the life-force of Jesus were draining from His body on the cross. Here He was, cruelly and shamefully hung on a Roman cross. He had been rejected and put to death by the very people He came to save; "the Seed" that would defeat the adversary as decreed by Yahweh Himself in the Garden of Eden.

I believe that these women also realized that there was more to all of the events that had occurred than was visible to the physical eye. They knew that a spiritual showdown was taking place. **"He shall crush the serpent's head and the serpent will bruise His heel".** Was this the bruising to which the Scriptures referred? Was it necessary for "the Seed" to be planted before it could spring up and offer life and liberty? These questions must have invaded the minds of the distraught congregation of women. The history of the covenanted people of God is covered with the blood of children, especially boys because Satan was always trying to kill the Messiah as soon as He came into the earth realm. The women of the nation of Israel have always been crying; their tears mingled with the blood of their slaughtered children, sacrificed by the devil and his minions in further defiance of God's sovereignty.

A Matter of Identity

Mary, mother of our Lord, knew that the child she was to bring forth was the Christ, the Promised One. She had been positioned, appointed and anointed to be the virgin prophesied by Isaiah to bring a child who would proclaim liberty to the enslaved human family and freedom from the legacy of sin of the first parents. But the truth is that Mary had already been in preparation for her appointment. She had spent time learning the truths contained in the Scriptures, she had lived a life pleasing to God and she was His faithful servant.

What effect did this knowledge of Jesus' identity have on Mary? It allowed her to prepare for the responsibility of teaching, training and exposing the Christ child to the Scriptures, the right environment and the right companions. We are certain that she understood the import of her privilege in carrying the Messiah. This is clear from her exaltation in the presence of her cousin Elizabeth.

Elizabeth, mother of John the Baptist and cousin to Mary also knew Jesus' identity. This knowledge was made known to her by the Holy Spirit, which came upon her causing the baby John in her womb to leap for joy. **Luke 1: 40-45.** In verses 42 and 43 we read;

And she cried out with aloud cry, and then exclaimed, blessed (favored of God) above all other women are you! And blessed is the Fruit of your womb. And how (have I deserved that this honor) should be granted to me that the mother of my Lord should come to me?

Mary then went on to testify of her experiences to Elizabeth and the two women fellowshipped, rejoiced and glorified God together. Elizabeth knew, always, the true identity of Jesus, the Messiah.

His Revealed Identity

The Prophetess Anna also knew the real identity of the Christ child. the Holy Spirit granted her the knowledge and discernment to realize her divine destiny in seeing the Messiah before her death; the baby Jesus was brought to the Temple, shortly after His birth. **Luke 2:36**. Anna proclaimed His true identity to all who were within the sound of her voice, to all who were looking for the Redeemer of the Children of Israel and the deliverance of Jerusalem from the control of the Roman enemy. **Luke 2:38.**

Anna knew the Lord's identity because it was revealed to her by the Holy Spirit. Read again the brief biography of Anna with which we are supplied by the Scriptures. Notice that we are told that she was a woman whose affections were completely dedicated and focused on the Lord our God. In Anna's life, she only had room for the Lord. To her therefore, God made the promise that she would see the Messiah with her own eyes in her natural life. Anna spent eighty-four years of her life worshipping the Lord in the Temple day and night and the Lord kept His promise. She saw the infant Jesus at His dedication in the Temple according to the laws of purification and dedication of the first-born child of a couple. **Luke 2:36-37**

Jesus declared His true identity to the Samaritan woman that He met at the well. In her discourse with the Lord, she referred to the promise of the Messiah. Jesus spoke plainly in confirming her unspoken question that He was indeed the Messiah, the Christ promised to the patriarchs. How did she receive this revelation? How did it affect her? What was her response?

She straightway ran to evangelize her neighbors. She had come face to face with the Christ and had experienced a life-changing, spirit-cleansing transformation. Her man-focus was dramatically replaced with a paradigmatic shift in her perspective on life and her God-given assignment. The Lord took up residence in her life; mind, body and spirit.

Her outlook and her future were changed by her encounter with the Messiah. There was no room for further questions when she received her revelation directly from the Lord; He told her that He was the Messiah of prophecy and promise. She was in the 'know'; granted divine knowledge.

These women received direct revelation of the Truth, total enlightenment and unequivocal confirmation as to the heavenly and earthly identity of the Lord. "He that hath an ear to hear let him hear and he that hath an eye to see, let him see". The women did! There was a heaven-directed reason behind the revelation granted to these women. The very nature of their individual assignments made it essential that they be given the inside track on the Presence of the Messiah in the physical realm.

Each woman was called to faithful service and spiritual warfare. Each was equipped, empowered and educated to oversee, supervise and participate in spreading the gospel of the Kingdom of God and to let the people know that God's Plan of Redemption is in motion. It is important that the divine operation is conveyed to the nations at the time appointed by the Almighty.

It was strategically and tactically imperative that the players, participants and handmaiden-warriors of the Lord be focused, motivated, knowledgeable, prepared, strengthened and committed to carry out the assignment for which they had been called by the Creator God. According to **Isaiah 48:17**, divine directions come directly from the Lord. It is the Lord that directs our steps, orders our lives and places us in strategic positions that enables us to perform those things which will bring to fruition His will and purpose.

It is important for us to understand that the Lord never imposes His purpose except He first gives the opportunity for refusal. Every child of God will be called to serve in the mission of publishing the Word of God to all the nations. There is no calling in Christ which is insignificant or inconsequential. We must remember Who it is that we serve. We might briefly summarize the process as follows;

1. Jehovah God discloses His identity
2. A divine revelation is made
3. A personal conversion takes place

4. An intimate relationship is established
5. A commission or assignment is offered
6. The opportunity to accept or reject is made available
7. There is a promotion to a higher calling in Christ
8. A warrior of the Kingdom is on active service
9. There is anointing for the appointment
10. The appointment/assignment honors/glorifies the Lord

Importance of Identity

It is very important that every child of God is fully convicted of their identity. I am persuaded that if Adam and Eve had accepted God's definition of who they were they would not have bothered about the words of the serpent. But instead of trusting the Creator, they relied on their own reasoning and admitted the doubt of the devil's lies into their hearts and minds. Eve felt that she was indeed lacking wisdom and that she was unlike the very Creator God who had purposed to make man in His image and after His likeness.

Eve believed the picture painted by Satan instead of the reflection of God that she was from the very beginning. Like Eve, women have allowed others to define us and we have taken on board their definitions to our detriment: appropriating them as our own. And these false identities have limited and restricted the woman of God especially in relation to service to the Kingdom. We must look to God, to His words, to the ministry of Jesus, to discover who we really are. He is our Creator and so He is the only true Source of revelation concerning our identity, purpose and destiny. Unless and until we know our identity we cannot serve the Omnipotent God who calls us His children, divine royalty and warriors.

It does not matter in what circumstances one finds oneself, if we have our identity fixed in our minds and our hearts we will stand. That is why Paul exhorted slaves and servants to serve their masters/employers diligently and with integrity because it is not the title that man attaches, which is important but that which God declares. So even if you are called a slave or a servant, worthless or unwanted, a pauper or a princess, a wife or a spinster, it merely amounts to a label; it does not determine your real identity in Christ or your standing in the Kingdom of Righteousness.

Jesus was not roused to argue with Satan about His identity as the Son of God and the benefits of that status. Instead, His response to Satan was a rebuke that spoke to the behavior of the tempter, not the standing of the Lord with His Father. As we studied before, He is our model, our standard. We need not argue as to our paternity or our heritage, if we are children of God then are we His heirs and despite our present appearances and circumstances, when Jesus returns we shall be like Him.

What would be the consequence of a soldier who goes into battle without any knowledge as to his identity? How would he know what was his assignment, his company, his side of the war? How would he be able to identify who is his enemy, on whose side he is positioned? How would he be able to distinguish between friend and foe?

It is essential that warriors know their identity because this allows them to know their enemy and fulfill their purpose. Do you know to whom you belong? Are you fighting on the wrong side in the Great War just because you have been tricked into believing a false representation of your identity? Falsehood is how the enemy undermines your identity and lies are how he convinces and uses you to do his wicked work of destruction.

The identity of every human being is founded in the Lord. As Christians, Christ-like in all our ways, we wear the uniform, the battle fatigues of the Army of Righteousness. We are first made by Him and then we are again purchased and saved by Him through Jesus the Christ, our Kinsman Redeemer. We are twice His!

There is no theory, philosophy, religion, action or reaction that can change this fundamental truth. We can choose any of a number of reactions or responses to this knowledge but it can never change the fact that God made us and then He saved us! He also made us to live to our fullest capacity, ability and abundance in Him and although we turned away from His provisions and His prosperity, He still reaches out for us in complete love with a heart of mercy, forgiveness, compassion and care.

It is He that made us, not we ourselves. **Psalms 100:3. (NIV)**

1. In the beginning was the Word and the Word was with God. 2. The same was in the beginning with God. 3. All things were made by Him and without Him was not anything made that was made. 4. In Him was life and the life was the light of men. John 1:1, 2 (KJV)

26. And God said, Let us make man in our image, after our likeness: and let them have dominion … 27. So God created man in His own image, in the image of God created He him; male and female created He them. Genesis 1:26, 27. (KJV)

The earth is the Lord's and the fullness thereof, the world and they that dwell therein. He hath founded it upon the sea and established it upon the floods. Psalm 24:1. (KJV)

Bloody Battles

The devil made war with women in the times before the Messiah's birth firstly because his purpose is to steal our joy, to kill our relationship with God and to destroy our ability to inherit the Kingdom of God the Father. In the second place, Satan has always known that the divinely pre-destined role of womankind is to make war with him, to engage in battle and bring forth the Seed that will activate God's weapon of mass destruction. (WMD). God's WMD will bring an end to sin and the evil reign of the kingdom of darkness, deceit and destruction.

The devil was first put on notice in the Garden of Eden. Paul informs us in **Colossians 1:26** that **"the mystery which was hidden for ages and generations, from angels and men"**, was not fully revealed until the triumph of the Lord Jesus the Christ. It was the devil's lack of comprehension of how God's Plan of Redemption would be unfolded on humanity's behalf that caused him to go all out to persecute all male persons that appeared to be the promised Destroyer of evil. **Luke 2:23.**

The manner of the fulfillment of God's plan was to astound for all times, all of His creation. He emptied Himself of His greatness and through the vassal of woman, as the Seed, entered into the world to save it as the Lord Immanuel. His desire and His purpose is to provide access to the Door to life everlasting and the restored Kingdom of God on earth. **Ephesians 2:9-12**

The devil still holds a special hatred towards the females of the human family. He seeks revenge for the birth of the Christ, for the birth and rearing of all new warriors and workers in the Kingdom, and for the birth of revelation in the spirit of women of their divinely ordained purpose of spiritual warfare. The enemy is equally challenged by the even greater spiritual 'Woman' betrothed to the Lord Jesus Christ; His Beloved, His Body, His Bride for which He paid the dowry, the bride- price with His very blood. That Woman is His Church.

Now the devil's hatred of womankind and his war efforts against our ministry and our commission is even graver than it has ever been as we approach the closing of this dispensation. He is running scared, making out as if he were a roaring lion, seeking to destroy as many souls as he can in the time left to him. But he is only faking. The real roar is the roar of victory that will come from the real lion; the Lion of Judah who will return in power and in glory and declare God's final judgment. The Lord Jesus will bring the war to its triumphant conclusion for the Kingdom of our Lord and our God.

Women know with certainty and confidence, we are ordained, appointed, assigned and anointed by God to be warriors in the battle between the Righteous One and the deceiver of the nations. The deceiver will stop at nothing to nullify our appointment and limit or lose our contribution altogether. The use of counterfeit spirituality that snares, traps and especially attracts women, in order to engage our energies in diversionary activities, is a proven method of success for the devil.

However, we must resist the devil and he will flee from us, says the Lord. **James 4:7.** We must turn to God, set our affections on

Him and run the race that the Lord has placed before us. The Lord who began a good work in us is able to complete it by His grace. Jesus promised that greater things than was accomplished by Him in His earthly ministry, is our legacy. We are all soldiers in the army, workers in the Kingdom, and possessors of the Spirit of victory that brought Jesus out of the grip of death.

We must stand together with our men, warriors all and fight. There is no excuse for taking a back seat in the Great War. The weapons of our warfare are designed to be unisex. They fit the male as well as they fit the female of the human family. The Robe of Righteousness is also from the same Designer! Remember by one man, that is by Adam and Eve, sin entered into the earth realm. By the same token, it is through the righteousness of one, the Son of Man, that justification is granted to all of us who accept the redemption work of Jesus our Substitute and Sacrifice

The Tears of a Woman

In every culture and country with which I am familiar, there is one expression that I have found common to them all, a concept that all agree on. That is, that it is unnatural and most abhorrent that a parent outlives a child. It seems to be one of those occurrences that are particularly soul-destroying. It goes against the natural order of nature, the accepted way of things. Parents expect to have the pleasure of seeing their children grow to maturity and carry on where they have left off.

Yet throughout history there have always been great pain and suffering caused to parents who experience the death of their child. The loss of a loved one is always difficult and its effect is never to be under-estimated. However, in many instances we can manage to take comfort for example when that individual has lived a long and fulfilling life. Accidents are part of life and self-neglect, self-abuse or disregard for self and life when they contribute to or culminate in death can be reasoned. But one thing is sure, regardless of what circumstances contributes or leads to the death of a child, the tragedy hits home so much harder. Even total strangers will sympathize with those that have suffered such losses.

The experience of my siblings bears out my views here. When we look through the Bible, we come across many incidents in which children die leaving distressed, distraught and almost deranged parents. As I think back on the women in the Bible, the image which first comes to mind is that of the women standing about at the foot of the cross of Jesus the Christ, as He hung in love and submission to the will of God, fulfilling the Plan of Redemption. Among the women was Mary the mother of our Lord.

As women, we can only imagine the anguish and the agony that she was experiencing. Theologians tell us that it is apparent that Joseph, her husband, had died some time before, so she stood as a lone parent watching the dreadful death that was her Son's portion. Jesus is the Son of God but He is also the Son of Mary. She knew He was the Son of God with power to vanquish all those who were inflicting pain and death on His physical body. But she also knew that He was indeed the Messiah and that His submission was evidence of His obedience to His heavenly Father and to the nature and character of His Divine DNA. She recalled the words He had spoken during His ministry, the proclamation of the Prophetess Anna and the comments of the Rabbis at the Temple when, as a twelve year old boy He stayed behind in Jerusalem.

And He said to them, How is it that you had to look for Me? Did you not see and know that it is necessary [as a duty] for Me to be in My Father's house and [occupied] about My Father's business? Luke 2:49.

During the course of His ministry, Mary had come to understand that He always placed God first. The physical torture to which Christ was subjected was the most reprehensible, the grossest that it was possible for Him to suffer at that time. He had been scourged almost to the point of death, and then cruelly made to carry the cross; it was not His, it was ours. Then, He was nailed to it.

Any mother will confirm that Mary's agony was equally intense at every level of her being. It was physical, emotional, mental and spiritual pain that Mary was experiencing. She stood face to face with the reality that **"He came unto his own and His own received Him not..." John1:11**. He had received disdain instead of honor, a crown of thorns instead of a throne of purest gold. His mother felt the rejection of her son, the Son of God, the promised Messiah of her people, in the very depths of her being. He did not deserve such an ignoble, painful and untimely death. Mary's heart was broken and bleeding. They had crucified her firstborn child, the only Begotten Son of God and He was their only hope, the hope of the human family.

Mary's sacrifice was also the Sacrifice of God the Father so that He could turn all our pains into joy and our sorrow into rejoicing. Again, let me repeat, the women who accompanied the Lord to the Cross understood very well that throughout the ages women have always suffered the brunt of the devil's onslaught against their families. They also understood that it is the role of women to be on the frontline and continue to war with the destroyer. The Sacrifice of the Seed was the agonizing pain and the restoration of power to the women of God; the Beginning and the End of their warfare. There are many examples that demonstrate this truth.

We can only imagine the anguish of Eve's first encounter with human death, the death of her son Abel. She was the first mother of the human family to suffer the loss of a child, the first to feel the full wrath of the enemy's attack on her offspring. Abel was in his prime, full with the promise of life and the joy of serving God when he was killed by Cain, his brother. This double whammy of pain and loss must have been unbearable. But God had clearly said that **"the wages of sin is death"** and the full import of the sin of eating from the tree now resulted in the death of one son at the hands of another.

So it was that the first death, funeral and bereavement was by a mother and father for the untimely passing of their child and the guilt, shame and loss of a son who was the first murderer. In addition, the hope that Cain or even Abel was the Promised Seed also died with the demise of Abel. The full realization that redemption and restoration was not through these two sons must have completed the tragic hat-trick, hitting home really hard.

But God proved Himself as ever merciful, faithful and true and gave comfort and renewed hope to our first parents, broken and grieving at the double loss at the tomb of Abel. He blessed them with another son, Seth, a substitute for Abel. Seth foreshadowed the Divine Switch, pre-ordained in God's Plan of Redemption. He sent our Substitute, Jesus the Christ to take our place in the tomb, our dead place and re-generate dry bones by the quickening of His Spirit.

And Adam knew his wife again; and she bare a son, and called his name Seth. For God, said she, hath appointed me another seed instead of Abel, whom Cain slew. Genesis 4:25 (KJV)

Let us look at the plight of the women in bondage in Egypt. The women of the Israelite nation experienced the death of their boy children at the command of the enemy through the person of the Pharaoh. It is too horrible to even imagine the weeping, wailing and unstoppable anguish that these mothers felt when the evil scheme of the devil was enforced and a newborn baby boy was killed. Despite the plans of the destroyer, God made a way of escape for the life of one of those infant boys to be saved, covered by the grace of our Lord and the faith of his mother. This mother felt in her spirit that there was something about this child of hers that would invoke the hand of God to protect his future. She was God's warrior and she fought a good fight of faith.

This survivor was prepared, equipped and positioned by the wisdom of his mother and the favor of Jehovah God, to lead the enslaved people of Israel out of Egypt and into nationhood and covenant with the only true God, the God of the patriarchs Abraham, Isaac and Jacob. The plan to destroy the Israelites, dishonor God's promise to Abraham and thereby make a liar of God was thwarted by Moses, Law-Giver, Prophet and Patriarch of the nation of Israel.

The women whose babies were killed suffered but they had no control over the fate of their children for the devil was engaged in acts of horror and violence. These people were in a position of helplessness. They could not challenge or change the scope of the enemy's operation but God made an escape for the savior of His chosen people. Satan's deadly campaign was motivated by fear of the birth of the Messiah but whatever he does he can never abort a miracle baby!

If all male children were killed in Egypt then there would not be a Redeemer. Furthermore if the males are destroyed, then the Israelites would become extinct and God's promises and His Word would be rendered void. This is the consequence which Satan constantly battles to achieve. He wants us to believe both at the individual and the corporate level that God is uncaring, a liar and an exacting taskmaster making impossible demands of His creation. His campaign still continues against the people of God.

But God is God and He is able to make the impossible look like 'a piece of cake'. He covered and protected Moses from the adversary and prepared him for his assignment. Moses therefore was also a type of the Messiah. This great man of God was able to accomplish great feats, spiritual and natural with the help of Jehovah God.

A similar fate to that of the women who lived in Egyptian bondage also befell the women living in Bethlehem at the time of Jesus' birth. Herod, the King of the Jewish people at that time was used by Satan to order the deaths of all boys born around the time that he was visited and notified by the wise men of Jesus' birth. To ensure that there was no chance of escape for the child about whom the prophecies were written; Herod ordered the deaths of all boys born in Bethlehem around the predicted birth time up to two years old.

Those bereaved mothers must have cried out to God with just one question; when will we get justice for our slain children? The fact is those mothers had lost their children as casualties and victims of war. Those killed in Egypt and those in Bethlehem were all casualties of the great controversy which occupies the Kingdom of God and is waged by the prince of darkness and his rebellious supporters, the demonic one third. His purpose is to deny us our inheritance and prove the impossibility of keeping God's commandments. Since we are made in God's image and His likeness, if we fail, God also fails; that is the premise of the devil's activities. The victory of our Christ has not lessened Satan's desire to undermine the authority, the righteousness and the justice of God's Kingdom.

We know well the story of Naomi who lost her husband as well as her two sons whilst the family sojourned in Moab to avoid the effects of a famine that was in Bethlehem, their home-town. Naomi was distraught at her loss and felt that her future had been taken away from her. So deep was her pain that she never envisaged a recovery. She even declared her name changed to Mara; a word which means bitterness. **Ruth 1:20, 21.**

Naomi was convinced that her life was basically over, she had no children and so did not have the promise of grandchildren to look forward to as one of the pleasures of old age. But Father God had another plan. He alone can turn the bitter tears of a woman into tears of joy; joy as she becomes the nurse to the child born to restore the name of her son to an inheritance with the Children of Israel. **Ruth 4:14-17.** Naomi's great grandson was King David.

So it is that even in the midst of the bitterest experience a woman can have, God will bring comfort. Often, we do not understand and perhaps it is not for us to have all the answers to these questions this side of eternity. Questions such as the following has often been asked: Why is it that our children die so young and our women must weep? Why are our children always under attack by the enemy? Why does the devil try so hard either to kill or destroy those who live? God knows, He really does; the adversary is determined to dishearten and dissuade us from trusting the Lord, believing His Word and accepting His unconditional, limitless love for us despite the apparent victory of death, disease and sin over our children.

We must stay focused on God and His will and purpose for our lives whatever challenges we come up against. We cannot allow ourselves to be distracted by our pain, destroyed by our grief or defeated by the enemy's ambushes and covert attacks. We just need to focus on the big picture. We are in a war against the kingdom of darkness; we are warriors and our loved ones will be taken hostage, they will be the casualties of this war.

So we have to know that being on the Lord's side is not play but we must also know that His is the side of Love, righteousness, eternal life and final victory over everything that seeks to destroy us and our loved ones. This includes Satan and all sin. Our faith is the faith of mothers who have suffered the death of their children, husbands, communities and yet still hold fast to the certain hope of the resurrected Christ Jesus to a perfect sin-free immortal life with our loved ones. Warriors take heart; **"weeping may endure for a night but joy comes in the morning"! Psalms 30:5**

CHAPTER 18

GOD GIVEN GIRL POWER

Their Father's Daughter

Mahlah, Noah, Hoglah, Milcah and Tirzah were the five daughters of Zelophehad. Their father was of the line of Joseph through Manasseh, his son. These five sisters were on the receiving end of what they considered to be stark injustice according to the law enforced among the Children of Israel. They were not prepared to take the perceived inequity without expending every possible effort to have their voices heard. They determined to present their grievance, claim and petition to that great man of God, Moses, their Prophet and Leader, despite the odds being stacked against them.

The **Book of Numbers 27:4-5** records their claim in the following manner;

> **4 …Give to us a possession among our father's brethren.**
> **5. And Moses brought their case before the Lord.**

According to the ordinances and the rules of inheritance as declared by Moses, only the men or sons of a family could legally claim a share in the possessions, the estate of a deceased father. Women, daughters, were not legally entitled and there were no provisions, clauses or exceptions that made provision for any entitlement or direct claim. There might have been discretion available for benefit to be bestowed indirectly; at the discretion of the men of the family. Women therefore had no 'locus standi'; a legally recognized right to share in the inheritance left behind by their fathers.

This was the state of play when Moses was ordered by God to divide up the lands to be inherited by the different tribes of the Children of Israel. The judicial requirement for qualification to an inheritance operated to the detriment of the daughters of Zelophehad and others in a similar position. They would be left unprotected, dispossessed and disgraced. Their father's name would be dishonored and removed from among the 'roll call' of his relatives, his tribe, and ultimately the nation because he had only daughters.

These five sisters must have been terrified of the road ahead; frightened for their future with no family funds to pay their dowry or bridal price, or to provide for their welfare if perchance they should remain unmarried. The customs of their people allowed them no recognized say in the affairs of their tribe; no voice and no vote. These were godly young women reluctant to challenge the status quo but burning with a sense of injustice and the absence of fair play, they were prompted to take action and I believe that prompting came by the Holy Spirit

The young women knew the law concerning daughters inheriting in the absence of sons. It had never been the custom or the practice in all their known history for women to be recognized as direct, legitimate claimants in this manner. To petition for equal treatment with sons was probably considered an outrage and evidence of rebelliousness, immodesty and a bid for equality with men.

It is certain that these five sisters agonized long and hard about the options available to them. They wanted to secure their future and at the same time ensure that their father's inheritance and his name remained in the annals of their people. After failing to find a satisfactory outcome through any alternative, discretionary avenues that might have been available to them, the sisters agreed to challenge the prevailing laws and the rules that were being compiled and implemented by the Law-giver, Moses.

"Give to us a possession among our father's brethren" was their appeal. After all, they explained, Zelophehad had not forfeited his inheritance through disobedience or rebellion, and since he was without sons, his inheritance should in all fairness be passed on to his daughters. Moses, that just and righteous man of God could have brushed their claim aside. After all, the laws were quite clear on the rules of inheritance. Nevertheless the Scriptures tell us that Moses **"brought their case before the Lord"**, the only true and perfect Judge.

The Lord declared them **"justified"** in their claim, correct in their presentation and He advised Moses to **"give them an inheritance among their father's brethren, and ...cause their father's inheritance to pass to them"**. The Lord further clarified the operation of the law and decreed that His judgment was now a binding statute and ordinance. Later on in the Scriptures, we read that further stipulations were added to ensure that a woman who was a direct beneficiary under this law would not be used to deplete the wealth of a tribe by marrying outside her tribe and adding her legacy to that of her husband's.

It is the will of the Most High operating on, or in us that empowers us to fulfill His plans, purpose and destiny for our lives. The daughters of Zelophehad were operating under a very special anointing which gave them the passion, the conviction and the determination to petition Moses and challenge the status quo. It was a powerful anointing that furnished them with the resolve and the strength to seek to bring about social and legal change.

I feel certain that their first inclinations were timid, faltering speculations. But as the anointing of the Lord took hold, they grew bold and fearless. What evidence do we have that these were anointed women? The Divine Himself confirms this by His declaration and judgment. He is the Giver of all good gifts to His children and He is Justice. The Lord would not have engineered, managed or ordered any situation or circumstance, which would unfairly and inequitably, cause hardship and pain to His people. The desire to pursue a course of action in order to secure an inheritance for daughters was a just and worthy cause. It was approved by God and it originated with him also.

6. And the Lord said to Moses, 7. The daughters of Zelophehad are justified and speak correctly... 11. It shall be to the Israelites a statute and an ordinance. Numbers 27:6-7, 11

These five sisters were inspired, motivated, and persistent in their efforts to bring about social change for the improvement and the status of women in their community. The sisters were not prepared to sit back, ignore the prompting of the Holy Spirit and allow a rule, custom, tradition or any familial, peer or other communal pressure to deprive them of their inheritance. They were possessed of a desire, a passion and zeal to press forward, face the challenges, the uproar, the outrage, the stress and possibility of defeat in order to challenge the strongholds of tradition and established legal precedents. The justice of God is the righteousness of God. There is no higher or greater authority to which we can bring our appeals. The sisters were successful in their pursuit; justified said the Lord, and so they were rewarded with the terms of their petition by the Judge of the nations.

What is Justification?

Justification is a divine act whereby an infinitely Holy God judicially declares a believing sinner to be righteous and acceptable before Him because Christ has borne the sinner's sin on the cross and has become "to us ...righteousness" (1 Corinthians 1:30). (The New Unger's Bible Dictionary: Merrill F. Unger. Revised and Updated Edition 1988. The Moody Bible Institute of Chicago)

Justification is generally to be understood as an act that releases an individual from guilt through the right/righteous act of another person. Justification does not relate to the merit of the guilty person but that of a substitute. So that in relation to God's grace it is manifested in the sacrificial death on the cross of His Beloved Son, our blessed Redeemer the Lord Jesus Christ, as a Substitute for sinful man. This operation of God's grace is declared by the Apostle Paul in **Romans 3:24-26,** in the following terms

24. All are justified and made upright and in right standing with God, freely and gratuitously by His grace (His unmerited favor and mercy), through the redemption which is (provided) in Christ Jesus.

25. Whom God put forward [before the eyes of all] as a mercy seat and propitiation by His blood [the cleansing and life-giving sacrifice of atonement and reconciliation, to be received through faith. This was to show God's righteousness, because in His divine forbearance He had passed over and ignored former sins without punishment.

26. It was to demonstrate and prove at the present time (in the now season) that He Himself is righteous and that He justifies and accepts as righteous him who has [true] faith in Jesus.

So it is by the propitiation of the blood of the Lamb that the Lord Almighty justifies those who would otherwise have no place, part or portion in His righteousness. It is a joy and a marvelous wonder that the Lord God uses the language of justification when He declared a change in the operation of the laws of the Old Covenant. He used the language of the New Covenant, **"justification"**, which comes only through Christ Jesus our Savior. The successful claim of Zelophehad's daughters for a right to their father's possession was God's response to their faith in His righteousness.

The Almighty's declaration of the Plan of Redemption in **Genesis 3:15** allows the daughters of man to be beneficiaries of Jesus' act of propitiation and atonement equally with sons; both received a right to be inheritors, legal beneficiaries in the Divine Father's Kingdom of Righteousness. The Law of God cannot be circumvented, nullified or made void. It is the same throughout all the eternities. His

Laws must be fulfilled. That is the reason that Jesus had to die because without the shedding of blood there is no remission of sin.

We could not save ourselves by any other means that we could concoct or imagine. God's Word declared the means of redemption and only the death of Jesus could pay the price and satisfy the justice of His righteousness. That is why the Apostle Paul reminds us that we cannot boast in our redeemed state because we cannot save ourselves. It is the blood of the Lamb of God that cleanses and it is His atonement, His righteousness which justifies. By His sacrifice and the justification He wrought on our behalf, we are heirs and joint heirs of His possessions, His inheritance and His Kingdom. **Titus 3:7**

The Creator God is an unchanging God and the blood of Christ establishes the New Covenant which brings life to all, equally. In Christ only is God able to declare us 'justified'. This He does, not on our own merit but through the perfect obedience and righteous character of our Lord Jesus which covers all those who are in Christ, and He in them. **1 Corinthians 1:30.**

By faith, the daughters of Zelophehad; Mahlah, Noah, Hoglah, Milcah and Tirzah looked forward in faith, caught the vision of the Lamb that restores us to the status of children, heirs and joint heirs. They laid hold of the legal right purchased by the Christ, to an equal share of the possession of their earthly father as well as their heavenly Father. **Romans 5:1.** Their claim was honored by God because of His mercy, His grace, His righteousness and His justice. In other words, God honored the terms of the New Covenant in Jesus as He was even then, already slain for the justification of the human family and intercedes before the throne of the Lord day and night. **Isaiah 53:11**

Likewise all His daughters, we who are children by adoption, are entitled to a share in His possessions through the atonement brought about by our elder brother, the Firstborn of our Father. In Him is our inheritance made secure. It is no secret that God equally welcomes the disadvantaged and the dispossessed of this world as much as the rich and the recognized. **Romans 8:29.**

We Shall Overcome.

There is a lesson for anyone in circumstances and situations that seem impossible of change. The legal, political, administrative and social institutions of the societies in which we live are not perfect and injustice is inherent to their functioning as is the presence of sin and fallibility to human nature. There will only be a perfect world when righteousness, justice, love and other godly attributes are the character of the sovereign ruler as well as of the citizens of that world. In other words, issues of injustice will no longer exist when we are again under the direct rule of God through the Lord Jesus. In the meantime however, we have a duty to partner with the victims of injustice and pursue changes that will reflect the character of our Lord and the character that should also be in us as the Holy Spirit sanctifies and perfect us to the image of God.

In such situations, we have a responsibility to fight for the will of God to be made manifest in the earth, in the same way that all those who are called by the name of the Lord must stand up for right. We must all be like the daughters of Zelophehad; pressing our claim and pursuing our cause for individual and joint rights. Each sister had an individual claim and together they presented a united, corporate front; there is power in unity and accord, in the physical as well as in the spiritual realms. This leads me to the next, most important point relating to unity and agreement of purpose. It is just as important and powerful that women support each other as sisters and agree in the spirit on matters of spiritual import; including spiritual missions and ministry as well as warfare.

One of the most prized experience of my life as a woman of God is the opportunity to join with other sisters in Christ to agree, touch and petition the Lord and watch as His love and His power is made manifest and our prayers are answered. He never fails to surprise me in the way that one is reminded of how awesome He really is and the faithfulness of His Word that says where two or three are gathered in His Name, He is present, ready to bless. And this promise is coached in words of certainty in that He says He **will** be in our midst. **Matthew 18:19-20**

I have proved Him over and over and so have my sisters. So when the world has fenced you in, placed limitations on your options, erected barriers against your progress, circumcised and circumvented your opportunities, denied your rights, sabotaged your potentials, deleted your possibilities, ransomed your hopes and dreams, ambushed your destiny and hijacked your heritage, make your petitions known to Almighty God, individually and corporately. In His providence and provisions, we can be more than conquerors.

Our Advocate and Chief Intercessor, Jesus the Christ will petition the Father on our behalf and His Word promises us that Jehovah will hear from heaven and answer. He never fails. **1 John 2:1.** There is power from on high waiting to anoint us with boldness, perseverance and faith. The Lord is the only One who can break the chains of bondage, oppression, isolation, alienation, disenfranchisement and exclusion. He came to set the captives free, to increase territory, fertilize barren wombs, give life and form to dead bones, restore honor, respect and parity in society and above all else, to re-inaugurate proper standing in the Kingdom of our God.

A Higher Authority

The pioneering daughters of Zelophehad were backed into a corner. Their relatives and the Elders of the tribe were unable to deliver the outcome the women were hoping for or offer any acceptable solution to their dilemma. Instead their pursuit of reformation may have caused consternation, frustration and maybe even anger. After all, they were trying to amend, change or render obsolete the traditions, customs, practices and enforceable rules and rights applicable to their nation. In other quarters there might even have been some sympathy, understanding and even regret for their situation. But the law was the law.

However, difficult circumstances and impossible odds are the fodder that God uses to demonstrate the fullest operation of His grace and His love in our lives. He is a God of the lost causes. He keeps a special channel, opened and permanently tuned, to receive the cries of those who find themselves drowning in the depths of despair, despondency and discouragement. He always hears when we call for His help and His favor.

The Lord Jesus is the fast track into the Presence of the Almighty for the petitions of those who are down-trodden, despised, dejected or denied. Mahlah, Noah, Hoglah, Milcah and Tirzah knew that there was One to whom they could direct their Final Appeal. They also knew that He had appointed an Advocate to present their petition in an appropriate manner, to Him. For these five sisters, Moses was that Intercessor. He was able to access the Presence and the ear of the Lord and present their claim for parity before the law, and justice for the dispossessed women of their nation

The daughters of Zelophehad were confident that their case was worthy of the attention of the Lord Jehovah and the efforts of the Prophet of the Most High God. They were determined to have their case heard by the highest authority so convinced and convicted were they of the justice of their claim. They could have given up after the tribal elders ruling but they did not. They placed their last hope, their faith and their salvation in the decision of God. Their faith, a gift of the Holy Spirit, was sufficient to motivate and propel them to approach the man of God and make their requests known. After all, faith without works is dead. **James 2:17-26**.

Their determination and their faith in the right of their cause is a further lesson to us; when we have embarked on a mission of right or righteous purpose, we must persevere in our efforts and not allow obstacles or enemy attacks to hinder us. The final authority in the spirit and in the natural is the Lord. And even when it seems that there is no hope, He is the highest Authority and the final word belongs to Him.

The Chief Advocate

The prophet Moses was a type of the promised Messiah. He stood between the Children of Israel and God; pleading their cause, interceding on their behalf, seeking instruction, receiving direction and representing the love and will of God to His people. Jesus the Christ is the Anointed One, the Messiah, the real deal. Not a type, a shadow or a representation, but the Promised Seed. He is our Chief Intercessor with the Father. **Hebrew 7:25.** In truth, the Son has always been our Advocate with the Father even before the very earth was established. It is He who defends us, intercedes for us, and fights for our future. He is the Lion of Judah, the mystery and the miracle of the Lamb who is become the Lion Defender of the children of God, redeemed by His blood and called by His name.

It is the Anointed One that stands before the Throne of Grace and claims victory over the usurper of the birthright and divinely ordained heritage of man; male and female, gifted to us by our Heavenly Father. The Lord Jesus redeemed us and **"as many as receive Him, to them has He given power to become the sons of God, even to as many as believe on His name". 1 John 1:12.** By His victory over death, sin and the grave, He has restored us to be heirs of our Father's legacy by His Holy Sacrifice that brings justification to those who are reborn, not of the flesh but of the Spirit.

The sisters were determined to change the social and legal order of their day by bringing about a change in the law that governed God's people. Their intention was clear. There was a defect, oversight or omission which caused hardship and suffering, fear and desperation. While there were many who felt that the status quo should not be disturbed, tradition should not be tampered with and the law could not be changed, the sisters had the conviction, perseverance, passion and faith that fuelled their righteous cause and kept them going. Their fire, fervor and faith came from the Lord and despite the appearance that they were 'bucking the trend' by petitioning change in long held traditions and practices; God was on their side and so they could not be deterred, distracted or denied.

There are many occasions when issues of social, political or legal reform must be pursued and the Lord always has His chosen people to carry out His will. Seeking to bring about such changes requires determination, passion, patience, perseverance and above all else, God-faith that the thing that one is trying to achieve is right and just both in the eyes of God and man. The sisters were chosen for just such a task and they proved themselves equal to the call of God on their lives.

Therefore, let us learn the lessons of the fighting sisters of faith; there is no area of life that excludes the will of God. In every situation that we face the warrior spirit gifted us by the Lord becomes an effective asset to fulfilling the Father's will. He is concerned about everything that impacts our life and desires us to be His instruments in the establishment or pursuit of justice, equality and harmony within the family of man.

The daughters of Zelophehad had their petition declared as justified and they were the happy recipients of God's justice, direct from His throne. Their weeping was turned to tears of joy and triumph. A new law declared the mercy, will and love of the Lord our God. The birthright of the sisters was restored to them and equally to all women in their position. We too, like these five sisters can lay hold on our birthright which was stolen in the Garden of Eden.

We too can do the same as the daughters of Zelophehad; when Jesus our Savior yielded to the will of God in another garden, the Garden of Gethsemane His obedience assured us victory over the plans, plots and diabolical designs of the devil to dispossess us of our Father's inheritance. When right, fairness and justice is on your side that means that God is on your side. Never give up! God is able to turn institutions and systems around that have operated to oppress, depress, abuse, misuse, divide and distract the hearts and minds of His people. There is nothing that is impossible for our God. It is His will that justice reigns; the authority to administer His justice and all judgment is given to the Lord Jesus by the Father. **Jeremiah 23:5. John 5:22-27.**

When we are in positions of inequality and unfairness, exploitation or exclusion, isolation or alienation, we too must look to our Advocate and High Priest, to the Judge and Enforcer of justice, by prayer and supplications with praise and thanksgiving. It is in the lost causes and the impossible circumstances that our God has the opportunity to make manifest to the nations, His perfection and His justice, His love and His glory to all who will call upon His name.

There is not an area of our lives that the Lord is not interested in, or a subject matter that cannot be addressed by His Word. There is no struggle or fight for fair-play, justice, equality, honesty, inclusion, recognition, appreciation or representation that is excluded from the operation of the principles, purposes and will of the Kingdom of God and His righteousness. In other words, as people of God we should not draw a demarcation line between social, political, economic, and personal acts of righteousness and a Christ-like character and Spirit filled lifestyle. We are warriors of the cross in whatever capacity and on whichever frontline we are positioned.

When Christ is the focus of our lives and God is Sovereign over all our ways, our every step is ordered by the Lord and all our thoughts are in subjection to His will, even as our actions must flow from the guidance of the Holy Spirit resident within our hearts. **Psalms 37:23, 24.** Wherever we find ourselves, whether at work, at the well, at home or at church, in social or political gatherings and functions or in private individual interactions, at the grocery store, in a queue at the bank or walking the dog, we must allow the Spirit to lead us and control all our thoughts, words, actions and acts and attitudes.

Even at the risk of being criticized, ostracized or penalized, we must always remember that we have an Advocate who will intercede with the Highest Authority, present our petitions, make our requests known and plead justification. Whether the battle is large or small, we can never give up, throw in the towel and allow the traditions and practiced tendencies of this present system of darkness or the attacks of the enemy to crush our spirits. The battle is not yours, it is the Lord's and He has already overcome the enemy so that we are more than conquerors in Christ Jesus. **Romans 8:37-39**

As women, we are all inheritors of the Kingdom of our God. Like the daughters of Zelophehad, we are entitled to a share in the inheritance of our Father, joint heirs with Jesus the Christ and heirs of His Father and ours. It does not matter where injustice might be, whether it is in the institutions of the world, the culture of our communities, or in the church of the Christ; we are partakers of the new covenant of the cross where there is no distinction, discrimination or division. We are all qualified to share in the justification secured at Calvary. **"There is therefore now, no condemnation to them which are in Christ Jesus." Romans 8:1.** Old things; old systems, old attitudes, old curses, old politics and old bondages are passed away, behold, all things become new in Christ Jesus our Lord. **2 Corinthians 5:17-21**

The attitude, approach and assignment of the sisters may be briefly summarized as follows for our study:

1. The sisters refused to accept the status quo. They did not believe that authority over their lives and their destiny rested solely in the hands of man

2. They would not walk away from, or give up their claim to their inheritance even though it appeared they were fighting a loss cause in the eyes of man. After all, they had tangible proof that God is a God of loss causes where it concerns His people.

3. Zelophehad's daughters believed in the justice of their cause and the right of their claim to their legacy. There was no reason that could explain why they should be excluded from a share in their father's portion.

4. They were convicted of the justice of their cause and were willing to challenge the accepted customs, traditions and laws of the day, regardless of the consequences. They had faith that God was a just God and that their cause was not frivolous.

5. The women were prepared to step out in faith and follow up with action that manifested their faith in God's justice. Their faith was not an abstract thought but propelled them to act. The pursuit of their claim was faith in action.

6. The sisters made sure that they followed the correct procedures and activated the proper processes for their claim. They ensured that they went through the appropriate channels and finally on to the hest authority through the Advocate provided by Jehovah to intercede on the behalf of His chosen ones. We too have an Advocate which is Christ Jesus, our Lord.

7. The daughters of Zelophehad did not become discouraged or disheartened about challenging a seemingly impossible wall of objection based on the customs established in their society. Rather, they made their appeal to the ultimate Authority and in so doing won their case; the right for themselves and all other women in the same position, to inherit from their father in the absence of sons. The Highest and ultimate Authority in our lives must be the Lord our God.

Job is a famed biblical character noted for his faith, his endurance and his ultimate victory in God as he stood firm in the face of great trials, testing and suffering brought against him by the adversary. He received the reward of his confidence and trust in the Lord. After having lost everything through satanic attacks, all was again restored to him. This included sons and daughters. Job prevailed and so demonstrated that God's faith in him was justified.

As a result of Job's suffering and travail in the physical and spiritual realm, he was divinely purified, gained godly wisdom, became spiritually matured and was made perfectly righteous. After all, Paul tells us that even Jesus the Christ was perfectly equipped for His office as our Redeemer and High Priest through the human experience of suffering that He underwent. **Hebrews 2:10** This spiritual growth and maturation of character that flowed from Job's experience brought about profound changes that impacted his life in all areas, his family and his community. Some of the changes may be summarized in the following way –

- ❖ Job loved with the heart of God: he prayed for his friends that had tried to discourage him and convict him that he deserved his trials. Note that Job's action preceded his blessings and his restoration by the Lord.

- ❖ He saw with the eyes of God. Job caught the vision of the Lord of the redemption and restoration of the human family, justified and made righteous by the Son.

- ❖ Redemption applied equally to male and female, sons and daughters. Travail and suffering of women became real and personal to him and he understood that the Lord redeems us all including His daughters by the sacrifice and suffering on the cross.

- ❖ As a result of the love shed abroad for all of the human family, all of us have a right to an equal inheritance of our Father's legacy; heirs and joint heirs of the Kingdom of Light. Therefore being after the heart of God and catching the vision of redemption, Job bequeathed an equal inheritance to his children, sons and daughters alike.

- ❖ This act was so unique that it is recorded in the Scriptures for our instruction, example, enlightenment and salvation.

It is no surprise that this man of God who experienced the working of righteousness and divine justice up close and personal acted the way he did; according to God's justice and God's way. Not only do we find that the daughters of Job were specifically named in the Scriptures but we are told that they were made to inherit equally, officially with their brothers. They were provided a legal right to inherit from their father's estate including his eternal, divine inheritance; an equal portion of righteousness and service to the eternal and only wise Jehovah God! **Job 42:13-15.**

CHAPTER 19

ON THE WARPATH

The Arsenal of the Warrior

The people of God are involved in a spiritual warfare that is intensifying as we approach a very critical time in the history of man and the plan of God for the human family on earth. Once again women must be ready, prepared, positioned, appointed and anointed to fight the good fight of faith. We constitute over half the world's population therefore, potentially, over half the human soldiers in the Army of the Lord. We must be in Christ, God-focused and Holy Spirit fuelled and fired up to wage a holy war against the enemy of our souls, our destiny and the Kingdom of our Father and our Lord;

> **For we are not wrestling with flesh and blood [contending only with physical opponents], but against the despotisms, against the powers, against [the master spirits who are] the world rulers of this present darkness, against the spirit forces of wickedness in the heavenly (supernatural) sphere. 13. Therefore put on God's complete armor, that you may be able to resist and stand your ground on the evil day [of danger], and, having done all [the crisis demands], to stand [firmly in your place]. Ephesians 6:12-13**

Why do I proclaim this battle cry to the women of the nations now? God's Holy Words have informed us of the situation and circumstances surrounding the state of the enemy's posture and position in many biblical texts, one of which we just read. And any doubt about its relevance today is confirmed by listening to the news, monitoring world events and walking around most of our neighborhoods. The world is in a terrible mess and the enemy of mankind and of Jehovah and His Kingdom authority is rejoicing.

But the Words of the Most High have already decreed the instruments and vessels of His response. It is my purpose to focus on the role of women in this spiritual warfare as decreed from the beginning; **'the woman will be at enmity with the devil'** says our Creator God. **"Surely the Sovereign Lord does nothing without revealing His plan to His servants the prophets". Amos 3:7.** And so by the mouth of His prophet Joel, He declared that in the last days His Spirit will be poured out on all His people in abundance and our sons and daughters shall prophesy. He further reinforces the equality and equity of His blessings by adding that **"upon the servants and upon the handmaids in those days will I pour out My Spirit!" Joel 2:28, 29.**

That old serpent, the deceiver, seized control of this earthly domain as a satellite of the kingdom of darkness. There is only one Way that we can have the faith and focus that we need to be empowered and impassioned to carry out the Lord's commission to warfare against Satan's domination of our nations. We can only fulfill Jehovah's plan, purpose and promise to mankind through the Holy Spirit. It is the Spirit of Christ indwelling our earthly temples that will provide power to press toward the mark of redemption and restoration in the strength of our Redeemer and the might of our God and Creator. We cannot employ the weapons of our warfare if we do not possess the Holy Spirit and unless we deliberately make the choice to serve the Christ our Lord, we are His enemies and of the army of the dark forces of evil.

If women ignore, deny or refuse our Commission in Christ as warriors against the warmonger and thief of our identity and our inheritance, we are supporting Satan in His treachery. And it does not stop there; failing to seize the opportunity to be justified by the

Christ, so that we have a clean slate and a fresh start in the Lord is a choice. It is a choice to continue in subservience to evil, in submission to the serpent and in collusion with the destroyer of the life and Deity-designed destiny of mankind.

Conversely, even the foolishness of God is beyond our comprehension and His ways as high as the heavens are in relation to the earth. In this spiritual warfare between the Glorious Two Thirds of the heavenly hosts and the Unholy One Third of the satanic supporters, there are only two sides. We can decide to be with The Two Thirds under the authority of the Commander-in-Chief, the Lord Jesus Christ or we can side with the One Third and their leader the father of lies and sin, the diabolical destroyer of life, Satan. There is no middle ground, no third way. There are only two sides in this war and no room for abstention.

There has never been a middle ground despite the attempts by the enemy to have us believe otherwise. He has inspired seemingly alternative forms of worship that purports to be a third way. They may be summarized in the following way:

a. Worship of the Most High God in some format that denies the identity, character and power of God
b. A true realization of self that elevates man to the status of god
c. Elevation of humanism which rejects God's moral authority in preference for a self-determined moral value system of humanity
d. Ultimate enlightenment through the esoteric arts and practices
e. A new way for a new age which recycles old age religions and beliefs

Joshua makes the subject matter under discussion, unequivocally clear and simple; **"Choose this day, whom you will serve"**. **Joshua 24:15.** There is only one Way to become a servant-warrior of the Creator God. Jesus said, **"I am the Way the Truth and the Life, no man comes to the Father but by Me"**. **John 14:6.**

Therefore there is only one Way into the Kingdom and one Way to make it through enemy territory and that is to be fully clad in **"God's whole armor [the armor of a heavy-armed soldier which God supplies] that you may be able successfully to stand up against [all] the strategies and the deceits of the devil". Ephesians 6:11.** If we neglect **'so great a salvation' (Hebrews 2:3)**, then we are choosing to continue to be enemies of God and of His Kingdom.

For God sent not His Son into the world to condemn the world but that the world through Him might be saved. John 3:17

For as many as believe on the Lord Jesus Christ that He is the Son of God, shall be saved. John 11:26. (NIV)

Death and hell can have no claim to blood-bought believers. The righteousness of the Christ is imputed to the saints justifying us before the judgment throne of God. If we love the Christ, we will also love our fellow humans and we too shall do the work that He does, as directed by the Father. The Lord Jesus was sent to save mankind from the rule of sin which 'works death' and eternal damnation in our lives. So that as many as believe in Him shall be reborn of the Spirit and of water through baptism, into the family of God. Those who do not believe that Jesus is the Son of God reject the Father also and therefore remain in sin and at enmity with God.

To be carnally minded is death. The carnal mind is enmity against God; for it is not subject to the law of God, nor indeed can be. Romans 8:6, 7.

17. For the desires of the flesh are opposed to the [Holy] Spirit, and the [desires of the] Spirit are opposed to the flesh (Godless human nature); for these are antagonistic to each other [continually withstanding and in conflict with each other], so that you are not free but are prevented from doing what you desire to do.

18. But if you are guided (led) by the [Holy] Spirit, you are not subject to the Law.

19. Now the doings (practices) of the flesh are clear (obvious); they are immorality, impurity, indecency,

20. Idolatry, sorcery, enmity, strife, jealousy, anger (ill temper), selfishness, divisions (dissensions), party spirit (factions, sects with peculiar opinions, heresies),

21. Envy, drunkenness, carousing, and the like. I warn you beforehand, just as I did previously, that those who do such things shall not inherit the Kingdom of God. Galatians 5:17-21

All such as try to enter into the Kingdom by some other way than through the Lord Jesus remain servants and soldiers of the prince of darkness and his army of destroyers. The enemy knows that his defeat was accomplished by the Savior yet he still seeks to destroy as many human lives as possible in order to deprive them of entry into the beauty and joy of God's Kingdom. The plots, plans, ploys and tactics of the enemy come in all different sizes, shapes, packages and trappings. Anything or anyone may be employed to deceive, distract, distort and dispose of the touch, teaching, call, commission, influence or indwelling of God by the Holy Spirit.

Satan will juggle the truth around so much and make lies and deception so attractive, so plausible, so comfortable, familiar and undemanding that only the presence of the Holy Spirit can enable the sin-befuddled minds of humans to see the truth of Christ clearly. The handiwork of the adversary is so well concealed, his strategies so subtle, the blurring of the lines between good and evil so cunningly air-brushed that were it possible even the elect of the Lord would be deceived. **Matthew 24:24**

The distinction between truth and lie, disobedience and rebellion, reverential worship in spirit and in truth and the practice of a form of godliness that denies the power of God, is impossible of discernment except we have our eyes firmly fixed on the Lord and His words deeply rooted in our hearts. There are philosophies and logic, scientific objectivity and idolatry that masquerade as alternative truths and new age illumination purporting to lead us to enlightenment and understanding of the meaning and purpose of life. They challenge the very existence or nature of the Divine, as expounded in the Holy Scriptures in an effort to beguile and bewitch and ultimately entice us to rebellion and forfeiture of our godly inheritance.

4. But because of His great love for us, God, Who is rich in mercy

5. Made us alive with Christ even when we were dead in transgression – it is by grace you have been saved.

6. And God raised us up with Christ and seated us with Him in the heavenly realms in Christ Jesus,

7. In order that in the coming ages He might show the incomparable riches of His grace, expressed in His kindness to us in Christ Jesus.

8. For it is by grace you have been saved, through faith – and this not from yourselves, it is the gift of God. Ephesians 2:4-8

There is no other name given among men whereby we can be saved and attain the Kingdom of Heaven. A thief and a hireling will not risk anything for the sheep but the true Shepherd will lay down His life for the sheep, even the one lost sheep that has strayed from the safety of his voice. **John 10:11-15**. Who is on the Lord's side? Are you, or have you chosen, actively or passively the things of this world, its present rulers or the inventions of man's mind and hands? The time is coming when **"every knee shall bow and every tongue confess that Jesus Christ is the Lord"** and Jehovah is our Creator and God above all others. **Romans 14:11, 12**

Have you set your affections on the things of the Lord, have you sought the Kingdom and the righteousness of God, are your treasures laid up where they can never decay? **Colossians 3:2- 17.** Are you in the camp of the enemy or among the soldiers of the army led by Prince Michael and the Glorious Two Thirds, so that when the final trumpet is sounded at the end of the war, you will enter into the rest prepared for the servants of the Lord?

Revelations 22:2 tells us that after the victory is secured there will then be **"the healing and restoration of the nations"** and **verse 3** assures us that there shall no longer exist anything that is accursed. The Scriptures go on to say in triumphant tones;

> **...And death shall be no more, neither anguish nor grief nor pain any more, for the old conditions and the former order of things have passed away and God will wipe away every tear from our eyes. Revelation 21:4 (NIV)**

> **And if anyone's name is not found recorded in the Book of Life (at the final judgment), he was hurled into the lake of fire' prepared for the devil and those who serve him. Revelation 20:15. (NIV)**

So are you ready to choose, to actively seek out Christ and the salvation He offers and declare your love and loyalty by joining the army of the heavenly hosts and the saints. Or, are you willing to make a choice for the devil by default? We are born in sin and to become a child of God and a citizen of His Kingdom we must choose for ourselves; choose to be heirs of the inheritance that God offers us in Christ or to be cohorts of Satan and his destiny of final annihilation

> **20. Behold, I stand at the door, and knock: if any man hear my voice, and open the door, I will come in to him, and I will sup with him, and he with Me. 21. To him that overcometh will I grant to sit with me in my throne, even as I also overcame, and am set down with My Father in His throne. Revelation 3:20, 21. (NIV)**

We have to make a choice and we do, actively or passively. Choosing Christ immediately brings us under His command and since there is a war that is raging, wherever we are, there is a divine commission to serve. Women of God, the Father put His confidence, faith and favor in us by His commission declared in **Genesis 3:15**. God's army is an equal opportunity, equal access army! Will you take up arms and the privilege and honor of following Him to victory?

State and Status

There are many women today, especially in western societies who feel that they have "arrived". We had goals, ambitions, expectations and dreams of achieving levels of success in the world and we have seen those come to fruition, due in great part to the ground work and sacrifices of an earlier generation of females. We have aspired to and become career women operating in the upper echelons of the professional and business classes. Many of us are motivated to achieve personal excellence in order to secure economic independence, sense of identity, and personal value.

Despite all the set-backs, suffering and sacrifices that our 'success' required, women have persevered in the hope of becoming the authors of their own destinies. As wholesale subscribers to the notion that money equals power, many of us have taken up its pursuit with a passion, determination and commitment unequalled in any other aspects of our lives. Financial freedom from the restraints imposed by dependence on fathers and husbands, promised us a greater say in issues affecting our individual and family's well being. It also promises a greater measure of participation and equality in contributing to the institutions and operations that shape our world and our place in it.

In view of our current perceived status, many of us now believe that we have succeeded in achieving equal standing with men in our societies. Generally speaking, especially in western societies, we now think that women are no longer relegated to the status of second class citizenry, en masse. We can therefore feel rightly proud of these accomplishments. However a closer look at the harsh reality of the balance of political and economic power in the worldly institutions and governments of our day may be a rude awakening. The majority of women, even in the developed nations still occupy under-paid and under-valued jobs merely to ensure there is food on the table and shelter for their families. And even the success stories do not necessarily find complete satisfaction in their achievements.

There are other women who have achieved their supposed success in finding and marrying Mr. Right or Mr. Rich. We have financial security and our status as a member of a select group or social class is indisputable. The house in the suburbs, the two and a half children, the appropriate dog, cat and car, the right friends and social circle and the sufficiently conservative, circumspect church all go to complete the picture of success. It is just as successful for some of us to be Mrs. Right as it is getting that promotion to CEO of the Company for others. These are just two examples of the passion and pursuit of women in today's modern world.

There is no implied or intended criticism of ambition, hard work and success in the world but of the priority that we give to worldly success at the expense of godly service, devotion and loving duty. Many of us who feel that we have reached that place of status and security that we desired are content to sit back and bask in the good providence of our positions and just cruise along in comfort, confidence and complacency. But let me just say to any woman who fall into the above categories; there is more to life than the accolades, achievement and applause that this world so highly esteems!

There is another dimension that was ordained for our fulfillment and to settle only for the standing ovation that echoes from the hollow hallways of society, is **"to fall short of the glory of God"**, the glory that the Almighty created to be our birthright, our legacy. We can be God's princesses, daughters of the Most High, royally appointed warriors in the Army of Righteousness, victors over death and inheritors of life eternal. Now which future will you choose, which outcome sounds like true success?

Our Lord is a gentleman and will not force His Way; the decision is yours! Even if your outward appearance says servant or slave, choosing the Christ will transform you from a pauper into a princess, a child of the Most High. Wearing the most expensive diamond does not compare to being a citizen of the holy and beautiful city, the New Jerusalem that will descend from heaven when Christ establishes His Kingdom on the renewed earth! **Revelation 21:10-27, 22:1-5!**

The satisfaction of material comforts and worldly fame is a welcome but temporary benefit that is confined only to this life-time. But this life is only a passing phase. Man is like the grass that comes up and then withers and dies. Eternity lies beyond death and what happens there is determined by how we live here and now. The treasures and achievements so highly revered, esteemed and sought after by this world, are not lasting and therefore cannot earn us a place in the Kingdom of the Eternal One. However, the ability to use one's talents and treasures bestowed by God, which does not bring with it any sorrow, for the purpose of the Kingdom, is success.

If eternal life is our desire and it is the answer to our search for eternal youth! (I tease!), then we must have a relationship with the Lord. By inspiration I will look at the situation of Lot's wife. She lived a very comfortable lifestyle in the city; the City of Sodom. Read about her fate in **Genesis 19.** Her husband was a wealthy man. She was blessed with children who had married well. She was satisfied with the standing she had achieved in her community and she relished the benefits and the amenities of city living. There were some unsavory characters, some disgusting practices and some questionable morals around but she was tolerant in her attitude and her approach to her neighbors. She tried not to interfere, criticize or condemn anyone for their choices.

Live and let live was her approach. After all, she knew what was acceptable for her and her children and she lived accordingly. Apart from all that, she had everything that a woman of her time could possibly want. In fact she was so content with her position that she never even contemplated the possibility of moving to another neighborhood. She was part of the elite, the in-people; anywhere else was too provincial, a step down.

When the angels of the Most High came with news of Sodom's judgment it was shocking. How could this be true? The invitation of the angels to re-locate her and her family was just too overwhelming. She would have to leave immediately, leave all her possessions; material and social, behind. She would have to start all over again. In addition to which, her married children refused to heed the warning and utilize the exit provisions that Abraham had secured for his nephew Lot and the members of His family. They did not believe the Messengers of God and the Words of Jehovah. They were not in right standing with God and so did not have the faith required to act on the holy message of the angels.

Many of us are just like Lot's wife. The situation as I have described above is not as far-fetched as we might think at first sight. Imagine giving up everything you have including all you have worked to achieve, at the drop of a hat. Would you be like Lot's wife or would you gladly heed the chance of escape offered by a message of deliverance from the Lord of Heaven and earth? Many of us are defined by our status and our material possessions as well as by what others think of us. Take these away and there is nothing of substance left to carry us through periods of testing and trials. The idols we have given center stage in our lives crumble like dust in the wind. We soon realize that our houses are built on sand not solid rock. **Matthew 7:24-27**

Pearl of Great Price

We can be so focused on the things that satisfy the lust and cravings of the flesh that we miss the important things of God that are eternal. I am by no means belittling the hard work and the achievements made by women in our present day society. I am proud of them. I am merely trying to point out that if we desire real achievement, satisfaction and a sense of purpose, we need to seek after a greater prize than that which perishes with the world and at the whim of governments.

We need to be like the rich man who was on the look out for a **"Pearl of great price"**. Once he found it, he went and sold everything he had in order to secure possession of it. **Matthew 13:45, 46.** It is the will of God that we likewise, recognize the pearl of great price, salvation in Christ Jesus. Attaining the Kingdom of God and His righteousness, pressing through all the material and moral morass that can tangle our minds and bodies and reaching toward the higher calling of the King; that should be our greatest desire.

I write, as I do throughout this study under inspiration for our personal understanding concerning Lot's wife and the destruction that came on her as recounted in **Genesis 19** and some of the lessons that the Holy Spirit has revealed to me. Lot's wife had no higher ambition, no greater purpose than the material, earthly wealth, possessions and prestige that she had already attained in the City of Sodom. It was for that reason her heart and mind were so entangled, so conflicted that she was unable to focus on the divine direction of the angels of God. All her affections and her heart's desires were completely tied up with her life as it was experienced in that condemned place. Lot's wife was not God-focused.

She knew about God, and she knew that the angels had been sent by Him to make a way of escape. Yet because she was not God-focused and was not possessed of God-faith, she was unable to anticipate life outside the city walls of Sodom. She was not looking for the City, whose Builder and Ruler is God. She was deceived, enticed and trapped by the temporary things, both material and immaterial, that appeal to the carnal nature of man.

The Scriptures tells us that we have to be willing to give up mother, father, sister, brother and even children in order to be obedient to the Lord and His holy calling. Notice that although Lot's wife went along with the angels, with her husband and daughters, all that consumed her mind and her heart was a desire for what was being left behind in Sodom. She was physically absent from Sodom, but spiritually present in her focus, her attachment and her desires.

God's mercy and His favor were lost on her. He had made a way of escape not because she deserved it but because of His mercy and His promise to His servant, Abraham. Lot's wife caught the vision, started on her journey out of that City of Sin but took her eyes off the prize. She hungered once more for the former things of her life. **But "if in this life only we have hope then we are of men most miserable',** says the Word of God. **1 Corinthians 15:19.** The culmination of the choices made by Lot's wife was death and damnation. She rejected the future that God had in store for her and so shared the fate of the City of Sin. **Genesis 19:26**

Positioned for Power

On the one hand, we have a brief biography of Lot's wife, who lost her salvation because she determined her identity and defined her status in relation to her earthly possessions and material worth. On the other hand, the Scripture gives us the shining example of Hadassah who risked the loss of the highest possible status in society, the pleasure and security of vast wealth, the love of a great king and the influence that goes with the position of a favored and beloved royal consort, in order to be obedient to the call of God on her life.

During the period of the Medo-Persian Empire, the Persian King Xerxes, also known as Ahasuerus in Hebrew, ruled over 127 provinces, stretching from India to Cush, the Upper Nile region. He ruled his kingdom from the citadel of Susa. To celebrate his success and impress his subjects, he organized a massive banquet and invited all the nobles and officials of the Kingdom. All the military leaders of Persia and Media, the princes and the nobles of the provinces were present. We are told that this festive occasion continued over a period of 180 days in which the King showed off the great wealth of the kingdom as well as the splendor and glory of his majesty. **Esther 1:1-21.**

In his celebration, the King wanted to parade even the beauty and majesty of his Queen, Vashti, in all her royal fineries. **"But when the attendants delivered the king's command, Queen Vashti refused to come. Then the king became furious and burned with anger"..."** Esther 1:12. This outrage was answered by the banishment of the Queen and the issue of a royal edict declaring every man to be the ruler over his own household, so that the example of Queen Vashti would not be emulated and wives would respect their husbands.

At this time, there was a Jew who had been carried away from Jerusalem by Nebuchadnezzar, living in the citadel of Susa. He lived with his adopted daughter Hadassah. King Xerxes made a proclamation to gather suitable young women to his palace for preparation for a period of twelve months. At the end of that time, he would choose a bride and a new Queen. Hadassah, thereafter known as Esther was also taken to the King's palace. There, after the appointed time of preparation, God's Word tells us

The king was attracted to Esther more than to any of the other women, and she won his favor and approval more than any of the other virgins. So he set a royal crown on her head and made her queen instead of Vashti." Esther 2:17.

At that time and even by today's standard, it was a great achievement for Esther to be the queen of such a vast empire. In spite of her good fortune and the amazing blessings she received from God, Esther did not allow these to change her. She was already in a position of favor with Jehovah God long before going to King Xerxes palace and finding favor in his eyes.

She had been brought up in the fear of the Most High God and she kept her faith with Him. She was a woman of God and was available for His service. She never imagined the nature of the calling that God had placed on her life. After all, He is able to do exceedingly, abundantly above all that we can ask, think or even imagine! But Esther knew that the palace of the Persian King was not her destiny, only a destination on the road to her divine legacy.

Esther had a King in her life long before she ever met the Persian King Xerxes. She was already royalty before that crown was placed on her head. She was already a child of the Creator God. Esther had already learnt the importance of obedience to the will of God in the teachings, faith and history of the Jewish people. And that is why when the time of testing came for her and her people; she turned to her real King, first. Esther, her attendants, her uncle and the Children of Israel went to put their petition first before the Most High that is; they fasted and prayed to the King of Kings and the Lord of Lords, at Esther's request.

The Father God blesses us so that we may be able to be a blessing to others. We often think that we can only bless others with a financial blessing. But God's blessings can take many forms. For example, being in a position to enable or empower an individual to provide for their family is a great blessing, or being able to put in 'a good word' in a difficult or challenging situation, on behalf of someone who may be powerless to affect their own destiny, is a sharing of your blessings and will be a delight to the Giver of all good gifts.

The Lord positions us where He has need for our service. This applies whether we consider our positions to be lowly or exalted according to the calculation of man. It is not about the place that we are in, the title by which we are called or the circumstances that got us there. Rather, it is always about the assignment of our God and the roles we are destined to play in bringing about His purpose. There is no purpose determined by the Father that is more important than any other. So wherever we are placed is the exact location that will enable us to be obedient to our individual calling and afford us the privilege to make war with the enemy.

Doing the will of God and fulfilling His plan for our lives is our reasonable service to the Eternal One. The level of achievement and success that we attain should not be measured according to the standards regarded by this world system but according to our faithfulness to the Kingdom of God. We are merely transients in a temporary posting to carry out a mission for the Kingdom. We must live by the standard of the heavenly system, of which system and Kingdom we are citizens.

It is wonderful to be a God-fearing man or woman but it is even more awesome to understand that we all have been called to serve. There is Kingdom-work to be done. There will continue to be a need for laborers, soldiers, servants and ambassadors to join in the Great Commission of our Redeemer to restore the authority and government of the heavenly Kingdom, on earth.

Esther was informed and trained to obey the will of God in her life and to understand the importance of that divine will to the posterity and prosperity of her people; the Children of Israel. She had the example and encouragement of her adopted father, Mordecai who refused to turn his back on the God of Israel and worship false gods, even when the threat of death hung over his head. Consequently, when great disaster and genocide hung over the Jewish people in the Babylonian kingdom, Esther was divinely located to accomplish that which the Lord had determined for her to do.

She had the influence, the conviction and the faith to follow through on the provisions that God had made for the salvation of His people. She could choose to stay quiet and God would have provided another way of escape for His people or she could accept that she was at the perfect place to be a warrior queen!

The consequences of the sacrifice required of Esther were a matter of life and death. The loss of material possessions and the worldly regard for prestige and influence did not shake her resolve to risk appearance in King Xerxes presence without a summons; an act that was illegal and could lead to his displeasure and her death, as easily as it might lead to her embrace and exoneration.

Esther was fully committed to be obedient to the will of God even if it led to her death. The saying "death before dishonor" was the maxim operating in Esther's mind and heart. She chose death rather than bring dishonor to her Father-God, her father Mordecai and her people. When Esther made her decision she was not thinking of Esther, the queen rather she was thinking of Hadassah, the young Jewish woman of God, warrior by divine appointment.

What is the profit of gaining the whole world, only to loose one's eternal life in the Kingdom of the King of Kings and Lord of Lords? Esther had completely surrendered herself to God. She was committed to the Lord and did not allow anything to distract her from her greater destiny. That destiny was to be the means, the live, biological weapon by which Jehovah God would save her people, His people again, from the destructive designs, plots and plans of the enemy of God to thwart the Redemption Plan of Heaven's Throne.

If Haman's evil plot had succeeded then the lineage of David could have been destroyed and the promise of Messiah would have been successfully aborted. And that was the plan of the devil. Mordecai's take on the situation was different. He had a God-perspective and faith that believed that even if Esther **"remained silent at this time, relief and deliverance will rise up from another place for the Jews". Esther 4:13.**

Let me remind my sisters and brothers, it is not because God cannot fulfill His purposes without a particular individual's help that we are called to fight in the Great war; it is that He loves us so much that He offers us the opportunity, the privilege and the honor to join Him in His work of redemption and restoration of our birthright.

Esther was created, prepared, positioned, appointed and anointed for **"such a time as this"**. **Esther 4:14.** She took the preparatory steps that were within her control, that is fasting and prayer, then leaving everything else to God, she stepped out in faith on her assignment. There are many times that we must make extra preparations when confronted with certain demonic attacks such as the planned extinction of the Jewish people against which Esther was about to make her stand. There are instances when we must fast and pray because as the Lord Jesus taught His disciples, there are some demonic strategies, assaults and opposition that **"cannot be driven out by anything but prayer and fasting"**. **Mark 9:17-29.**

Activating the Miracle

So determined was Esther to do the Father's bidding that she embraced the possibility of death and still yielded to the task to which she was assigned. However, there are lessons that we can learn from Esther's preparation before going into battle and engaging the enemy of man' salvation.

1. Esther made an accurate identification and assessment of the problem and the enemy.
2. Esther brought her petition first to the King of Kings, Jehovah God.
3. Esther asked that all the Jewish people fast for three days, both day and night.
4. She and her maids also joined in the Fast before going into battle.
5. She clothed herself in her royal robes to demonstrate her command of the situation and her armor/covering by her Sovereign Lord, the Divine One.
6. Esther carefully chose her location and timed her appearance according to divine guidance before King Xerxes.

7. Finally, she acted confidently and strategically in making her request known to King Xerxes.

Hadassah also called Esther was only able to stand in the gap because of –

a. her God-given position of influence and prestige, in spite of her humble origins
b. her God-fearing upbringing and her refusal to turn her back on her roots, her heritage as a part of the covenant people of the Lord
c. her God-focused attitude to life, accepting that worldly wealth and status even as the queen of one of earth's greatest kingdom, amounts to zero if one is not in right standing in the Kingdom of Jehovah God.
d. Esther did not focus on revenge, only on redemption, not on the adversary but on the Redeemer

The attacks of the enemy may not always be recognized as a matter of life or death naturally but they always are spiritually. He always battles to destroy our future in the Kingdom of God. It might not be apparent to us that the physical survival of a nation is at stake when we are in situations that require us to make a stand for God. But whatever we are positioned to accomplish for the Lord is for the survival of men and women who are potentially **"a peculiar people, a nation of priests ..."** within the spiritual realms and heavenly places. **1 Peter 2:9**

We do not need to see this now or understand how our seemingly small contribution fits into the whole plan but we can be certain it does. Furthermore we must understand and accept that there is no trivial, small, unimportant or unnecessary assignment from God. When humans fight in a war, they send their soldiers, spies, covert operatives to infiltrate and operate from deep within enemy territory as well as on the obvious frontlines or secondary positions. What might appear to be an insignificant action might be the very linchpin on which victory or failure stands or fall.

It is also instructive that Esther did not focus on gaining revenge on Haman, the enemy of her people, of herself and of God Most High. Her faith was in Jehovah God and He declares to us that vengeance belongs to Him. He has promised us that He will be an enemy to our enemy and we shall overcome all those who fight against us for His name's sake. In fact Jesus teaches that we should pray for our enemies. **Romans 12:19.**

There is no position too unimportant for achieving the overall success of the mission. If we as humans are able to grasp this in the natural, then even more should we be able to appreciate the chance to be undercover agents, covert operatives and super-(natural) soldiers in the Special Forces and Combat Units of our Commander-in-Chief, Jesus Christ the Lord.

Satan will always seek to manipulate and exploit the status and standing of women by distraction and deceit so that they become puffed up with pride, revel in a false security, feign satisfaction, harbor conceit and get comfortable with complacency. His purpose is to attempt to undermine God's sovereignty. Esther could have deluded herself into thinking that she had achieved her position in the Persian kingdom all by herself; her good looks, her charm, her sexuality or sensuality etc. Or, she could have believed that having achieved such a standing in such a kingdom, she should forget, despise and hide her humble beginnings, her family, her people and her God and look out for herself. In other words as we say in today's world 'look after number one'!

Likewise, Esther could have allowed fear, that is, the fear of death according to kingdom customs either for going into the king's presence without an invitation or of being identified as one of the condemned people, the Jews. But perfect agape love casts out fear and our obedience to God is an outer working of an inner love of the Lord. Esther's love for the Lord and her faith in His plans for her life gave her the confidence to overcome any misgivings that may have crossed her mind as she prepared to meet her destiny.

Esther's decision and subsequent action was based on a simple truth; she was a faith-focused, Word-wielding warrior of God fearlessly fighting the vicious and venomous attack of the adversary. She did not succumb to the soul-satisfying egotistical accolades that were heaped upon her or the flattery bandied about the royal residence and the courts by self-seeking sycophants.

Instead her actions were birthed out of a fully surrendered heart and a mind in submission to the will of God. She knew that God had proven His faithfulness to her people and certainly to her personally, as evidenced by her individual history and so she determined to believe the Lord for a miracle and depend on Him to make a way. Yet even if she should fail she would remain faithful to her covenant with Him.

38. For I am persuaded beyond doubt (am sure) that neither death nor life, nor angels nor principalities, nor things impending and threatening nor things to come, nor powers,

39. Nor height nor depth, nor anything else in all creation will be able to separate us from the love of God which is in Christ Jesus our Lord. Romans 8:38, 39

In other words, Esther was prepared that **'neither life nor death would separate her from the love of God'**. And loving God means obedience to His call on our lives. Her weapons were not carnal but spiritual as she went into battle against the principalities and powers of darkness and the traditional domain of the "Prince of Persia" with whom the archangel Gabriel did battle in **Daniel 10:13**.

It was the boldness of the Spirit of God and the strength of the Lord which carried the woman of God into the presence of King Xerxes. Her submission to the purpose of God for her life impacted the survival of her people and magnified the name of her God, our God, throughout all the regions of a pagan kingdom. And even today, the Jewish people celebrate the story of Esther; her courage, her obedience, her faithfulness, her love and her selflessness in defeating the deadly enemy of the Children of Israel and the whole human family. Haman was a servant and slave of the prince of darkness. The annual holiday of Purim is an enduring memorial of Queen Esther, warrior of the Most High.

The gift and the right of free will that the Creator God bestowed on the human family means that whether we choose to use our positions and our possessions to fulfill God's will is completely up to each of us. Esther made a choice which affected the fate of the Jewish people and informed a Kingdom of idol worshippers of the true God. As we saw earlier there was another Queen positioned to influence a kingdom for good or evil and she chose to perpetuate the evil will of Satan. That queen was of course, Jezebel.

Jezebel chose to serve a false God, joining the army of darkness and trying to wreak destruction on the people of God. The Jezebel spirit too is still rampant today and the aim remains the same; to war with the people of God and the Kingdom of Love.

Warriors of the Lord, emulate the example of the great warrior queen Esther! Women of the Kingdom, guard against the spirit of Jezebel which can parade and pretend to be a prophet but is really intent on plotting the downfall of all that is holy, righteous and worshipful of the Lord God Almighty! Esther's faith and her love fortified her heart, mind, and body so that with agape love overflowing, she exemplified the Christ-like quality of self-sacrifice; a quality and trait that all warriors must seek to possess, live and die by if necessary. The absence of love's operation in our lives is a sure sign that we do not belong to the family of God. The Lord declared its importance by His Word:

My command is this; Love each other as I have loved you. Greater love has no-one than this that he lay down his life for his friends. John 15:12, 13.

We know that we have passed over out of death into Life by the fact that we love the brethren (our fellow Christians). He who does not love abides (remains, is held and kept continually) in [spiritual] death. 1 John 3:14

CHAPTER 20

POLITICS, POSITION AND POWER

The Power for Good and Evil

There is a biblical character whose very name invokes an image of evil personified; treachery, rebellion, hatred against God and His prophets to her very bitter and awful end. Her life perfectly demonstrates how rejection of God is a choice to serve the enemy and how far that service can reach into the very future and the legacy bequeathed to our children. The person to whom I am referring is Jezebel, wife of Ahab, King of Israel to whom I have previously referred. **1 Kings 18-21. (Chapters 18-21)**

In fact she has come down through the pages of history, name and all, as a warning to God's women and a byword for iniquity; spiritual fornication, harlotry, idolatry, carnality, blasphemy and aggression towards the Kingdom of God. According to the Revelation of our Lord to the Apostle John, the spirit of Jezebel will continue to infect and replicate itself to the very end of days, working against the will of God and the prophetic anointing in the earth realm. **Revelations 2:18-29**

Jezebel was a servant of the devil. Instead of enmity with the enemy, there was collaboration. She joined with the accuser of God's people to bring about their destruction. We manufacture or blindly follow after rituals, practices, customs and cults that have nothing to do with worshipping the true God. And we work ourselves into a frenzy to convict and convince ourselves and others that these paths also lead us into the presence of the Holy God, our Maker. We dress up our ideas, our so-called wisdom and knowledge with the importance of man's limited, polluted vision and values, and parade them as alternative truths. But all the perceived wisdom of man and woman is foolishness in the eyes of God. And the self determined salvation of the soul is only falsehood, deception and idolatry. There is only one Way and one Truth; Jesus the Christ is the Way and He is the Truth.

Like Queen Esther, Jezebel was also a queen with the power to affect the Kingdom of Israel for good and for God. Instead she chose to follow an iniquitous lifestyle aggressively opposed to the Kingdom of Light. She professed a religion superior to worship of the God of Israel and pursued every avenue of darkness to impose and enforce its observance even to the slaying of the prophets of the Most High. A brief comparison between some of her achievements and Esther's will be instructive.

One queen used her position and status to fulfill the design of the Father Creator, the other to do the work of the enemy of God and mankind; Satan. One queen glorified God through her obedience, the other glorified self and sin. Esther served and saved a nation for God, Jezebel sought to destroy a nation through the worship of Baal; she led the people of God into idol worship and rebellion against godliness, holiness and the supernatural favor of Jehovah. One queen called a nation to prayer and fasting to secure the favor of Jehovah God for the benefit of them all while the other queen channeled the devil's revenge against the prophets and the people of God to their national detriment.

Today, we are all faced with the same choices as Esther and Jezebel. We can be yielded in service to the Lord or we can be self-serving and thereby sacrifice our selves to the service of the adversary of God's Kingdom. Regardless of the presentation, packaging or promises, it all comes down to a matter of choice. We can choose to be either for or against the Lord Jesus. We can devout all our energies to the acquisition of wealth, fame, career, professions, husbands, material or intellectual property but in the final countdown, have we gained salvation or a place in Satan's kingdom, life or death, redemption or condemnation. Are we self-centered or Christ-centered, a vessel for the manifestation of God's glory or a vassal of the destroyer and his treachery?

There are no accidents or coincidences in the plans of God. When we find ourselves in a particular place, at a certain time, with the correct credentials to affect the Kingdom of God for good or ill, we must be so sure of our assignment that we choose according to the will of God for our lives. We are always where we are for God's purposes, if we live in submission according to His direction and His guidance by the Holy Spirit.

But the devil, who is a liar, will try to tempt and thwart God's plans and manipulate us into disobedience and sin. The awesome thing is that whatever the devil designed for deceit and defilement, God is able to turn around for righteousness and redemption. And, although we follow a path that leaves us in a place of poor choices and disastrous decisions, Jesus the Christ died to give us the opportunity to turn away from sin at anytime we choose; not by our will-power or force of character but by His Spirit, His mercy and His grace.

A Mother's Legacy

The Bible tells there was a ruler of Judah, sitting on the throne for six years who was so driven by ambition that grave acts of murder and infanticide were committed to attain that crown of the kingdom. The monarch to whom I am referring is Athaliah, daughter of King Ahab and daughter of Jezebel either by birth or marriage. **2 Chronicles 22:2.** This is the only time on record that Judah was ruled by a female monarch but it is a testimony of what can happen when Satan is the originator of one's choices, ambitions and goals; the master of one's life and beneficiary of one's actions. Jezebel left a legacy that her daughter Athaliah inherited, embraced, cherished and show-cased in her own life. **2 Kings 11**

Athaliah married Jehoram who was the King of Judah. His reign was short but marked for its idolatry because he walked after the ways of the House of Ahab, his father-in-law. They worshipped Baal and reveled in the ways of the flesh, obviously disdaining Jehovah God, His law and His prophets. The seeds planted and nurtured in the viperous bosom of Jezebel bore a harvest of bitter fruits. Its venom and wickedness infected her children and all who fell within her influence.

After the death of Jehoram, his son Ahaziah became the ruler of Judah. He also followed in the footsteps of his parents and worshiped Baal but circumstances transpired that he was destroyed along with other sons of the House of Ahab, under the command of Jehu, acting as the hand of God. The reign of Ahaziah lasted for only one year and he was buried. **2 Chronicles 21:6.** The influence of Jezebel had been passed on to her children and grandchildren; a legacy of satanic submission and service. This fact is confirmed in **2 Chronicles 22:3-4.** It tells us that Ahaziah:

Also walked in the ways of the house of Ahab, for his mother was his counselor to do wickedly. 4. So he did evil in the sight of the Lord like the house of Ahab, for they were his counselors after his father's death, to his destruction."

The actions of the bereaved mother following the death of her son could only have flowed form a heart of stone; a heart given over to the control of the kingdom of darkness in which evil graduates to its fullest horror in the minds and hearts of the life surrendered to the prince of darkness. Athaliah was a woman surrendered to wickedness. She chose to serve the devil and she held nothing back. Ambition for domination drove any semblance of humanity from her and resulted in the perpetuation of a heinous act of homicide:

When Athaliah the mother of [King] Ahaziah [of Judah] saw that her son was dead, she arose and destroyed all the royal descendants. 2 Kings 11:1.

These royal descendants were her grandchildren! She set about killing them all so that she could achieve her ambition; domination. She desired to elevate herself, to sit as ruler on the throne of Judah, unopposed, unchallenged by the hereditary heirs that were her own flesh and blood, her grandchildren. She literally bequeathed to them a legacy of violent death. This is the maturity of wickedness, idolatry, rebellion, rejection of righteousness and disdain for the work of redemption of the Christ.

Athaliah demonstrated the fruits of self- will, self-determination and self-promotion. All the teachings and self-realization experiments that elevate self to the status of godhood while they ignore and disavow the existence of Jehovah God, will ultimately lead to personal destruction and eternal damnation. Religions and rituals that turn away from the Bible and Jehovah God and invite exaltation of a power, force or philosophy that comes from any source other than God are counterfeits. They are designed by Satan to trap the human family and keep them captives of sin, death and hell. We were not created for darkness but for light and without light we mutate into hideous creatures of iniquity whose thoughts and actions are evil, continually.

Athaliah had been so long exposed to and submitted to the rule of darkness that her humanity was mangled and her heart and mind could only conceive evil desires and ambitions. She had lost sight of the existence of the true God, the value and necessity of His Word, laws and statutes. The soul and spirit of mankind has an eternal need to be in relationship with the Lord. Satan perverted love and replaced it with fear. His promises of wealth, power and influence to mortal man can only be achieved through violence, deceit, destruction and a sacrifice of life; the life of children, grandchildren, relatives, friends, colleagues or anyone that might impede the spread of evil within the earth realm. And finally, the lost soul will be sacrificed on the altar of pride and idolatry; the loss of everlasting life in the Kingdom of Love and Righteousness.
Jeremiah 17:5

The Triumph of Good

Athaliah had reached the pinnacle of devil-worship. It does not matter the fineries that might frame the form of worship that one chooses, if God is not the centre of your devotion, adoration and reverential worship then it is Satan that is getting your glory, loyalty and obeisance. It might not appear to be so and many will hotly dispute it. But as we discussed earlier there are only two sides in this war and it is not possible to have ones practices reflect godliness but one's personal character reflects the attributes of Satan. Athaliah was the ruler over the Kingdom of Judah for six years. **2 Kings 11:3, 4**

However, in the seventh year, seven signifying completion in divine business, Jehoiada the priest of God took decisive steps to remedy the wrong perpetrated against the kingdom of Judah. He was the husband of Jehosheba who had stolen the baby Joash, son of Ahaziah, (Ahaziah was her half brother) from among the king's sons before they were slain by their grand-mother. She hid him with his nurse in the House of the Lord! The priest secured a covenant with the military arm of the Kingdom of Judah when he presented the rightful heir to the throne, the young child Joash. Jehoiada commanded them; setting out a plan to seize the throne for the young heir. Athaliah was slain with the sword beside the king's house.

And Jehoiada made a covenant between the Lord, the king, and the people that they would be the Lord's people – and also between the king and the people. 2 Kings 11:18.

Achieving positions of influence and power within the social, political, economical, professional or religious sectors and institutions of society certainly affords us great opportunities to do commendable service for the Kingdom. But attainment of such positions should not be regarded as an end in themselves. Power without God-purpose is pointless. After all, every appointment is subject to the will of God. **Daniel 2:21.**

Some of us might even achieve exalted positions pivotal to piloting change for the betterment and improvement of people who might otherwise suffer reproach, oppression, exploitation or abuse. But if we are only occupied with self, ego and worldly honor we will miss the opportunity to serve for which God positioned us. The legacy of Jezebel and Athaliah did not die with them but carried on with their descendants. This is a reminder that we should be careful what inheritance we leave our children and those who come after us; we must teach our children and tell them of the God of salvation. This too is our battle as mothers.

Like Esther, some of us will be seen, recognized and celebrated as our choices and actions impact the very survival of a community or a nation; glory to the Lamb we are blessed to be a blessing and all men can call us blessed! But we do not have to be in high profile positions of power or influence to affect a huge work on behalf of the Kingdom of God; the person that is considered least in the eyes of the world is the very person that is the greatest in the sight of the Almighty. **Matthew 20:25-28**.

In our little corner of the world, our small sphere of influence our contributions to the war effort might seemingly be insignificant in the natural realm by our community or church and remain un-noticed, un-announced and un-celebrated. But like the widow whose small contribution of her two mites **(Mark 12:42-44)** received the recognition and commendation of the King of kings, if we do all that we are appointed to for the honor and glory of God, we too will receive His applaud! It is not the applause of men that is important but the approval of the Almighty.

The Unknown Cook

The little boy whose mother prepared him a lunch of five loaves and two fish though unknown to us and unrecognized even by the beneficiaries of Christ's miracle nevertheless played an important role that brought glory to the Lord on a grand scale. I am sure that she did not have a clue as she sent her child to Christ's crusade that her preparation and provision of simple food for her son would be the very seed from which a great harvest would be manifested. The feeding and sustenance of thousands and the magnification of the Messiah throughout the ages hinged on the act of love of a mother who cooked a pack lunch for her son! There are many lessons that this mother can teach us. Here is a brief list for our benefit and blessing:

- **Always plan in advance and be prepared for any eventuality that might arise**

- **It is important to make provisions that will feed both the body and the spirit**

- **Even a child must learn to sit at the feet of Jesus and learn Truth**

- **A child can comprehend the things of the Kingdom of God**

- **Adults can learn natural and spiritual lessons from children**

- **Children belong to the Lord and can be instruments for His service**

- **The principles that build character when taught and modeled at home will inform, guide and sustain children in their decisions when they are away from home and as they grow into adults. For example, generosity, honesty.**

Bringing up God's Children

Women of God, the importance of raising our children in the fear of the Lord cannot be exaggerated or over-emphasized. There is a war that is raging and our children are a huge part of the struggle.

They are a natural prey for the devil and his cohorts. He will do any and everything to capture and control the minds of our children.

Children are the future of this world and they are the future warriors against Satan. He recognizes that the way to destroy the human family is by ceaseless attack against our children. It is a strategy that will destroy both parents and children alike. And do not be lulled into a false sense of security. He uses all modern technology to gain advantage. The media is at his disposal and it is maximized to its fullest extent in influencing and manipulating the minds and hearts of children. **Ephesians 2:2**

The devil's aim is to undermine the foundations that we have established for our children in Jehovah God and Jesus our Redeemer. The methods and means that the devil uses in his attacks are numerous and diverse, subtle, misleading, seemingly innocuous but deadly in their final effect. Parents, we have to be on guard, aware, informed, girded, and Holy Ghost powered to fight for our children's salvation. Do you understand now why God offers us a commission as His warriors against the enemy?

We must be God's women, grounded in the Scriptures, trained and equipped to fight on the home front as fiercely and as ferociously as in any battlefield. All the skills that come from the conditions imposed on womankind, such as patience, endurance, discernment, self-control, and discipline, long-suffering and so on will be absolutely essential in the warfare for our children. The devil has taken the hostility into our homes and now we must go after him armed with our spiritual weapons in the strength of our Lord and King, the conquering Lion of Judah.

After all, we might be home-makers like the heroine Jael, taking care of the needs of our families, when the Lord presents us with a chance to strike a blow for the Kingdom, for His people, the Body of Christ. The task to which the Lord calls us might not be considered important in the estimation of the world but the mere fact that God assigned us to it proves its significance. Every soldier knows that from the smallest to the biggest task that they carry out, each forms an important part of the whole. That is why Paul exhorts us not to esteem any part of the body more highly than another. **1 Corinthians 12**

Enlarging a Homemaker's Territory

Jael, the wife of Heber, the Kenite, was in her tent, minding her home affairs, when an arch-enemy of the people of God came face to face with his fate the moment he entered her territory seeking an accomplice. Jael was used of God to fulfill His Word, spoken by the Prophetess Deborah, Judge of the Israelites at this period in history. She did not leave her home to go in search of an act of valor or fame but the Lord brought the opportunity to excel in His service right to her door. The Scripture records the story as follows in the Book of **Judges 4 and 5.**

Sisera was the Commander of Jabin, a King of Canaan. Sisera with his vast army oppressed the Children of Israel for twenty years. The Lord spoke through the Prophetess Deborah, the Judge and Leader of the Children of Israel at that time, to send Barak son of Abinoam, with the ten thousand men who followed him, to go and take the victory God had granted against Sisera.

Yet despite the fact of a ten thousand strong troop, Barak knew that if he was to succeed then the pattern established historically, of his people's military victory, must be adhered to. That tradition was to place the Lord at the head of their advancing army. God had spoken by the mouth of His servant Deborah and so Barak refused to go against the enemy of his people unless the Prophetess herself went with them!

In the book of Hebrews, we read Barak's name among the list of the great men of faith hailed as examples to us by the Apostle Paul. Barak gained this recognition because he was able to recognize the voice of God and His presence with the Judge and Prophet of Israel at that time, God's woman, Deborah. It was just as essential as it ever was to have God's duly appointed leader of the nation of Israel riding into battle at the head of the army, whether the Prophet and Judge was a man or a woman. His faith was based in the Lord and it was His ability and prerogative to appoint whomever He wills to whatever position He desires. Barak's identity or self-esteem was not lessened; he did not need to monopolize praise for the eventual triumph of the battle to validate his worth to the Lord and his nation.

The result of Barak's faith and his honoring of the Word of the Almighty allowed the Lord to demonstrate His glory in exalting even the least in the world so that the Lord's strength could be demonstrated in human weakness. **Judges 4:9** – tells us that the Prophetess told Barak:

... The honor will not be yours, for the Lord will hand Sisera over to a woman.

God had another plan to bring about the fall of that great Commander of Canaan's army. A 'sleeper operative', a warrior was already in place. Jael's husband Heber had separated himself from his clan, the Kenites, descendants of Moses' brother-in-law, and moved near to a place called Kedesh. This move, this circumstance meant that Jael was now perfectly positioned to influence the future of the people of God when the opportunity to strike a blow for good and God presented itself.

There were **... Friendly relations between Jabin King of Hazor in Canaan, and the clan of Heber the Kenite. Judges 4:17**

Sisera knew the state of relations with the clan of Heber and so when he found himself in flight and fear for his life running from the army of Barak, he sought to hide in the tent of Jael, wife of Heber. Sisera was so certain of her support that he asked her to lie, be his accomplice if necessary, to protect him from the hand of the soldiers of Israel. But the Lord had been drawing the heart of Jael to Himself; He offered her the opportunity to find her real identity and her true purpose in Him as His warrior for righteousness.

The enemy of God's people imagined his evil ways were supported and condoned by Heber's wife but he found out too late for his salvation that she was the Lord's handmaiden; arm of His justice and His righteousness. Sisera exulted in his high profile role as persecutor of the Lord's people and when faced with revolt, defeat and humiliation he ran for cover. He ran to a place that seemingly offered him safe passage and protection but as the Scriptures declare in **1 Thessalonians 5:3 "For when they shall say, Peace and safety; then sudden destruction cometh upon them, as travail upon a woman with child; and they shall not escape."**

Jael killed him as he slept in her tent and delivered his dead body to Barak. Jael had gone beyond the point of compromise; she was not a spectator in the war, she was a warrior.

There was great rejoicing in the victory over the enemy and praise, honor and thanksgiving went up to the God of Israel. In my spirit, I feel that this action, in which Jael drove a peg though the temple of the commander of the enemy's army was a timely reminder to God's people; a foreshadow of the triumph of the Seed of the woman, who would crush, destroy and nullify the head and rule of the serpent forever.

Many blessings were heaped upon Jael. And we see that these blessings are echoed in the blessings that Elizabeth declared over Mary the Mother of Christ when she learned of the pregnancy of the Virgin. Compare **Luke 1:42** with the following text:

Blessed above women shall Jael, the wife of Heber the Kenite be; blessed shall she be above women in the tent. Judges 5:24

Jael's act was the turning point in the fortunes of the Israelites at that time. The Scripture tells us that

On that day, God subdued Jabin, the Canaanite King before the Israelites. And the hand of the Israelites grew stronger and stronger against Jabin, the Canaanite king until they destroyed him. Judges 4:23, 24 (NIV)

Jael was positioned to serve God and to bring about victory for His people. He was able to use the faith and the actions of a homemaker, seemingly not in a position that would or could be considered of significance to anyone but her family, at a time when women were regarded as mere property of their fathers and husbands, to alter the outcome of hostilities and the fate of a nation.

Jael was available to be used by God. She was given a chance to choose her side in the war. We do not know much about her history but despite the friendly or seemingly neutral position of her clan, the possibility of causing diplomatic disturbance and the apparent betrayal of the political status quo that assured her people peace with Canaan, Jael acted in obedience to God's call to warfare and in so doing she increased her territory and was blessed indeed! **1 Chronicles 4:10.**

It is certain that she recognized her guest and the role he played in oppressing the Israelites. She also knew that there was a war and she made a decision to choose the side of God's people. Jael faced the hard truth, there is no middle ground; one is either for or against God. Trying to live in no-man's land and placate the enemy by keeping quiet in the face of evil is wrong and really amounts to a choice for evil.

We can each choose Christ or acquiesce to the devil's agenda. But to desire the Christ is to deny self and be totally, absolutely and completely committed and submitted to the will of God and His purpose for one's life. Every child of God has a mandate for service. Jesus the Lord has and so too do all who are named by His name.

But you are a chosen race, a royal priesthood, a dedicated nation; [God's] own purchased, special people, that you may set forth the wonderful deed and display the virtues and perfection of Him Who called you out of darkness into His marvelous light. 1 Peter 2:9

The Keeper of the Ward-Robe, The Keeper of the Book

Another example of a woman, who was available at just the right time to serve the higher purpose of God, is the Prophetess Huldah. It was her blessing to be a light-bearer for the Lord and guide the rulers of the nation of Israel in the way of the Lord; mapping the course of a King and his administration to turn the nation of Israel back to the proper worship and reverence of God and the refurbishment of His Temple. She influenced the government and the governing of a nation.

Josiah became a King of Israel when he was only eight years old. He had been brought up to walk in the ways of King David despite the idolatrous ways of his father and his grandfather; earlier kings who lived and died in rebellion against the way of the Lord. At the time of his rule in Israel there was much idolatry in the land, practiced even in the temple of the Most High. When he was eighteen years old, he began to take an active and consistent interest in the re-building and re-furbishing Temple Project. As a result, when the high priest Hilkiah, discovered the Book of the Law of God, he passed it on to Josiah's secretary, who read its contents to the King.

The Book of the Law opened the King's eyes and awakened him to the apostate condition of the nation. The King sent out his top ranking officials, including the priest to go and seek for guidance, truth and instruction from the Lord. **2 Kings 22: 13.** His envoys went directly to the Prophetess Hulda for answers, for counsel and for divine direction in their desire to perform the perfect will of God. King Josiah was in search of truth and purpose not just for himself but for the whole kingdom of Judah. The Word of God promises each person that we will find the Lord when we seek after Him with all our hearts. **Jeremiah 29:13.** The Lord had a lady in waiting; He had appointed and anointed the Prophetess Huldah for just this time and just this purpose.

Notice that when the priest and the top officials of the Kingdom wanted information concerning Jehovah they knew exactly where to go; there was no debate, no proverbial scratching of the head. There was a woman of God, a prophetess, the keeper of the Ward-robe who was also a keeper of the Word of God, of the Book. Appropriately for the keeper of the ward-robe, clothing, that she should also be keeper of the wisdom of God's law that furnishes us with the righteous dress code of His Kingdom! I will speak on clothing in the final chapter of this book. The Prophetess declared **"Thus says the Lord, the God of Israel"**. She spoke the Word of the Lord for the nation as well as for the individual, the King who had sent his officials to inquire.

In a time of great desolation, desperation and dismay concerning the wrath of God and His prophesied judgment against Israel, the eyes of the nation's leaders looked to the woman of God. They knew she had a personal relationship with God and that she was His anointed servant. The Prophetess instructed, counseled, advised and directed the King and his officials in the statutes and ordinances of the Almighty. This is a task that she could only have performed because she was prepared, trained and ready to stand in the gap at the Lord's command. Through the Holy Spirit her Sword was sharpened to perfection cutting through the illusions, the lies, the pretences and the apathy of the people called by the name of the Lord. **2 Kings 22:14-20.**

The Prophetess Huldah also conveyed God's promise to King Josiah as recognition of his obedience in serving God with zeal and valor. In compliance with the counsel of the Prophetess, the King went out with a new mission, a new direction and an extraordinary anointing to 'clean house' and establish the Name of the Lord once again in its rightful place among His people. The faith, force and fervor of the King in pursuing the will of God, is honored by the record of **2 Kings 23:25**, which states;

Neither before nor after Josiah was there a king like him who turned to the Lord as he did – with all his heart and with all his soul and with all his strength, in accordance with all the Law of Moses. (NIV)

Josiah became a true servant of the Lord whose life was a testimony for the glory of God.

His mission was revealed, launched and sustained by the counsel of the handmaiden of the Lord. She maintained her integrity in God despite of the profusion of idol worship that invaded and consumed the lives of God's people. The Prophetess Huldah was ideally situated to impact the life and reign of this king of Judah. Her service to the nation was one which caused the name of our God to be glorified and His worship to mark the lifetime achievement of a King for an eternal reward.

The Prophetess Huldah was surrounded by the forces of evil; idol worship was the dominant practice of the day and the kingdom. Yet she did all that she could to equip and prepare herself to serve the Lord at a moment's notice. Surrounded by the enemy and his servants, the woman of God remained fully armored, confident and secure in the provisions and protection of Jehovah God.

4. Yes, though I walk through the [deep, sunless] valley of the shadow of death, I will fear no evil, for You are with me; Your rod [to protect] and Your staff [to guide], they comfort me.

5. You prepare a table before me in the presence of my enemies, You anoint my head with oil; my [brimming] cup runs over. 6. Surely or only goodness, mercy, and unfailing love shall follow me all the days of my life, and through the length of my days the house of the Lord [and His presence] shall be my dwelling place. Psalms 23:4-6.

On the Wall

It would not have been a part of Joshua's plans to include the role and the fate of an enemy in the furtherance of his military strategies and tactical planning in the push to overthrow the rulers of the city of Jericho. Joshua was a direct witness of the history of God with His people. He was one of only two that were part of the original exodus from Egypt. He had seen the wonders, signs and miracles that were the tools of his people's liberty at the Hand of Jehovah. He therefore would certainly not have been surprised that God uses whoever will trust in Him to bring about His will. And Joshua was all about fulfilling the commands of the Lord.

Rahab was an inhabitant of the city of Jericho, a native of that community. She was not a Jew and was not brought up according to the religious teachings, customs or practices of the Jews. She was a lady who earned her living by selling her favors to men with money, power and influence in the city. In fact she was even known to the King of Jericho. In her world she was a success. Rahab had acquired material wealth and a status that reflected her success. She occupied a prime piece of real estate in the city and actively cared for the needs of her relatives.

Yet by the Spirit we can discern that in her heart she experienced a sense of lack; an emptiness that she was unable to fill with all her endeavors and her achievements. In her natural mind that should have been enough. We may infer from our own sense of incompleteness and dissatisfaction when we live a life dedicated to sin, that perhaps, even her mind felt abused, soiled and degraded by her profession. The exchange of her self-esteem for the things of the flesh was a poor one. Even the worship of the gods of her people was not enough to give her the peace that comes with a truly prosperous life.

Rahab's desire was much deeper than she could fathom. A desire placed in her heart by the Creator God and although she was unable to put her finger on the root cause, she knew it was there. There must have been other young women looking from the outside in, who assumed that Rahab had it all, especially those from families with little or no wealth, or worldly status. After all, Rahab was able to dress in the latest, most expensive and favored fashions of the day. Physically, she was desirable to men and her associates occupied the upper echelons of the society. Rahab was the equivalent of a Hollywood Queen, one to be envied and emulated in the eyes of the world.

Today, in our own communities, there are many disenfranchised individuals who can only hope to attain a livelihood if they become a part of the illegal economy. Many women find themselves in compromising, undesirable positions based purely on the economic security that is anticipated or promised. Quite often these expectations are never fully realized, proving to be outright lies that most often leading to personal exploitation, abuse, manipulation and a life of crime and self recriminations.

Deep calls to deep and so our spirit will always be seeking to connect with the Source of Life, with the Eternal part of itself located in the Person of the Creator God. The only way to re-connect is through Jesus the Christ. He is the Way, the Truth and the Life; the only Door to the Divine. Jesus did not come into the world to condemn us; to tell us how bad and sinful we are and that hell is our destination! Rather, He came to offer hope and access to the Kingdom of God, so that regardless of how lost we are in sin, how worldly we are in our mind set, attitude, approach and ambition we may still be saved, sanctified and restored to fellowship through Jesus the Christ.

Rahab caught a glimpse of a different possibility, promise and prospect with the arrival of the Hebrews. Everyone in Jericho and the surrounding region had heard the stories of the mighty and miraculous deliverance of the people who worshipped an invisible, incredible God. They had been freed from four hundred years of slavery in the great dynasty of Egypt. It was reported, although not always believed that their God had empowered their leader to perform supernatural feats on their behalf and so won their freedom.

In the empty hours of the night and early morning, when she had some 'alone time' after her last client left, Rahab would look out from her window, over the great wall, and wonder what it was like to be an Israelite with such a mighty God who took such interest in the welfare of His people. She had prayed often, making sacrifices to the gods of her people. But still she felt empty, lonely, worn out, depleted and defeated without the comfort and security of a companion of her own; a husband that cared just for her. All there was ahead of her was more of the same meaningless existence, the promise of a futile, fearful future as she got older, beauty fading and her attractiveness and ability to retain her clientele diminishing.

Then one fateful day, the fabled people of the wilderness, on their journey to their "Promised Land" were encamped outside the city walls of Jericho. Rahab had an excellent view of their camp which stretched into the distance as far as the eye could see. There was an air of suspense and excited fear inside Jericho. Everyone knew that the presence of the Children of Israel was trouble. They had apparently been within reach of Jericho a long time ago, forty years previous it was said but they had turned away into the wilderness and the expected attack did not happen. Not a single person in the city believed that history would repeat itself. One thing that was unanimously agreed however; if their God really did all the things claimed and rumored throughout the city, then the King of Jericho and the inhabitants of the walled city had good reason to be scared.

Joshua 2:11

The more Rahab listened to the stories, the more her spirit began to long after and crave the God of the Jews as her own. Her eyes were irresistibly drawn to the view from her window of the Hebrew Camp spread out in the plains below, on the other side of the river. Such a God who defended His people against all their enemies would be able to help her find new meaning and direction in her life. Maybe He could free her too from all the constraints and restraints that was a result of her lifestyle. Perhaps He would give her a new start in life; she could become a dress-maker perhaps or even a wife and mother. Rahab dreamed and hungered for a life of worth, honor and peace. **Joshua 2:8-13.**

We do not of ourselves seek after the Almighty. He seeks after and longs for us. **"All we like sheep have gone astray".** Isaiah 53:6. I believe that there began to be a thirst in Rahab; a longing after the God of the Hebrews. I believe that the Spirit of God began to work conviction in Rahab's mind and heart. A conviction that would work towards her salvation; her conversion, redemption and restoration to a right relationship with the Creator God and a corresponding realization of the responsibility of reaching out for her divinely designated destiny as a child of Jehovah. There was a spirit of warfare within her fighting to find expression. And all the while it was God calling her to take a stand.

The Father God always presents us with the opportunity to make a choice to serve Him or to turn away from Him. Rahab's chance turned up on her doorstep, literally. She was supernaturally and strategically positioned to offer assistance to God's covenanted people in a time of war. Rahab had learnt from her own experiences that personal gain, status and favor in the high places of society did not lead to fulfillment or lasting satisfaction in life. Serving a higher cause, the cause of Jehovah God held the promise of a more rewarding future.

The two young Israelite men in need of a safe house to escape the soldiers who had detected their presence in Jericho was the trigger that propelled her towards personal breakthrough. In their moment of need she was given the opportunity to help them and by so doing help herself and serve their God. Their acquaintance might just provide the avenue for her to get answers to her questioning, self-searching puzzlement about the God of the 'Wilderness People'. All her craving, her longing and her desire reached a climax at the moment she needed to make a decision to aid or betray them. Either she must risk the wrath of the King of Jericho if discovered or surrender to the benevolence, mercy, kindness and will of the God of the Jews. She needed to step out in faith or shrink into fear. The Lord gave her the gift of faith and she immediately transitioned from darkness and death into His glorious light and life.

In Him was Life and the Life was the Light of men. John 1:4

Recognizing the Right Side of the Wall

Walls are built to keep people in as much as they are built to keep people out and depending on the side of the wall you are, it may be difficult to appreciate this perspective. The walls of Jericho stood between the Children of Israel and their inheritance, the Promise Land. As much as it needed to come down to let them in, once Rahab chose the side of God's people, its fall would let her out, signaling her liberty. The wall separated her from her future, her freedom to start over as a new creature in Christ. **Colossians 1:13-14**

Being on the inside of the wall was the living symbol of her bondage to idolatry, to a life of immorality and degradation despite its obvious material and social perks. Rahab had an appointment with destiny. It was her privilege to activate her destiny by fulfilling her assignment; to give shelter and protection to the two Hebrew spies. Throughout all of her life, her rough and tough times, her time of unknowing ignorance of the great Eternal One, He had her in His mind. Often times when we are busy getting on with our own plans or doing whatever we think we need to do to survive, we are completely unaware of the higher purpose and the heavenly calling that God ordained from the beginning of time, just for us.

For I know the thoughts I have for you, says the Lord, thoughts and plans for welfare and peace and not for evil, to give you hope in your final outcome. Jeremiah 29:11.

The fact is, with our carnal viewpoint, we are much more practiced at recognizing or identifying the walls that are keeping us out, preventing our access to what we feel will make our lives complete and successful; excluding us from some benefit that could be social, economic, political or ecumenical. However, we often fail to recognize that there might also be a wall that is keeping us hedged in, restrained and limited in vision, blind to our options and opportunity for freedom in Christ, without divine intervention.

In other words, the problem may not be about getting in but about getting out. It is easier for man, pre-disposed toward sinning from our birth, to get into sin than to get out. The love and leading of the Lord, a direct intervention through the Holy Sprit is the only way out. Sometimes the wall is irrelevant to our captivity or limitations. Our freedom is first of all a spiritual reality. And whether it is evident physically or not should not deflate, diffuse or defeat us in worship and witness for the Lord. Even in the natural world, soldiers continue to be soldiers even if they are captured by the enemy. Our freedom lies in the Messiah and that cannot be affected or prevented by any wall designed by the enemy.

The issue of our comfort zone will rear its tentacles drawing us away from the window that allows us to look beyond the wall and see the people and the Kingdom of God and His amazing love and plans for our lives. We get so content, so complacent, and so comfortable that we do not perceive that we are in poverty, spiritually. We do not appreciate that God is able, willing and ready to increase our territory that we might attain to the fullness of His promises for our lives. For Rahab, the walls were preventing her from learning about the one, true God. It was an obstacle, a hindrance and a test of her desire to respond to the working of the Spirit of God in her life. The walls of Jericho were Rahab's blessing in disguise!

When God presented Rahab with the chance to get from behind those walls, to let in the Light, to gain her liberty, she was ready to take the risks, to go against the odds, against the king and his soldiers, against her neighbors and against the gods of her people. She confronted her fears head-on, and placed her hopes, her faith and her future with God's people. **Hebrews 11:31**

Again let us be reminded; what was intended by the devil for the control, corruption and final destruction of Rahab's life was utilized and made to serve the divine purpose of the Lord. He alone is always able to turn things around for good when we submit to Him. It is demonstrably clear that all things including all our bad experiences, disappointments, pain, sorrow, tears, misfortunes and heartache; all things work together for good to the appointed of the Lord. **Romans 8:28**

Rahab's future became tied in with God's people and her posterity remains to this very day. Rahab had no idea of who she could be in Jehovah God but He knew the purpose for which she had been born. He knew the plans that He had for her; He had already deposited the seed of promise in her spirit and it was always nestled in the possibility and potential of her natural and spiritual world. Despite appearances to the contrary, Rahab was positioned for the promise of prosperity and perpetuity.

Rahab chose the "better way". Her position; geographical, social, and political, was employed in the service of the King of kings and Lord of lords. Who would serve a lesser when one has the opportunity to serve the Greater? She was called of God to be:

- A savior to the Hebrew spies and to her family
- A witness to the saving power of God; even to the saving of a heathen prostitute.
- A survivor of the destruction of Jericho.
- To be a wife and mother.
- To be numbered with the people of God as an ancestor of Jesus Christ.
- A partaker of the promise of God's covenant with His chosen people.

There is not one single person beyond the reach of God's love and the redemptive power of the blood of the Lamb. It might appear to someone seeing with the eyes of this carnal world that this or that individual is too steeped in sin, long lost to the human family as a valuable individual but that is never the case with the Eyes of Love, the eyes of our Lord and Savior. Jesus gave His life as atonement for all our sins, no matter how heinous; in Him there are no lost causes in the battle for souls.

The blood of Jesus cleanses and makes new, giving us a fresh start and a clean slate. There is no stain too stubborn, no crime too grievous, no sin so vile, and no behavior too abhorrent that the blood cannot wash away and His righteousness cannot cover. To partake of the salvation that He offers, we must

a. turn our minds, emotions, will and hearts over to Jesus,
b. accept His love, mercy, and grace,
c. believe and accept Him as the Beloved Son of God,
d. repent of all our wrong-doing,
e. confess Him as personal Redeemer,
f. ask Him to be our Savior and Sovereign Lord
g. He will in no wise cast us off, ignore or deny us. **Romans 10:9-13**

It is the Lord's delight and His purpose to redeem us to enjoy the favor and fellowship that He shares with His followers and with His Father. So many times we go about with an unrealized, unfulfilled potential waiting to come to fruition in our lives. Yet in our complacency we are content to limit ourselves and in so doing limit what God can accomplish by and through us for the Kingdom.

Many of us are content to pursue earthly treasures and pleasures which are only for a time or season. Alternatively, we get bogged down in self pity, self- analysis, regret, betrayals, hatred or a hundred other emotions all manufactured or magnified by the devil to distract us. These missives invade our minds and hearts and separate us from our true identity, status and destiny. It does not matter where we have been or where we find ourselves right now, it only counts what we do from here on out. Faith in Jesus the Christ is an investment in a guaranteed glorious future.

It is time we stand in the authority of our Lord and submit to His plan for our lives. As the Psalmist says in **Psalms 34:90, "They who seek the Lord shall not want for any good thing"**. There is nothing in and of this world that should separate us from the love of the Almighty. And since we show our love by our obedience, then we should indeed be pleased and privileged to accept the responsibility, trust and opportunity that He has ordained for us to be His Spiritual Warriors. Who will we disappoint, God, the family of man, ourselves or all of the above? Are we ready to risk everything in this world for the honor of serving our Lord and bringing glory to His name?

Ruth was ready to be His warrior, Jael was ready, Prophetess Huldah was ready, Rahab was ready and Queen Esther was ready. **"If I perish, I perish"** declared the Queen. Are you prepared to place your all on the altar; life, love, loyalty and labor? We are not our own, we are twice His; by creation and redemption. When we give ourselves to the Lord we merely return what is truly His! Are we willing to be a Hannah and give back to the Lord the most precious gift that He has given to us, His love through His Son, our Redeemer? Jesus the Christ said **"Render therefore unto Caesar the things which are Caesar's and unto God the things that are God's". Matthew 22:21.** We belong to God and so all our talents, treasures, tangibles and intangibles are His; totally.

> **Then Jesus said to His disciples, If anyone would come after Me, he must deny himself and take up his cross and follow Me. For whoever wants to save his life will lose it, but whoever loses his life for Me will find it. What good will it be for a man if he gains the whole world yet forfeits his soul? Or what can a man give in exchange for his soul? For the Son of Man is going to come in His Father's glory with His angels and then He will reward each person according to what he has done. Matthew 16:24-27 (NIV)**

> **For the grace of God that brings salvation has appeared to all men. It teaches us to say "no" to ungodliness and worldly passions, and to live self-controlled, upright and godly lives in this present age, while we wait for the blessed hope – the glorious appearing of our great God and Savior, Jesus Christ, who gave Himself for us to redeem us from all wickedness and to purify for Himself**

a people that are His very own, eager to do what is good. Titus 2:11-14 (NIV)

Your beauty should not come from outward adornment, such as braided hair and the wearing of gold jewelry and fine clothes. Instead, it should be that of your inner self, the unfading beauty of a gentle and quiet spirit, which is of great worth in God's sight. 1 Peter 3:3 and 4 (NIV)

I tell you the truth, Jesus replied, no one who has left home or brothers or sisters or mother or father or children or fields for me and the gospel, will fail to receive a hundred times as much in this present age (homes, brothers, sisters, mothers, children and fields – and with them, persecutions) and in the age to come, eternal life. Mark 10:29-30 (NIV)

CHAPTER 21

DRESS TO IMPRESS

☙

What Is Your Worth?

We live in a world today that places great value on what you look like, where you eat, how you dress, where you hang out, whether you are part of the in-crowd, the hip club and the paparazzi parade. It is a big deal who you have been seen with, how much money you have or who names you as friend in the famed and higher echelons of society. And these are just a few of the things that are used to determine the importance, status, influence and success of an individual in a world fast approaching the last days of this dispensation; the end of the time of the Gentiles.

> **18. In the last days (in the end time) there will be scoffers [who seek to gratify their own unholy desires], following after their own ungodly passions. 19. It is these who are [agitators] setting up distinctions and causing divisions – merely sensual [creatures, carnal, worldly-minded people], devoid of the [Holy] Spirit and destitute of any higher spiritual life. Jude 18 and 19. (Verses)**

But placing faith in the value system of this world and using that as a measure to define one-self underestimates the potential that God placed within us to become great in His eyes, in His Kingdom. But even more importantly, we ignore the worth that He placed on us when He risked His Kingdom to implement a plan for our redemption that required the Son of God becoming a man and being sacrificed to redeem us from sin, even unto a cruel death.

The love of God declares our true worth, a value that can attach to us for all eternity, if we so choose. He will not force us to love Him in return; His love is unconditional. But we cannot inherit eternal life while we remain in our sinful state regardless of how much we are loved by God; righteousness, holiness and divine justice cannot tolerate sin and there must be a separation between carnality and spirituality, between the just and the unjust, between light and darkness. Our final destination is our choice; we can live eternally or die the final death, it is not up to God, it is up to us. All He can do is love us and give us the chance and the choice to decide if we are worth His love and His Sacrifice or even if we care. The time for our decisions is even now at the door.

The Prince of this world is on borrowed time and he knows it. He is running around trying to destroy as many souls as he can before the return of the Prince of Peace, the Messiah of the human Family, Jesus the Christ. Satan has worked incessantly since Eden to keep us away from the love of God. The family of man has clothed itself in sin and displays all its vices, its crimes and its chains of captivity as though they were proud trophies of success, power and achievement. They are not. They only indicate that we have succumbed to the folly of idolatry and the ravages of evil and iniquity. We are pawns of Satan in his diabolical scheme to seize God's Sovereignty. Every thought of Satan is to destroy and he is happy as long as he can claim some small victory over the Christ and His Father, our Loving Creator. And if it takes the form of inciting, deceiving or tempting one soul into sin and therefore support of his seditious acts against God, then the serpent is satisfied.

The human family made a choice in the Garden of Eden to sin and since then continues to choose darkness rather than light because our sins are of the darkness and the kingdom of darkness. But we were created to love and worship God. We lived and basked in the beauteous light of His Presence in Eden. Then the devil came in and disruption, destruction and death followed in his wake. We stepped outside the relationship of love that we had with the Father and we lost our home in Paradise.

But God is not willing that any of us should perish and suffer the final death. He planned and provided for our redemption and restoration to our former glory in His Kingdom through the Messiah, the Promised Seed of the woman. His Son's obedience and submission to Heaven's Law purchased our freedom from bondage to Satan. **Romans 4:4-8.** We have a 'get-out-of-jail-free' card, if only we avail ourselves of it. We have the choice of life and death and right now we have the right to choose life. Jesus our Kinsman Redeemer is the Light of the world and anyone who chooses may repent of their sins; their past mistakes, rejection and rebellion and accept the Christ as Lord of their life. The Holy Spirit will embrace you and fill you, teach and train you in the Way.

[The Father] has delivered and drawn us to Himself out of the control and the dominion of darkness and has transferred us into the Kingdom of the Son of Love. Colossians 1:13

Covering Your Nakedness with Designer Clothes

It has become an important consideration to ensure that the person who designs our clothing is famous and popular. The labels on our material possessions will determine how much money we have spent and therefore our status as aspiring or accomplished individuals in our society. However, in choosing our designer clothes the following are some of the considerations that we take into account:

b. The right design or style for the event
c. The designer
d. The fashion house; the label
e. The attention that will be received
f. Making headline news
g. The reputation that will be acquired

h. The value in the future

These issues are not so different to those that we should apply when making decisions about our eternal garment.

a. The right design - clothing with longevity that will lasts for eternity
b. The Best Designer – He is the First and the Last
c. A cloak of Righteousness from House of Gethsemane Garden or filthy rags from the Garden of Eden
d. Attracting the attention of God or that of man and Satan
a. Clothing that will be cast into the fire after the Great Judgment Day
b. Clothing that will be the righteous clothes of God's Kingdom of Love
c. Clothing of purest white, bright and shining purchased by the Christ.

The final decision that we make in choosing the clothing that covers our nakedness is a matter of life and death. I have heard people say "fashion is important' but I doubt they realize quite how important in the divine plans of mankind's destiny and destination. The first piece of information that we need to know is that the Lord is the First, Great Designer and He is the Last, Great Dresser of the human frame. His garments are unisex but every person must be trimmed, pared and prepared to fit into them.

The size and the style are not dependent on your personal statistics but on whether you are ready to be pared, processed, trimmed and tailored to the size needed to fit the garment; the garment is one size and all must fit the that one size. The Designer cannot and will not make alterations to suit us; we must all conform to the style and size if we desire to wear His design. This point was the subject of a sermon that I heard preached a few years ago and it made an astounding impact on all those who heard it.

Finally, the cost of this Designer's clothes has already been paid for by our Big Brother, Jesus. All we have to do is to freely ask and freely receive this garment from its Designer in exchange for all the other filthy rags that we wear and consider valuable. The filthy rags to which I refer are materialism, pride, idolatry and all sins against the Father. **Isaiah 54:6.** The garment paid for by our Brother is the Cloak of Righteousness, the clothing of the Firstborn! I know that the presentation of this issue of nakedness, shame and holy covering is unusual but it starkly recognizes our perspectives and perceptions on fashion in today's world. It deals with a most important issue, who are you dressed to impress? The paparazzi, your colleagues, friends, foes or your father, your heavenly Father that is!

Nakedness and Shame

Did you know that sin will steal your clothes? It will steal your covering and leave you naked, ashamed and isolated. Giving free reign to the desires of the flesh and failing to deal with deceit will always leave us uncovered, exposed to sin which works death, disease and ultimately destruction in our bodies. The Robe of Righteousness which is the very light of the Lord, His purity, holiness, glory and love, was the original covering of Adam and Eve in Eden. **Psalms 104:1-2**. It is also with this robe that we are re-clothed upon our rebirth into the family of God through Jesus the Christ. He covers us with His Robe of Righteousness which He has kept pure and undefiled although He was in this sin polluted, wickedly corrupted world and subjected to temptation the same as every human being.

> **I will greatly rejoice in the Lord, my soul will exult in my God; for He has clothed me with the garments of salvation, He has covered me with the Robe of Righteousness, as a bridegroom decks himself with a garland, and as a bride adorns herself with her jewels. Isaiah 61:10**

In the face of sin which is the violation of God's commands, the covering of righteousness falls away leaving us naked and ashamed again. **Micah 7:9.** Check out the experience of the sons of Sceva who faked their belief in the Christ and suffered the humiliation of exposure and the true state of sinful man in **Acts 19:13-16**

13. Then some of the traveling Jewish exorcists (men who adjure evil spirits) also undertook to call the name of the Lord Jesus over those who had evil spirits, saying, I solemnly implore and charge you by the Jesus Whom Paul preaches!

14. Seven sons of a certain Jewish chief priest named Sceva were doing this.

15. But [one] evil spirit retorted, Jesus I know, and Paul I know about, but who are you?

16. Then the man in whom the evil spirit dwelt leaped upon them, mastering two of them, and was so violent against them that they dashed out of that home [in fear], stripped naked and wounded.

Let me share right here this word of revelation; it is a good thing for us to recognize our nakedness as Adam and Eve did. It means that our conscience, the Spirit of God in us is not dead but awake to our fallen state. Shame and guilt further indicates that we are aware that we have broken God's trust and acted contrary to His statutes. Nakedness means the absence of God's righteousness, exposing the fallible, selfish, self-seeking, self-centered foolishness of human nature. Confronting our nakedness and feeling shame is a necessary first step to repentance. **Genesis 3:7**

The devil stripped Adam and Eve of their covering, their clothes in the Garden of Eden through his lies and his deception. While they remained in right standing with God and lived in submission to divine directions, the first parents were not ashamed of their bodies for they reflected the glory of God. **Genesis 2:25.** There was no need for Adam and Eve to feel ashamed or guilty because they were pure in heart, mind and body; righteousness was their natural covering and in the absence of sin, there was no shame or guilt to be experienced. Moses reflected the same glory after only forty days continuously in God's Presence on Mount Sinai.

The truth is there are so many people who are walking around naked and do not even realize the condition of shame in which they have become comfortable and content. We need to take the same steps to secure covering as did our first parents in Eden. Adam and Eve's first response to their nakedness was to seek to cover themselves with leaves. The covering that they were able to provide for their shame was at best temporary, insufficient and ineffective for the purpose.

Generally speaking, why is clothing so important to human beings? Some of the reasons may be summarized as follows

a. Cover intimate and private parts of the body – modesty and privacy
b. Protection against the elements
c. A mark of identification e.g. of status, profession, culture, religion etc.
d. Pre-requisite for access into certain events, locations etc.
e. Maintenance of good health
f. Guard against sexual sin and crime against the person of another

But we should find the right clothes that will cover our filthy, vulnerable state and not resort to our own feeble and inefficient attempts; attempts that can be likened to that of Adam and Eve. Their efforts to design and clothe themselves were futile just as in a spiritual sense the many and varied attempts to regain right standing with the Creator amounts to nothing but wasted effort.

For we have all become like one who is unclean [ceremonially, like a leper], and all our righteousness (our best deeds of righteousness and justice) is like filthy rags or a polluted garment; we all fade like a leaf, and our iniquities, like the wind, take us away [far from God's favor, hurrying us toward destruction]. Isaiah 64:6.

In His love and mercy God made coats/clothes of skins to cover Adam and Eve. In order for God to make these coats to provide the appropriate physical covering needed by Adam and Eve in the hostile environment which followed their sin, it is accepted theology that He must have sacrificed the life of an animal(s) to secure the fabric; the skin used to make their coats.

For Adam also and for his wife the Lord God made long coats (tunics) of skins and clothed them. Genesis 3:21

In effect, that was the first blood sacrifice of innocent life on the earth and all because of man's sin. The sacrifice was the first that symbolized the requirement of blood and therefore death that would be necessary before man could again wear a Robe of Righteousness, the garment with which we were originally covered by the Creator. I would not be surprised to discover in the eternities to come that the animal that was first slain for the purpose of clothing man was a lamb, much like it was the Lamb of God that died to redeem the human family. It is His righteousness that covers our sin and shame like a cloak.

What are the substantial points to note concerning the clothes that God provided for Adam and Eve?

a. Required the sacrifice of life and a spilling of blood
b. Provided complete, comprehensive, effective covering for both
c. Supplied the design for future clothes that would be appropriate
d. Fabric and style of clothes that protected their skin from harm by the elements and a hostile nature
e. Clothing that was durable and therefore signaled long-term planning and approach to the matter of covering. Note that fig leaves by comparison were suited only to short term usage in temperate climates.
f. The coats were a physical reminder of divine truths; the pair needed to depend on God's provision in all things: the blood

sacrifice that was needed for the atonement of sin, the godly garment, the Robe of Righteousness that God must provide to cover man's spiritual nakedness
g. The Eternal One must be the Source of the Sacrifice.
h. Demonstration of God's continuing love, care and concern for the welfare of the human family despite their rebellion
i. The coat was a reminder of God's promise to redeem and re-clothe them again in His glory through the Seed of the woman.

I would like us to pause for a while and think about the lengths to which the devil will go to keep us naked and ashamed and hiding in darkness, refugees from the Father's Kingdom of Love. Adam and Eve hid themselves from the Lord in Eden after they sinned and lost their righteous covering. Today, vast numbers of the human family is still in hiding from the face of a loving and grieving Heavenly Father. **Genesis 3:8-11**. Satan's efforts to get God to walk away from the human family were still operating even while Jesus was on trial and being put to death on the Cross.

Symbolically, Satan sought to strip His clothes from His body to humiliate Him, to cause people to turn away in disgust, guilt or shame, to repudiate the righteous covering that Christ brings to the human family, His family.

"They cast lots for His garment". Matthew 27:35.

But this attempt, enacted in this physical, natural realm achieved the very opposite. **Psalms 22:18**. The Lord was prepared for this experience, an act foretold by the Psalmist David. Jesus was all about fulfilling the Laws and the Prophets; it is the purpose for which He came into the world.

The important thing about Jesus was not His physical apparel but rather His spiritual adorning of purity and light. His covering of righteousness is the shining 'Shekinah' glory of God and of such intensity and brightness that when He was lifted up on Calvary's Cross, His righteous Light shone forth and drew men all over the world to Him as He prophesied it would. **John 12:32 -36** It was impossible for Satan to disrobe the Christ; he tried and failed.

For the [Lord] put on righteousness as a breastplate or coat of mail, and salvation as a helmet upon His head; He put on garments of vengeance for clothing and was clad with zeal [and furious divine jealousy] as a cloak. Isaiah 59:17

Battle Fatigues

The Lord Jesus is the Commander-In-Chief of the Army of God's Kingdom and we have a commission to wage war against the serpent until our Lord shall put a final end to his campaign of hatred, wickedness, destruction and rebellion against the Most High God. Women of God, warriors all, put on the full armor of warfare and stand with the Lord and the Righteous Two Thirds to conquer the great adversary of our hopes, our homes, our heritage, and our Holy and Righteous Father and God.

Finally, notice that not even a thread on the garments of the three Hebrew boys was burnt when they were taken out of the fiery furnace into which Nebuchadnezzar threw them for refusing to worship the idols of Babylon. In the physical realm their clothing was flammable; able to be destroyed by the natural fire. But because the Lord protected them, throwing His own perfect garment over them, they could not be touched!

This physical manifestation of the endurance of natural clothes reminds me of the clothes worn by the children of Israel while they sojourned under the protection of God in the wilderness for forty years. Their clothes never got old, did not wear out; how awesome is that! This infusion of natural clothing with miraculous qualities is indicative of the durability, longevity and eternal nature of our spiritual clothing supplied by our Great Designer. The righteousness of the Hebrew boys was a spiritual thing and likewise could not be destroyed, penetrated or even damaged by the efforts of the enemy. The holiness of God is indestructible, incorruptible and more brilliant and perfect in adversity. The clothing of the boys did not even smell of the smoke! In this way we are given evidence that the trials and tribulations through which the saints of God must pass; the wars fought by His warriors, will not leave a mark, a stain or smell either.

Women of God, you are God's warriors and as such must be clothed appropriately in the battle fatigues of your warfare. The armor of God provides the battle dress and weaponry that will give us the victory in Christ Jesus, by the power of the Holy Spirit. The command to **"Put on the whole armor of God"** is an imperative that must be obeyed. Failure to comply with God's command is a sin and will render us vulnerable to attack and annihilation by the enemy.

However before we can be His warriors we must first clothe our nakedness with the righteousness of our Lord. This is clearly demonstrated to us in the order and the process that was set up by God to dedicate and set Aaron apart for his office as High Priest and his sons as priests in the tabernacle of the Tent of Meetings; God's mobile Temple among the sojourning Children of Israel. **Exodus 40:12-16.**

The Robe of God's Priestly Nation

It is clear that Aaron as High Priest and his sons as priests were all required to undergo an identical process of purification; they received identical, first garments. But as Aaron held another, higher calling as the High Priest, his additional garment of office was placed over the linen tunic and girdle. Jesus is our High Priest and so it is His Robe of Righteousness that assures entrance into the Presence of the Father. After the priests were washed with water and the High Priest anointed with oil by Moses, God required that they be clothe in white linen tunics (the breeches being under-garments of personal modesty might have been worn during the washing). **Exodus 39:27-29.** Jesus is our Water, the Holy Spirit our anointing Oil and His Righteousness and Truth, our white linen tunic and girdle; our cloak of righteousness. As warriors, our battle fatigues will be placed over our garment of righteousness as Aaron's high priestly robes were added over his tunic. We are a nation of priests but like the Levites we are warrior priests.

Every one of us must dress to impress the Bridegroom so that we will not be thrown out of the marriage supper of the Lamb. The Designer of the eternal garments for the Kingdom of Love waits eagerly to clothe us; He gave His very life's blood to purchase our righteousness and therefore our right to partake of the marriage supper of the lamb.

The light of Christ's righteousness is still shining today; it is a spiritual energy Source that lasts for all eternity. It shines in the thickest darkness and the darkness retreats and scatters before its path; the darkness has never overpowered it. **John 1:5.** It is so perfect, so strong that in the eternities we will have no need for the sun, the moon and the stars. The Lord Himself will be the Light of the City. Let us all make our calling and election sure as Children of the Light; Light-bearers and Warriors of the Kingdom of Light, Love, and Righteousness.

22. I saw no temple in the city, for the Lord God Omnipotent [Himself] is its temple.

23. And the city has no need of the sun or of the moon to give light to it, for the splendor and radiance (glory) of God illuminate it, and the Lamb is its lamp.

24. The nations shall walk by its light and the rulers and leaders of the earth shall bring into it their glory.

25. And its gates shall never be closed by day, and there shall be no night there. Revelation 21:22-25

Arise [from the depression and prostration in which circumstances have kept you – rise to a new life]! Shine (be radiant with the glory of the Lord), for your light has come, and the glory of the Lord has risen upon you! Isaiah 60:1

The sun shall no more be your light by day, nor for brightness shall the moon give light to you, but the Lord shall be to you an everlasting light, and your God your glory and your beauty. Isaiah 60:19

23. Thus says the Lord: Let not the wise and skilful person glory and boast in his wisdom and skill; let not the mighty and powerful person glory and boast in his strength and power; let not the person who is rich [in physical gratification and earthly wealth] glory and boast in his [temporal satisfactions and earthly] riches;

24. But let him who glories glory in this: that he understands and knows Me [personally and practically, directly discerning and recognizing My character], that I am the Lord, Who practices loving-kindness, judgment, and righteousness in the earth, for in these things I delight, says the Lord. Jeremiah 9:23, 24

As for Me, this is My covenant or league with them, says the Lord; My Spirit, Who is upon you [and writes the law of God inwardly on the heart], and My Words which I have put in your mouth shall not depart out of your mouth, or out of the mouths of your [true, spiritual] children, or out of the mouths of your children's children, says the Lord, from henceforth and forever. Isaiah 59:21

And he said to me, These are they who have come out of the great tribulation (persecution), and have washed their robes and made them white in the blood of the Lamb.

15. For this reason they are [now] before the [very] throne of God and serve Him day and night in His sanctuary (temple); and He Who is sitting upon the throne will protect and spread His tabernacle over and shelter them with His presence.

16. They shall hunger no more, neither thirst any more; neither shall the sun smite them, nor any scorching heat,

17. For the Lamb Who is in the midst of the throne will be their Shepherd, and He will guide then to springs of the waters of life; and God will wipe away every tear from their eyes. Revelation 8:14 –17

The [Holy] Spirit and the Bride (the church, the true Christians) say, Come! And let him who is listening say, Come! And let everyone come who is thirsty [who is painfully conscious of his need of those things by which the soul is refreshed, supported, and strengthened]; and whoever[earnestly] desires to do it, let him come, take, appropriate, and drink the water of life without cost. Revelation 22:17

Amen. Even so come Lord Jesus. The grace of our Lord Jesus Christ be with you all. Revelation 22:20-22 (KJV)